C000174323

ONE WORD OF TRUTH

One Word of Truth

The Cold War Memoir of Michael Bourdeaux and Keston College

Michael Bourdeaux

DARTON · LONGMAN + TODD

First published in 2019 by
Darton, Longman and Todd Ltd
1 Spencer Court
140–142 Wandsworth High Street
London SW18 4JJ

ISBN 978-0-232-53414-6

A catalogue record for this book is available from the British Library.

Printed and bound Bell & Bain, Glasgow.

To Gillian, my first wife, who worked tirelessly for Keston in its early days.

To Lorna, my second wife and editor, without whose encouragement and practical help this book would never have been written.

Hoping that my three grandsons, Nicholas, Christopher and eventually Oliver will read this book.

Contents

Note on the Title

The title is the penultimate sentence of Alexander Solzhenitsyn's Nobel Prize speech, which reads in full: 'One word of truth shall outweigh the whole world.' He is pleading for the artist or writer to cut through the miasma of propaganda worldwide and speak with honesty, at whatever the sacrifice. His words are as relevant today as when he wrote them nearly fifty years ago. To a world where, still, 'fake news' of one sort or another engulfs us, Solzhenitsyn calls us from the past: 'And the simple step of a simple courageous man is not to partake in falsehood, not to support false actions! Let *that* enter the world, let it even reign in the world – but not with my help. But writers and artists can achieve more: they can *conquer falsehood*! In the struggle with falsehood art always did win and it always does win! Openly, irrefutably for everyone! Falsehood can hold out against much in this world, but not against art.'

Solzhenitsyn was not permitted to deliver this in person, but, much later, in 1983, came to London to accept the award of the Templeton Prize, which he won in that year. I had the privilege of spending time with him.

Acknowlededgments

My thanks go to all staff and Council members of Keston College, without whose dedication and frequent shafts of brilliance the College could never have existed. Many of the 150 or so people who brought this work to fulfilment could not be named, but this book is a permanent testimony to the multiple roles they played.

Victoria Watts and Andrew Lenox-Conyngham persuaded me to continue looking for a publisher when I was discouraged and wanted to drop the project. My thanks now go to Darton, Longman and Todd for the enthusiasm with which they have taken it up.

Two people delved in the archives and answered all my queries and checked references. Without the unfailing help of Malcolm Walker, in earlier years, and of Larisa Seago recently, I could not have completed the work.

I have benefited from the patience and practical suggestions of several who have read the manuscript whole or in part: Roland Smith, Alyona Kojevnikov, John Briggs, Keith Clements and Xenia Dennen. Most thanks are due to my wife Lorna. She has toiled over the editing from beginning to end and improved my work immeasurably. All these have made suggestions and corrected mistakes, but those which remain are mine.

Messages of Support

In June 2019 Keston College began its celebrations marking fifty years since its founding. We received messages from two Russian former 'dissidents' whose work and plight we had publicised many years ago. I read out their messages (translated by Alyona Kojevnikov) and they produced an unforgettable impression on the assembled company. I am delighted to reprint them as the introduction to this book.

Both Alexander Ogorodnikov and Viktor Papkov were members of the 'Christian Seminar', a study group for young people, adjudged to be a criminal offence by the powers of the time. Alexander was incarcerated in a mental hospital in 1976 and two years later received a nine-year sentence in one of the worst labour camps. Viktor's sentence, although less severe (three years), was even more ludicrous. First, he was tried for stealing state property, which he had not done, and the case was dismissed. However, a new charge of forging documents was brought, alongside 'parasitism' (refusal to work). Keston kept their names alive during their incarceration and they were both released early when their cases were brought up with the Soviets by President Reagan and Mrs Thatcher.

***

Dear Father Michael!

Dear Xenia Dennen!

From the bottom of my heart, it brings me great joy to congratulate you on this memorable occasion – the 50th anniversary of Keston College.

Grateful memory recalls images of times not so long past: the stifling, socially suffocating reality of "developed socialism" and crumpled pieces of tissue-thin paper covered with microscopic writing, detailing the suffering and pain inflicted by the heavy hand of a state that drove us into the narrow space between the Criminal Code and the dictates of the builders of communism, and the modest hope granted to us through your voluntary emissaries, to bring our cry, our grief and what King Solomon called "hope full of immortality" to the Free World.

You were the champion of our suffering voice that was being smothered by the heavy burden of communism! Your compassionate support blunted the fury of the punitive energy of our persecutors, those storm-troopers who dared to challenge Heaven!

Together with you we held our ground in this epochal struggle against unprecedented persecutions and trials, brought down on us by a totalitarianism which proclaimed itself, in all seriousness, as the new faith to bring down every faith in the world, clearing its blood-soaked path with stupefying propaganda and unrelenting violence.

With love and gratitude,

Alexander Ogorodnikov

Christian Seminar (on Problems of Religion and Revival)

Moscow, 15 June 2019

***

Dear Father Michael!

On this momentous occasion, please accept our heartfelt congratulations to all the staff of Keston College, and especially to you. Yours was the inspiration and able leadership that yielded the unique achievements of the College for decades.

In the bitter years of our struggle against communist oppression, you raised your voice in our defence, your work lightened our burden and your true compassion shaped our fates.

We shall never forget this. Your Christian endeavour was that of a man who extended a helping hand to us at a time when we needed it most. We heard your voice and the voices of those you called to come to our support. That response was enough for us to stand firm in our fight for freedom, a freedom toward which we continue to strive.

On this year of the 50th anniversary of Keston College, thank you once more, Father Michael, for what you did for us.

May God bless you, your family, and all those who worked selflessly for and with Keston College.

Victor Papkov

Tatiana Lebedeva

Christian Seminar (on Problems of Religion and Revival)

Moscow, 15 June 2019

Preface: A Time of Transition

It was 1989 and the world was changing. During my life I have been eyewitness to several extraordinary events, into which I was propelled by the unseen hand of God. One of these brought me unexpectedly to participate in a moment of history, when a tiny nation measured its strength against the might of the Soviet regime. No one could have predicted that the Christian faith of the Lithuanian people would predominate, but their path of prayer and suffering was to lead to freedom for church and nation.

In the previous year, 1988, Mikhail Gorbachev's reforms had enabled the Russian Orthodox Church to claim new freedoms and there was a reversal of the atheist policies of the seventy years since the Russian Revolution.

After a failed attempt to visit Lithuania in 1960, still a part of the Soviet Union and barred to tourists, twenty-nine years later I was finally on a plane to Moscow with an onward ticket to Vilnius, the capital. Just a few months earlier I had visited Moscow for the first time in over a decade, my original visa refusal reversed at the last minute, allowing me to travel to Moscow for the Millennium of the Baptism of Rus'. This was the celebration by the Russian Orthodox Church marking its thousand years' history since 988.

An unprecedented opportunity arose to visit this tiny, beleaguered Baltic state, but again I was refused a visa – until the decision by the Soviet Embassy was suddenly overturned after an intervention by the Foreign Office. Lithuania had been part of my life since the 1970s, when news first reached me of the new struggle by the Catholic Church for religious freedom.

The last Soviet religious prisoners to be held, carefully documented by Keston College, were Lithuanian Catholics and now they had been freed. Bishop Vincentas Sladkevičius, released after nineteen years in prison, was able to reclaim his diocese of Kaisiadorys. With other bishops, a delegation visited the Vatican. The rebuilding of destroyed churches had begun. The Queen of Peace Church in Klaipieda had been the subject of dispute since its construction, a quarter of a century earlier. The parishioners built it with their own hands and paid for it themselves, immediately after which it was confiscated. Now, to great rejoicing, the faithful celebrated its return.

A petition was signed by 31,000 people for the restoration of the mother church, Vilnius Cathedral, which had been commandeered by the state authorities as a store for books and later an art gallery. In what seemed like a miracle, the Bishop of Vilnius, Julijonas Steponavičius, was returning, after twenty-nine years of prison and house arrest, to reclaim his cathedral and his diocese. Out of the blue I received his personal invitation, just two weeks before the event on 5 February 1989, to be a guest at the re-consecration.

I caught the last possible plane out of Moscow on Saturday, 4 February. Met by a delegation of lay believers at the airport, they drove me to a private house for supper. The next morning, Sunday, a car called to collect me. At the chancellery there was a bustle of bishops and priests surrounding Bishop Steponavičius, a small figure, undiminished by suffering, who found time to embrace everyone around him.

After a brief exchange in Russian, I found myself sitting alone with him in the back of the official car. The driver threaded his way through the familiar streets, being forced to stop at intervals as the crowds on the pavement pressed forward to receive the Bishop's blessing through the open window. He told me that his illegal punishment (without trial) had been for refusing to forbid the teaching of the catechism to children. These long years, nearly half a lifetime, had been a time of prayer, of supplication for an event which he did not believe he would live to see. Now here he was, impeded by ever thicker crowds as we approached Gediminas Square, the heart of the city, where the cathedral stood.

I appeared to be the only foreign guest and I was not aware of the protocol, as the way ahead to the cathedral was blocked by a sea of bodies. Was it even safe? As we got out, a friendly hand guided me to walk behind the bishop as he strode purposefully forward. I had a vision which has stayed with me. In my mind I was following Moses across the Red Sea. Marshalled lightly by civilians (not police), the waves parted and a clear path ahead appeared. As we progressed, slowly, while the Bishop exchanged greetings with the crowd along the way, one peculiarity struck me. There was no cheering. There was a quality of silence, broken only by the intake of ten thousand breaths and the waving of flags in national colours, gold, green and red, still officially banned. Prayer, not cheering, greeted our progress, as I followed behind.

As we reached the outer walls of the cathedral, I sensed that Bishop Steponavičius was re-consecrating himself as well as his cathedral. I felt the same, in what was one of the most solemn moments of my life. Television cameras rolled, as they would for the next three hours or more, while the Bishop began by praying as he processed around the exterior of the building. Entering through the newly restored west door, he did the same inside and then prostrated himself for several minutes before the altar. Only then was the consecration mass ready to begin. A priest had conducted me to a position of honour in a reserved section in front of the congregation. Sitting with me were Lithuanian dignitaries in priestly robes or national costume and a scattering of Russian Orthodox priests. I later found out that not even the Vatican was represented at this most significant of events.

The mass lasted two hours, the congregation now joining fervently in prayer or song at every appropriate moment. Following this, young people in their local costume, differing according to each region, walked up the nave to present flowers (yes, in a northern midwinter) to the Bishop, who placed them on the altar. Some spoke; one of these was Nijole Sadunaite, just released from a labour camp, addressing the Bishop in the name of all political prisoners.

A whirlwind of events followed. A succession of new friends, some of whose names I knew as former prisoners, guided me around their ancient city. With jubilation they pointed out a notice on the wall of a building which, until recently, had been the museum of atheism. The words read, 'Museum closed. Property of the Vilnius Curia from 1 March 1989'.

Next, my friends conducted me to a first-floor office overlooking Gediminas Square. Sitting at a desk, then standing in greeting, was Professor Vytautas Landsbergis. His was a new name to me, but he had emerged as head of Sajudis which means 'Movement', a clever short form reflecting Gorbachev's policies. Sajudis, was already an illegal party pledged to secure Lithuanian independence. Landsbergis eventually became the first head of state of a free Lithuania. Finally, there was a festive dinner at which the first edition of a new Christian magazine was presented, *Kataliku pasaulis* (Catholic World), another milestone.

On 7 February the press announced that the Reverend 'Miklas Bordo' had been a guest at the great event.

I had already become convinced that the Soviet Union had no future. Now, in those few days in Lithuania, I was certain of it.

Chapter I
Praze-an-Beeble – A Cornish Childhood

'Praze, Praze' – 'Alleluia! Praise the Lord'. The scene of this exchange between the guard and a passenger was Praze-an-Beeble station, in the days before Dr Beeching swept it away. I never actually heard this and it may have been mythical, but the story was too good not to be true and went its rounds beyond the village.

The name of the Cornish village in which I was born and bred is itself slightly controversial. 'Praze' does not feature on the oldest maps, because it was built only in the nineteenth century on a lode of tin, housing for a mining community. No one ever called it Praze-an-Beeble, but the Ordnance Survey insists on this, repeated on the road sign as you approach from Camborne in the direction of Helston. The Great Western Railway had never heard of this either and for as long as the station existed, 'Praze' it was (on the delightful old line: Helston (for Culdrose and the Lizard Peninsula), Truthall Halt, Nancegollan, Praze, Gwinear Road (mainline stop for Penzance and Paddington). This little train was the magic carpet to adventure – it would take us, after all, via two changes, to the enchantment of St Ives, where we used to spend our holidays during the war, when more distant travel was out of the question.

There are several Prazes (French-Cornish for 'meadow'), but only one Praze-an-Beeble, the suffix being the name of the tiny river which flows past the primary school I attended until I was eight. The river then finds its way to Trenwheal and Townshend, where it joins the bigger Hayle River and finds its way out into the estuary and once-industrial town of the same name ('Hayle' means 'estuary').

Our village itself, though, was far from romantic. In reality it was ugly, consisting originally of a main street with terraced houses on both sides and no front gardens. In the high noon of divided Methodism it supported a 'top chapel' (long since closed) and a Wesleyan chapel halfway down. The only buildings of any real note were the post office, now listed, and the St Aubyn Arms at the bottom, opposite the 'Plan' (plantation), with its war memorial to the victims of the Great War.

Continuing towards Helston, up Station Hill, the *nouveaux riches* who had amassed a few hundred pounds built their semis and constructed them well. Amazingly, somehow my grandmother, Anne Bourdeaux, her sister, Auntie Mabel, and later my father's brother, Uncle Bryan and his wife, Auntie Della, lived side by side in the middle of this road – and none of them had any significant money behind them. The opposite side, in my younger days, was an open field, with the road leading to a railway bridge and beyond that the station.

Praze School was a few hundred yards away to the east, following the course of the stream, which, with the blacksmith's shop, was a constant distraction on the way to school. Most important of all and the social centre of the whole community was my father's bakery, with the proud sign on the wall, 'A. C. Bourdeaux and Sons'. My father, Richard Bourdeaux, was the elder of two by eight years; Bryan was his only brother and there were no sisters.

The Family Bakery

The story of the founding of the bakery is a sad one, but the outcome was a triumph over adversity. My father was born on the last day of 1907, in Birmingham, not Cornwall, though my grandparents moved 'home' when he was a toddler. My paternal grandfather, Cecil, fought in the First World War, but was one of the innumerable men who suffered from a gas attack, was invalided out, and could never work again. His young wife, Anne Carah Edwards, was a woman of considerable determination, humourless, but with warmth concealed inside. There was little compensation and she knew that the two boys would have to make their own way in life very shortly. Continuing education was scarcely an option where there were no pennies, so she established a village bakery business in the heart of Praze.

My father was a weekly boarder at Hayle School up to the age of twelve, where 'Boss' Wagner and a few taps on the wrist taught him beautiful handwriting, but much else was lacking. His real education came later. When he was old enough to go away, his mother scrimped and saved to send him to the National Bakery School in London. He had lodgings in Streatham and flourished, returning with all the certificates and a high degree of competence.

While his mother was engaged full time in setting up and running the bakery, which needed a wellspring of determination and toughness, the upbringing of Bryan was largely in the hands of Auntie Mabel, my grandmother's sister. Bryan would have liked to train as an engineer, but the family's limited resources did not permit this. Neither did he want to work in the bakery, so he took charge of the shop and deliveries of bread and cakes to the outlying farms. In those pre-supermarket days, there was money to be made by driving a van on its rounds, down many a rutted farm track, at the end of which the farmer's wife would buy a week's supply of bread, 'splits' (soft rolls) and *'saffern cek'*. I came to know this side of the business well and enjoyed helping our trusty Griff Hart, carrying the loaves and counting the money. When well established, this supported two vans, but of course they disappeared with the advent of the supermarket. When Uncle Bryan was in the shop, he worked alongside my grandmother, which can't have always been easy for him.

Once war broke out, my father learned that his was an essential trade, which he would combine with duties as captain of the Home Guard (to be taken with seriousness, as invasion was a real possibility and there were rugged coastlines on both sides of the county within a short distance). Bryan volunteered for the RAF, hoping to become an engineer, but, with his bakery experience, the Government decided otherwise and put him in the galley as a cook in the Navy. He worked on a supply ship and, despite seasickness, surprisingly came to love the sea itself. He was, for a time, on that terrible run around the North Cape, delivering supplies to Murmansk, which may eventually have reached Leningrad under siege and saved lives there. To my knowledge, though, he was never permitted to set foot on Russian soil. Much later there was an award of service medals to those who showed such gallantry, but Bryan died far too early to receive one. He would have deserved this accolade, and to many in Russia he was a hero whose name they never learned. Rising to the rank of Chief Petty Officer, while engaged in action on a convoy to Russia he slipped and severely injured his back, from which he suffered for the rest of his life. On the deck of HMS *Bulldog* where he was serving, he witnessed the German surrender of the Channel Islands.

When the war ended the two brothers worked together again (my father was 38, Uncle Bryan 30). After much discussion, Bryan eventually offered to sell his share in the business to my father. This enabled him to leave Praze with Auntie Della – true Cornish from the neighbouring village of Leedstown – and they moved with their two sons, Paul and John, to the Scilly Isles. Buying a small confectioner's and tobacconist's shop in Hugh Town, St Mary's, Bryan revelled in the new life. Harold Wilson used to be a regular visitor to buy his paper when in residence. Bryan ran it alone until he retired and the shop, though sold out of the family, still bears the Bourdeaux name (as does the thriving pottery a mile away established by his younger son, John). Paul was educated at Truro School and became a career specialist in primary education.

Praze and Crowan

If you continued up Station Hill, you would walk under a heavy black railway bridge, long since demolished, and then come to a long granite wall which was a daily feature of my life when I started school. Leaving the station entrance on the left, we follow the wall, which in those days often crumbled and fell down in places through neglect. We are, in fact, on the east side of the Clowance Estate, on which I would live for the first eight years of my life, and then during school holidays for the next ten years.

This was, in the nineteenth century, the home of the St Aubyn family, which gave its name to the one pub in Praze. After the Great War they sold up and moved north to their preferred estate, Pencarrow. The Glanvilles, who had made their money in the local mines, bought the old house and its land, farms, pond, kitchen garden, iron-age tin quarry and magnificent ancient woodland. They were never up to the maintenance, whether through absence of tradition or lack of money to employ enough servants to keep the place going, I never knew. By the start of the Second World War, the golden age of Clowance had long since passed. Gone were the social events which used to grace the lawn in front of the house leading down to the lake; gone were the comings and goings of the Cornish gentry up and down the main drive; gone was the weekly ceremonial drive in full finery past the Lodge, when the gatekeeper would rush out and swing open the gate to give passage to the landau as it began its ascent across the Demmon (*'demesne'*?) Fields to Crowan Church.

Praze itself was a child of Methodism and had no parish church. Crowan was the old settlement and Praze has always been in its parish, as is neighbouring Leedstown. Pevsner dismisses the church as 'All granite, severely restored 1872, with a West tower of three stages, unbuttressed.' This may be true, but it had a certain grandeur, with its tower standing proud just below the higher ground at Blackrock to the east, part of the granite and tin central spine of West Cornwall, where the fields give way to tin mining and the relics of engine houses rise stark from the gorse and heather.

Crowan – St Crewenna – owes its dedication to one of the innumerable Cornish, Breton, Irish and Welsh saints whose lives are entirely lost in history. Not even a legend relating to the life exists. I write 'the' life, not 'his' or 'hers', because I was always told as a child that no one knew whether Crewenna was male or female, and I have heard no word on this since. Inside, Victorian restoration or no, it has a plain dignity, enlivened by several monuments to the St Aubyn family going back to the fourteenth century. Its bells, except during the enforced silence of the war years, rang out regularly (and still do) over a peaceful landscape.

The glory of Clowance was always in its grounds, rather than in the great house itself. Once again it does not impress, but Pevsner is unduly dismissive: 'Plain house of seven bays and two storeys, granite, with a one-storey Tuscan porch of four columns, apparently early c19.' That is all. He makes no mention of the Georgian orangery or the stables at the rear, so full of character.

For the duration of the war the Government commandeered the house, leaving Mrs Glanville installed in a tiny flat, and two aged sisters, the Misses Chipman, isolated in the stables. Naturally, the whole place deteriorated rapidly under the succession of British, then American, troops, followed by Italian and, after D-Day, German prisoners of war. Mrs Glanville continued in residence, but could never even begin to restore Clowance. All the occupants of that time would be amazed to see it now: an upmarket timeshare, with well-appointed units built in part of the gardens, but the rest of the grounds being increasingly restored, Heligan-like, to former splendour. There is a new grand entrance forged through the old wall (now rebuilt) and the woods just south of the entrance to the former station.

So it was to the Lodge, the gatekeeper's house, that my mother brought me, a few days after my birth in Camborne Nursing Home on 19 March 1934.

My mother had benefited from a broader education than my father and would have flourished at university, if such a move could have been afforded, or even contemplated, in such an isolated community. Her father, Horace Blair, was a Devonian, who spent his life, apart from service in the cavalry in the Great War, as a schoolteacher and later, from all accounts, a good headmaster of small local schools.

These appointments moved him around. He was teaching at the little school in the fishing port of Porthleven, near Helston, when my mother, Lillian Myra Blair, was born in 1908. She would live, like my father, to be 91. She was the eldest of four sisters and

I had the gift of three beloved Cornish aunts. Dolly was the sporty one, who virtually grew up on a bike, and later moved to London to marry Uncle Will, an architect. Hazel came next, always bubbling with good cheer and commanding a responsible job as a bookkeeper in Redruth, which was her married home for many years. Last came Joan, with the warmest heart, who worked in Truro in the war. Then she devotedly looked after Nanny and Papa Blair in their old age. Nanny had had polio when young and she wore surgical boots, but that didn't keep her off her bike or prevent her from joining in everything, including rowing, even when they later moved in retirement to Tresillian, on an upper tidal reach of the River Fal.

The Blairs had moved to Praze after the Great War, where Horace was headmaster in the 1920s and 1930s, and it was there that my mother and father met. They never lived for a day outside the village, leaving it only for holidays and visits to family.

Far from being an educational backwater, there were inspirational teachers in Cornwall, and in my mother's schooldays Anne Treneer was the outstanding figure. She published two autobiographical books, the second of which, *Schoolhouse in the Wind*, gives a fine insight into conditions in Camborne in the 1920s. What Anne writes is so vivid that it is worth quoting her at some length, especially as she mentions my mother.

'As I reached the school gates girls would be streaming in from Redruth and Portreath; from Lanner and Carnkie; girls from as far afield as St Day and St Agnes. Girls from Hayle, Gwithian and Conner Downs; girls on bicycles from Praze… I felt especially drawn to the country children, children who, on Saturdays and Sundays, were living almost unchanged such a life as I myself had lived at Gorran and Caerhays. Lillian Blair and her sister from the schoolhouse at Praze especially used to remind me of myself and my sister. They would come sometimes, on nipping days, with little hot bottles of water in their pockets to warm their hands. Bicycling is cold work in winter for the first mile or two.'

My mother trained on the job to be a primary school teacher at eighteen. This was her sole professional career, which she gave up when I came along. She did do some supply teaching later on, but it was the Second World War which launched both my parents into prominence in the local community.

The five years before the outbreak of the Second World War were as idyllic as any childhood could be. From the outside the Lodge looked like everyone's dream cottage: granite, gabled, walls pierced by delightful tiny diamond-shaped lead-paned windows. I'm sure my mother managed to clean them, but how must remain the secret of a determined woman. She bore her drudgery without ever a word of complaint. There was one irregularity in the plan of the house. The front door was shielded by a picturesque porch with a small circular lookout in the wall. Here the gatekeeper used to sit on a granite bench, peering out and awaiting the arrival of a carriage, before opening the gate. ('Best-Gate', it was sometimes called, though it was a wooden structure and far less imposing than that of most other manors.)

Inside, the Lodge was minuscule: kitchen, scullery and living room downstairs, two small bedrooms and box-room upstairs, with no corridors or landings. The box-room, otherwise known as the 'spare bedroom', would one day house an evacuee, followed, near the end of the war and ten years younger than I, by my brother Neil. The heating was adequate for such a small house: open grate, with a single hob, just large enough to boil a kettle, in the living room; coke-fired Cornish range (prototype of the Aga) in the kitchen. There was no heating in the bedrooms. The coalhole was a shed to the left of the back door, where ivy picked its way through the holes in the slated roof.

But the main feature (unbelievable to reflect on today) was the absence of a bathroom or even of running water. There was no tap in the house, though the scullery had a washing-up basin with a plug and soak-away. All water had to be run from a single tap outside the back door, through which my mother had to carry in water for washing, bathing and doing the dishes, after heating it in a cauldron on the Cornish range. We all used to take turns in a hip bath, though eventually we fell into the habit, once a week, of trailing down to Granny Bourdeaux's on Station Hill, where the plumbing was more than adequate.

The family joke – and shame – was (need one say it?) that there was no inside toilet, though why the Elsan had to be situated a good 30 yards away at the extreme top end of the back garden, where it yielded to the woods, is anyone's guess. Did I say Elsan? This was a chemical installation, which came only much later. Before that, my father would joke about what he called the 'long drop' into a pit. I can illustrate the narrowness of my early horizons by stating that I felt no particular shame in later inviting the occasional boarding-school friend to stay. I remember that one had to negotiate the path in pitch black, with a torch, but running the gauntlet of a herd of cows which had often invaded the top of the garden.

Such was my home until the age of 18. All my schoolwork in the holidays, of which I did a great deal, was either by daylight or, at one time, by candlelight when I studied late at night. Later, there were some semi-efficient Calor Gas lights, which, the saying goes, were thrown down the nearest tin-mine shaft when electricity finally arrived. This was symbolical of welcoming progress, but they would have been valuable antiques today. Restored, extended and prettified beyond recognition, the Lodge is now offered as an upmarket holiday home.

To me, none of these features was a deprivation. The compensations, if I needed them, were life-forming. Nature's parade began at the back door, where birds sometimes came to drink at the surrounds of the tap. I hardly ever experienced a night elsewhere until I was eight. I would awake to the sound of the dawn chorus and the cows (in the Demmon Fields opposite, if not in the back garden). My love of the open countryside has been with me ever since, and I'm grateful now to be living in Iffley, a village through which the Thames flows.

I loved looking for birds' nests and would find dozens in a season: I learned to distinguish the mottled eggs of blackbirds from the blue of the thrushes and to marvel at the domed domain of the wren. I would look at, sometimes touch, but never damage a nest. No one ever thought of feeding the birds as we do today, for there was such an abundance for them – also, wartime food regulations would not have permitted it. Rooks nested high up in the elm trees beyond the toilet. When I was a teenager I did occasionally shoot at them with my father's two-two rifle (courtesy of the Home Guard) and singular lack of success. This was because the farmer-fathers of some of my friends hated them for stealing the crops, so I was only helping the local economy. I later shot rabbits, too, always handing over to my mother the job of gutting, skinning and cooking them.

The garden was small, but surrounded the house and my mother kept it impeccably: rambler roses, yucca plants which flourished so well in Cornwall, a shaven lawn, a yew tree on the road side and a towering holm-oak, overshadowing the defining feature of the garden: a tiny stream which flowed its whole length, from beside the toilet shed at the top, to where it disappeared under the drive at the bottom, to emerge in the woods under a conker tree the other side and gently snake down to the Clowance lake between lush, fern-covered banks. It was, of course, the jewel of my early childhood. It was gentle. It never flooded, though occasionally the fringes froze when the temperature dropped to un-Cornish depths for the odd day in the winter. I never knew nor cared to find out where it originated. Its importance was the constant challenge it brought into my life. In my earliest days I would make mud pies there. Then, as friends began to come round, we would dam it or throw in sticks or leaves, racing them to declare a winner as one emerged from the undergrowth around the holm-oak or, more adventurously (and with only rare success), from the egress the other side of the drive.

There were always friends – at various stages through my childhood Michael Pearce (the butcher's son), John Trewhella (a leader, because older), the gentle big boy, Tom Roberts from Crenver Farm, who was my best friend, even though he was older and we eventually went to different schools. The woods were just one adventure playground, tree-climbing or playing our favourite game, when we were old enough to be daring. 'Meet moppie'. This was a game of chase and tig, where a certain tree was declared 'home' and one would guard it. The rest of the mob would fan out and try, after a given number of minutes, to regain the tree without being touched by the guard. The greatest adventure, though, concerned Mrs Glanville, who hated my friends and me playing in the woods, claiming (rightly, but impossibly) that they were her private property. She would sometimes come and virtually join in the game by chasing us. She never caught anyone, but would continue to our front door and confront my mother, who would squirm, but would never tell us off, except in a voice which made it obvious that she knew that we would be out there again within five minutes.

My Parents

Why did my parents choose to live in this place, their first marital home? It was economic necessity, not aesthetic attraction. There was simply no spare money to buy a house in the early days of their marriage, and rented accommodation nearer the bakery was scarce. They had intended to move soon and were saving from the day of their marriage (Boxing Day, 1932), but the war intervened and made any such considerations impossible. My mother paid the rent meticulously on each quarter-day. She would count out £12 in single notes in a ritual I well remember; then I would take it down to Mrs Glanville. That was less than one pound a week, though how good value that was compared with my father's small and irregular profits from the bakery, I can't say.

My parents always had a telephone from the earliest I can remember. You had to pick it up and wait. Then the voice of Joyce Webb from the post office would boom down the line, 'Number, please' – and you had to dictate the number to her. If it was just a local one, you would state the figures only. We were 'Praze 29', later '329'. If you wanted to make a more distant call you would state the destination and then you had to wait until the operator in the other exchange had time to pick up the connecting phone and plug a lead into the little hole at her end. Then you could hear the number ringing which you had called. Everyone used to say that Joyce knew every piece of news in the village, though I expect in truth that she was too busy to listen in to many conversations.

Even more strangely, we had a car from my youngest days. The first model was a tiny three-wheeler 'trike', yellow and green, with a rounded nose, front seat for two, tapering at the rear, where there was a jump-seat, just big enough for me when I was tiny. It wouldn't pass any safety regulation today, though if any still exist, they must be valuable items in a vintage-car collection. When I grew a little, my father replaced this with an Austin 'Big Seven', navy blue, narrow, but with two recognisable seats at the back. Amazingly, we became the envy of many during the war. We were allowed to keep the car and have a limited petrol ration, strictly for travel to and from work, or for Home Guard duties.

My father never walked the less-than-a-mile to work, but came home by car for lunch, always expecting it to be on the table sharp at twelve and finding it so. If he was on 'early turn', he would leave at about five, returning for a cooked breakfast equally on the dot of eight. Then he would come home around half-past-four, giving him a long evening, which he would often spend playing cricket, but never doing any gardening.

My mother's regime was to present the family with three cooked meals a day (she would do this even when I began taking her grandchildren down to Cornwall in the 1960s). The food was simple, but nourishing, and we never ate less than well, being supplemented by goodies from the bakery: fresh-baked bread, splits and cakes every day or as needed. During the stringent rationing of meat during the war, it was always in abundant supply, a bartering process probably having taken place. My mother had a repertoire of about ten dishes and usually we knew what to expect on each day: Sunday joint, cold leftovers on Monday, meat again on Wednesday, lentil stew on Thursday, fish on Friday and Cornish pasty (of her making, never the bakery's) on Saturday.

Shopping in those days was not complicated. Tradesmen plied their rounds. Every week we saw Walters the fish-man and Pierce the butcher. Then there were slightly less frequent, but equally essential callers: Rapson the coalman and Toms the paraffin-man. The latter played a special role in my childhood, for in him is enshrined my first memory of being truly naughty. His van would stop in the semi-circular space off the road, outside the gate into Clowance. He would sound his horn and I would be the first to run out. When he opened the door of his van, there was a cornucopia of apparatus, taps, cans, wicks, candles, all beckoning irresistibly. My ploy was, while Mr Toms' hands were both engaged in holding a can and turning a tap to make the paraffin flow from the tank, to throw gravel or small stones into my mother's cans waiting in a row to be filled. My mother, who could never tell me off and never did until her dying day, stood by, embarrassed but helpless, while Toms chased me when I ran off to look for more stones. My father was never there to administer the strap.

On Friday afternoons, until I went to school, my mother would take my father back to work and drive me with her into Camborne to do the extra shopping. Camborne, to this day, is little more than a grand version of Praze, with its plain granite houses and scarcely a garden visible, but I used to love going into the shops, especially Liptons, which was a delicatessen in today's parlance, full of tempting local produce. Parking was always outside the shop. I would sometimes sit on guard and run inside if the local policeman came to tell my mother to move on, because she was causing an obstruction. Then there was the bank (Barclays, in the market square which never housed a market in those days), which I was never permitted to enter when young, and so I came to think of it as a temple of secrets.

The other regular excursion outside the house was to church on Sundays, walking on the straight uphill path across the Demmon Fields. At first it was mornings only, then Sunday School in the afternoons, taught by the teenager Joyce Soady, who would later spend her working life in my Dad's employment, then evensong as well, when I was old enough to sing. Dad would always go on ahead, because one of his main hobbies was bellringing. He was, for many years, captain of the tower and, after the war, came to know many Cornish churches, because he would organise ringers' outings, where visiting teams would ring the local bells on light summer evenings or on Saturdays when there was no cricket.

I never remember objecting to going to church. It was what one 'did'. But it was here, in all the simplicity of the hymns, that I learned the first rudiments of music, a love of *Hymns Ancient and Modern* – later revised and re-revised – which has never left me. I enjoy singing some of them even today, but remember the unexpurgated versions well. When did anyone last sing of 'the rich man in his castle, the poor man at the gate'? My mother (alto) and my father (a very light tenor) soon had me in the choir and I found I had a voice. I would later be in the Philharmonia Chorus in London at the time when it enjoyed a worldwide reputation, but from my first day to this, except once or twice at university, I never had a singing lesson.

Old Joe Orchard pumped the organ bellows behind in the Vicar's vestry. At the console sat a delightful old man called Mr Ursell, with imposing silver locks, who played the tracker-action organ really rather well, and whom we children, inevitably, called 'Mr Rehearsal'. He had a brilliant pupil, Marion Goldsworthy (later James), whose playing was always a joy and a stimulus, and I remember she once wrote a piece of music for me, a setting of the *Nunc Dimittis* for a nativity play we put on. 'Creating' this, as the professionals say, gave me a pleasure rarely exceeded by the rich experiences of later life. In Crowan church choir only men and boys were robed in those days, while the ladies and girls would sit in the front two pews, sopranos on 'decani' led by Joyce Soady, altos (often my mother was the only one) on 'cantoris'.

I never became 'high church', though the first vicar I remember, the Revd Herbert John Skewes, used to love his festal processions and I admired the copes that he wore. In the earliest days, before I joined the choir, when he came past my seat he would swirl his robes and grin at me: I would pump my arms simultaneously in excitement, a physical quirk signifying enjoyment which would be with me throughout my childhood. No one, though, according to the inevitable local lore, could replace the late Canon Adams, who preceded my childhood.

Nor was I deprived of family holidays. I remember two (1938 and 1939) which were occasions of utter delight and adventure. The Scilly Isles, virtually unknown as a holiday destination in those days, now priced out of reach for many people, were local and easy of access by a daily sailing. My parents took me to Penzance for my first trip on the sea. The crossing, just under three hours past Land's End, could often be rough, but for me it was an adventure beyond imagining. On arrival, the *Scillonian* unloaded its contents of holidaymakers and supplies from the mainland on the quay of Hugh Town. Eric met us in his tractor and loaded our cases on the cart behind. We piled on and he drove us through the fields, now in summer bare of the daffodils which were the basis of the islands' economy, to his father's farm. Every morning I would be up with the farmer and go out and about, feeding the livestock and collecting the new-laid eggs. One of my earliest memories, when I was four, was running in joy to the farm with an egg clutched in each hand, tripping over and crushing them both in my little palms. How I howled, as if a tragedy had descended.

At the outbreak of war, in the Home Guard, my father had professional training from the soldiers billeted at Clowance. Thereafter, following a hard day's work, he would spend long night-time hours, patrolling the local hills on the lookout for 'Jerry'.

They never found the Germans, but there were inevitably some occasional false alarms. One I remember in particular was a series of expeditions to Polcrebo Downs investigating strange lights in this uninhabited area. Eventually, they found a courting couple illuminating their tryst by illegal torchlight. But this was not the end – the lady concerned was one of the Jewish schoolteachers evacuated from the East End of London – and her name was Grunsberger!

Dad's Army came into play during the day, when military discipline crept into the bakery. The team there were not misfits – far from it – but they were all, for one reason or another, prevented medically from joining the forces. It was Frank Hosking, the eternal joker, who couldn't see much beyond the end of his nose, who, overflowing with energy, initiated army drill. Every movement up or down the floor of the bakery had to be preceded by the order, 'One, two'. If a long-handled wooden paddle, used for pushing loaves to the back of the oven or retrieving them when baked, needed to be moved from one oven to the other, it could be done only if the order, 'Shoulder… arms' came first. So 'One, two' became my father's shorthand for imposing discipline on me at home, or even on my mother, when he thought she was being slow. This was one of his almost limitless fund of standard sayings, on which he would draw right up to his death, only ten days after my mother's, in 1999. One, especially reserved for me, when my thoughts took me on a journey outside the room was 'Behold' (short for 'Behold, the dreamer cometh').

Neil was born in 1944, two years after I had started as a boarder at Truro. From the first, he was brilliantly skilled in everything practical, good at everything I could not do. He filled the gap at home, because Edith, our evacuee, by this time had gone back to London for good. Later it became obvious that Neil's gifts would not be fulfilled by work in a bakery. He decided not to inherit the family business and instead set up a successful building firm which constructed or renovated many houses on the Lizard peninsula and eventually he worked in more distant parts of Cornwall, too. The knock-on effect of this was that, when my father retired, there was no one to take the bakery over and it passed out of the family. Sadly, it was eventually demolished and is now replaced by a block of flats.

In the village my father had a nickname for everyone, none of them complimentary, some of them unrepeatable in print. We had the 'Silver Tenor' in the church choir, 'Holy Joe' for a lay reader, 'the Hoss' for Arthur in the bakery, who was as slow and reliable in his job making bread as he was opening the batting for Praze cricket team.

There was a young Ghanaian who studied at the local pottery, for whom my parents had a special soft spot and he was often welcomed in our house. He played tennis well and always beat my father. All this seemed natural to me at the time, but now I see that my father was amazingly liberal minded for someone of his background and education. The real test – and I shall never forget it – came when German POWs were confined in Clowance during the last days of the war. They had to go out under guard to help on the land where, as far as I know, they were well treated, but when they returned, they were confined to barracks. Their limits were the paths in front of the manor house, which ended at the front wall by our cottage. The POWs could exercise here under supervision and one day my mother and father invited two of them in for a cup of tea when they stopped at the gate outside the Lodge. The NCO in charge surprisingly gave permission and stood guard outside. I was there, home on holiday from school, but had not yet begun to learn German. Expressing themselves in halting English, the Germans were obviously thrilled to be allowed inside a private house, which they could not do on the farms. They began to come regularly and a real friendship developed. I'm sure that, without my knowing it at the time, my enlightened parents made an inestimable contribution to the international aspect of my education.

Evacuees

My mother also found herself during the war in a senior local job, which was, in a sense, more challenging than my father's. I don't know how or why she was selected to become a leader of the Women's Voluntary Service (WVS) in Praze. On the face of it, I would have expected the overall bosses to have considered her too mild for an awkward administrative task which involved social work and prying into family circumstances, sometimes of people she did not know well. She became the Billeting Officer for the stream of evacuees who appeared in Praze from the East End and eventually from Bristol, when it came under heavy attack. It must have been her experience as a teacher that persuaded the authorities to choose her.

The evacuees arrived on a special train at Camborne station in 1940 and a whole segment of them, allocated to Praze, were put in the care of my mother, to bring them in a bus to the school. Even to summon people from all the local homes must have taken considerable organisation. Of course, there were many spaces in the houses where men had been called up and even women had gone 'up country' to serve in various war capacities.

What my mother had to guard against, though, was farmers or their wives looking from head to toe at these poor children from deprived backgrounds, before choosing the strongest among the boys as sweated labour. The scrum was unimaginable, a tale which my mother sometimes recounted. Somehow, though, she imposed discipline and by the evening the schoolroom was empty. Many of them, by their clothes and shoes, exhibited a poverty which she had never before seen.

She did not come away empty handed, however. In perhaps the only action where I know my mother to have done something with an ulterior motive, she kept back for herself a waif-like eight-year-old, blonde and fair-skinned, who looked as though she had never had a square meal in her life. And indeed so she ate for the next four years. 'Any more, Auntie?' (eni moah, a'ee?) in her inimitable Cockney accent became another household saying, current among my children even today.

Edith West came from the poorest of backgrounds. I know my mother chose her, two years my senior, to be the sister I never had. It must have been a shock suddenly to find the box-room at the Lodge occupied, and my self-centred little world suddenly split open by the intrusion of an alien being. The truth is, though, that as soon as we could understand each other's language, we got on very well. We probably argued over food every day until I went away to Truro School two years later, but in all other respects we did develop a real relationship and shared everything in our lives. I don't even remember feeling jealous when she was left at the Lodge when I went away.

We had our arguments now and again, but we always resolved them in a friendly way. The only time that Edith went running to my mother was when I hit her over the head with a butterfly net. I don't remember what she had done, but knowing my hot temper, inherited from my father, I expect it was trivial and probably my fault.

Often, however, foster parents from around the village would come running to my mother with problems and grumbles, and it was here that her diplomacy came into play. Sometimes evacuees' mothers would appear unannounced on the train from London to visit their offspring, but they were welcomed and none found any significant fault. The evacuees had their own local welfare officer, though, who frequently brought unjustified complaints to my mother's door. It was this person's arrival one evening which occasioned the only unpleasant event I ever witnessed at home. This lady was sitting by the fire berating my mother. My father and I were in the room and listened in silence – until he suddenly leapt to his feet and shouted, 'I've listened to you enough. There's the door. Never come here again.' She was the only person ever to be expelled from our house, but she caused no more trouble. She was the same person who had shone the lights on Polcrebo Downs.

The evacuees were not only well treated; they experienced, even in wartime, little luxuries and a style of life that they could never previously have imagined. Edith's cousin Siddie Barlow loved it so much that he returned after the war and bought a smallholding in Praze. For many years our first-ever newsagent in the village, who converted an old house in Fore Street into a shop, was 'Baigent' (no one ever used his first name), a former evacuee who made a good living there.

Edith herself went back home when she was twelve, to experience the joys of puberty with her mother, though not before one day I heard her exclaim, 'Ee, me spuds are coming out', which I didn't understand at the time. We not only kept in touch after the war, but she several times came to stay. We met a few times in London when I began my National Service and she took me to the old Sadler's Wells to see *Carmen*, with Constance Shacklock, my very first experience of professional opera, introducing me to a lifetime of devotion to this great art form.

Ours remained strictly a brother–sister relationship. Edith grew into a beautiful young woman and eventually married a GI, Bob Halvorsen, emigrating to live the rest of her life in Lincoln, Nebraska, where I visited her in 1969. On trips back to England she visited my parents several times, bringing children and eventually grandchildren with her. When my mother and father both died in 1999, she sent me a beautiful letter and contribution to their memorial fund.

I must conclude this chapter with another Praze evacuee story reflecting lack of local prejudice during the war years.

My great-aunt Mabel Edwards lived alone, after taking charge of Bryan, one house below her sister, Granny Bourdeaux, on Station Hill. When the evacuees arrived, she took one in, Rosie Obler, who turned out to be Jewish, though I don't suppose Mabel knew this on selection day. Rosie, Edith's age, was even more waif-like than Edith, but my father got to know her. She could sing. He would perch her on the counter of the bakery shop and ask her to go through her repertoire, something which Rosie always remembered with affection. Auntie Mabel, when she discovered Rosie's religion, insisted on the strictest observance – provided she was brought up as a Christian, too. There were many Jewish children in the contingent. There was no synagogue west of Plymouth, but the many Jewish children were supposed to attend a class of some sort on the Sabbath in Camborne. Auntie Mabel ensured that Rosie never missed. But Mabel was also strict in her own Anglican observance, so Rosie had to accompany her to church on Sunday mornings and also attend Sunday School in the afternoons. This seemed to suit Rosie and she flourished. I think this was remarkable for a person like Mabel who had never had a child of her own and who hardly ever set foot outside the village, except to go on a church outing.

Later Rosie, too, married a GI and emigrated to California. It was many years before I came back into contact with her, but when I did it was both sad and joyful. She wrote me out of the blue, I think after recognising my name from the press.

She, I discovered, had had a sad life. In Los Angeles her husband had been murdered in the street, as an innocent passerby. Her son moved out and did not leave a forwarding address. Her only other child, a daughter, had learning difficulties, but they were a devoted couple, sustained by Rosie's job in a bank. She sent me her short memoirs of wartime life in Praze, featuring both my parents and Auntie Mabel, in which she wrote that her childhood experience in Praze was the happiest time of her life. Written in a simple, natural style, these pages brought back a flood of memories, which we all enjoyed with tears and laughter. I was thrilled, many years later, when she and her daughter came for a holiday in London, and I was able to meet them.

School

The biggest change, of course, to my early life was when I started school at four. 'Crowan' School, as it was officially named, was actually in Praze, and at our dawdling speed from the Lodge often took half an hour to reach. My mother arranged for Ethel Faull, a 'big girl' (probably all of ten) from one of the local farms, to call for me daily. On my first two days, Betty Allen, older and knowing all the ropes, called out, 'Please, Miss! Michael hev wet hisself.' Everyone thought that was natural enough. No one mocked me and I quickly fell into a routine, picking up reading and writing seemingly without having to make much effort. I would, though, sometimes be bored while the others chanted, from a big wall chart, 'The cat sat on the mat.' Miss Ella Veale, who lodged on Station Hill with Auntie Mabel, was a kind and excellent teacher, followed a year later, when I 'went up', by Miss Poole. Occasionally we saw Mr May, the formidable but efficient headmaster, who often called on me to read out loud in class. 'Arithmetic' was always my best subject. I found an old green school textbook which had belonged to my father. He had never completed the answers, so I started to fill them in, and soon found myself going on to algebra, which did not have any place at Praze School.

But these were now war years and my parents had a problem. How would I be able to develop at my natural pace in this rather restricted setting? They announced, in 1942, when I was eight, that I would soon be going to Treliske, the preparatory department of Truro School, as a boarder.

This decision by my parents was one of extraordinary foresight and, without question, was the first turning point of my life. What persuaded them that this was the best solution? They obviously did not consider that waiting three years until the enforced move from Praze to Camborne Grammar School at the mandatory age of eleven was an adequate solution (quite apart from the difficulty of travelling daily nearly four miles each way with the wartime lack of transport).

For them the fee of £100 *per annum* would be a sacrifice almost too great to bear, but they had just enough to pay this and to buy all the items on the clothing list and I soon faced a new life.

Chapter II
Truro School: High on the Hill

During the war years and subsequently (until 1952), when Europe was only just beginning to recover, Truro School turned me – and many of my contemporaries – into internationalists. Here was an educational achievement which has been the foundation of my whole life. A small number of masters (not many mistresses) who, through age or minor disability, could not serve in the forces, ran a school where hardly a day passed without the broadening of our horizons. At the same time, the strict Methodist values – taught, but humanely imposed – sank into our very bones.

Treliske

I do remember a traumatic event at Treliske, the prep school, on my second or third night away from home. I had not even got to know Mr and Mrs Stratton, who ran the establishment virtually on their own. They called us in the middle of the night: 'Get up, come down to the air-raid shelter.' We didn't know and weren't told what was happening, but, with dressing gowns on and wrapped in blankets, we were led down several flights of stairs and into the mysterious basement, which we had never seen. We were there for several hours on two consecutive nights. Later I learned that there had been a serious aerial bombardment of Falmouth Docks. My parents could see a red glow in the sky vaguely to the east of where they lived and had been worried, thinking that Truro, too, might have been under attack.

Treliske was a nineteenth-century mansion converted to house some 30 boarders, five or six to a dorm, upstairs in the main building, and about the same number of dayboys. I was, of course, homesick at first, but soon became used to the new life, especially as there were so many interesting activities. The Strattons taught us all subjects between them. Mrs Stratton, helped out by a matron ('Miss Matty'), was kindly, never raised her voice and looked after all our needs in a homely way. Her husband was authoritative; all obeyed him unquestioningly, but he did not arouse excessive fear and rarely needed to resort to heavy discipline. He could, of course, in those days impose beatings, which he did with a soft slipper, but only very occasionally.

From Mr Stratton I began to learn French and enjoyed it from the first; I've often reflected on how enlightened it was to teach a foreign language at that age during war years, while the culture it represented was uncontactable. Yet we were protected from the war in our cocoon, and apart from the air raids during those first nights, I don't remember that it impinged on our lives in any serious way. Our diet must have been restricted, but we never went hungry. The grounds were extensive, or at least to us seemed larger than they were, being surrounded by a golf course, which was out-of-bounds, but still used and maintained. We occasionally found golf balls in our woods and earned the odd sixpence by returning them to the players. The woods were of pine and dropped a generous supply of needles ('fuzz'), which we used to thatch our little houses made of sticks or to furbish tracks for our dinky toys which we raced and garaged with endless inventiveness.

Love of sport began here. We played soccer in the winter. The same front lawn of the former estate had to serve as a cricket pitch in the summer. As groundsmen could not be employed full-time during those years, Mr Stratton often mowed the pitch himself and we had to go out in a rota to dig up – very carefully with penknives – the invasive plantains and daisies.

It was on this pitch that I first exhibited my evil temper in a social context. I'm sure that my all-forgiving mother had not been nearly severe enough in curbing this at home. Jack Nash was batting and I was fielding at mid-off. He hit the ball in my direction and I dropped it. He used a nickname which I had acquired through my tendency to blush when embarrassed and shouted out, 'Rosie Cheeks, Rosie Cheeks – can't catch for toffee!' I ran over to him and administered a punch right on his own pale cheek, which soon swelled up, so that he carried a ripe black eye for several days afterwards. Mr Stratton, who was umpire and coach combined, dismissed me from the field and summoned me for a severe interview soon afterwards. I was mortified and never physically assaulted anyone again. I escaped a beating and have the feeling that Mr Stratton understood the circumstances which he had witnessed. He also informed my parents and my mother was duly ashamed.

Under the strict rules prevailing in boarding schools of those days, my mother and father could visit me only once in three weeks, but more often would have been difficult anyway, considering conditions in the depth of the war. There were trains from Praze to Truro, via Gwinear Road, but then a long walk from the station to Treliske. As the car could not be used for private purposes in those days, when we started term we had to load our tin trunks onto shared taxis at Truro station and a few pence would be added to our bills for this service.

There was good time for reading and I quickly learned the value of the well-stocked junior library. Having the leisure, I would pick up a book that appealed and read it: only too rarely in later life would I have such an opportunity. We were not guided in any way. My chosen shelf was the one which contained the complete works of Richmal Crompton, the *Just William* series. I devoured every one of them and the exploits of William's gang remain in my mind even today.

During the school holidays I immediately reintegrated into home life as it had been earlier. It must have been during this time that my parents taught me the rudiments of tennis, which was to become important to me later. A local farmer lent a corner of a field and he helped to mow it himself. My mother was responsible for measuring out the court. Somehow she acquired lime to mark it, using an ancient and rickety contraption which relayed the white mix, via a series of cogs, from a small rectangular trough to the front wheel, which inscribed the lines on the uneven turf. It wasn't a good surface to play on, but it encouraged quick reactions to an erratic bounce and I ever afterwards preferred to play – and eventually umpire – on grass.

My parents put me in for a new 'Governors' Scholarship', which I won. It was worth £100 a year, but that virtually covered the fees and, beyond keeping me clothed, they never had to pay for my education again.

Truro School

'Big School' – Truro School, on the other side of the city – was a different world, a macrocosm after the microcosm of Treliske. I went there in 1944, after two years at the prep school, aged only ten. New perspectives opened out overnight. The outlook from the windows could not have been more different from Treliske. The splendid school song says it all:

> *High on the hill, with the city below,*
> *Up in the sunshine we live.*
> *Would you ascend to us, listen and know,*
> *This is the warning we give:*
> *When we are told*
> *This is pure gold,*
> *Let it be gold in its ring,*
> *Little we care*
> *What it may wear –*
> *What is itself, that's the thing.*

The song didn't seem to attract too many ribald versions, though I remember 'What she may wear' being substituted for the penultimate line. It was reputedly penned by an old Truronian, Joseph Hunkin, later to become Bishop of Truro. It was a gloss on the school motto, *Esse quam videre*, taken from some obscure Latin author and continued *bonus maluit* – 'He preferred to be good rather than to seem to be good', which is an excellent guiding word, to which I would like to think I, as well as thousands of other Old Truronians, have tried to remain faithful.

High on the hill we certainly were. From that day to this every passenger in every train pulling out of Truro and heading over the viaduct towards Plymouth has been able to see the school on the opposite side of the valley. The Victorian clock tower stands out now, as it did then, dominating the ever-growing number of new buildings further up the hill behind. I slept and worked for ten years in that grey pile, behind which, in those days, there was just the science block, a two-storey classroom building and an asphalt playground. The only other outside installations were a fives court, long since demolished, but well used as a sort of cricket net, and a primitive loo block, which existed during my whole time at the school.

Below were two small boarding houses, Pentreve, half hidden in the trees, and Epworth on the other side of Trennick Lane, the road to the school. But the glory of the site was the terraces, cascading down from the school frontage. In my early days, they were gardens, not well managed during the war years, but later turned most successfully into rather constricted grass tennis courts. Behind, further up the lane, playing fields rose one above the other to the top of the hill. The lane led to a country path through Pencalenick Woods, all within our bounds, and just beyond was the village of Tresillian. I could often visit my grandparents there on Sunday afternoons and sometimes I went out on the Fal in the little rowing boat they kept on the mudflats, navigable at high tide only. Opposite them lived Robert Shaw, later to become a Hollywood star, whose father was the local doctor.

Robert was to exert an influence on me he could never have imagined. At school he was already a brilliant actor. He complemented what we read in the classroom by demonstrating his power on stage. He stood at the adapted reading desk of the school chapel, a makeshift theatre, and proclaimed, 'Friends, Romans, countrymen, lend me your ears. I come to bury Caesar, not to praise him.' His stunning declamation riveted me at the age of just eleven, in the context of a production by Freddie Wilkes, who, as director, always showed gifts equal to his teaching of French and German. Freddie sought out talent and nurtured it. Robert's subsequent career, as the 'Old Man of the Sea' and in many other films, as well as his success as a novelist, is on record. I never, to my knowledge, exchanged a personal word with him, but he remained a hero, not least on the rugby field, where he had a rare turn of speed as a wing three-quarter.

In subsequent years Billy Faull played the female lead in *The Taming of the Shrew*, but my next real highlight was Shaw's *Saint Joan*, in which my friend, Derek Jaynes, at the age of fourteen, played the lead and held the Truro world in his hands as he lamented the sound of the 'blessed, blessed church bells', which 'she', in captivity, had been deprived of hearing. Neither Billy nor Derek made a subsequent career of acting, but all of these drama heroes exerted a subtle influence on their contemporaries.

I was not an actor, but I did have a walk-on part in *Saint Joan*, where I had to stand still and listen to the Inquisitor's interminable speech. Freddie Wilkes was well known for distributing signed and inscribed copies of the programmes to the actors, for which he would choose apposite words from the play in question. My programme read, 'They also serve who only stand and wait' – Milton was pressed into service because there was nothing in Shaw's text which fitted.

These early days were intimidating. From being a big boy at Treliske, I was suddenly a midget in a world inhabited by giants (Keith Vyvyan was at least six feet six and seemed to me seven feet tall). Biggest of all – by reputation, rather than stature – was Warne, the head boy. He was terrifying. On my first day, Buddy Rich warned me to keep well out of his way, which I did and he never noticed me. He never had a Christian name, as far as we knew. It was enough to hear the words, 'Warne is coming' and his little subjects fled in terror. John Warne subsequently, I heard, forged a career in the Secret Service.

Outside the classroom, my early days were spent in the junior boarding house, Pentreve, and on the playing fields. Here, too, there was stimulation. Our housemaster,

David ('Leaky') Phillips, was also an actor and often appeared in Freddie Wilkes' plays. The focal point of our week was after Sunday-evening chapel, when we gathered in the master's study. With one lamp shining in a pool of light he would read Sherlock Holmes – always Sherlock Holmes – in an understated but riveting voice. Every detail of the unabridged plot would come across with menace and sarcasm (in the Holmes–Watson dialogues). Why 'Leaky' I don't know. What I do know is that in those war days the BBC was short of actors and sometimes he would disappear on the train up to London to record a role in a radio play. When it was broadcast we were allowed to listen with rapt attention.

Methodist Education

Over the whole institution a remarkable man presided: E. H. Magson. Dr Egbert Hockey Magson (1881–1961) was a headmaster of the old school. As with Warne, he had only to speak and he would hold us all in thrall. He was only 63 in 1944, but seemed, to us, much older. He moved slowly, but with absolute authority. He would conduct assembly in the school hall nearly every day. He always found an apposite reading or reminiscence which came to form the basis of our life's standards and morality.

These daily offerings were but the hors d'oeuvres. The meat came on Sunday evenings. Yes, we did have visiting preachers, who were sometimes well known. As we were a Methodist foundation, every President of the Methodist Conference would visit us once during his term of office. But it was Dr Magson who commanded most attention and I can remember some of his sermons even today, over seventy years later. One evening he had a blackboard (pulpit props were unheard of in those days) turned away from us. At the dramatic climax of his discourse on double standards, he turned the board towards us, and there was his text:

No man can serve two masters: for either he will hate the one, and love the other; or else he will hold to the one, and despise the other. Ye cannot serve God and mammon (Mt. 6:24).

There would have been hardly a boy in the chapel who knew the word 'mammon', but nor was there a boy who would ever forget it after that evening.

Sitting on the platform were also the depleted staff and the choir, but also not far from Dr Magson would invariably be his wife. Mrs Magson (I never knew her Christian name) was portly, seemingly ancient, but also with a dominant personality. So commanding was she that she 'suggested' we should give up our free Sunday afternoons to her 'voluntary' classes. She was a devout Methodist of the old school and the main theme of her sessions was temperance. She would drum into us the horrors of alcohol and the benefits of a life free from it. She enjoined us to sign the 'pledge', which was easy to do, as neither wine nor spirits had ever passed my lips at that stage. We did have communion from time to time in the chapel, but the tiny individual glasses were filled with some dark juice, never the fermented fruit of the grape. My first taste of sweet Cyprus sherry in my parents' home would come long after the war and the departure of Mrs Magson, vows taken in her presence by then long forgotten.

Memories of early years in the classroom are dim, but we were a much larger group than in any public school today. This was due to two factors: the war-induced paucity of staff, and the presence of Kent College. They had arrived from Canterbury as evacuees and integrating them must have demanded a miracle of administration, but our safe haven worked for them and a handful of their staff. Wonders of organisation were accomplished behind the scenes. Just as suddenly Kent College disappeared and our classes became smaller.

I was the youngest in the class, until, somewhat later, Peter Stephens arrived, younger by eight weeks. He would go on to be head boy when I was his deputy in our final year. Together, in those restricted circumstances, we both acquired the beginnings of an international outlook. He later learned Swedish to add to his French and German and went on to study at Lund University, before becoming a professor of New Testament theology and eventually President of the Methodist Conference. He died in 2019.

With School Certificate behind me, I went on to concentrate on languages and English in the sixth form. To my eternal shame, I had failed Latin. I have to say that, alone among the subjects I was studying, our instruction was poor. 'Agricola', as he was universally known, was a very nice man, but he lacked the teaching skills necessary to coax us through a subject the worth of which we doubted. I had to do a re-take in a subject demanded for Oxbridge entry in those days.

Why did I take up German? It seemed a natural progression from French, but later I came to see there was much more. Freddie Wilkes had something special about him. I began German soon after the war had ended. Looking back, one might have expected comments from him on the victory, but his approach to the language ignored recent politics and he taught us classical German culture. Eventually, for us, Goethe and Schiller stood beside Racine and Molière as great writers in the European tradition. This was a lesson beyond literature, one of tolerance and broad-mindedness, of world values.

English, too, flourished remarkably at Truro. Mr E. B. 'Bert' Willday was, from time immemorial, Second Master. He was stern, but with a dry sense of humour, sometimes expressed in a quirky way. He loved incongruity – for example, in the contrast between Christian and surnames. He quoted more than once the name of a fellow pupil of his at school: Justinian Stubbs, which he persuaded us was funny. He was the organisational genius who made the timetable work faultlessly decades before the advent of computers. Many years later it would be my privilege to preach at his memorial service.

But it was in the classroom that I came to know Bert. His passion for Shakespeare taught us to understand the language and love the drama. When he took us into the Forest of Arden in *As You Like It*, we felt we were among the trees. We could soon quote

Macbeth's speeches and he was as good on the poets of Palgrave's *Golden Treasury* as he was on Shakespeare.

Early Travels

After the war Germany and even France were closed to us, so it was an adventure to step on to foreign soil for the first time. This was a daytrip to France with my parents during our holiday in Jersey in early September 1950. In St Malo and Dinard I heard, for the first time, a language I had been learning spoken on the street. School exchanges were impossible in those days, but we were encouraged to take up French penfriends. More excitingly, my parents arranged for me to spend a month in Paris with Alain Bardinet and his family over Easter 1951, when I was seventeen. I was bowled over by the experience. The Comédie Française, concerts, opera, the sights and sounds of Paris all crowded in together. Alain later came to stay in Praze and he loved the countryside. Decades later, married to an English wife, he came to revisit my parents.

At Truro my rugby skills improved through the years and eventually became important in my life. The 1951–2 season was unforgettable. Our team beat every school in Cornwall and those from Devon which we played. Our forwards never received the ball and plunged back into the ruck of bodies, as so often happens these days: their one aim was to get the ball out to the wings. As open-side wing forward, I was free to roam. It would be wonderful now to watch a video of how we played, but alas this has gone for ever.

My first visit to Germany was in this totally unexpected context. I was invited to play for Cornwall Schoolboys on a goodwill tour to Hanover and, as the only one in the team with some knowledge of German, I became captain. This was over the Easter of my last year in school and my first experience of being a 'diplomat'. We all witnessed the extent of devastation – by us – in what had been a great city, where rebuilding had barely begun. Rugby never really took off in Germany, but their youth teams, as might have been expected, grafted well and had good discipline, though lacking in experience.

I have indelible memories from our first game in Hanover. I was defending underneath our posts about ten minutes into the match when I intercepted a pass and ran some 80 yards to the scoreline. I just reached the line ahead of fifteen chasing Germans. After our victory, one of the spectators came up to me and said, '*Der Versuch war vortrefflich*' ('the try was excellent'), but the finishing touch to the day was after changing. A middle-aged man came looking for me in the pavilion and said (in English): 'Do you remember me? I'm Hans.' It was indeed one of the soldiers whom my parents had made welcome in their house seven years earlier and to whom they had written about the trip. Hans had come all the way from Essen, 170 miles away, to see me.

Unbeknown to me at the time, the match was reported in the *Western Morning News*. My father's short-sighted baker, Frank Hosking, was first to pick up the paper, peered at it minutely, and danced down the bakery waving the paper, 'Mike 'ev bloody scored – told you 'e would!'

A New Headmaster

We had long since had a new headmaster, A. Lowry Creed, who came to us from Kingswood, also a Methodist school. Lacking Dr Magson's charisma, he was an efficient, rather cold, bureaucrat. Indeed, he was the essential new man who would guide the development of Truro School into its difficult post-war years. Few warmed to him, but he had the right skills. My parents saw him from time to time and he convinced them of my progress, but he never relaxed to any informality with them. Peter Stephens, an excellent mimic, would repeat his expressions as if he were in the room and his favourite was a chilling, 'You know the rule' to any boy in disgrace whom a prefect had brought to him.

Mr Creed (he never had a nickname) summoned me early in the autumn of 1950, having seen my results. 'Bourdeaux,' he said (never any informality in those days), 'I want to try something with you. As you know, Truronians always do well in Modern Languages at Oriel College, but you have time on your side. We will put you in for a scholarship next year, but now I want to experiment. I'm going to send you to sit the entrance exam at St Edmund Hall.' This was unexpected: I had never heard of the Hall, but it was an order.

So it was that, not yet seventeen, I found myself in December 1950 on a train for Oxford, distant and unknown, via Reading. On arrival in Oxford, I walked through the city, down the High Street and to the porter's lodge of St Edmund Hall. The greeting was warm: 'Ah, Mr Bourdeaux [I had never before been so addressed], yes, we're expecting you. You are to sit your exam tomorrow, but meanwhile we are putting you to stay in the Queen's College next door.' Coming from warm and damp Cornwall, and rarely having set foot outside the county, suddenly to find myself in the formality of the front quad of the Queen's College and to feel the biting frost on my nose was a culture shock. I found it a disquieting place. There was no heat in my room and I lay awake almost the whole night trying to keep warm under a thin blanket.

The following day the Hall next door was a different world. The informality of the small quadrangle, colourful even in December, enveloped me and I loved the tiny chapel, with its burnished wood panelling. I can't remember the exams, but I was summoned to the Old Library, long and narrow, dimly lit, to be greeted breezily by faces illuminated at the far end of the long table. The Principal Dr A. B. Emden and the Vice Principal Dr J. N. D. Kelly introduced themselves and made me relax at once. I don't know what impression a raw sixteen-year-old from the provinces made on them, but I felt sufficiently at ease to be drawn out in all sorts of ways. We talked of my French and German studies and my village background. They asked about my teachers and what they had done for me. Then came an awkward moment: 'Ha, Mr Bourdeaux,' Dr Kelly said, 'I see from what Mr Creed writes that you like tennis.' I replied – and I can remember the words as if I spoke them yesterday – 'Yes, I am passionately fond of it.' Dr Kelly: 'Apart from being passionately fond of it, are you any good at it?' I did not know then that the Hall was on the cusp of achieving an outstanding all-round sports record which would never be surpassed. Whatever I said in my confusion must have been satisfactory, for a few days later a summons to Mr Creed's study imparted the information that the Hall had accepted me.

'Of course,' Mr Creed said, 'we still expect you to sit the exam at Oriel next year.' Oriel offered me a place, but it had been love at first sight. It was the Teddy Hall dons, really, with their warmth and informality, who swayed the issue.

There was no tradition then of a gap year, and I marked time for the 1951–2 academic year. I was deputy head boy, so I had administrative jobs. I now had my own room, privacy and a radio, which helped me increase my knowledge of music during the early days of the Third Programme. Once Mr Creed called and he was not well pleased, with his conservative tastes, that I was listening to Stravinsky's *Rite of Spring*. He thought the *avant garde* was not for Truro School.

This was the opportunity to widen my reading of French and German literature. I also acquired a *Teach Yourself Italian* book, which I enjoyed going through on my own. Though I never became fluent, this stood me in good stead for many visits to Italy later in life.

Starting a Tennis Team

I had not been successful in being selected for the cricket first eleven in 1951, my next to last year, which I had hoped for, and this jolted me into taking an independent decision. I said I would not play any more cricket, but tennis instead. There were some horrified reactions from both staff and boys. We were, after all, a 'cricket and rugby school' and had never fielded a tennis team. Mr Creed sent for me and offered his backing, provided I could take on some of the organisation myself. A few other masters were encouraging and offered coaching. We had some facilities, with tennis courts on the 'Terraces', where the ground-staff had made a good playing surface, even though the surrounds were restricted in area.

Mr Stedeford took charge of selecting the team and helping to find fixtures. At that time the school was strict in its Sunday observance, so there was no play on the Terraces in front of the school, in full view of any visitor who made his way up the hill. Behind the science block, higher up at the back, there was a very poor asphalt court and play was permitted on that surface on Sundays, inadequate though it was. I never did consider Truro's strict Methodism to be hypocritical, but that was the nearest it ever came to it. Years later I came back as a visiting speaker and the new headmaster, Derek Burrell, arranged a reception with wine. How times had changed!

Tennis led to my parents becoming involved with the school as never before. My mother was secretary of the little club in Praze, so early fixtures were provided by their visits. We could not play them away because there was only one court. In my last summer, several of the stalwarts had left and younger players were waiting to emerge. As captain, I chose as my partner an inexperienced but athletic fourteen-year-old, Ben, who was keen to learn. This was Benjamin Luxon, who would become one of the world's leading baritones, for whom Benjamin Britten would one day write a leading role (*Owen Wingrave*). Several times in the future, in the Philharmonia Chorus, I would enjoy listening to my former tennis partner singing solo. At a time when most opera singers were static, Ben was powerful and athletic on the stage.

I represented Cornwall at tennis that summer, but as I was never resident in the county again, I was not selected to play in subsequent years.

Singing

My last year, therefore, was filled with extra-curricular activities. I began to develop a bass voice and singing played a bigger role in my life. Sammy Way was our music master, whose tastes did not reach much beyond Mendelssohn and Stanford in B flat, but he was an inspiration to the school choir. Our weekly anthems on Sunday evenings came to be a feature of the week. Subtly, music and the teaching of the sermons were creeping into my bones.

The choir was an activity for boarders only. The division between boarders and dayboys was really experienced only on Sundays, as the latter were not there, so could not sing in the choir and they were about a third of the school's strength. The dayboys used to come either on foot from Truro or by train from Camborne or Redruth, with a few from up the line at St Austell. In the classroom there was no distinction, nor was there on the sports field. The division into four 'houses', named after three previous headmasters and 'School', affected field sports only and dayboys and boarders found themselves alongside each other in the same houses. There were rivalries, however. Dayboys, who of course did their prep at home, often outshone the boarders academically, so there was no division there, but occasionally they felt deprived by missing out on Sunday activities and choir (we had school lessons on Saturday mornings). It is sad that this was before the era of portable tape recorders, so no vestige of our music of those days remains. On special occasions we sang the first part of Handel's *Messiah* and once, after the service, *Acis and Galatea.*

On Sunday mornings chapel or church were compulsory for boarders. Here was the only religious division that ever entered our consciousness. The Methodists would go a short walk down the hill into the centre of the city to attend St Mary's Methodist Church, while we Anglicans had much further to walk – up the other side of Truro to Kenwyn Parish Church, where the service, as I remember, was invariably boring and adult-orientated, so different from school chapel which was to come later in the day. There was, in fact, an Anglo-Catholic parish much closer to the school than Kenwyn, but we were never allowed inside, as Kenwyn, presumably, was the next best thing to Methodism.

There was a ritual attached to the trek back from church. On the last Sunday of the school year the leavers, on crossing the Truro River, would throw their hymn books and mortar boards, which we had to wear on the walk, from the parapet into the river. This custom, which began to attract the joyous attentions of townspeople, was also a disgrace to the school, so it was terminated before my last year.

Music began to play a more important part in my life. On occasion we went to musical performances in the city. There were oratorios in the Methodist chapel, and some of the great singers of the day would come. I heard Isobel Baillie sing often, also Constance Shacklock and Eric Greene (one of the best-ever Evangelists in the Bach Passions).

The Misses Radford in Falmouth were enterprising women and put on professional opera locally. They performed Mozart's *Il Seraglio,* which their friend Sir Adrian Boult conducted. In my last year the BBC Symphony Orchestra came to play in Truro Cathedral and some of us were invited to join a 'Cornish Teachers' Choir' to perform Vaughan Williams's *Benedicite*, my first experience of a great conductor and of singing with a symphony orchestra. The cathedral, however, played a surprisingly small role in my Truro life, except on this one occasion.

I did, however, have my first 'religious experience' connected with Kenwyn, or rather the vicar, who prepared me for Confirmation at fourteen. He was a tall man with enormous feet, in whose classes we used to vie with each other to see who could stare longest at his feet without attracting his attention. There must have been a spark, however, because I remember on that Whit Sunday of 1948 the sun shone brilliantly. I thought to myself that this was really Pentecost and the words lodged in my mind, to be endlessly repeated to myself during the day, 'The Spirit of the Lord is upon me'. Bishop Hunkin of Truro confirmed me that day, but I had been too young to meet him properly and he died soon after.

So my Truro days came to an end, if not in a blaze of glory, then full of experiences which would guide my tastes and interests for the rest of my days. At the very top of the list must be '*Esse quam videre*', the quiet, steady inculcation of honesty, openness, loyalty and adherence to high standards, which should be the essence of any good education. The thought of National Service looming at the end of the school year was daunting, but it proved to be an experience which would change the direction of my life forever.

Chapter III
Secret Classrooms (Cambridge)

The equivalent of today's 'gap year' was universal and enforced back in the 1950s, though for boys only, not girls, and for us, it was not one year, but a minimum of two. It was called National Service. For many, this dreaded time was an unwelcome intrusion into the years of education and there were innumerable horror stories about how recruits wasted their time or worse. One person I admired at Truro School, Dudley Hobbs-Webber, joined the Naval Air Arm and was killed when his plane crashed into the sea. Others were sent to Korea, where the war between North and South was in full spate.

National Service

I was just aware of the Soviet Union as our ally while I was at Truro School, yet within a few months Russia had become my life and would dictate my university studies, an academic year abroad, a career, and even whom I should marry.

There was a choice: Army, Air Force or Navy, though no guarantee that the authorities would offer what you put top of the list. I was lucky. By the end of August my call-up papers had arrived: to present myself at the RAF reception centre at Padgate, near Warrington, then in Lancashire. The North West was a world totally unknown to me at the time, though my arrival was eased by a chance encounter on the train.

On leaving Praze station, the train's little compartment brought me face to face with David Jewell, destined to become a lifelong friend, and who would be a distinguished schoolmaster and eventually Chairman of the Headmasters' Conference (as it then was). David was as full of self-confidence as I was intimidated by what lay ahead. He was going to join the RAF Regiment, a tough regime, like the commandos, for which he was eminently suited, and in which he would become an officer, following a family tradition. But for the moment, we were going to present ourselves together as recruits. Our travel document designated a change of trains at Crewe, though with several hours' overnight wait there. In those distant days, station waiting rooms had a certain comfort and ambience. As I would one day tell his boys when, as head of Repton, David invited me to speak, 'The first night I met your headmaster I slept with him. Not in a bed, you understand – but on a table – a very large table, in the waiting room at Crewe station.'

How much we actually slept I can't remember, but we arrived at Padgate in good time for the deadline and we received a number and the rank of AC2 (Aircraftman).

Assignment to a hut followed, then kitting-out, a medical examination and our first parade, which was as brutal as I had expected.

I had a problem with the local accent. Although fit and disciplined from life and sport at boarding-school, I was awkward at drill ('square-bashing'). Once the NCO in charge shouted to me, 'Hoy there, are you with us?' I heard '*Withers*' and responded, 'No, I'm Bourdeaux' – to general hilarity.

After a week we were sent to RAF Hednesford, on Cannock Chase, Staffordshire, for eight weeks of initial training. The only bright spot was our proximity to Wolverhampton, where we could go on the bus to watch Wolves, then in their finest days, and captained by the great Billy Wright. I acquired a new sporting interest to set beside my rugby and tennis.

Towards the end of this time, a dreaded day loomed – posting – which would designate the way we were to spend the next two years of our lives. Not for me, though. I had failed in my attempt to be selected as an officer cadet, so I was soon to say goodbye to David. The fateful word came – 'Administrative Orderly' – RAF-speak for truly the lowest form of life: carrying out someone else's orders, lighting office fires, making tea, slopping out the ablutions, for two years, with the prospect of rising to LAC (Leading Aircraftman) at some time in the future – but not even the hope of learning a useful trade.

There was one saving grace in the undemocratic society which was Her Majesty's Forces of the time: the right of appeal. I took my life in my hands and appealed. My interview with a senior officer was amazingly congenial. I had never talked personally to an officer before, but it was a different world. He offered me my first civil cup of tea, leafed through my papers and said 'Hm, you're a linguist. There's a need for interpreters to help our occupying forces in Germany. Why haven't you applied?' I replied that no such option had appeared on the pre-posting forms we had had to fill out. 'Well,' he went on, shuffling his papers, 'could suit you. Are you interested?' Was I interested? I was ecstatic. 'Go home, then, for your long weekend leave and report back to take your interpreters' exam in ten days' time.'

Going back home to Cornwall after nine weeks away was a comfort, but my happiness was short-lived. I developed, in those short days, an abscess under a back tooth. It knocked me out completely, so, after the extraction, the doctor prescribed a week's rest and provided the certificate.

On my return to Hednesford I immediately enquired about the German exam. Officialdom responded (approximately) in these steely tones: 'Too late! The exam has already taken place. You're back to your original posting. You'll leave as soon as the word comes through.'

'But surely there's another exam coming up?'

'Sorry. You have to move on. You can't be redrafted to wait for a lot of recruits who are behind you.'

Once more I summoned the courage for a second time to request an interview. This time it would be with the camp commandant, a Group Captain. I wish I could remember his name: I owe him one of the great debts of my life.

Again, I was put at my ease. I handed over the medical certificate which I hoped might provide a lifeline. After poring over it for a moment, the Group Captain said, 'This is most unfortunate. Let's see what we can do. You were going to be a German interpreter. I think I've heard of something else – a Russian course for National Servicemen which began recently. Are you interested?'

I wonder today what I said in reply. He picked up the phone on his desk. 'Give me Records Office at Gloucester, please.' [This was apparently where the postings were administered and recorded.] 'I've got a young man here who's interested in the Russian course. Is there another one starting? Yes – in two months' time… There are vacancies? I'll ask him.'

Russia – at a Distance

The rest of the conversation vanishes into a cloud of euphoria, but the outcome was decisive. The CO said he was sorry, but I would have to wait a while until my posting came through. This wouldn't be until just before the start of the next course, but it was definite that my name was on the list. I would be reporting to Coulsdon, Surrey, at the beginning of March. I could now go home for some extra leave and when I came back I would report to the library, where I could start to teach myself Russian, if I could find a book.

So it was that this thoughtful man kick-started my career and pointed me in a direction that I didn't even know existed when I left Truro School six months earlier.

The weeks in the library passed quickly. A humane regime did indeed prevail there. Recruits were mostly too busy to use it, so duties were few, and there were an NCO and a junior officer in permanent charge. Apart from tidying up a few shelves, I had no duties at all. I was soon working away at *Teach Yourself Russian*, with its blue and yellow jacket. It was difficult and – as I was soon to discover – inaccurate in places, and the guidelines for pronunciation weren't that helpful, either. But when I reported to Coulsdon on 1 March 1953, I at least knew the alphabet and some basic vocabulary, though conjugations and declensions remained a mystery.

These few preceding weeks gave me, in fact, a flying start in what was to be the beginning of a highly competitive eighteen months. Before arriving in Surrey, I had been told that after two months there would be a decisive exam. The more successful candidates would move on to Cambridge for a one-year interpreters' course. The rest would continue with Russian, but at a lower level, to be trained as technical translators at Bodmin, Cornwall, then posted to Germany to work on radio intercepts. Either sounded attractive, but the chance of going to Cambridge University to study at the Faculty of Slavonic Studies would be an opportunity to be striven for.

From the moment of attachment to the Joint Services School for Linguists (JSSL), Coulsdon, I entered a new world. My rank immediately became 'Officer Cadet' and there was an issue of white flashes to sew onto the shoulder pads of our uniforms. Those from the Army and Navy received the equivalent insignia. It was strange to see navy blue and khaki uniforms after having floated for months in a sea of light blue ones. The camp was run jointly by the three services, but the parade ground rapidly faded into the recesses of memory. Everyone in charge called us 'Mr' and treated us with deference. There was even an issue of civilian clothes for us to use during evenings and weekends.

We had to line up for roll call occasionally, but nothing was allowed to impede our progress to the classrooms, which, like our barracks, had only recently been cleared of full military occupation. There was, though, one other constant reminder that we were military personnel. Next door was the notorious Caterham Barracks, the parade ground of which was dominated by RSM (Regimental Sergeant Major) Brittain, reputed to be the Army's most fearsome figure. Yes, he was separated from us by a high wall, but when he was on parade, every single word he shouted penetrated even our classrooms in a strange, jagged counterpoint to the gentle and mellifluous Russian which we were attempting to assimilate.

We all signed the Official Secrets Act at the outset – a solemn oath which turned out to be meaningless. From that day to this no one has ever entrusted me with any information which falls even remotely into such a category. It did, however, give one the feeling that the next 18 months were going to be important – for the country, as well as for us. The nearest I ever came to learning a military secret was to learn the parts of an aeroplane in Russian, few of which I can now remember.

Coulsdon not only recognisably belonged to the world of civilisation; it was also situated in the south, within a short train ride of central London, where I would be able to go to concerts in the newly-built Royal Festival Hall (possible even on weekdays, if there wasn't too much work to do), and our increased pay as officer cadets just about allowed this occasionally. But there was also, for me, the rival blandishment of home comforts.

My Auntie Dolly (Dorothy, the sister next down from my mother in age) had moved to London to marry Uncle Will, an architect. She had been the sporty one, but now she put her energies into maintaining a magnificent garden in Woldingham, which was only five miles from Coulsdon, so I had a refuge – and Cornish pasties – at weekends for the next two months. Uncle Will, too, was welcoming in his stiff and formal way and with a clipped London accent, but he became my real friend, because he had a collection of records and superb equipment on which to play them. LPs were just coming in and Uncle Will was beginning a collection, so there was never a dull moment during my weekends. He particularly loved piano concertos, especially, by Rachmaninov and Schumann, a new world for me.

Uncle Will's other passion was cars: vintage cars. He had a bull-nose Bentley in one garage, which he never used, but maintained in such a state of polish that, when he switched on the light at night the car itself flashed. His second car was a more usable open-top Bentley and one of the great delights of a fine Saturday afternoon would be to go for what he described as a 'spin'. I never acquired his passion for cars, but loved the countryside.

Every day for the next 18 months would begin with grammar, followed by oral exercises and the production of *rasskazy*, talks or mini lectures to be given by each of us to the whole class, sometimes on set topics, sometimes on subjects of our own choosing. Later in the day, after we had acquired the first elements of grammar and sentence structure, there would be the study of elementary texts. We progressed eventually to readings from Russian literature, first the great poets, Pushkin and Lermontov, both of whom also wrote beautifully simple prose, then later the more complex structures of Tolstoy and Dostoevsky. In the afternoons there would be lectures: Russian geography, the Soviet armed forces, reminiscences by individual instructors of their earlier lives. Some had taught in Soviet schools; others had been in the Red Army. Significantly, ours was not an 'anti-Soviet' school, let alone a 'spy school'. There was a studious avoidance of direct anti-Soviet propaganda, though every instructor could have told colourful stories of the recent war – and sometimes did during informal gatherings in the bar. In the main, we were left to draw our own conclusions about Stalin or the Soviet system. This was a clever stricture on the part of the higher powers. We assimilated a new world of culture without being put off Russia for life. I was reminded of my experience of learning German at school.

I shall never forget the first few days of formal instruction at Coulsdon. We sat quietly in the classroom, awaiting with apprehension what the first lesson would bring. Mr Ojolikov came in and began without preamble: 'Today I will teach you the Russian alphabet. It is very easy.' And teach it to us he did, within the day, so that by the evening we would never forget the 36 characters, including hard and soft signs (ъ and ь) and the – at first unpronounceable ы ('ye<u>r</u>y'). 'You – the gentleman in the front row: have you ever seen a camel?' 'No, Sir.' 'So you do not know what noise it makes?' 'No, Sir.' 'I will teach you – *uuiii* – especially loud when it's on heat. Now all say it together… Luckily, it is never found at the beginning of a word, only after a vowel, when it's easier.' So our new instructor became our friend from the first day.

On the second day he came in and, business-like as usual, said, 'Yesterday we learned the Russian alphabet. Today we will learn the vocabulary. The first two letters of the alphabet a and б – a and b – put them around the other way, ба – repeat them – баба. There you are – "baba" – the Russian word for a grandmother. If you remember that one word, you have the essential basis of Russian.'

On the third day he came, his face swathed in laughter. 'On the first day we learned the Russian alphabet. Yesterday we learned Russian vocabulary. Today I will teach you Russian sentences: *умер Сталин* ("umer Stalin") – **Stalin has died!** That is the only sentence you will ever need to know in Russian.' At which point he collapsed in a paroxysm, shaking all over, not able to express himself for several minutes. So there we were: selected players in a Cold War drama, but confronting what might be a different world from the one in which we had started the course the day before yesterday. The news had been picked up, doubtless by graduates of an earlier course, at a monitoring station somewhere, and we were among the first in the world to know. I can't remember how many more sentences we learned on 5 March 1953. It was a rare excursion into politics.

Cambridge

March and April sped by and I graduated to the select course at Cambridge University, all set to train *kursanty* (the universal name for students) as interpreters from the Army and the RAF. Our equivalents in the Navy went to London. Those who were to become translators went to Bodmin for a further nine months, followed by a posting. For us, Bodmin would follow Cambridge, but that would bring us to the end of National Service, so no posting would follow: only 'demob'.

In all, five thousand young men were on the JSSL Russian course between 1951 and 1960, of whom some 1,500 became interpreters and 3,500 translators. This student body, when eventually dispersed, would make an academic contribution to the life of the UK. Not only would Russian, for the first time, become a subject taught at many universities: the ex-*kursanty*, even if they did not follow up these studies, would forever have an understanding of Russia imprinted on their minds.

The immediate aims of JSSL were pragmatic. This country did not have a reservoir of Russian speakers. In the post-war years our Eastern ally, Stalin, turned his back on his friends, as the Red Army imposed communism upon all the countries of what would soon become the Soviet bloc. The military build-up, with the growing threat of nuclear weapons and the struggle between the Soviet Union and the US for superiority, did indeed alarm our government of the time. Its response was both imaginative and practical, demanding detailed organisation and the recruitment of a whole cadre of instructors whose security had to be monitored with extreme care.

On the course, as well as serious study, there were endless moments of hilarity, as one might imagine from a cast of characters including Alan Bennett; Michael Frayn; Eddie George, the future Governor of the Bank of England; and the novelist D. M. Thomas, my fellow Cornishman. At the same time the work was intensive and unremitting. Every day lessons occupied six hours of our time, followed by two or three hours of homework. We learned vocabulary from pocket-sized wordlists during the odd moments. The threat of expulsion from the course was a weekly reality. Fail the Friday test two or three times and you were out, or demoted to the translators' course. The final sanction was to be RTUd – the dreaded acronym for 'returned to unit'. This would be no joke: there was a brutal war in Korea and many National Servicemen fought in it. The general work ethic was so strong that, even without such threats, the failure rate would have been almost negligible. Everyone who qualified for the course in the first place had the ability to last the pace.

One curiosity is that for decades the story of this byway of Cold War history remained largely undocumented. There was nothing secret about it, despite the Official Secrets Act. At Cambridge, university undergraduates and dons mixed daily with *kursanty*, if not in the classroom, then around the colleges where we could freely socialise.

After Easter in 1954 we moved to Bodmin in Cornwall. Its military camp, the 'finishing school', called Walker Lines, next to the barracks of the Duke of Cornwall's Light Infantry, was an open campus. Its inmates moved around the sleepy town at leisure, where the local people took us to heart. Our unit could subscribe officially to *Pravda* and *Izvestia*, so each day aeroplanes brought bundles addressed to 'JSSL, Walker Lines, Bodmin'. Much later, in the 1970s, any residual idea that JSSL was still secret was blown apart when the *South Bank Show* 'recruited' a choir of former *kursanty* and we performed Russian folk songs on TV.

Full documentation had to wait over forty years until 2002, when the late Harry Shukman, one of the first graduates of JSSL and recently retired don at St Antony's College, Oxford, joined with Geoffrey Elliott, retired investment banker, to produce *Secret Classrooms: An Untold Story of the Cold War* (St Ermin's Press, London). The book contains controversial elements. One of its themes is the inevitable rivalry between London and Cambridge *kursanty*. It has never been fully explained why the senior course was divided into two. It was rumoured at the time, probably correctly, that London was the much harder school. The names Bolsover, Hingley and Toms, months after we rejoined their former students in Bodmin, still struck terror into the London alumni. Here is how Elliott and Shukman characterise the two places:

> If Cambridge was Chekhovian, London's tone, set less by the shadowy George Bolsover than by its first director Ronald Hingley, might best be called 'Stakhanovite', if anyone now remembers that persistently overachieving worker who became a propaganda icon of the Soviet era. But it was far from grim and it achieved results.
>
> The contrast with Cambridge was comprehensive, from the personalities involved, the teaching style, the discipline and the staff down to the students' accommodation. The two institutions, or more precisely their leaders, were fiercely competitive in a way that perhaps only those used to navigating the undercurrents of academic life can appreciate. Hingley, who was highly critical of the Cambridge operation, though he got on well with Liza Hill personally [first professor of Slavonic Studies at Cambridge and head of the course there], recalls George Bolsover harrumphing that Liza 'would be better off bringing up a bunch of squalling brats' than pretending to be an academic.[1]

According to one London *kursant*, Brian Toms, Hingley's replacement as director in 1955, was 'totally without imagination … his exhortations were never more than low-level threats, his criticism akin to jeers'. Even if this is an exaggeration, we never had anyone remotely like that in Cambridge.

---

1   p. 148.

These raw edges were still smarting fifty years later when the book appeared. Ronald Hingley, who moved to Oxford after a long stint teaching in London, was upset by it and wrote a lengthy rejoinder which he circulated privately.

It would take me well beyond the scope of these memoirs to go into the whole history of JSSL. Nor is this now necessary, for the recent book is so well researched and lively that I would be doing little more than repeating what Geoffrey and Harry have so brilliantly documented. I will confine myself, therefore, to a few personal recollections which may add a little colour to the picture.

Cambridge could not accommodate us all, living space then as now being at a premium. We were farmed out, first to Newmarket, then to Foxton. Our Newmarket mansion was spacious, having previously belonged to a racehorse owner and looking out onto the racecourse. Every morning during the summer that we were there, some of us, at least, could look out of the window and watch the magnificent horses being exercised along the edge of the heath. The spacious rooms which provided our grandstand were not as luxurious as this might imply, because each was shared between four, without subdivisions, and the furniture was basic. However, among my fellow-occupants was John Dunstan, an erstwhile classmate at Truro School.

Some students found Newmarket dull at weekends, but I occupied myself fully, playing for the town tennis team and joining the choir of the parish church, meeting a welcome everywhere.

Most of the enduring memories of my Newmarket summer focussed on the famous bus ride. This acquired a life and mythology of its own. It was, in fact, more than half an hour each way along a dull, flat road, but the fertile minds of the *kursanty* soon enlivened it. Yes, out would come the wordlists, to be studied with especial assiduity towards the end of the week when the feared test would take place. We were always puzzled to know why we had to learn, for instance, the Russian for a capercaillie, a bird of which I had never heard. Perhaps the compiler was preparing us for reading Turgenev, rather than an encounter with Soviet paratroopers who had landed on the Scottish moors.

More memorably, though, instead of rugby chants or the bawdy songs which had been the staple of our square-bashing barracks, a whole series of tribal songs evolved. I don't know whether our group devised these or whether they were the legacy of previous courses, but there is one which stuck in everyone's mind.

One of the word-list highlights was *dostoprimechatelnosti*, which has no convenient single-word translation. It means 'things you ought to see when you visit a place' and is the exact equivalent of the German, *Sehenswürdigkeiten* (I suppose 'sights' might do as a translation in most contexts). Anyway, the *kursanty* found the word immensely appealing and set it to the tune of 'Glorious things of thee are spoken', the German national anthem, *Deutschland über Alles*, composed by Haydn (the theme of a set of variations in one of his last string quartets). The Russian word fits it beautifully – in the plural for lines 1, 3, 5, etc., in the singular (without the final *i*) for the even lines.

Never since have I heard Haydn's tune in all its splendour without thinking of the Russian for 'notable sights'.

After six months we moved to Foxton Hall, a country mansion in a small village on the other side of Cambridge – but the bus journey was much shorter and never generated the same mythology.

So, eventually, we moved to Douglas House, a former nurses' home in Trumpington Street, Cambridge, and life became easier. The study centre was an anonymous, but unguarded, group of adjacent terraced houses, Salisbury Villas, in Hills Road, on the way to the station. Anyone who wished to find out what was going on there could have walked in off the street and looked at the notice board.

Brilliant Teachers

Dominating the whole Cambridge enterprise, with a studied dignity and humanity which seem to have been lacking on the London course, was Professor (later Dame) Elizabeth Hill. Elizaveta Fyodorovna Hill was, it seemed to us, a cross between formidable academic and Russian princess, though she was neither of those. Her origins – and original status – were more humble, though perhaps more colourful. She came from a prosperous Scots-Russian merchant family in St Petersburg. Whishaw-Hill & Co had been trading in coal with Russia since the eighteenth century. She was christened 'Bessie May', but later changed her name by deed poll to Elizabeth (Elizaveta) and adopted her father's first name (Theodore) as a patronymic. She learned English and Russian from her parents, French and German from a series of governesses. But she was born at the wrong time, the very beginning of the twentieth century, so she could derive no lasting privilege from her origins. The Bolshevik Revolution saw her family immediately ruined; she was cast adrift in London, a rootless teenager with no money. She and her two sisters began living in high-class hotels, awaiting the money that never came, but as hope dwindled, so did their standard of living. Eventually it was two rooms and a gas-ring in Putney.

Liza deserves a full biography. Her life is a fascinating story of determined achievement in the face of the adversity of the years of her youth. Until it is written, one has to make do with her rather unsatisfactory autobiography, an entry in the *Dictionary of National Biography* and a good account in *Secret Classrooms*.

Her father became a door-to-door salesman and played auction bridge for money. Liza herself, when she was old enough, secured a post teaching languages in a girls' school in North Wales. Somehow she wrote a doctorate in London, without having done an undergraduate degree, and it was accepted in 1928. She met Doris Mudie, a fellow exile from Russia, who owned a house in London and who became her lifelong companion. Doris was still an active presence, with no defined job that I could ever work out, on the course in Cambridge. Liza lectured at London University's School of Slavonic Studies in the 1930s and, in a rather murky enterprise, apparently infiltrated by Soviet intelligence, she set up a Russian course for regular Army officers in London, organising a follow-up study period living with a Russian family in Paris. Appointed to a lectureship in Cambridge, she later became the first-ever Professor of Slavonic Studies there, a remarkable achievement for one who had never been a university undergraduate.

In 1950 she was the obvious person to establish the branch of JSSL at Cambridge, a post for which she immediately displayed an outstanding aptitude. The university had few undergraduates studying Russian and the sparsest roster of dons, though quality ran ahead of quantity. Among them was, most prominently, Nikolai Andreyev, who delivered a memorable series on Russian history on the course. His daughter, whom I remember as an infant when I was a guest in the Andreyev house, later became a specialist in Russian military history at Christ Church, Oxford. He had been for two and a half years in the Soviet camps after the Second World War and he occasionally broke the 'no-politics' rule by recounting the horrors he had endured. Edward Sands (on Pushkin) and Peter Squire (on the Decembrists of the early nineteenth century) were others regularly borrowed from the university to lecture on the course, but the one who truly influenced me was Alexis Vlasto, of King's College, whose systematic lectures on grammar at the beginning of every morning were the bedrock of our subsequent knowledge.

The majority of the personnel, however, were Liza's non-university recruits. They were a talented and colourful group, fully deserving of the tribute Elliott and Shukman eventually paid them. For me, one pair stands out: Gretch and Pavlov (seconded from Coulsdon). They were a husband-and-wife team, never known by any other than their surnames. They had been members of Stanislavsky's touring company from the Moscow Art Theatre who visited Paris in 1925 and defected, rather than return to put their heads into the noose which was tightening around all aspects of Soviet society as Stalin began to exercise his authority after the death of Lenin. Their joint readings conjured up for us the whole world of Russian theatre and its great playwrights, Chekhov, Gogol and even Pushkin. Sometimes, too, they would give individual readings from the classics of Russian prose and poetry. Their influence was largely responsible for the talented dramatic efforts which *kursanty* produced during the years of the course.

Another teacher to whom I owe an immense amount, as I was in her small conversation class, was Mrs Hackel. Liza claimed that she belonged to a religious order in London and changed her clothes on the train to Cambridge. Whatever the truth of that, she always looked like a nun to me, who had never before met a Russian one. Previously she had been married and had escaped to the West by swimming across a river with her late husband, a Russian German. Small of stature, round and dressed in black from head to foot, including a headscarf, she was the prototype of the Russian *babushka*. We called her *maisky zhuk* ('mayfly', which is in fact a black short-lived flying beetle). This may sound disrespectful, but we adored and feared her at the same time.

We were six in her class, far too few to escape her intense individual scrutiny. We had to prepare *rasskazy* (mini lectures) for her and discuss them after we had delivered them. Often she would interrupt us with the terrifying phrase, of which we lived in constant apprehension: *takovo slova nyetu* ('There's no such word'). More often, though, we managed to please her and her face would become wreathed in smiles as she dubbed us *molodyets* ('clever young man') – and I see her face even now, years after her death, whenever I hear that common expression. Her son, Sergei Hackel, before his premature death, became a married Orthodox priest. Much later Fr Sergei and I developed a friendship and a strong working relationship. Like his mother, he had the characteristic of being outspoken, rather than a sycophantic adherent of the Moscow Patriarchate, to which jurisdiction he belonged. He wrote an outstanding book, *Mother Maria Skobtsova,* the story of a nun who perished in the Nazi prison of Ravensbrück. I often wondered whether, when writing it, Sergei was thinking of his mother and the fate which might have befallen her.

Mr Vlasto and Mrs Hackel: these were the two who built up the basic knowledge of grammar and how to use the Russian language. I had the good fortune to have been in their classes for a year.

When Liza Hill spoke, every word held her young audience. It is said that she took only one term's sabbatical in the whole time the course lasted. She did sometimes give a general lecture for everyone, usually on some aspect of Russian literature, presented with brilliant characterisation and wonderful pronunciation, whether in Russian or English. The courses ran, in the main, smoothly and brilliantly. The wobbles were brief and usually hilarious.

I remember one, affecting the dramatic productions which were such a feature of JSSL life. The winter of 1953–4 was cold, very cold, a winter such as we do not encounter now. The keen *kursanty*, with the drama instructors, planned to produce Griboyedov's *Gorye ot uma* ('Woe from Wit'). When it came to the point of moving from rehearsals in Salisbury Villas to a performance at the Cambridge Arts Theatre, which was always at our disposal on Saturday mornings for the compulsory Soviet film, it turned out the place had been double-booked. No production would be seen on the Cambridge stage. Immediate back-up plans were put into place, probably by Alan Bennett and Michael Frayn, to produce the play on ice, in fact, on the frozen River Cam, to give it a more authentic atmosphere. Needless to say, this never occurred, but discussing the prospect kept us amused.

I didn't know Bennett and Frayn well, because they were one course ahead of us. We were 'F' Course, the sixth intake – three a year – since the inception of the enterprise, so there were always three groups of students at different levels working at Salisbury Villas. 'E' Course had the gifted actors and Peter Woodthorpe starred in the first-ever Russian-language production of Pushkin's *Boris Godunov,* never to be forgotten by those who saw it. On another occasion, when the play was *Revizor* ('The Inspector General') by Gogol, the protagonist came looking for the mayor – who was asleep in his house. '*Speet*' ('He's asleep') came the interjection from the doorman. '*Speet* back' came the universal chorus from the *kursanty* audience – to Liza's horror at the indignity to which this most solemn thespian moment had been subjected. The cells of *Beyond the Fringe* germinated in Salisbury Villas.

The one time I had a private interview with Liza she showed the warmth beneath her formal exterior. The Australians were about to play Cambridge University at cricket. I asked her for a half day off for the first day and she granted us the whole day from 11 a.m., time to be there for the Friday start.

At the end of the year the whole of 'F' Course, Army included, assembled to hear an address from Lord Tedder, Air Chief Marshal of the RAF, quite the grandest occasion I would ever witness while a member of HM Forces. Bodmin, the 'finishing school' to which we graduated, was a very different place, yet much of the mythology generated about JSSL seems to relate to it. We were, to our shock, back in uniform, billeted again in huts, but not dumped in the middle of Bodmin Moor, as some later accounts seem to imply. The regime, from the commandant down, was relaxed, however, and we were 'demob-happy', as the saying of the time went. There was now a visible end to this strange interlude and by the end of the summer of 1954 we would be free of all military discipline.

Back to Cornwall

On 26 January 2005 the BBC broadcast a misleading documentary on Radio 4 called *Samovars on Bodmin.* The strange title (why not 'on Bodmin Moor'?) heralded 30 minutes of delight featuring the recollections of Alan Bennett, Michael Frayn, Eddie George and Harry Shukman. Oddly, it represented Bodmin as the focus of all the activities, whereas Bennett and Frayn had begun their friendship on the Cambridge course and there was no mention of the translators, who were posted to active service intercepting Russian traffic on the airwaves.

Many of the *kursanty* had never been to Cornwall before, but it was a fine summer and they loved it. Classwork was less intensive than it had been in Cambridge. Ostensibly we were learning how to repair an aircraft engine (in Russian, not in practice), but the threat of being RT'd no longer hung over us.

There was time for music, drama and exploring the Cornish countryside, despite the paucity of local transport. We had an accomplished choir from Cambridge, now augmented by naval personnel, who had joined us from London. We sang the death scene of Boris (from Mussorgsky's opera) with real style and we also recorded folk songs, later transferred to tape, including a solo from me ('Twelve Robbers').

Apart from the local pubs, the main focus of activity off-campus seems to have been the Parish Church of St Petroc, scene of a series of liturgical dramas, encouraged by the welcoming Canon Harmer. Just before my time, the *kursanty* paid tribute to the spirit of Cornwall by producing *The Vespers of St Petroc,* which 'featured a liturgical ballet, the Magnificat, the Journey of the Magi, after which the whole company swept out in procession… leaving the church in darkness and silence until the church bells rang out'.[2] This must have been quite a performance, as instructor Dmitri Makaroff, a great thespian and later to become an Orthodox priest, played St Petroc and the programme proclaims that other roles included three bishops, a king, a queen, attendants, demons, clerics and a certain mysterious 'Madame Bibi' – who perhaps wandered in from another plot.

My parents, of course, awaited my transfer to Bodmin with impatience. It seemed odd indeed, after a two-week Easter holiday at home, to be taken to Bodmin in my father's car. The clock read 38 miles, but the journey was not convenient, with no bus going from Bodmin to Praze and the slow rail journey necessitated two changes. My parents had moved to a new house in the summer of 1952, just after I had left Truro School, leaving behind a cottage full of love, character, coke fires, Calor Gas and candles. Though the rent had been negligible, it was far too small and now, for the first time, they would own their own house. They chose a vacant plot of land up a slope behind Crowan School. It was custom-built, following plans by Uncle Will, three bedrooms, but a bit four-square and without any frills: we were still in a period of austerity in the aftermath of the Second World War. My room was pleasant and comfortable, though, with a splendid outlook eastwards across fields and up to moorland. The view westwards from the upstairs landing took in St Ives and the sea to the north-west and the outskirts of Penzance to the south-west.

Over the years, my mother turned this former field into an attractive garden, not alas sheltered from the west wind, but eventually, as the shrubs matured, they formed a good windbreak, just as all good gardeners plant in Cornwall. Their pride and joy, though – and mine – was the asphalt tennis court under my window. Of course, they built it with me in mind and I would spend many happy hours on it, but the unyielding surface was not that gracious to play on. The court, however, proved to be popular that summer with my tennis friends among the Bodmin *kursanty*, who somehow made their way to Praze. I solved the transport problem by buying a 'BSA Bantam' – a two-stroke motorbike, not the most reliable or safe mode of transport, but a sign of moving up in the world. However, it served its purpose and helped me get home for a proper weekend (unlike Cambridge, there were no activities on Saturday mornings).

So, after a break of eighteen months, I was able to take part in Praze village life again – tennis matches on Saturdays, church on Sundays, and I continued this in one way or another for the next five years, up to my leaving for Moscow in September 1959. On some long summer evenings a few *kursanty* headed for the coast at Fowey.

Scottish Interlude

The tailpiece to JSSL, after our final exam, was our recall to do training as reservists. Officially, the word was that we would be called to serve two weeks every year for the foreseeable future. By the summer of 1955 Bodmin had closed, to be replaced by

---

2   Elliott and Shukman, op.cit., p. 93.

Crail, on the east coast of Scotland, near St Andrews, north of Edinburgh. On arrival we had to be kitted out: this time with full officer's uniform. At demob the previous year we had passed out as pilot officers, promoted after an 18-month stint as officer cadets. Now we were to be flight lieutenants and smartly dressed in a new uniform. I reflected on the overturning of the WOSB's (War Office Selection Board, pronounced 'wasbee') decision of nearly three years earlier not to select me as an officer. Those of us who had now completed a year's Russian at university had no need to revise and there was no compulsion to do a stroke of work.

Crail itself was a tiny – and then isolated – fishing village, full of character. The officers' mess was pleasant, comfortable and welcoming and we had individual rooms to sleep in. I had many friends among this intake of reservists. We had money – a substantial payment for this two weeks' work – so a group of us hired a car for the middle weekend and I thus gained my first-ever view of the Scottish lochs and highlands.

I looked forward to a lucrative extra holiday for years stretching into the future, but some form of government cut operated and we were never afterwards recalled. Perhaps the rationale was that by 1956 the world was changing and the Cold War was receding into history (as we naively thought). It was, after all, the year of Nikita Khrushchev's denunciation of Stalin. Still to come, though was the Soviet treachery in Hungary in November of that year. Probably the real reason for ending reservists' training (though JSSL itself was to continue with fewer and fewer numbers until 1960) was that Russian was now taking off at British universities and the Government felt that it now had a sufficient and replenishing pool of talent on which it could draw in an emergency.

Thus concluded for me the most decisive period of my life. Often have I speculated on where life would have taken me, but for the toothache and the perspicacity of that group captain at Hednesford. I might have become a parish priest. Who knows? The non-secret classrooms of the Joint Services School for Linguists changed all that.

Chapter IV
Two Halls

Two Oxford halls were to dominate the next five years of my life, but no two institutions could be more different than 'Teddy Hall' (St Edmund Hall or SEH) and Wycliffe Hall ('Wickers'). Life in both became more conventional than it had been in the JSSL, but it was no less formative: a degree in Modern Languages was followed by one in Theology.

A 'State Scholarship', as it was then called, followed by a 'County Scholarship' (from Cornwall), covered tuition fees and living costs. How different life was for students (and their parents) in those abundant, distant days!

St Edmund Hall

'Come on, Hall.' In the 1950s every playing field in Oxford seemed to resound to the raucous voices of the supporters of Teddy Hall. One college dominated the whole range of sport. Those in residence in 1954 included Mike Smith, later to be captain of England at cricket, and he also played fly-half at rugby for the university. There were internationals in rowing, amateur soccer, lacrosse and rugby.

The outstanding sportsman in my year was Peter Robbins, who played wing forward for England when not sharing my French language sessions. I knew him already, as we had been in the same RAF intake at Padgate. We attended the same translation class at the residence of Madame Hottot in Plantation Road, a lady of great spirit and charm. She took to Peter's huge frame on first sight and, whenever he was late or missed a class, she would excuse him, '*Le rugby, je suppose*'. Peter made an impact on all who met him, whether in personality around the Hall or physically on the rugby field.

My last year, 1959, was also the acme of achievement: Teddy Hall won the inter-college cups (Cuppers) at rugby, soccer, athletics, tennis and – for the first time ever – went head of the river in 'Eights Week' on the Isis. The national press picked this up and praised our achievements. This was too much for the *Oxford Magazine*, which queried our admissions policy and engendered a sharp reply from Dr J. N. D. Kelly, now Principal, who nine years earlier had questioned my tennis prowess at my admission interview.

Indeed, there had been a proclivity to admit outstanding sportsmen, but gifted players who also had academic ability tended to put the Hall at the top of their list. There was a backlash: the Fellows realised that the great morale which existed at the time must be sustained by academic achievement as well as sporting ability and soon academic ability began to dominate selection.

The Hall was then uncomfortably small, even for its 250 undergraduates, so there was only one year 'living in', before we had to 'live out' and find accommodation ('digs') with a landlady. I also had to share a study – something unthinkable today. Because we were both from the West Country, Ron Truman (from Torquay) and I were put together in a rather shabby, noisy top-floor study overlooking the succession of buses rolling down the High Street. We got on well in what was called the 'Slums' and tried to admire the Examination Schools opposite rather than the buses which stopped or changed gear below us. Ron's and my parents became friends and he disproved the belief that all Aularians were sporty. Ron specialised in Spanish and I could see that he was destined for an outstanding academic career. We had separate bedrooms, of course, right at the top. Every morning Alf Blay, our 'scout', would bring in a jug of hot water for shaving. There was no central heating, either, but we survived.

That area of the Hall is now dominated by modern concrete buildings, principally the Wolfson dining hall, with residential accommodation above, completed in the late 1960s and early 1970s. They have transformed the less-seen part of the college. In his official history, *St Edmund Hall: Almost Seven Hundred Years*,[1] Dr Kelly sets out the record of a remarkable period of expansion.

What I did not know when I came up to the Hall was its Cornish connection which Kelly recounts, appearing dimly through the mists of time. The first-ever documented reference to its existence is in a rental book belonging to the (now disappeared) Osney Abbey for 1317–18. Curiously, it was John de Bermingham, the Rector of Iffley, where I now live, who first purchased the site where the Hall now stands and passed it on to Osney Abbey.[2]

The Abbey was prosperous and let out property as 'academical halls'. For *Aula Sancti Edmundi* it was receiving an annual rent of 35 shillings from John de Cornubia (Cornwall), a Master of Arts, who came from Egloshayle (today part of Wadebridge). Records indicate further West Country associations: two more of the earliest principals, Robert Luc and John de Bere, were from Cornwall and Devon respectively. By the beginning of the fourteenth century there were at least a hundred such institutions in Oxford: St Edmund Hall is the only one which has survived.

Teddy Hall, though, was never to become the West Country's Oxford refuge in the way that Jesus College was for the Welsh. Even the 'Cornish choughs' which appear with such prominence on the Hall's coat of arms rather sadly represent a bird which was virtually extinct in the county by the time I was in residence (happily, at the beginning of the twenty-first century the choughs were both re-introduced and at the same time began spontaneously to re-colonise one or two sites on the remote Cornish cliffs).

Nothing of the early buildings remains, but the first scholars must have known and used the adjacent Norman church of St Peter-in-the-East and its atmospheric crypt. The

---

1   Oxford University Press, 1989.

2   For the fullest account of this early period, see J. N. D. Kelly, op. cit., Chapter 1.

church was deconsecrated and happily came into the possession of the Hall in the late 1960s. It underwent a successful conversion into a spectacular library, opened in 1970.

The association with St Edmund is tenuous. Born in Abingdon about 1170, he was the first graduate of Oxford University to become Archbishop of Canterbury and the first to be canonised. When the university was petitioning Pope Gregory IX for the canonisation, the document refers to the fact that he had built a lady chapel 'in the parish in which he was then residing'. Dr Kelly maintains that the lady chapel of St Peter-in-the-East exactly fits the date architecturally and that there is no other building in Oxford which does.[3] Tradition places his residence as having been on the ground now occupied by the Hall's main buildings. Nothing is known about his teaching of undergraduates, if indeed it took place, but the association of the name of St Edmund with the Hall existed from 1240, the year in which he died in France while on a journey to Rome. He had set out to plead a cause with the Pope, begging for the appointment of a papal legate to countermand King Henry III's attempt to exercise his authority over the powerful barons. He never completed his journey, dying at Soisy, in Burgundy, on the way and being interred in Pontigny Abbey, where his great shrine is known as that of 'St Edmé'.

The distant history of St Edmund Hall held all too little interest for me when I 'came up' in October 1954. The atmosphere of its ancient quadrangle, the smallest of all those in the older Oxford colleges, was spellbinding, though. Its flowers, window-boxes and vast wisteria on the north wall were widely admired by visitors; there was subtle harmony in its buildings, even though they dated from such different periods (sixteenth to nineteenth centuries).

This quad was not only small: it was hospitable, an open space which formed the unofficial social centre of the college, deprived as it was of the great buildings which many other colleges enjoyed. With two-thirds of its undergraduates living out, they had nowhere else to assemble except a tiny junior common room and bar. Around the central well the atmosphere was invariably convivial, whether in summer or winter, and was often enlivened by celebration of the latest sporting triumph. This rarely developed into full-scale rowdiness and the undergraduates respected the sanctity of the grass, on which only Fellows were permitted to walk, though they rarely did so. Oxford quads did not, as a rule, encourage such intimacy.

As there was no second quadrangle, the Fellows' rooms all looked out on this space and they could observe every character and every move. Those who lived in contributed significantly to the spirit of the Hall, which was its most distinguishing characteristic. We in no way envied the bare and forbidding magnificence of Tom Quad at Christ Church. No Dean of 'the House' could ever socialise with his undergraduates in the way Canon Dr John Norman Davidson Kelly did. More than any other being, alive or dead, he was the epitome of that communal spirit. As a bachelor, a keen

---

3   Kelly, op. cit., p. 9.

sportsman himself, his 'family time' was when he descended from his lodgings and appeared in the quad, where he knew everyone by first or nicknames.

Dr John Kelly

Dr Kelly influenced my personal formation, first of all in the chapel, once described (apocryphally?) by an American tourist as 'the cutest little God-box in all Oxford', which he never missed. It was indeed tiny, but the woodwork, in the style of seventeenth-century Grinling Gibbons, glistened. Towards the end of my time it also acquired Ceri Richards's painting of Christ at Emmaus, the modernism of which aroused national controversy at the time. But now the slight distortion of the figures, Christ's hands in particular, seems just right. Those, after all, were the days when *The Times* music critic described an Oxford Bach Choir performance of Stravinsky's *Symphony of Psalms*, in which I sang, as 'worshipping God with broken bottles'. The chapel was always crowded and I learned a new choral repertory with our singers, augmented by voices from the ladies' colleges.

Dr Kelly's Anglo-Scottish voice was moderated to perfection for those intimate surroundings and was imposing even when he was reading a list of benefactors of the Hall. Clad in the resplendent scarlet robes of his Oxford DD, he invariably made a colourful entrance. Less spectacularly, but still formal, he arrived at the Old Dining Hall for dinner at the head of his small bevy of dons with an equally formal aura. Someone once described his arrival as 'looking as though he had come straight from heaven'.

Though – unlike some of Dr Magson's – I cannot remember a single sermon, I must have assimilated a great deal, for it was during this time that the conviction gradually grew in me that I should offer myself for ordination. There had not been a sudden revelation, rather a gradual strengthening of conviction. All the past influences – Christian home, Methodist school, Russian culture at Cambridge – were coming together to give me a clear vision of my future direction. It was never that I would be a parish priest, rather that I felt it right to offer my linguistic talents to the church worldwide as a servant.

It was with Dr Kelly that, sometime at the beginning of my third year, I first broached this subject. 'Dear boy,' he said, 'I had always had such hopes of you, but I never thought it my place to mention this. Yours is a late vocation – but they are almost always among the best.' Yes, that's what he actually said. He certainly knew how to inspire confidence in a young man, however shy of talking of such a sensitive subject. I had, after all, feared he would point out my utter unworthiness. He cemented a key issue of my future: 'You must come back to Oxford for two more years. If you reside at Wycliffe Hall, I can be your New Testament tutor.' And so it would be. Dr Kelly was the world authority on *Early Christian Doctrines* and *Early Christian Creeds*, which were his great and unique contribution to scholarship. I had the privilege of spending many private hours with him and coming to know him as a friend and motivator.

We had social – or rather sporting – contacts, too. Dr Kelly introduced a 'Principal's Tennis Handicap Prize'. He had often appeared at the side of the court while I was playing for the Hall. Squash was the game at which he was reputed to excel. I thought it would be fun to invite him to sign on as my tennis partner and that he would be honoured to take part in his own tournament. The captain of the year gave us a generous handicap, as Dr Kelly was by some years the oldest contestant. To the Principal's immense embarrassment (and certainly intense pleasure) he won his own prize in its inaugural year. Dr Kelly was fast for such a solid figure. At the back of the court, which he occupied most of the time, he lumbered a bit, but had an excellent eye and a huge sweep of the racket. We won five rounds. I don't know what he gave himself as his own prize, but for me he chose a copy of Bernard Berenson's *Italian Painters of the Renaissance,* which was my introduction to a subject of which I knew little.

As well as being too small, SEH was not even fully independent. The Queen's College next door had retained certain rights, particularly over the appointment of every principal up to, but excluding, Kelly himself. During my time, in 1957 the Duke of Edinburgh visited the Hall to deliver our new statutes, giving us total independence.

The student body almost doubled between Kelly's first and final year. Even more important than buildings was the expansion of the governing body during that time. The Hall, when I arrived, was fortunate in the calibre of its small number of Fellows. When Kelly took over in 1951 there were – incredibly – only five of them. By the time I graduated in 1957 there were eleven – and now there are over eighty, excluding Honorary Fellows.

Those to whom I was closest were Revd Graham Midgley (1923–99), who embodied the very spirit of the Hall, with his room on the quad and his succession of large (but well-trained) dogs, so frequently in evidence. He was an English don, became Dean in 1956 and – after a short ordination course in the summer of 1957 – Chaplain as well, replacing Dr John Cowdrey (History) in that early group. Bruce Mitchell (Anglo-Saxon and English) brought an Australian informality to his relations with all he met. Reggie Alton – also an English don (what strength we had in that sector) – doubled up as Bursar and had the most compelling spoken voice. He was also a fine cricketer and an expert on handwriting. In my supplementary contribution to his *Times* obituary (5 January 2004), I wrote:

> The small chapel of St Edmund Hall, Oxford, often resounded in earlier days to Reggie's magnificent declamation. In particular – and it was certainly engineered by the chaplain – he would often be appointed, early in the academic year, to read Ecclesiastes XII. 'Remember thy Creator in the days of thy youth,' he would declaim, and then fix his eye on the choir, augmented in those days by ladies from another college, 'and all the daughters of music shall be brought low.' His voice transfixed the company of undergraduates and they will never forget it.

With Dr Richard Fargher I made progress in French literature, but it was Russian which provided most of the stimulation. It seemed an automatic decision to drop

German, which I had been accepted to read. Following prelims at the end of the second term, there were choices, so Russian became my primary subject, with French secondary, but linguistic achievement was supposed to be equal in both. I chose nineteenth-century literature in each language, which would entail substantial reading, but all of it stimulating and widening my vista on each culture. Paul Foote, of The Queen's College, charming and personable, picked up where JSSL had left off with Russian language. We had to study philology and I chose the history of Russian. More important was a decision from which I benefit even today – to do a paper in medieval Russian literature and the history of the Kievan state.

Dimitri Obolensky

If I had to choose one intellectual experience which stood out above all others during these first three years in Oxford, it was to listen to – and eventually to become a friend of – Dimitri Obolensky. Professor Prince – later Sir – Dimitri was one of Oxford's influential personalities in the post-war years and up to the 1980s. As I wrote of him on his death on 23 December 2001 in his *Guardian* obituary:

> Sir Dimitri Obolensky… had, whether in English, French or Russian, the most beautiful speaking voice – deep, resonant, with a slightly studied perfection, as if he required some reflection before delivering a sentence with every inflection in place.
>
> The Russians loved it; his speech recreated a bygone era, the expression of which they thought had been lost for ever. He adored curious words from the old time: a 'reject' could be a *shanterapa*. How? Serfs used to be lined up to see who had a voice good enough to sing in the church choir. In the aristocratic French of the time, the master would say to a failure, 'Il ne chantera pas!'…
>
> Those who heard his lectures on the conversion of the medieval Kievan city-state of Rus to Christianity in AD988, and the subsequent effect of this on Russian medieval culture, will never forget the experience.[4]

No single work of Russian literature or music ever surpassed in its influence on me the cumulative effect of these lectures. They opened up a historical perspective – especially the world of Byzantium – of which I had known nothing. Prince Vladimir, who became a Christian and was baptised in 988, Vladimir Monomakh, the peaceable and magnanimous ruler of a city-state and the (rather less historical) figure of Prince Igor became living realities for me and peopled my imagination. Obolensky's tutorials, always one-to-one in those days, were special events. With his exquisite politeness and tolerance of views differing from his own, he never uttered a harsh word. His pen would be busy while an essay was read, then there would follow discourse, picking out strengths and weaknesses and delivered as though it were a composed lecture.

---

4   *The Guardian*, 4 January 2002.

Every essay should have a beginning, a middle and an end, and must engage the attention of the listener from the first sentence: I never forgot that.

When, after graduating, I returned to Oxford to read theology, there was the possibility of proposing a paper of one's own choice, not necessarily bound to any aspect of the syllabus, provided the Theology Board approved of the plan. I thought how wonderful it would be to study the history of the Russian Church and Dimitri and I worked out a course, which was accepted. This gave me a whole term during my second year of theology when I could renew my personal tutorials with him. I added much to what would become my professional knowledge at this point. In those distant days, Oxford University led the world in the study of the Russian Orthodox Church, but this did not persist into the twenty-first century.

Music – Always Present

The diet of music on offer was not quite as rich in the 1950s as it is today, but much of it was available free within the colleges. After my day came the proliferation of excellent specialist small choirs, which today select their members from over the whole range of the colleges. I knew little renaissance music, but the choirs of the cathedral, Magdalen and New College, supplemented by visits of the Alfred Deller Consort to the free Balliol concerts on Sunday evenings, supplied what was lacking.

My Oxford musical experience was dominated by two institutions, the Oxford Bach Choir and the University Operatic Society. Apart from occasional visits beyond Oxford, all the choir's concerts were staged in the Sheldonian Theatre, a fine Wren building, but as uncomfortable then as now. Oxford still lacks a concert hall. The Bach Choir opened up a whole new world of music and showed me what fine choir trainers and conductors could achieve. The first was Thomas Armstrong, soon to be knighted, and with us sadly only for my first year, before being called to London to take up a post as Principal of the Royal Academy of Music. Apart from having a clear and decisive beat, he was a choir trainer through and through, having been in charge of the music at Christ Church Cathedral for many years. Subsequently in London I would sing under many of the world's most renowned conductors in the Philharmonia Chorus, but not a single one talked about the music itself in the way that Tommy Armstrong did. He had known all the English composers of his generation personally – Vaughan Williams, Herbert Howells, Gustav Holst – and his modest method of telling stories about them would grip the choir's attention.

In my first term we sang Beethoven's *Missa Solemnis*, tough music by any standards, but he put us through our paces without ever raising his voice or losing his temper. Then, in his final term, Sir Thomas Beecham invited the Oxford Bach Choir to sing with his Royal Philharmonic Orchestra. We sang *Sea Drift* by Frederick Delius, with Bruce Boyce as the baritone soloist, a work not often performed these days. Real spice came with Borodin's *Polovtsian Dances* (alas, in English) and the few sung bars ('Italie, Italie') in Berlioz's 'Royal Hunt and Storm' music from *The Trojans*. To add to the electric excitement of singing under Beecham in the Sheldonian, he invited us to repeat the concert in London in the Royal Festival Hall, which had only just been opened.

Thomas Armstrong's successor was Sydney Watson, who followed him at the cathedral also. Sydney was also a great raconteur, though much funnier, with a stutter which he cultivated for effect, making even the most banal joke hilarious. 'In m-m-music, as in l-life, the fewer in the b-b-bar the better!' Sometimes by the time he reached the end, you had forgotten the beginning, but you found it hysterical anyway. Sydney trained us to sing many more masterpieces: *Requiems* by Brahms and Verdi, Holst's *Hymn of Jesus*, Vaughan Williams's *Sea Symphony, Five Tudor Portraits* and Stravinsky's *Symphony of Psalms*. Herbert Howells came to hear his *Kent Yeoman's Wooing Song* and Vaughan Williams – one of his last public appearances – his new Christmas oratorio, *Hodie*. When we were rehearsing the Stravinsky, Professor Spicer, who was sitting in front of me, passed around one of those tiny, black throat sweets, popular in those days. Not yet being familiar with Stravinsky's style, he coughed and spat out the sweet, which stuck to the printed page. He then claimed to have sung it as an extra note and said it fitted well into the composition! Nevertheless, we were moved by the work's spirituality.

Just as enjoyable as the music itself was the social side. Monday rehearsals were in a venue which caused much merriment. They took place in the lecture theatre of the University Museum, to reach which you had to make your way between the dinosaurs, both excavated and reconstructed. We sometimes used to bet whether Sydney could get through a rehearsal without reference to the prehistoric marvels, all just encountered. David Jewell and I met up again in Oxford and always sat together for the Bach Choir rehearsals.

The Operatic Society was an institution of the time. Its purpose, in those days, was to give undergraduates the opportunity to become well acquainted, as performers and listeners, with a whole range of opera. Every week an individual, who had volunteered the previous term, would present a concert performance of an opera in the Holywell Music Room, with predictably mixed results, but the system did familiarise us with the variety of opera – with piano, but minus orchestra.

Each year, though, there was something more professional. Professor Jack Westrup would put on a fully staged performance in the Town Hall, aiming to present to the British public a work which he considered unjustly neglected or even totally unperformed. To him the world of music owes the first stirrings in the UK of interest in Monteverdi's operas.

I couldn't afford the time to sing in the chorus of these productions, which rightly demanded many rehearsals, but I did volunteer to be publicity officer for the performance, during my third year, of a double bill, Ravel's *L'enfant et les sortilèges* and Stravinsky's *Oedipus Rex*. An undergraduate whom I met through these productions was John Cox, a year behind me at St Edmund Hall, who then had his first opportunity as a producer. John, who is now an Honorary Fellow of the Hall, found that an amateur talent transformed itself immediately into a life's work and this launched an outstanding career.

One semi-professional operatic opportunity came the way of a small group of enthusiastic amateurs almost every term: the Chelsea Opera Group's eagerly awaited visit. They were establishing a tradition of regular visits to Oxford and Cambridge to present concert performances of Mozart operas. They would bring with them a professional orchestra and soloists, but in each place they needed a local chorus. A group of us were delighted to oblige – and found ourselves face to face with rehearsals under the conductor, Colin Davis, then in his twenties and unknown, but he would soon have an international reputation. We were almost the first to benefit from his humour, enthusiasm and musical insights before the whole world was to come to know them. There was never a dull moment in rehearsals: he once told the basses to sing a chorus in the *Magic Flute* 'as though you've got the whole of Wookey Hole inside you!'

I hope I did fulfil, at least to some extent, the Principal's expectation of tennis prowess. There was, in those days, no play in the winter, but my summers were filled with exciting tennis when I played for the Hall for five seasons, forming a partnership with Bob Hughes. I was elected captain in 1959 (my status at Wycliffe Hall permitting my continuing eligibility to play for Teddy Hall) and in my last two years we won Cuppers, the inter-collegiate competition, for the first (and second) time.

Wycliffe Hall

After my degree in Modern Languages in 1957 I immediately switched to Theology, with the challenge of compressing the normal three years into two. Also I knew no Greek, so I had to teach myself during the summer vacation. It was gratifying to find how the Russian experience of learning an inflected language prepared me mentally to take on the challenge of Greek.

Coming back in the autumn of 1957 for a completely new course of study demanded full concentration, but there was also the discipline of living in a theological college. My ties with the Hall remained strong through my weekly visits to study the New Testament with Dr Kelly. Wycliffe Hall ('Wickers') though, introduced me to a new society, new parameters of life, new standards and ideals.

Wycliffe was, in the mid to late 1950s, a remarkable place intellectually, but housed in buildings which were then hardly fit for purpose. In those days it consisted of two large converted North Oxford houses, with an adjacent principal's residence. It was pleasant, however, to have a room in the Hall for two years and to be living within easy walking distance of the city centre. My natural affinity was with the more traditional Anglican style of Crowan parish and the chapel at St Edmund Hall. Life in this community was more circumscribed than anything I had experienced for the last three years, but it looked outwards as well as inwards. Daily chapel was compulsory, but we could come and go as we wished after dinner. The majority of the students belonged to the evangelical wing of the Church.

The Principal, John Taylor, eventually to become Bishop of Sheffield, did not have an easy personal manner, but he was an impressively organised man with the widest range of contacts. Excelling as an administrator, he appointed challenging permanent staff as lecturers and personal guides in the realm of Anglican spirituality. The Principal looked after the placement of his students, responding imaginatively to their wide range of needs and competence. Most exciting for the students was a weekly series of visiting speakers who opened our eyes to the role of the Church in the world.

One breakfast time I found myself sitting next to Fr Trevor Huddleston and then a little later to a bishop, known as Archibald of the Arctic. From the former I absorbed, during his frequent visits to Oxford, the degree to which the Church could be involved in human rights issues and I felt passionately about racial justice in South Africa before I did about the persecuted Christians in Russia (about whom I still knew almost nothing).

The New Testament, now in Greek, took on new colours as I visited Teddy Hall weekly to read it and discuss its theology with Dr Kelly. His study, high up in his lodging and overlooking the quad, became familiar to me, and in the second year of study we went on to Christian Doctrine, his special area of expertise.

A permanent strong influence at Wickers was Stuart Blanch, who became my tutor in Old Testament, and with whom I first came to grips with its contents. His lectures were a source of never-ending delight, enlivened as they invariably were by the most touching human details. He had not been a chaplain in the RAF for nothing and, when I heard of his eventual elevation to bishop and archbishop, I thought how wonderful this was for Liverpool and then York. He also monitored my essays in his tutorials and intellectually I found this whole new area of study a revelation. I would have loved the opportunity to have deepened this study by learning Hebrew, but there was no time.

Stuart could be hilarious at times and once taught us a lesson in patience. His example of the opposite came in a sermon, in which he told the story of how the most mild-mannered of men can sometimes be goaded beyond endurance. A solemn senior clergyman was sitting in his study, waiting for the rain to clear, so that he could make his way to a cricket match scheduled for the afternoon. He looked repeatedly at the barometer fixed on his wall. It said 'Fair'. He brought it down, put it on his desk, he tapped it and it went higher instead of lower – but the rain continued. This went on for several hours during the morning. Eventually, the cleric picked up the barometer and threw it through the glass straight out of the window: 'Get out, you bloody thing – go and see for yourself!' he shouted. Stuart and I kept in touch. He invited me to York to play tennis with him in his lounge, which, he said, was large enough to turn into a court, but I never managed to visit him there.

Among our colleagues were foreign visiting students, beneficiaries of scholarships from the World Council of Churches. Fr Karekin Sarkissian was from the Armenian community in Beirut. He once gave us a lecture in which his impassioned thesis was that ancient theological differences between his church and ours were of little account and we should achieve intercommunion. He also talked of his love for Armenia itself, his community's homeland, but which he had never been able to visit because it was under Soviet domination. Later in life, after the collapse of communism, he was able not just to visit it, but to go there as Catholicos, the elected head of the Armenian Church. Sadly, he died before I was able to take up his invitation to visit him there.

Two real 'Soviet' students joined us, both Lutherans from the Baltic States. Kaide Rätsep was a pastor from Tallinn, Estonia, and was taciturn, to put it mildly. Janis Veyś was personable and studied, successfully, for an Oxford BA in theology. Sadly, he later abandoned his faith and adopted a public anti-religious position. He had undoubtedly been subverted by the KGB from the outset. While I was in Moscow subsequently, he visited my parents for a short holiday and received a Cornish welcome.

Stuart Blanch was always supportive of my efforts to develop my Russian work, but it was John Taylor who encouraged me to use my languages in the service of the Church. He, it was, who contacted the World Council of Churches and advised me to apply for one of their scholarships. On offer, if successful, was the possibility of going to the Greek Theological Seminary at Halki, on an island near Istanbul, long since – and scandalously – closed down by the Turkish authorities. More exciting, though, because of its Slavonic connections, was a new opening to study at the Serbian Orthodox seminary in Belgrade. I applied during my last year at Wycliffe and was successful, thrilled at the prospect of learning another Slavonic language and revisiting Yugoslavia, where I had gone once on holiday during a university vacation.

'But God judged differently,' as the monk Pimen said, when writing the history of the Time of Troubles in Pushkin's *Boris Godunov*. In May 1959, during my very last weeks, I saw a notice on the board of the Taylorian Institute, Oxford's modern-language library, which conveyed a message in these approximate words: 'The Soviet Government has signed a cultural agreement with the British Government. The British Council urgently seeks Russian graduates to participate in this first exchange, all expenses paid, and for the duration of next academic year at either Moscow or Leningrad Universities.' With a mixture of regret and excitement, but with lasting consequences, I had to renounce my Serbian scholarship.

I was about to embark on a new and decisive phase of my life.

Chapter V
Moscow Panorama

When I opened the curtains of my tiny room, there it was spread out before me: a panorama of Moscow, in the autumn every building dulled by the almost perpetual mist and rain or, later, sharp-edged in the snow. Even on the worst days I could see the Kremlin; on the best it drew the eye, magnificent even at the distance of some four miles, the gilded domes sparkling, it seemed, with inner light. Closer were the oval perimeter of the Lenin Stadium and the faded glory of the Novodevichy Convent, walled and pink. From our perch, Stalin's outrageous skyscraper on the Lenin Hills, the eighth largest city in the world lay before us.

We were the first group of exchange students to spend a year in the Soviet Union, seventeen of us, divided between Moscow and Leningrad. We had been hastily recruited: Harold Macmillan and Nikita Khrushchev had signed an exchange agreement only in May 1959, long after most students had made firm plans for the next academic year. For the Soviets, we later discovered, it was a matter of urgency: for several years they had been training a cadre of young specialists ready to investigate scientific research in some of our elite universities. Our training, apart from the Russian we had learned in the past, had been less than basic, the inside of a day at the Foreign Office: two sessions separated by a generous lunch, enlivened, it must be said, by an enlightening presentation from Mr Hugh Lunghi, who had not only had long experience in the Moscow Embassy, but fourteen years earlier had been a key figure in administrating the Yalta Conference. Many years later we would go together to the Livadia Palace and he would point out the chairs and the retiring rooms of Stalin, Churchill and the ailing Roosevelt.

Within a few days we were sailing on the *Mikhail Kalinin*, first class, via the Baltic capitals to Leningrad, an idyllic week when the sea was often so calm it mirrored the discs of the sun and the moon. Our group was depleted: one was in Moscow already, another would come later; two others received no visas, one of whom, Nick Slater, was the nephew of Boris Pasternak, and another had, it was rumoured, smuggled a Polish girl across the border. Two were women, both heading for Leningrad. My visa was granted for me to study Russian history, which had been part of my course – but I had not mentioned that it was *church* history, nor that I had a degree in Theology.

However insecure we felt, we were aware that this was more than an adventure: a solemn obligation lay on our shoulders to make this exchange work and to secure its future for the sake of our successors in years to come.

Culture Shock

For the only time in my life I kept a diary. I used it as the basis for my first book, *Opium of the People*,[1] but it disappeared for years and I thought it had either vanished in one of our moves or been stolen, possibly by the KGB, on the one occasion we had a break-in at the future Keston College. But when I began my research for these memoirs it was easily found and I have used it for this chapter. It consists of just under four hundred pages, mainly of typescript, but with some entries by hand. The text is evenly divided between diary entries and carbon copies of my letters home. The two complement each other, as I deliberately wrote extended letters to my parents to record what would easily pass the censors, confining much that was more personal and critical to the diaries.

In retrospect, I note too much self-indulgence and self-pity which so many of these pages portray. I can, though, now explain this. My five years of Russian studies had not prepared me for what it was like actually to live under the Soviet system. However much variety and stimulation there had been at Oxford, even when travelling I had always been in a protected environment. This evaporated the moment I stepped off the ship, climbed aboard the night train to Moscow and was installed in my student room. My first letter home describes MGU (Moscow State University):

> It is a skyscraper of 30 storeys and in dimension is one of the largest buildings in the world. To be living in such a monster is a peculiar experience and it is very difficult to find one's way round, especially as each of the four wings is symmetrical. So you can reach a room and be sure it's yours, even with the right number on it, and then find that you are in entirely the wrong 'sector', as they call it … The building is a self-contained town, with its own shops, cinemas and sports facilities… The rooms are quite well designed, with space for all the books and clothes I have. They are in pairs, each separate from its neighbour, but sharing a shower, washbasin and toilet inside the main door. On each corridor there is a kitchen.'

We arrived in Moscow on 13 September 1959, just as the first *sputnik* was about to crash into the moon. The Soviet Union was agog and the country collectively joined in the countdown as the moment approached. The rocket emitted a regular beep. At midnight it abruptly ceased and huge cheering broke out all over the university. The Vice Rector greeted our group next morning, reminding us, with some irony, that our 'happy arrival' had coincided with an equally happy and just as momentous event.

It was not only the building which was forbidding and alien to anything I had known. The place was buzzing with Soviet students, but no one wanted to socialise. We had expected curiosity, perhaps instant camaraderie, but when a student came near us, his manner was awkward and intrusive. We felt – and all of us shared this

---

1   Michael Bourdeaux, *Opium of the People* (Faber and Faber, London, 1965). Second edn. A. R. Mowbray & Co Ltd, Oxford, 1977.

impression – that this act of friendship was cold and designed to monitor what we were doing. It would be months before any of us was invited into a Russian home, and we later learned that the political powers in the university had specifically warned the students against any close association, saying that we would all be spies who had received special training.

The culture shock we experienced could not in any way compare with that of some other groups of foreign students. There were hundreds of Africans in our year: very soon they would move to populate the Patrice Lumumba Friendship University nearby, but this was still under construction in 1959–60. Most of them had five-year scholarships, but came with no knowledge of the language and had to undergo intensive linguistic study before they could even start. For them the disorientation was shattering: unlike us, they had no background for Russia and were there to receive free education, including political, not to assimilate another culture. These students gravitated naturally to us and felt much more at home with their 'colonial oppressors' rather than with their Soviet 'liberators'. They had no prospect of returning home even during the long summer vacation. I made friends with at least a dozen of them, not one of whom seemed influenced by communist ideology. Indoctrination must have been foremost in the minds of the organisers of the scheme, but at the cutting edge they failed dismally.

This applied to the francophone Africans, too. In December I made one friend in this group, Fatumata Touré, who arrived heavily pregnant. Her husband, nephew of the President of Guinea, had been detained at home by some important business. In a state of depression and not knowing a word of Russian, she immediately fell ill and was admitted to hospital in a great distress. I was the only person she could speak to, as not a soul in the hospital knew French, which obviously added to her misery. After a few days I took a decision, backed by the hospital, to order a taxi and bring her back to her room in MGU. Here I could call to see her every day and brought her the only food she had, but soon two students from the Belgian Congo and Cameroon took this over and became her friends, too. I arranged for the Catholic Chaplain at the American Embassy, Fr Dion, to come and see her. When her baby was born in the New Year, all went well.

There was also a large Chinese presence in MGU. They were the diligent ones. Once, returning to the university on foot late at night, in the company of David ('Boris') Thompson, the other resident in my binary accommodation, we saw hundreds of lights burning in all parts of the skyscraper. David said, 'Just imagine: behind every one of those windows there's a Chinese – working!' Their studies were cut short the next year, however, when Chairman Mao fell out with 'Nikita' Khrushchev and every one of them had to leave precipitately.

The KGB

It was I, though, who almost suffered an even more abrupt departure. In shock – and in fear that the text might be found and confiscated – I failed to record much of the detail in my diary and the significance of what happened did not fully dawn until later.

It all began in the Bolshoi Theatre just two and a half weeks after my arrival. We used to obtain our seats cheaply – and excellent ones they were – through the *Inostranny otdel* (Foreign Relations Department) of the university. It was easy for the KGB to plant one of their agents in an adjacent seat.

By this time I was feeling both homesick and lonely, despite keeping contact with some of the other exchange students, who were busy settling into their new studies. I had hoped quickly to make Russian friends, but this was not happening, so it was easy to set me up by putting a friendly Russian next to me in the Bolshoi. Anatoli was a doctor from Minsk, he said, and introduced me to a protégé, Alyosha, whom he had adopted, he said, when the boy's parents were purged and perished in Siberia. A few more anti-Soviet remarks – the like of which I was hearing for the first time – and I was hooked.

The doctor invited me to Alyosha's birthday party the next day in the Moskva Hotel, where they were staying. Any qualms I had stood no chance against the excitement I was feeling (precisely the sort of situation our briefing should have warned us against and did not).

On arrival at the designated room, I was taken aback to find that there was no party – only the two of them. Anatoli went to fetch a drink, while Alyosha told me he was a believer. 'In Belorussia we are all Christians,' he said, 'and the churches are full of young people.' The trap had been sprung. I accepted a 'vodka' and immediately began to feel my head swirling. The vodka had been spiked and I was passing out after only a couple of sips.

What happened next was surreal. Anatoli came to lie beside me on the bed, while Alyosha looked on. Hands moved – gentle pressure was applied. At that very moment someone burst into the room. Flash bulbs popped – but I was not undressed and nothing had happened. I shot upright and dashed out of the room, thinking only of the new winter coat I had left downstairs in the cloakroom. I found the *talonchik* (plastic ticket), grabbed my coat and ran outside, where fortunately a taxi was waiting. It took me straight back to the university, where I reflected in shock on what had happened.

I rang the British Embassy and made an appointment for the next day to see Kenneth James, who, as the Cultural Attaché, was directly in charge of our group. He would one day be 'Sir Kenneth' and our ambassador in Poland, then Mexico. He suggested immediate repatriation, but offered me the chance of staying on, if I could face it. My Cornish granite prevailed, so I decided not to quit.

I remember some years later, under the pretext of a 'drink' in a pub near the Foreign Office, being intensely questioned as to whether, after all, I might have been compromised. Had I been, the Soviet tactics would have been to release a photo dossier some years later, almost certainly in the mid-1970s, when the work of Keston College was beginning to achieve recognition. Homosexuality 'among consenting adults' was, of course, at that time still illegal: proof of any such activity would have been devastating for my future career. This attempt, maladroit though it was, left a deep scar. From then on I *knew* the KGB, and the experience affected my view of the Soviet Union.

True Kindness

Soon after recovering from this shock, I began to experience the real warmth of the Russian character, which, in many contexts, communism had all but obliterated. The ubiquitous 'collectives', where each cared for all and all for each, were, I judged, a sham, sometimes no more than an excuse for denouncing those who did not fit in.

Babushki – the old ladies with headscarves – were almost a race apart and penetrated every corner of the Soviet Union, whether it was sweeping the snow off the streets, monitoring every floor of every hotel in the role of *dezhurnaya* (women on duty) or meticulously polishing every square inch of brass in the churches. It was two of these, though, who revealed a heart of gold behind an exterior which was often forbidding.

The first encounter was almost too trivial to note, yet I have never forgotten it. To this day an essential adjunct to Russian culture is the cloakroom. You do not enter a public building still wearing your outdoor clothing (and to enter a private apartment you must also take off your outdoor shoes). So every building has its spacious cloakroom, with rows of pegs and plastic *talonchiki* guarded by an often-ferocious *babushka* overseeing the *garderob*.

One day in November I went to the Lenin Library, opposite the Kremlin in central Moscow, to do some work. As I handed over my coat, the *babushka* inspected it and reprimanded me, '*Molodoi chelovek, u vas veshalki net*' – 'Young man, you have no tag on your coat'. 'Sorry,' I said, 'it broke.' She almost refused to accept it, but took it with a withering glance. When I returned several hours later the tag was beautifully, meticulously replaced by a new one.

My encounter with Olga Sergeyevna at just about the same time led to a friendship which was to endure for my whole year in Moscow.

In search of an open church, I had set out for the old village of Kolomenskoye, now long since engulfed by Moscow's gargantuan suburbs, but then in the countryside some distance beyond the end of a tramline. The unpaved roads at that time of the year were almost ankle-deep in the mud which quickly seeped over the top of my overshoes.[2]

Olga Sergeyevna was sitting in the park, a huddled, bent *babushka* of about 65, dressed in black from head to toe. Her padded jacket filled her out into a shapeless bundle, while the only touch of colour was the fawn shawl wrapped tightly over her head, covering it completely except for her eyes and pale cheeks. She demanded

---

2   For a fuller account, see Bourdeaux, *Opium of the People*, pp. 82–4.

to know how I had got myself into such a mess. She took me to a pool of melted snow, stood me in the middle of it, seized a clump of grass in her fist, bent down and proceeded to scrub off the mud with that makeshift tool that became efficient in her hands. She then took a clean handkerchief out of her pocket and continued. I was overcome. We talked and it soon emerged that she was a believer. She asked if I would accompany her to vespers, which of course I did, standing beside her for almost three hours.

At the end, I was in the process of saying goodbye when she invited me to come home with her for supper. We walked two miles (along a cleaner path), reaching one of Moscow's countless blocks of flats. We climbed to the fifth floor, walked along a broad, empty corridor, pervaded, like all Russian living quarters, by the smell of mingled stale cabbage and cooking fat. Her flat was a single room, just large enough for a high bed with an iron frame, draped with antique lace, a table and five upright chairs. The walls were bare, except for a mirror, a paper icon in one corner and two dresses hanging on a rail. There was no cupboard and she kept her crockery, pots and pans in a box under the bed. The only ornament was a green rubber plant by the window.

She talked incessantly of how happy she was to have an unexpected guest, sent by God. I said that during my two months in Russia I had never seen the inside of a Russian home. She pressed me to share her supper: *'Kushaite, kushaite'* ('eat, eat'), to refuse to do which is an insult at a Russian table. She produced uncooked salted fish and milk from the space between the double-glazing of the window and a hunk of dry bread from the communal kitchen along the corridor. Between us we used all the utensils she had: a glass, a mug, two knives, one plate and one teaspoon.

The church was her life, she said, and how delighted she was now, since her recent retirement, to be able to give almost her whole being to it. For ten hours or more a day she would sweep, scrub and polish every surface in the building which had provided her solace since she lost her husband in the war.

I met Olga Sergeyevna several times. She was always the same, treating me as if I were the only guest she had ever had in her life and bursting into tears of gratitude for any little gift I could find to bring her. Whenever I became depressed, either at the rudeness of the Russians or at the all-pervasive and crude atheism surrounding me in most contexts in Moscow, I would think of her. The image of that dumpy figure and cheerful face would invariably give me real support.

The British Community

For the British community, which was small in those days, our arrival was something of a diversion. Married couples wanted to adopt us and make sure that we had enough to eat. Our allowance was generous by the prices of the day and was, of course, reciprocal, the Russian students in the UK receiving the equivalent. Each month we received 1,500 roubles, approximately 50 per day, almost £2 by the tourist exchange rate of the time (£1 equalled 27 roubles). With this we could eat, buy metro tickets and go to the theatre or a concert at least once a week and still have something left over.

Once we came to know some of the British community, invitations began to flow in our direction. I expect, too, that they found our youthful observations in an environment so different from theirs to be refreshing and without too much political pre-judgment. Apart from diplomats and their wives (there were no female diplomats in thosee days, the secretarial pool excepted) there was a handful of newspaper correspondents and Douglas Stewart, of the BBC, a distinguished reporter, like so many who were to follow him. I met Dennis Ogden two or three times, correspondent for the *Daily Worker*, before it acquired the name of *Morning Star*, and who, as a communist, enjoyed privileges of travel and access systematically denied to the others. However, it says much for the other correspondents that they accepted him socially and invited him to their homes. The others teased him about the amount of freedom he enjoyed, as the only one whose articles were not subject to censorship – 'Freedom? Yes, to hang myself,' he rejoined.

Before long, our group became known not only for the verve of its conversation, but also for its collective appetite. It was not for nothing that we became known as 'the locusts'.

For me, there was something different and special which the others could not share in the same way. Only one or two displayed an active interest in the Church, but I had studied Theology and had early on decided that investigation of the religious situation was to become my main preoccupation. I easily persuaded myself that this was a logical extension of my official subject, Russian medieval history.

There was a weekly Anglican service in the study of Ambassador Sir Patrick Reilly. On the first floor of the old British Embassy on the bank of the Moskva River, directly opposite the Kremlin, this had not only a warm and welcoming atmosphere on Sunday mornings, but also what is still the most dramatic view of the Kremlin from any vantage point in the capital. It was said that Stalin hated having the British looking in to see what he was eating for breakfast and was determined to evacuate the aliens, but he never succeeded and it is still in use as the ambassador's residence, although there is now a new building for the embassy itself. From time to time, as I walked up Gorky Street (which reverted to its pre-revolutionary name of *Tverskaya ulitsa* after communism), Moscow's main shopping street, leading away from Red Square, I would glance at the former Anglican church of St Andrew's, just down a side-street to the left. It was all too visible as a red-brick monument in Victorian gothic style. It was then in use as a recording studio for Melodiya, the concert agency. I never imagined that thirty years later the church would be restored to the community, though for some time disputes persisted and it was still occasionally used for recordings. In 1994 Queen Elizabeth II visited it, which helped regain the legal title to the property.

For the first few months a lay-reader, Dr Alistair Cameron, a scientist, read matins and preached with considerable insight. He was due to leave at Christmas, however, and there was no other permanent resident to replace him. Every two months or so the Anglican chaplain from Helsinki would appear and conduct communion for two consecutive Sundays, but his was a difficult job. He could never stay long enough really to know his congregation or their individual needs. From time to time other clergy appeared, most notably the Revd Francis House. He gave up his Christmas at home to spend extra time in Moscow, where he had visited as a member of a World Council of Churches delegation, in preparation for the forthcoming application by the Russian Orthodox Church to join, eventually accepted in 1961. We had a long and detailed conversation about my perspectives on the religious scene.

Gradually, though, I was drawn into a more active role. I was asked to train a choir to sing carols, not only at the Christmas services, but also in various diplomatic locations around Moscow. Not many diplomats could regularly attend rehearsals, but we got by and all the performances seem to have been successful, bringing pleasure to many people, not least to non-Christians, such as Burmese and Japanese diplomats invited to the Canadian and American embassies, where we were invited to sing. On a visit to Spaso House, residence of the American Ambassador, Llewellyn Thompson, I first met Gillian Davies, the Welsh nanny of the Ambassador's young children, who later became my wife.

Organising this choir led to my being invited to conduct the services after the departure of Dr Cameron. Selby Martin, aide to the British Ambassador, Sir Patrick Reilly, made this suggestion, and many times we gathered in the elegant study of the Ambassador himself. Through this Selby became a friend, and his autobiography reminisces about these days. I do not seem to have preserved any of the notes I used for my sermons, but it was a fine opportunity, the first I had ever had, to preach systematically to one congregation. Indeed, at Wycliffe Hall there had not been many opportunities to preach at all.

Music

I had long since learned that Moscow offered the most amazing opportunity to hear music, week in, week out, of world-class standard. I doubt whether there was a louder buzz in any of the great musical centres of the world at the time for a number of reasons. Not only did Moscow have a reservoir of genius, but it was little known 'live' to the world at large. This was largely because even those musicians who were listed (unofficially) as safe to travel abroad – and many were not – could do so only under the most restrictive conditions. *Goskontsert* (the State Concert Agency) made all their engagements for them, and they were accompanied by minders who ensured that they would not make private contacts without reports on these going back to the KGB. Stepping out of line would put a question mark against future foreign trips. Further, the drabness of Soviet life highlighted the fantasy and delight of live music in general – not only the Bolshoi Ballet – as an experience to take one out of oneself for a few hours. All this added to the intensity of concerts, not only for a British student, but for the Soviet public, too.

In April 1960 I was to participate on the periphery of a remarkable musical event. One of the quirks of the excessive official control of music at the time was the perceived necessity to slot high-profile events into exchange programmes or formal series of concerts which we would probably today call festivals. Thus it was that Aaron Copland and Lukas Foss came to Moscow for a week of 'American and Soviet Music'. Dmitri Shostakovich had visited Oxford as Isaiah Berlin's guest in June 1958 and to receive an honorary degree, but, in the West – as indeed in Russia – his personality was an enigma. In 1960 he had not yet met Benjamin Britten and Peter Pears. Later, their friendship and mutual admiration would enrich them all.

I was nearing the end of my exchange, by which time I was a frequent guest, courtesy of Gillian, at Spaso House. Mr Thompson asked me to see him. He said he was looking for someone who knew about music to help him host a reception for Shostakovich and Copland. Would I be interested? I received a front-row seat for the concert and an invitation to attend the reception at Spaso House afterwards. 'You have a job to do,' he said. 'Mr Shostakovich doesn't like receptions and is likely to leave after fifteen minutes. Please engage him in conversation and try to keep him longer.'

The programme featured a violin sonata and piano quartet by Aaron Copland, followed by a new quartet by Lukas Foss, played by the Borodin Quartet, then new short pieces by Shostakovich, Kabalevsky and Khachaturyan. Finally Sviatoslav Richter played Prokofiev's last piano sonata.

At the subsequent buffet supper at first I was in a corner of the Blue Ballroom at Spaso House talking to Copland. When Shostakovich came into the room I brought him over to talk to Copland and they seemed to enjoy each other's company. Then it was Shostakovich on his own. Socially he was difficult, initially appearing ill at ease, but he gradually warmed to the occasion and did not attempt to leave when Copland moved away. We talked about Oxford and his visit two years previously. 'His nervous twitches and loud clearing of his throat ceased and his faint voice became stronger,' I wrote. As well as being hosted by Isaiah Berlin, he had made friends with Dimitri Obolensky, my former tutor. He was disappointed not to have met Britten; he rated the *Serenade for Tenor, Horn and Strings* as one of his finest works, and much wanted to invite him to the Soviet Union. He had a high regard for William Walton, but had barely heard of Vaughan Williams. Shostakovich had spent the best part of two hours at the reception, and for something like half that time we were engaged tête-à-tête. It helped, of course, that I had heard Shostakovich's music on many occasions and seen him come to the concerts, where he would always acknowledge the applause with a shy bow and hurry off the platform as quickly as he possibly could. Most notably, I had heard the Moscow première of the *Cello Concerto No.1*, with Mstislav Rostropovich, who at that time was only just becoming known outside the Soviet Union.

By this time, now aged 53, Shostakovich had weathered the crises caused by Stalin's dictatorial intrusion into his work. He had survived and was now ready to break the mould. He would meet Britten and Pears on his next visit to the UK. Their friendship and professional collaboration developed rapidly. At Britten's home they developed a mode of communication which they called 'Aldeburgh Deutsch'; he invited the two to spend time at a composers' 'rest home' in the Caucasus. Rostropovich and his wife, the soprano Galina Vishnevskaya, visited them, and Britten wrote a song cycle for them, *The Poet's Echo*, set to Pushkin's words, with Rostropovich accompanying on his 'second instrument', the piano. It was fascinating to hear of Shostakovich's admiration for Britten just before the two met.

Other wonderful occasions were too numerous even to list. Perhaps most exciting of all were the evenings on which Sviatoslav Richter played. His concerts were never announced far in advance, but word would travel with electric speed around the musical community and hours before the appointed time crowds would gather outside the concert hall to besiege the lucky ticket holders. In later months my contacts at the American Embassy procured the magic ticket. I missed one event, though, which would have perhaps been the most unforgettable experience of all. Luckily, my British friend, Martin Dewhirst, who always had his ear closer to the ground than anyone else in our group, found out about the death and funeral of Boris Pasternak. On 2 June 1960 Pasternak lay in his open coffin at Peredelkino, the writers' colony (another Soviet feature now disappeared from Russian life). Richter came and played Bach and Beethoven uninterrupted for three hours, while Martin sat at his elbow.

Other great performers I heard were already legendary, but their world reputations were the more mysterious, due to the restrictions on their travel. Among them were David Oistrakh (violin), Emil Gilels and Lazar Berman (piano). I saw all the basic repertoire of Russian operas at the Bolshoi, which in those days commanded some of the most lavish resources in the world: *Khovanshchina* and *Boris Godunov* by Mussorgsky, *Prince Igor* by Borodin, many works by Glinka and Rimsky-Korsakov, Prokofiev's *War and Peace*, as well as several ballets. To this day, so few of these are performed with any regularity outside Russia that nothing could ever have replaced this formative musical experience.

I was always on the lookout for religious music, which was absent from the concert repertoire. Masses, passions, requiems were all virtually unknown to the Soviet public, so on those rare occasions when individual works did surface, there was overwhelming interest. It was the musical equivalent of going to the Hermitage Museum in Leningrad and seeing Rembrandt's *Prodigal Son* or a Leonardo Madonna. Thus I attended the first Soviet performance of Bach's *Magnificat* for forty years, Szymanowski's *Stabat Mater* and an organ recital, including some of Bach's chorale preludes, which the programme did not name because of their Christian connotation. I missed a performance of Mozart's *Requiem* because I was away.

One evening which was totally unexpected (this time a grapevine whisper did come my way) was the first performance – so it was said – of Rachmaninov's *Vespers* since the Revolution. This occurred in the little church 'of All Mourners' tucked away in the 'Beyond Moskva River' (*Zamoskvorechye*) area behind the British Embassy. This was in the context of a service of Orthodox vespers, probably with no permission sought or given and no advertising, and it would be twenty years before any performance would be permitted on a concert platform.

Atheism

It is now more than thirty years since the enforced atheism of the Soviet Union began to disappear. It was Mikhail Gorbachev's policy, from his election in 1985 or soon after, that changed this, so it is only those born before 1980 who experienced an atheist education and they are now beginning to produce a second generation which has not lived through this. It is difficult for these young people to imagine just how all-pervasive was this atheism, not only in its Stalinist apogee before the Second World War, but also in the subsequent Khrushchev years.

I was not, at this time, aware of the physical aspect of the renewed persecution of religion which became such a notable feature of Nikita Khrushchev's policy from 1959 until he was deposed in 1964. However, the propaganda accompanying it was everywhere. As a student, perhaps I noticed it especially strongly because, obviously, the younger generation was its special target.

Every student, from kindergarten to university graduation, had to undergo systematic ideological indoctrination. By the time they reached the exalted level of Moscow State University they should have become model atheists, yet this was far from universally true. Not only were there still (at that time) eight theological seminaries and two academies on Soviet soil, educating priests for service in the Russian Orthodox Church: the Roman Catholics also had a seminary in Lithuania and so did the Armenians in Echmiadzin, near Yerevan. Protestants, however, had nothing, not even a correspondence course.

One student was expelled from MGU while I was there – so a newspaper article attacking him wrote – for belonging to the ancient sect of the Old Believers. Quite often students would ask questions about my faith, exhibiting curiosity rather than hostility towards my position. One student, a girl called Maya, came to my room once and looked at the books on my shelves. When she saw a Bible she expressed the most intense interest, never having set eyes on one before. She was a student of English literature, well read and speaking the language well. She said that it was grotesque that the authorities should deny her access to this essential tool for her understanding of such poets as Milton and T. S. Eliot. I promised to try to find a Bible for her. However, like so many students who risked a conversation on a forbidden or difficult subject, she disappeared and failed ever to make contact again. This was a constant and distressing feature which blighted incipient friendships: the political watchdogs obviously monitored such relationships closely and were never slow to warn the student against developing them.

At university level, the core subject for every single student, arts or science, was *diamat* (dialectical materialism), the code name for Marxism-Leninism, which included atheism within its syllabus. I could have attended a lecture on this every day, and did once or twice in my early weeks. I soon found it so unutterably boring that I decided to take future lessons as read and drew a line under it. The observation of behaviour during these sessions, however, was not without its significance. Every lecture was two hours long, incorporating a short break which most students filled by smoking. During the first hour the lecturer, I observed, read from a textbook and some students (not all) scribbled down what he said, so virtually reproducing a set text, which could have been more conveniently read and annotated by the student in the first place. I expected that the second hour would be filled with lively questions and answers. The opposite happened. The lecturer droned on. The students became progressively drowsy and asked not a single question. One lecture did, however, become more animated – not because the students had woken up, but because they began throwing or catapulting balls of paper at each other, the lecturer seemingly oblivious to what was happening.

It was, I always believed, God's choice for my life that I should arrive in Moscow during the very month in which the growing anti-religious campaign acquired a public profile. Its flagship was the monthly journal *Nauka i religiya* ('Science and Religion'), the first issue of which appeared in the newspaper kiosks in September 1959. I bought the first and subsequent issues, and acquired the whole run, which is now held in the Keston archives at Baylor University, Waco, Texas. To some extent its tone was measured in its early issues, but reading it helped convince me of the reality of the incipient persecution of religion.

The Novodevichy ('New Maidens') Convent was reputed to be, during these years, the prime centre of Christianity in Moscow, so my first visit there was on 18 September, five days after my arrival in Moscow. Only one of the six imposing churches within the walls was open for worship. As a counterweight to this, another had been turned into a museum and now contained one of Moscow's foremost atheist exhibitions.

What immediately struck me was the primitive level of the propaganda I observed in the (former) Kazan Cathedral, on the Nevsky Prospekt, which I visited on a short stay in Leningrad. It claimed to be the primary anti-religious museum in the Soviet Union. With profuse illustration, its panels described the exploitation by the Orthodox Church of the peasants in the sixteenth and seventeenth centuries. A chart showed the relative wealth of all the monasteries in 1647, claiming that they owned one-third of all Russian land at that time.

When I published my first book, *Opium of the People* in 1965, I described Soviet anti-religious propaganda as 'unbelievably naïve'. To this day, I believe that it hindered its own cause. I wrote of it then:

> Not many Russian intellectuals take [the Museum of History of Religion and Atheism] seriously any more, though official figures claim that the number of visitors rose from 250,000 in 1956 to half a million in 1960… There is hardly an item which anyone with the remotest claim to scholarship would have dared include.

Among the captions – and there were many others on such topics as Jonah, the Gadarene swine and mustard seeds – was:

> The ark Noah built could not have accommodated all the animals which then populated the earth, which disproves the legend of the flood. The biblical story about it served as a weapon against agitators and implanted an attitude of patience and submissiveness in the downtrodden masses.

Then I went down into the crypt. I wrote the following:

> The culminating section… is a chamber of horrors depicting the tortures of the Spanish Inquisition; and it looks suspiciously as if the instruments were borrowed straight out of some local prison where they could have been in recent use.

Forty-three years later I visited the cathedral again and witnessed the final stages of a magnificent restoration.

My visit to Leningrad in 1960 included attending a lecture by the now-ignominious ex-professor of Old Testament at the Leningrad Theological Academy, Alexander Osipov. He had defected from the Orthodox Church very recently, announcing his apostasy in *Pravda* on 6 December 1959.[3] I was staying in a university dormitory and announcements of Osipov's lecture, 'How I Lost My Faith in God', were everywhere on notice boards and the walls. One of our exchange students resident in Leningrad had attended an earlier one and, after the lecture, a student had stood up and asked the question, 'Judas received thirty pieces of silver. How much did you get?' to which he had replied with an amused shrug. Here is how I wrote up my own impression of Osipov's lecture, attended by about two hundred students, comfortably filling a large lecture hall:

> The whole hall immediately fell under the spell of his presence. His penetrating blue eyes alone could hold an audience, as they flashed out from above his luxuriant brown beard, beginning to grey where it curled. This power was heightened by his rich, finely modulated voice, which he reinforced with dramatic gestures from his large expressive hands…

His lecture covered more or less the same ground as the *Pravda* article. Questions followed in the usual Russian pattern of the submitting them in writing. I took the initiative of sending one forward:

'In your *Pravda* letter and in your talk you did not mention the historical existence of Christ. How can a person who has studied the Bible as a historian completely ignore the fact on which the Christian faith is founded?'

The answer came back:

---

3   For extracts from this text, see *Opium of the People*, pp. 109–115.

'There are two theories about the life of Christ: 1) that he existed; 2) that he did not. The latter theory has been virtually proved to be the true one since the discovery and decipherment of the Dead Sea Scrolls a year or two ago...'[4]

I found the intellectual dishonesty of this reply astonishing, the more so since the vast majority in the room would never have heard of the Dead Sea Scrolls, as they had not been written up in the Soviet press at that point. Even during my later visit to the Leningrad Theological Academy students who had heard of them but never seen them implored me for copies of the texts.

Christian Churches

One of the odd aspects of my life in Moscow was the almost total absence, for me, of any formal postgraduate education. I was officially inscribed in the medieval department of the Faculty of History, with a brief to research the history of Byzantine–Russian relations in the tenth to twelfth centuries, the period covering the conversion of Russia to Christianity in 988, for which my studies with Dimitri Obolensky and Nicolas Zernov had prepared me.

It was a shock to find that I barely existed on the agenda of my supervisor, Professor Boris Alexandrovich Rybakov. He was a pleasant enough man, but was entirely preoccupied with travelling away from Moscow and abroad to lecture and to continue an excavation which he was conducting in Bulgaria.

However, I soon began to put this absence of any pressure to produce work to good use. Many people had been asking in the late 1950s how many churches were open in Moscow. No one knew and the Moscow Patriarchate was silent on the question. 'Modern' maps of the time erased many of the churches, even when they were open and operative. But in Moscow someone gave me an older map, and the churches were all marked. This precious document would guide me to all regions of the capital, as I formulated the idea of seeking them out more or less systematically.

Over the ten months that I was in Moscow I found out the answer – approximately thirty-five.[5] This was out of some six hundred, including private chapels, which had existed in a much smaller city before 1917.

The destruction or desecration of the rest – apart from a handful preserved as museums, such as the cathedrals of the Kremlin – was a barbarous betrayal of a heritage. Some of the churches had been razed to the ground, but, as throughout the country, usually the solid building was itself valuable enough to be converted to some other purpose. In the countryside, the church was often the only stone structure in a village of wooden houses and would be used for a store of agricultural implements, a *Komsomol* youth club or a cinema.[6]

---

4   Op. cit., p. 120.

5   Op. cit., p. 206.

6   See Alexander Solzhenitsyn's prose poem, 'Along the Oka', translated in Michael Bourdeaux, *Patriarch and Prophets* (Macmillan, London, pp. 154–5).

In Moscow there were at least two notable but contrasting examples of churches which had disappeared entirely. One was the little 'church above the gate' (*Nadvratnaya tserkov'*) at the entrance to Red Square. The whole structure was torn down, gate and all, in Stalin's day, in order to free access to the square itself, used twice a year in May and November as a parade ground to show off Soviet military might. Today one does not have to use any imagination to know what it must have been like: it was completely rebuilt in the 1990s, following original plans and photographs.

An even greater insult to Moscow's believers was the destruction of the Cathedral of Christ the Saviour. This had become Moscow's main cathedral after the closure of those in the Kremlin. It was built originally in the early nineteenth century to celebrate Russia's victory over Napoleon (one might have presumed that such symbolism would have saved the structure, at least for preservation as a 'museum of history'). The Wikipedia entry accurately describes what happened:

> On 24 February 1930, the economic department of the OGPU sent a letter to the Chairman of the Central Executive Committee asking to remove the golden domes of the Christ the Saviour Cathedral. The letter noted that the dome of the church contained over 20 tons of gold of 'excellent quality', and that the cathedral represented an 'unnecessary luxury for the Soviet Union, and the withdrawal of the gold would make a great contribution to the industrialization of the country'. The People's Commissariat of Finance did not object to this proposal. On 5 December 1931, by order of Stalin's minister Lazar Kaganovich, the Cathedral of Christ the Saviour was dynamited and reduced to rubble.[7]

The ruling atheists added insult to injury by filming the act of destruction, for subsequent use several times in anti-religious propaganda documentaries. Presumably this special treatment was because the additional symbolism associated with the status as the patriarchal cathedral overrode the historical significance. Further, it was on the banks of the Moskva River in a prominent position, barely more than a stone's throw from the Kremlin.

But there was a corollary to this story – or rather two, if one takes it up to the present. The original plan was to replace the imposing cathedral with an even larger structure, designated to become the tallest of all Stalin's skyscrapers in Moscow. Topping it all would be the most dominant statue of Lenin ever erected. However, the marshy ground by the river made an unstable foundation. The *babushki* of Moscow declared that the ground was cursed from the moment of the destruction of their cathedral. To their immense delight, cracks began to appear in the skyscraper's walls before it had reached half its planned height. The head of Moscow's 'reconstruction' team decided on drastic action. There was a humiliating climb-down and the structure was demolished. So it came about that Moscow's great open-air heated swimming pool

---

7   See Wikipedia, 'Cathedral of Christ the Saviour, Moscow'.

appeared in such a central location, giving forth during the winter a constant cloud of steam, which I used to think of as incense to the god of atheism.

The next act, sixty years later, was the reconstruction of the Cathedral of Christ the Saviour in the most lavish style possible, with money levied in large part on the business community of Moscow by Mayor Luzhkov. The builders followed the basic plan, but added an underground car park and an office complex in the most ambitious church building scheme undertaken in Russia for a century. No tourist can miss the new cathedral, but Russians were divided in their opinion of its artistic merit. Moreover, the cost, Muscovites claimed, could have provided for building churches in the needy suburbs.

Some former churches, which I observed as I walked for so many days around the streets of Moscow, had been desecrated to the point where their origins were no longer recognisable. A church on Red Square became a public toilet, no doubt an essential convenience for the crowds which constantly thronged there. It has now been rebuilt.

If you continued your walk beyond GUM (the State Universal Store), with its frontage directly on the square, you would come to what once had been a row of churches along the street called Varvarka, later renamed Razin Street by the Soviets (and now reverted to its original name). In 1959 they stood out and were recognisably some of the most outstanding small churches in Moscow. Soon after, the whole area was obscured by the construction of the monstrous Rossiya Hotel which was eventually pulled down. The churches are now splendid once again. One of the most beautiful of these in 1959 bore a plaque outside announcing that it was the 'Moscow Watch Repair Centre'.

Surrounding central Moscow was a circle of twelve ancient monasteries, their massive walls originally forming part of the city's defences, as well as providing a refuge for flourishing monastic communities (there are no monastic orders in the Russian Orthodox Church). I visited all of these in turn to discover, of course, that not one still served its original purpose. The closest active monastery to Moscow was at Zagorsk (originally and now again Sergiyev Posad, commemorating the name and preserving the remains of St Sergius, Russia's most revered saint), which I would visit on a number of occasions during my Moscow year.

I was able to go inside most of them, discovering that almost invariably the monks' quarters had degenerated into slummy and overcrowded tenements. The *Uspensky sobor* (Dormition Cathedral) in the Simonov Monastery was a dye-works, the Novospassky (New Saviour) Monastery allegedly housed 'historical archives', according to the plaque, though there was no access to them. The Andronikov Monastery, more interestingly, housed a collection of ancient icons.

By far the most intriguing was the Danilov Monastery, surrounded by the most forbidding wall of all, through which there was no access. Although there was no exterior designation of its purpose, a *babushka* told me that it was now a juvenile prison. It was Moscow's first monastery, founded in 1282 by Daniel, the son of Alexander Nevsky, when he was only twenty-one. It had also been the last monastery to keep its doors open during Stalin's reign, holding out until 1930 and housing the last vestige of an institute of theological education under the redoubtable Bishop Feodor. Stalin's henchmen eventually came to arrest the last thirty monks and took them out with their bishop to be shot.

As I walked around Moscow and recorded my thirty-five (the accurate number was more likely forty) 'working' churches, as the Russians called them, I could never have imagined that every single one of those which had been desecrated would be rebuilt and re-consecrated in my lifetime. There are now reported to be over six hundred.

The Official Church

Some of the most frustrating experiences of my year in Moscow were connected with my attempts to encounter the Church on an official level. To attend the liturgy and from time to time to meet members of the congregation was not difficult. Even young people, of whom there were some, would occasionally exchange a few words. But to engage priests in conversation? That was rarely possible and to set up any relationship with the Patriarchate itself or with any other structure of church life was impossible.

In retrospect, one can understand this, however frustrating it was at the time. The explanation is clear enough: the clergy could already feel the chill wind of persecution after a decade or more when their circumstances had been just a little better.

In my attempts to unlock the door to the Moscow Patriarchate and penetrate its interior I had one key: a letter of introduction from Michael Ramsey, then Archbishop of York, who was more than helpful and enthusiastic about my extended visit. A copy of this which I had brought secured my entry into the building in Chisty Pereulok ('Clean Lane') which then housed the Patriarchate and was formerly the embassy of Hitler's Germany. A man in tattered working clothes took me to a room at the end of a corridor where Alexei Buyevsky introduced himself as a lay administrator of the Patriarchate. What he did not say, of course, was that he reported to the KGB, which was later revealed, but this had to go with his appointment. I had previously forwarded the letter itself to his office, but received no reply. I mentioned this, whereupon he fished in a drawer and produced my communication, saying that for some time he had been expecting me to come.

Mr Buyevsky offered help in any way he could. He presented me with a book, *The Russian Orthodox Church, Organisation, Situation, Activity*, which, he said, would answer every question I could conceivably want to ask. He would also supply a list of churches which I should visit and tell me by phone when the Patriarch was celebrating the liturgy, so that I could attend. He promised also to make an appointment for me to see Metropolitan Nikolai, responsible for the foreign relations of the Church, after his return to Moscow, which would be in a few days. This was on 5 November, but it would take until 29 April for the interview to happen.

Our conversation was warm and friendly, but I soon came to realise that Buyevsky was the only person representing Orthodox officialdom whom I could see with any ease. The key that I had didn't quite fit the lock.

A week after meeting him I went to Zagorsk, and he had promised that someone would greet me officially and introduce me to those I wanted to meet. But when I arrived, after a train journey and a walk through the town to this most impressive complex, almost a walled city, no one knew I was coming. However, guarding the entrance was Fr Bartolomei, who arranged for another monk to accompany me on a tour, which included part of the seminary. The Vice Dean talked briefly and gave me a collection of photographs of the seminarians at work and worship, but there was no contact with the students themselves. I noticed that in the large assembly hall the picture behind the president's chair was of Lenin, but when I looked at the photograph in the album of the identical place the photograph had earlier been of the Patriarch. It struck me at the time that this was a small but symbolical warning to the students that it was communism that was in charge of their destiny, not the church authorities.

The tour continued through the impressive museums, which I could enjoy in isolation, but when this was over I was abruptly handed my coat. I had hoped to stay on a further four hours to be able to attend the evening service, but it was abundantly clear that my time was at an end. When I asked to see the library, the reply was that it was closed because this was a 'short day'.

Again, at the Theological Academy in Leningrad in May 1960 the message from Mr Buyevsky about my visit had not arrived, or had been removed from the in-tray. Here Professor Pariisky, the 'Inspector', was almost rude on the phone and when I called to see him, he made me show him my MGU accreditation before he would start to talk. He chose to discuss the Anglican Church and delivered a tirade, telling me that it was divided within itself, whereas all Russian Orthodox Church believers lived in harmony. I saw the chapel, the dining room and the library, even though it was partially closed for refurbishment. On the shelf of English books, there were the *Oxford Dictionary of the Christian Church* and those by Dr Kelly, my tutor, on early creeds and doctrines. These were apparently gifts from a delegation of Anglican monks which had recently visited the Academy.

Professor Pariisky did, however, ask two students to accompany me to the bus, leading to one of the most worthwhile discussions I had during my year in the Soviet Union. They told me they both came from Christian families, though some of their fellow students were converts from atheist backgrounds and had even been members of the *Komsomol* (Young Communist League). No reconciliation, they said, was possible between Christianity and Marxism, so they had chosen a hard path in life. Viktor came from the south of Russia, where his father was a 'worker' and his mother a tough and wise person. When his younger brother had wanted to enter another seminary, at Stavropol, state officials had come calling and delivered their threats, but his mother had dealt with them firmly, sent them packing, and now his brother had begun his studies.

The two could not have been more decisive in their condemnation of Alexander Osipov, who until recently had been their professor of Old Testament. 'Traitor' was the word they used and they called him a rat in slightly more godly language. Even so, they had learned much from him. They set out complex reasons why he might have betrayed his faith – possibly including some kind of infiltration into his private life, and thus moral compromise.

This was the only time in my year when I wished that I had been studying in Leningrad rather than Moscow, because it would have added untold richness to my life if I could have developed my friendship with these and the other students whom I would have met.

My eventual interview with Metropolitan Nikolai was so short as to be a virtual non-event, though in view of his death the next year in unexplained circumstances, as the noose of persecution tightened, it was more significant than it seemed at the time. Here is an extract from my diary:

> …after eight months of waiting … I was in and out in five minutes, and he gave me no time to ask a single question. He treated me like an official delegation from the Anglican Church, asking me about the state of health of some of its most prominent members, whether the Archbishop of Canterbury was going to retire, and whether Hewlett Johnson was still alive… I had a list of five questions to ask him. I was about to start on these… when he got up to go, and so the interview was ended.
>
> Unknown to me, he was already under immense pressure and he did not know how to react to this strange foreign student who suddenly appeared in Moscow.

The Baptists

The warmth that was lacking in my official contacts with the Orthodox was present in good measure with the 'Evangelical Christians-Baptists' (to give them their official title), though, did I but know it at the time, they were about to face even more bitter persecution than other believers. Moscow then had one solitary Baptist church and I visited it in my second month, after which I would attend it frequently.

One of the pastors was always on duty at the front door to look out for visitors, for by this time the location in a side-street in central Moscow was well known. He would take the visitor upstairs to the gallery of the church, where a special front seat was always reserved.

My host was Ilya Mikhailovich Orlov who spoke reasonable English and had studied in England, at Bristol Baptist College, from 1956–8, a golden interlude when restrictions on church life had eased considerably, but for a short period only.[8] Finding such familiarity – hymns I knew, a loud organ, a warm greeting – in such a place was, in its way strange, but gradually, over a number of visits, I came to realise that I

---

8   For a full account of these students, see *Opium of the People*, pp. 162–9.

was being shielded from really meaningful contacts. Pastor Orlov would stick close to me and even drive me in his car (what a privileged man he was) to the nearest metro station, so that there was never the opportunity to talk privately to any of the congregation.

Nevertheless, I came to admire the sermons preached – at great length and usually three in each service – by men denied any access to theological education. It was strangely touching to sing 'Silent Night' (so slowly that the tune was scarcely recognisable) on Christmas Eve. I would love to have been invited to sing in the choir, where there was more than a smattering of young people, but obviously this was not possible, either. Often members of visiting delegations were invited to address the congregation, invariably packed and responsive, but this was always done via an interpreter, so there was a safeguard in the message which was transmitted. I would have spoken in Russian and clearly this would not have been acceptable, so I was not invited to do so. They told me, too, that Billy Graham had recently paid them a private visit, but he had been permitted only to observe, not to speak.

I was filled with warmth for these people, who had russianised their Protestantism and made it entirely their own. I was happy and comfortable in their services and admired the directness of the message in their preaching. Without my knowing it, I was being prepared for the central role that the fate of the Baptists would play in the middle period of my life. Whenever I met the Protestants in the Soviet Union I would have the feeling, 'Communism can't win here' and I once recorded those words in my diary,[9] even though this was in the context of the Lutheran Church in Estonia, which I was to visit near the end of my year in the Soviet Union.

9   Ibid., p. 184.

Chapter VI
Seeking a Way Forward

Moscow State University did 'the class of 59' proud at the end. Our exchange was reciprocal, so the Soviet students in Britain travelled, as did we, seeing some of the show places of the Soviet Union. Our group left by train from the Kursk station on 4 June, bound for Orjonikidze (now called Vladikavkaz again), via Rostov-on-Don, a two-day journey. We were among the first tourists of the year – and perhaps the first non-Soviets ever – to go by bus over the mighty Georgian Military Highway and the Krestovy Pass (2, 400 metres), only just open after its winter closure, taking us beneath Mount Kazbek, the highest peak in Europe.

As we descended, with no forewarning, a landslide blocked our way. Our minder was horrified, not knowing how to handle such a crisis. Eventually we were diverted to an empty 'summer camp'. The local Georgians in a remote village, Pasanauri, had never seen foreigners before, but the word quickly spread about our presence. This gave them an opportunity to overwhelm us with their impromptu hospitality, a lamb was slaughtered, and we drank Georgian wine before continuing our journey the next morning.

Evading our minder, who tried to stick all the closer to us, after the debacle of the previous day, I caught a local bus from Tbilisi, the present capital of Georgia, to Mtskheta, the ancient ecclesiastical capital. Opposite the town, on the other side of the River Kura, the majestic Djvari Monastery, subject of a poem by Lermontov, glistened on a hilltop. I waited for an hour at a designated point for a boat to ferry me over. None came. In the distance I could see a dam with a path over it. I walked to it and began to cross. About halfway a soldier jumped out at me from behind a pillar, rifle at the ready and with fixed bayonet, which he pointed at me. I needed no order to march back; he opened the door of his guard-post, pushed me inside and slammed it shut. My terror instantly dissipated: there, already installed, were fellow students, Martin Dewhirst and Tom Webb, grinning sheepishly. An officer appeared and conducted an interrogation. In all honesty, it was neither long nor particularly threatening – indeed, one might call it almost polite. We simply told the truth: that we had wanted to visit the monastery, having no idea that there was a 'military installation' on the other side of the dam. He wrote out a statement to be signed by himself, the soldier and all three of us. The whole incident didn't last more than an hour, after which we were released, on condition that we return to Tbilisi immediately. This was the only arrest of my life.

Fifty-seven years later (2017) I was invited to a conference in Tbilisi for my second-ever visit. A friend, former Oxford student, the Revd Malkhaz Songulashvili, drove me to the Djvari Monastery. As we were crossing the road over the river I recognised the place of my arrest, I cried out to stop and Malkhaz took a photo of me, including the little stone guardhouse where I was interrogated. It was still there.

In 1960 we continued by overnight train from Tbilisi to Yerevan, capital of Soviet Armenia, with a visit to Echmiadzin, where the Armenian Church has its seminary, and the next day to Lake Sevan. We returned to Georgia and the port of Sukhumi.

It was there that I saw the Black Sea for the first time. After a visit to Lake Ritsa we joined a comfortable steamer, to call at Sochi, Tuapse, Novorossisk and Yalta. Denied an official visit, we bought bus tickets for Bakhchisarai, the former capital of the exiled (that is, ethnically cleansed) Crimean Tatars, but the militia inspected our documents at a roadblock just outside the town and turned us back. A taxi appeared out of the blue and took us to our ship free of charge, the driver telling us apologetically that we had strayed into a 'forbidden zone'. It would take me over thirty years to reach Bakhchisarai, an enchanting place celebrated by Pushkin.

The boat continued to Odessa, then by train to Kiev, where the atmosphere in the great Monastery of the Caves was oppressive. Kiev was, after all, the scene of the Baptism of Rus' in 988. There were still a few monks there, but they seemed too afraid to talk. I could, however, wander around on my own for several hours. This was 22 June. I eventually learned that I was one of the last foreigners to visit this historical site, now mostly in ruins, damaged during the Nazi occupation, before the regime closed it. When I returned in 1988, to witness the marking of the Millennium of Russian Christianity, I would be among the first foreign visitors after the hasty reopening just in time for the celebrations. This place would forever after be symbolic for me: religion persecuted, religion freed. Our trip had lasted three weeks and opened my eyes to the variety and diverse ethnography of the Soviet Union, though we were far too short a time in any one place to gain more than a superficial impression.

Gillian's Moscow Experiences

Gillian, then aged twenty-four, a primary school teacher, had applied for a job as governess for the children of the distinguished American Ambassador, Llewellyn Thompson. Jenny and Sherry were then nine and four years old, but, far from their creating a full-time job, Gillian discovered that Russian and Chinese servants were on hand to look after the girls while she worked as a part-time teacher at the Anglo-American school. She soon found herself also an unofficial social secretary and personal assistant to Mrs Thompson.

Gillian and I met through music. I was leading a group of British residents to sing carols at various embassies. On our visit to Spaso House, the residence of the American Ambassador, we were shown into the Blue Ballroom. As we began to sing, I was a little put out by the addition of a mezzo, who dared join in after not having attended our practices. I had to find out who she was. We went to a few concerts together and she told me her intriguing background.

Gillian was born in Tredegar, Monmouthshire, daughter of Ethel and Arthur ('Artie'), a Baptist family. Ethel was a schoolteacher and Artie a coal miner, who, like my father, had left school in his early teens. Gillian specialised in music, trained as a primary school teacher and worked in a tough area of Bristol. After three years she was looking for a move and noticed an advert in the paper: the American Ambassador in Moscow, Llewellyn Thompson, was looking for a governess/teacher for his two young daughters. Mrs Thompson interviewed Gillian in London and a few weeks later she was packing her bags for the US and Moscow.

When Gillian accepted my proposal of marriage, this would mean her leaving Moscow after only two years. There was no time to lose, as the rule of the day decreed that I, as a prospective curate, had to marry before ordination, which was due to take place at the end of 1960. My time in the Soviet Union was going to end in June, so we had to make all our arrangements before even meeting each other's parents. The four of them formed an immediate bond and worked hard on the wedding preparations.

There was a further complication. Before meeting Gillian I had made arrangements to end my academic year in Moscow with some extensive travel: by train via Kishinyov (now Chisinau) to Bucharest, Sofia, Istanbul and Greece, including Mount Athos. I kept to this, but cut it short.

So the baker's son would marry the miner's daughter! Gillian willingly became an Anglican in preparation for our marriage, and was confirmed in Moscow by Roderick Coote, Bishop of Fulham, who had a distant pastoral oversight over Moscow, which he occasionally visited. The wedding took place at Holy Trinity, Drybrook, Forest of Dean, in August. David Jewell was best man.

Before our meeting, Gillian had had many experiences as a result of her job, including travel in the USA, but most remarkable was one in Moscow. The autumn of 1959 was 'let's join hands across the sea' time, when the Cold War was to be warmed a little. Diplomatic exchanges led to a unique initiative. Mr Khrushchev, impulsive as ever, sent a message saying that he would like to meet Ambassador Thompson informally one weekend. He replied that this would cut across his only family time, so the whole Thompson family and their governess received an invitation to spend a weekend at the Khrushchev *dacha*. Nikita Sergeyevich wanted Jenny and Sherry to meet his grandchildren.

One Saturday morning in November 1959 the American party embarked in an embassy car with Soviet police escort and made their way out through the suburbs to an un-signposted road deep in the country. Passing through several security posts and into a heavily fenced area, the company was divided, with Gillian and the children given their own *dacha* with servant. There was a walk shared by the young Khrushchevs and the Thompson children. In the evening Gillian had to accompany Jenny and Sherry to a meal and put them to bed, babysitter provided, but the word came that she must not eat, because she was invited to the later banquet.

A slightly different, but not contradictory, account appears, as seen from the perspective of Llewellyn Thompson's daughters, in their biography of their father,

The Kremlinologist: Llewellyn E. Thompson, America's Man in Cold War Moscow (Johns Hopkins University Press, Baltimore, 2018).[1]

At the appointed hour a car appeared and drove Gillian to the main complex, where she was greeted not only by Khrushchev and the Thompsons, who were already waiting, but by virtually the whole Politburo, the party comprising some twenty people. This was, incidentally, one of those rare occasions when the wives of senior Soviet officials appeared. Gromyko, Mikoyan, Adjubei (Khrushchev's son-in-law and editor of *Izvestiya*, the official Soviet newspaper) and others, who had been only names to Gillian, were all introduced. As the evening wore on the toasts became more frequent and boisterous. Mr Thompson drank lightly, but not the Russians. One particular round of toasts was proposed individually to all nationalities present. Ukraine (Khrushchev) and Armenia (Mikoyan) featured separately, presumably to increase consumption, but so did 'Anglia' (Gillian forbore to point out that it should really have been 'Wales'), upon which the whole Politburo rose to drink her health.

The next morning there was a knock at Gillian's *dacha's* door. There was Mr Khrushchev in person, demanding to take her and the children on a ride through the snow in his personal *troika* (sleigh with three horses). Gogol has a wonderful passage likening Russia's headlong dash to its destiny to that of a *troika* ('birdlike troika'), virtually out of control. Mr Khrushchev's driving seems to have been only slightly more sedate, but he had obviously taken a liking to the young and rather modest 'English' lady and wanted to impress her. A few months later (May 1960) there was to be the 'U2 incident', when Garry Powers was shot down in his spy-plane from the skies high above Soviet territory, after which the Moscow ice froze over again harder than ever – but the excursion to Khrushchev's *dacha* deserves a footnote in the history of Soviet–American relations.

Marriage and Life in Enfield

'Marriage before ordination' was not the only rule. If you had been abroad, you had to adapt afresh to the discipline of a theological college, at the same time as getting used to married life.

Thus at the end of September 1960 I found myself back at Wycliffe Hall, now living out in married accommodation which we had to find ourselves. This was the only time that the Church itself paid for my education, though what precisely I was supposed to be studying was never made clear. Gillian found work as a supply teacher. The three months gave her an opportunity to get to know Oxford.

Prior to going to Moscow, I had visited the Revd Graham Buston and Enfield Parish Church. This, by now, had rather faded from memory, but I liked the town and its well-kept marketplace in front of the beautiful church. On a conducted tour around the parish I was warmly received by a variety of people, so on return from Moscow I decided to continue with my plans of taking up a curacy there. We invited Graham and

---

1   p. 204.

his wife Josephine to our wedding. A shy, rather diffident man, Graham was kindness itself in his personal relations. Josephine had brought private means into the family and they were thus able to buy a curate's house for us in Little Park Gardens, a very pleasant unmade road just round the corner from the church. This was necessary, because I was to be the second curate, the Revd Sydney Matthews already occupying the official curate's house.

Before this there was a crisis which almost led me to abandon my plans for ordination. It is hard now, looking back over almost sixty years, to remember how hidebound by convention the Church of England then was. Graham, he later told me, had been horrified, when he came to the wedding, to find that I had grown a beard, which I had done at Gillian's suggestion. When I was back from honeymoon he wrote a letter saying that he 'expected' that I would have shaved it off by the time I arrived in Enfield. This letter almost cost me my vocation. Gillian and I paid an anxious visit to Enfield, but he was immovable: the people of this rather staid suburban parish simply would not understand ... I never did discover what exactly it was that they would not have understood, but the episode caused real anguish, because Gillian did not want to be bullied, and I felt protective towards it, as the offending beard was 'hers' in the first place. We did pray about it – at length – and the decision was close: I would not sacrifice my immediate plans in order to hold out against what was virtually an order. I have often wondered if my Enfield career would have been less satisfactory if I had been permitted to keep the beard – and I wonder what Graham would have thought, had he lived to see Rowan Williams's splendid growth when he was Archbishop of Canterbury.

My ordination was in St Paul's Cathedral on St Thomas's Day, 21 December 1960. Our preceding retreat was in the Royal Foundation of St Katharine, a place of prayer in the heart of London's dockland, run by the Mirfield Fathers, who provided calm alongside stimulating conversation. The Bishop of London, Montgomery Campbell, conducted my ordination as deacon, which was attended by both sets of parents and a large supportive contingent from Enfield. I felt calm, blessed and truly called, after such a solemn ceremony, to serve the people of Enfield. I was left with a lasting impression of the Anglican Church at its best.

As soon as we were settled into our first house and I had been inducted into the regular pattern of traditional Anglican worship, my doubts disappeared. Enfield was exactly right for me at that time. It provided a structure, so necessary after not having had a regular home since leaving Cornwall for National Service eight years previously. Everywhere there was the warmest of welcomes, leading to many friendships.

Graham Buston ran the parish with meticulous care. At our Monday morning staff meetings, work around the parish was distributed between the three of us. Sydney Matthews, as the senior curate, was a late vocation, and we quickly formed a team where each knew his role and we worked well together. I was soon convinced that I was, at least for the time, following the right path. Graham monitored my sermons as a deacon and always had something positive to say. He also had the driest sense of humour. Waiting some weeks for the opportunity to teach me how to conduct a funeral, we experienced a hiatus. 'Why don't they die,' said Graham. Soon they did. I learned how to officiate and these occasions, preceded by a visit to the grieving household, were important to me. After a year I was ordained priest, so Graham taught me how to celebrate the Eucharist and to officiate at weddings. These, too, deepened my spiritual life, as they continued to do even when, for most of my later years, such opportunities would be reduced.

As a matter of record, my salary was £390 a year, our house being free of rent and rates. The parish paid my Church of England pension contributions, which continued in one way or another for my whole life and for which I would never cease to be grateful. Gillian, of necessity, taught full time in a primary school.

I loved my designated work in charge of the youth club. Young people regularly crammed into our house on Sunday evenings after church, among whom was a future cabinet secretary (Andrew Turnbull). Gillian brought in a later wave of even younger people when she started to train probationary choristers, among whom was a future bishop (Salisbury), then aged five. The music in church was ambitious and a constant delight – and I was invited to participate in the selection process of a new organist in my second year, leading to the appointment of Eric Pask. He had a day-job at the Bank of England, but had boundless energy and professionalism of the highest standard for the organ and the choir.

Graham also insisted that Gillian and I should benefit from as much free time as possible and develop interests outside the parish. We easily followed this advice and joined the Philharmonia Chorus in its heyday, with weekly rehearsals in central London and an average of one concert a month under world-famous conductors, mostly in the Royal Festival Hall, but including the excitement of a visit to Parma in 1963 to sing Verdi's *Requiem* in the beauty of the opera house, the Teatro Regio.

Graham had a vision for me, even if that could not be precisely defined at the time. He encouraged my determination to keep up my study of religion in the Soviet Union, hard though it was to find ways of following developments. There was also the 'post-ordination essay', mandatory at the time and which would eventually become the nucleus of my first book. Graham also encouraged me to accept invitations which began to come from neighbouring parishes to talk about these experiences, sometimes from the pulpit, sometimes to the various local societies which then proliferated. On these occasions my listeners always expressed something more than a polite interest, especially when they heard about the current 'atheist campaign' which I had seen with my own eyes. It was always frustrating not to have any practical suggestions as to what my audiences could do to follow up on an experience which was invariably new to them.

I hoped that the next step would appear in due time as a progression from Enfield. Might it be an academic post? This was only a vague hope, because there was no teaching post anywhere in the world which offered specialisation on religion in Russia. There were no missionary societies aiming to supply aid for the countries of the Soviet bloc – at least none in the UK, nor any that I had heard of in other countries. Only later would I discover the magnificent work of Aid to the Church in Need, a Roman Catholic organisation based in Rome and at that time active in France, West Germany and the Low Countries, founded by the redoubtable 'Bacon Priest', the Dutch Premonstratensian, Fr Werenfried van Straaten. Amnesty International would soon take up the cause of religious and political prisoners in the USSR, but it was not founded until in July 1961 and initially consisted of just one researcher, Bruce Laird.

Gradually the urgency of finding a way forward grew as the years of my curacy began to draw to an end. The obvious field was ecumenical relations. I did have French and some German as well. It was an exciting time in inter-church relations, especially with so many churches from Eastern Europe, including the Russian Orthodox Church, joining the World Council of Churches in 1961. I therefore hoped that there might be work for specialists in the ecumenical field, and I was one of the few who had had first-hand experience of life in the USSR.

I just waited for the openings to present themselves, but they never did, even after I began more actively to pursue them in my third year at Enfield. I simply did not realise at the time – though later I became convinced of it – that professional ecumenism was a club, to put it mildly, to which you either belonged or were outside of. For some reason, I did not belong from the first. I wondered if, despite my education and qualifications, I lacked the smoothness of the born diplomat. Later, when I began to write about the persecution of the Church, there were other, more obvious, reasons: writing about this was inconsistent with being active in inter-church relations. Very much later in my life I would come to see that focusing attention on the suppression of religious liberty would be a contribution to the ecumenical debate. The church diplomats – the professional ecumenists – would fulfil their own role, different, but an essential element of the whole scene.

I supported the Fellowship of St Alban and St Sergius, a loyalty which I had originally forged under the aegis of Professor Nicolas Zernov when I was at Oxford. Its dedication to eventual unity between Anglicans and Orthodox seemed to me at the time realistic, however distant the prospect now seems in the twenty-first century, and while at Enfield I served as a member of its council. The Revd Basil Minchin was its secretary, but, for my taste, there were too many ex-Anglicans in it who did genuinely 'love Orthodoxy' and had become converts, but too few who had a knowledge of – or even a real desire to learn more of – the situation of the Russian Orthodox in their homeland.

Gillian and I made a joint decision that we should start a family, and in April 1963 Karen was born. This was a happy time, despite our being penurious, with dear friends from Enfield being chosen as godparents. I was occasionally able to supplement my salary, if holiday time was available, by continuing to accompany American tourists around Europe for American Express and later Caravan Tours, something I had done regularly since starting this as a vacation job while at Oxford.

Journalism

At the very beginning of my time in Enfield, one event took place which launched me into journalism and provided an experience which would later encourage me to develop this, although it would not immediately lead to any openings. Just a month after beginning my new work I had my first article published. In those days I was a regular reader of *The Observer*, so while I was doing my final term in Oxford I reviewed my Moscow experiences and sent in an article. In the excitement of ordination and moving into our house, I had almost forgotten it when I received an acceptance notice and *The Observer* published it on 29 January 1961. There isn't much I would like to change. Even after over fifty years, I stand by what I wrote, with only a modification of emphasis here and there. It did, however, in the eyes of diplomacy (church and secular) type-cast me as a critic, not only of communism, but also of the Moscow Patriarchate's subservience to the regime. The aura of gadfly would buzz around my head for the rest of my life. Also, later, I heard a suggestion that the British Council would not welcome forays by its future exchange students into the field of human rights.

Perhaps the editorial lead-in was sharper in tone than my text, but it was not unfair. It read:

> How a Church can best continue its work in a country where religion is barely tolerated is the question raised here by a former theological student at Oxford, who spent a year in Russia under a British Council student exchange scheme. He feels that the Russian Orthodox Church is not meeting the challenge.[2]

I quoted from conversations with clergy I had met in Moscow who looked forward to the coming triumph of communism as a great opportunity for the Church. One priest stated:

> Monasticism has no future in this country. In the past its duty was to spread a high moral tone among the population at large, but now this is done by the Communist Party. It is inevitable and right that many monasteries have closed down … and the numbers inside them will continue to dwindle.

Although I heard his message, later I realised that these were the words of an intimidated man, terrified of being reported as anti-communist. I went on to criticise the naivety of foreigners who visited one of the handful of open churches, saw it packed with worshippers and cited this as proof of the freedom of religion in the Soviet Union. Almost the opposite was true, I pointed out: over-full churches simply proved that too few were open.

I portrayed something much more positive also: a summary of my conversations with two theological students (their names changed) whom I had met in Leningrad:

---

2   *The Observer*, London, 29 January 1961.

Boris opened his heart to me, while Pyotr listened avidly and agreed warmly with most of my comments. They were both from Christian families, but said that many of the students in the seminary were converts to the Christian faith from the ranks of the Komsomol. Boris had had much trouble from this organisation before he decided to offer himself for ordination, and they had used all means short of violence to dissuade him.

On the Church's attitude to the State, he was definite that no reconciliation was possible between Christianity and Marxism... [All priests] combat materialism with every means at their disposal... They fully realised the deadly seriousness of the opposition they would meet. They said they were desperately short of books to give them weapons for their struggle, even the Bible being unobtainable.

I ended with a eulogy to the faith of the *babushki,* some of whom I had counted as my friends in Moscow and from whom I had learned much. I was looking for the positives and, I hope, achieved something of the balance which would later characterise the work of Keston College.

Opium of the People

Gillian and I received leave of absence from Enfield to work at the British Trade Fair in Moscow for three weeks in May 1961, the very setting up of which fed the positive views about the progress in international relations. We were both so busy working that we had virtually no time for conversation with Russian friends and nothing significant occurred which changed my views. We worked (and received salaries which seemed to us princely at the time) in unaccustomed fields: Gillian modelled Kangol hats, to Russian women the height of fashion, and I explained the latest developments in Lancashire weaving technology!

The received wisdom of the time was that relations with the Soviet Union were improving and the advent of Nikita Khrushchev was pushing this forward beyond expectations. Despite his quick temper, he showed good humour and a human side of which the previous post-Stalin leaders had had a limited endowment.

I was the guardian of a truth which was a secret to the world at large. The Foreign Office was poorly informed about the renewed persecution under Khrushchev. There had indeed been two better periods for the Russian Orthodox Church. During the Second World War Stalin allowed some churches to re-open in order to boost the morale of the people. A second improvement occurred in the late 1950s, after Stalin's death, when the rebuilding of churches was possible for a short time.

I had been an eyewitness to the shattering of this truce and I was the bearer of bad news, which not everyone wished to believe. Allegedly, a 'Bourdeaux view' circulated in the FCO. I continued to work away quietly at recording more permanently my Moscow experiences, drawing on the details of my Moscow diary to back up my assertions. I had enough spare time to do serious work on this and by about a year after the publication of my article in *The Observer* I had written a first draft of a book.

At this distance it is hard to recall how complete in the early 1960s was the general ignorance about all aspects of the Church in Russia. It was nearly twenty years since the publication of Paul Anderson's *People, Church, and State in Modern Russia* in 1944. Since then, Matthew Spinka's *The Church, in Soviet Russia* had been published in New York in 1956, but had not circulated in the UK. In the early 1960s the gap was slowly being filled, most notably by a detailed book by Walter Kolarz, *Religion in the Soviet Union* (Macmillan, 1961), which mapped all the religions of the country and exhibited objectively the fruits of a lifetime of study, aided by his job at the Central Research Unit of the BBC at Bush House. As I read it I annotated it extensively. I wrote to Walter Kolarz and he invited me to call on him in his Maida Vale home, but sadly he died before we could meet. However, his widow, Shura, took me to heart: she became a lifelong friend and an influential figure as my work developed.

Kolarz's work provided a kind of framework for me in the planning and organisation of my own first book. Even though he had not lived to document the new wave of measures taken to suppress the church, he knew his subject better than anyone, and it provides, even today, a perspective of religious life in the USSR in the decade after Stalin's death.

My own book was based on a general knowledge of Russian history and a flux of conflicting personal experiences. I then went on – controversially – to describe my personal encounter with the Moscow Baptists. I asked myself this question: 'If I had met a potential convert to the faith at the university, a person from an atheist background, to whom I wanted to introduce Christianity, would I take him initially to an Orthodox or Baptist church?' My answer was to haunt me: 'In most instances, taking everything into consideration, I would probably advise a potential convert to go to the Baptist Church.'[3]

This remark was honest at the time, but it was overstated and I should have given a more nuanced view. Would the potential convert respond more readily to the direct appeal of a Baptist sermon or to the enveloping fold of a beautifully sung liturgy, itself the more poignant for being repressed in so many places? Some would doubtless respond more directly to an archaic language, Church Slavonic, than to the modern Russian. With hindsight, I now realise that I had not fully appreciated the intrinsic place the Orthodox Church occupied in Russian culture. I had simply not seen the Church at its best: my conversations with priests had been short and timorous (on their side and through no fault of their own). A priest would have doubtless addressed a young Russian differently. This remark was another judgement which marked me, even though my studies would bring me ever closer to the spirituality of the Orthodox tradition.

---

3   Bourdeaux, *Opium of the People* (1965), p. 171.

The eventual last chapter of *Opium* was not in the first draft. Indeed, before the end was written, the first manuscript was doing the rounds of the publishers. On the way, one particularly hurtful letter came from a prominent Christian publishing house, saying that my views did not coincide with those of the Archbishop of York (Michael Ramsey), so it was inadvisable to publish. But when, in 1964, I did receive a positive response, it was from a literary publisher which enjoyed the highest reputation. T. S. Eliot was a non-executive director, whom I did not meet, but I corrected all the proofs sitting at his desk surrounded by his photographs and first editions. Once Faber had agreed to publish, events moved fast. They assigned to me an editor, Mary Kay Wilmers, barely older than myself, but with distinguished literary gifts, who made sure every word was in place. We worked together positively over several months before her superiors insisted on something else, which changed the nature of the work. 'We need a new last chapter,' they said. By this time I had begun to find out more, especially from a book published in French. Nikita Struve's *Les chrétiens en URSS*[4] broke new ground and, unambiguously expressed, set out the tragedy which had befallen the Russian Orthodox Church since my Moscow sojourn only three years before. Living in Paris among the Russian émigré community, he managed to document the renewed persecution in a systematic way from returning travellers and from the new *samizdat* (unpublished documents) which were beginning to circulate in Russia. Here was my model.

---

4   Paris, 1963. Second edn, 1964.

Chapter VII
Be Our Voice

I pinned my hopes on an advertisement in the *Church Times* in 1963 for an assistant in what was then called 'MECCA' – the Missionary and Evangelical Council of the Church Assembly. I thought I might be a candidate – but beyond receiving an acknowledgement of the application there was silence. I waited for months, but heard nothing more. I had to assume I had not been shortlisted and eventually I read of the appointment in the press. I was bitterly disappointed. I had not then heard of the successful candidate, announced as 'The Revd. R. C. M. Jeffrey'. I am sure they made the right appointment.

This was, of course, a blessing in disguise and 1964 soon began to offer different perspectives. Not only was I busy thinking how to respond to Faber's request for a new last chapter, but I also found balm in Gilead – literally – for my application for a Wyndham Deedes Scholarship from the Anglo-Israel Association to study for six weeks in Israel was successful. Unaided by any advice from on high, I had to begin to make decisive plans to leave Enfield. Our house was needed by a successor and it was not done to stay on for a fifth year in a first curacy. The expectation was that a young man would do something different for a second curacy, but I received no offers or even suggestions.

The Last Chapter

I had not lost my sense of vocation, but the task of updating my manuscript and providing a new last chapter hung heavily. The only way to write a new final chapter would be, surely, to visit Moscow again for the first time since 1961. This was easier said than done, as I had almost no money. However, by using a small advance from Faber, I was able to sign up for a cheap 'educational visit' to Moscow and Leningrad with a group of Russian teachers scheduled for April 1964. We were closely monitored, herded together and subjected to endless propaganda about the superiority of the Soviet system. I broke free to meet one or two of my remembered Moscow contacts and began, amid reluctant conversations, to assemble some isolated pieces of the jigsaw.

Then a second visit in 1964 suddenly emerged. I had continued my association with American Express, and now they signed me up to accompany the University of Michigan Alumni Association on a trip around Scandinavia and the Soviet Union. I had clearly not put a foot wrong earlier in the year, and found myself – on what would be my last visit for a decade – in Leningrad and then Moscow for the first five days of August.

The Pochaev Documents

Shortly before leaving this time I had received a letter from my old mentor, Professor Nicolas Zernov. He enclosed a photocopy of documents he had received from Moscow, which were subsequent to the information in Struve's book. Here were detailed accounts, in semi-legible and uneducated hands, of Soviet cruelty at the Pochaev Monastery in Ukraine. There had been repeated attempts to close it down, stoutly resisted, by the monks and parishioners in the local village. The authors were believers who worshipped in the monastery, one the mother of a monk who had been subject to psychiatric abuse, incarceration in the local asylum and the infliction of mind-bending drugs by injection. The 'illness' was belief in Christ. At least, I thought, here would be a basis for my next enquiries in Moscow. I would ask my friends, with whom I had renewed contact only four months earlier, whether they knew of anything similar happening in other places. With the content of the documents and the names of the signatories firmly in mind, I set off to meet my American group and to continue via Scandinavia for Moscow.

The first evening there was nothing on our schedule. I had arrived that morning on the Red Arrow train from Leningrad, so I had time to set off to visit the Christian family who, I knew from my recent visit, had their ears close to the ground and would be able to give me some clues about events since I had last seen them. I told them of the Pochaev documents. 'Do you know of anything similar happening in other provincial areas of the Soviet Union?' I asked. 'Provincial areas – what do you mean? It's happening right here in Moscow,' came the reply. 'You only have to go to the Church of St Peter and St Paul – or rather to the remains of it – to see what these barbarians have been doing. They blew it up a couple of weeks ago on the pretext that they wanted to extend the Moscow Metro beneath it. Go and see for yourself.'

I was soon in a taxi – thinking that I must act at once, as it was well known that KGB vigilance often took a day or two effectively to operate, and on this first night I might not have a tail. So it turned out. I was soon at the square, which I had sometimes visited as a student. I stopped the taxi a few streets short, so as not to attract attention, walking the last few hundred yards. On the square a shocking sight greeted me. Where the church had stood in the middle of the open space there was a pile of rubble, the top of which I could just make out, two or three bent crosses on top of the heap. But the main part of the ruin was hidden by a wooden fence some twelve feet high.

Making sure I was not being followed, I walked, trying to appear nonchalant, up to the barricade. In typical Soviet fashion, it hadn't been erected with the greatest efficiency. Some of the planks were out of alignment and there were spaces in between, which widened near the top. I couldn't see that much, but I noticed two *babushki*, one of whom was trying to haul the other up by her elbows so that she could see through the wider gap.

'I must talk to them,' I said to myself, but didn't dare approach them right by the fence. I waited a while until they moved off and followed them down a side street.

Checking again I wasn't being followed, I came up to them from behind. 'Can you tell me what's been happening here?' I asked. They jumped as if electrocuted. 'Don't worry,' I said. 'I'll just move on. I won't bother you any more – don't be afraid.' 'Bother us? We're not afraid,' said one. 'Who are you?' 'I'm a foreigner, just arrived, and I wanted to find out more about what is going on here.' The other one put her hand on my shoulder: 'We need you,' she said. 'Follow us.'

This I did, a long journey some forty-five minutes into the suburbs. I kept my distance behind them, not exchanging another word, as they boarded a bus, then a tram, followed by a walk, it seemed almost into the country. We reached a little wooden house, one of those doubtless scheduled for demolition to make way for the faceless high-rise blocks which still disfigure the suburbs of virtually all cities of the Soviet empire.

They led the way inside, a comfortable little room with a stove, a bed, simple kitchen equipment, an armchair, a table, all crammed into a small space. A third *babushka* was there. 'I've brought you a guest,' explained one of the first two. Turning to me, she said, 'Who are you?'

'I've already told you. I'm a foreigner come to find out more about the persecution of the Church. This is my first evening and my friends told me to go to the square where I met you.'

'Yes, but who are you really?'

'I'm a believer, I studied here four years ago.'

'But why did you come to Moscow now?'

'I received some documents – they were letters from Ukraine describing the terrible things happening to a monastery.'

'Which one?'

'Pochaev.'

'What were the documents?'

'They were written by two women, Feodosia Varavva and Yefrosinia Shchur, mother of Anatoli, one of the monks…'

Their faces turned white. There was a stunned silence, then a cry, muffled in tears: 'We wrote those documents. I'm Feodosia and this is Yefrosinia'.

I couldn't speak. I waited for them to go on. 'We brought those documents to Moscow last year, hoping to find a foreigner to give them to. It was difficult, but eventually we found a French schoolteacher from Paris. We never heard whether she was able to take them back with her.'

'She did. I've seen a copy and read them. This was the reason why I came to Moscow: to try and find out whether what they said was true and to ask for more information. This is my first evening.'

'It's ours, too. We arrived today and immediately heard about the destruction of the church, so we went there – and found you! We were wondering how this time we would contact a tourist who would take our new documents.'

'What do you want me to do with them? What can I do for you?' I asked. The reply was instantaneous and decisive: 'Take the documents back, then be our voice and speak for us.'

Here was the kernel, in words loud and clear, as to how I should go about my future work and what its essence must be. A hard struggle would lie ahead, with many years of further preparation before I could even properly begin. And yet the objective was unambiguous. My task was not to give my own interpretation: I simply had to speak as a medium for the voice which I had heard so decisively and which I must find ways of continuing to hear.

The *babushka* whose room it was began to take a wad of writing out of a drawer – and there they were, more documents in the same handwriting, with the same signatures. In our emotion it was difficult to think or talk rationally, but of course I agreed to take the documents. Here was I speaking to the mother of one of the persecuted monks. I could only be bold, though at the same time I must exercise prudence, as well as restraint in not directly naming the brave people whom I had met. Soviet border control was severe, with the KGB increasingly controlling those known to have had contact with Soviet citizens. The penalty for discovery of the documents would be serious: certainly arrest, possibly a trial. Who knew what the consequences might be? But I could not possibly refuse. I wished that I could have been returning home next day, mission accomplished, but there were still three days to go. All I could do was to keep the documents on my person and hope for the best. I have absolutely no memory of passing through the customs. I think I kept them next to my skin – at least they would have to undress me to find them (X-ray machines not having come in by then). I avoided contacts with other local people during my remaining time in Moscow. As departure day approached, I became increasingly nervous and must have shown it. When it came to the point, I appeared to busy myself with the Americans under my care. I showed my passport, walked straight through and was soon on the plane.

What could I do with this wad of paper, some twenty sheets in number? My first decision was that I could not incorporate them into the book. This would have been far too sensitive and might establish a direct link between the authors and me, not least because of the timing of my visit to Moscow. The documents must be removed from any possible connection with me. Handing them to the British press might well have resulted in the right sort of publicity, but the timing might have established a connection with my visit. It would be better if they were not announced to the public in the UK.

Further, I lacked both sound advice and contacts. After discussions with Russian friends in London, the letters passed via an intermediary to Bishop Antony of Geneva, of the 'Russian Orthodox Church Outside of Russia (ROCOR), as it was then called, who released them at a press conference. Bishop Antony was a leading figure in the 'anti-communist' branch of the Church which was not in communion – or even contact – with the Moscow Patriarchate. Choosing him was perhaps not the wisest decision, as the world press considered ROCOR to be too politically motivated to be a reliable source. They did not make the impact they deserved. After all, Bishop Antony neither knew me nor the extraordinary story which lay behind their arrival in the West. In a curious way, that did leave the way open to me, as a kind of 'secondary source', to tell the story more graphically. I now had the material and the motivation to write a strong final chapter for the book. Here I could tell the story of Pochaev, quoting from the earlier documents which had come via Nicolas Zernov, but highlighting aspects from what I had learned from 'my' documents. So it turned out: my Chapter VIII, when published the next year, hit the press with some considerable force.

There were consequences. Perhaps the most important was that the Soviets never did succeed in closing down the Pochaev Monastery. World opinion had been alerted, and it seemed that now the Soviets wanted to hold back from such a scandalous act against one of the most influential monasteries of the Russian Orthodox Church. It would become a show place, and a limited number of monks were to be permitted to live and worship in it. Foreigners, especially a group of Americans, were soon taken there on an official visit and this was reported, in an act of supreme cynicism, in the *Journal of the Moscow Patriarchate*. To such visitors everything appeared completely normal.

The mantra of the time was that only quiet diplomacy could be effective in defence of religious liberty in the Soviet Union. I never contradicted this and believed it had its role, but this paled in comparison with the urgency of publicly revealing the abuses. The Pochaev experience led me to the certainty of this future policy, which I would practise for all my working life: quiet diplomacy in relations with the Russian Church or the Government could never replace responsible publicity as an effective tool for highlighting cruelty, deception and oppression, though the two approaches should go forward hand in hand.

For many years it was not safe to tell the Pochaev story, neither in lectures nor in writing. I eventually wrote it up and told it in the introductory chapter of my book, *Risen Indeed*, published in 1983.[1] Following an invitation to preach at Holy Trinity Church, Brompton, my experience appeared in the Alpha Course, a primer in adopting the Christian life for those who had not yet made the decision. Nicky Gumbel, its founder, quoted my experience as the direct intervention of God into one's life in an unexpected way. So it happened that this event became widely known, even abroad, in places which adopted the course, and this helped promote the future work of Keston College. As the Pochaev documents and their origin were to play a significant role in the future direction of my work, it is worth pausing for a while on their substance.

---

1   Darton, Longman and Todd, London, and St Vladimir's Seminary Press, Crestwood, NY.

The addressees of the Pochaev documents which Nicolas Zernov passed to me were the 'Eastern Patriarchs of Jerusalem, Antioch, Constantinople and others'. The detail was concrete and recounted in the simplest possible language. The authors of these documents designated the communist regime as the 'Antichrist'. They read in part:

> We cannot pass in silence over the barbarous mockery of Father Yosif, the [former] abbot, known in the world as Yakov Varnavvich Golovashok. He is seventy years old. In September 1962 Father Yosif was half beaten to death by the godless executioners. They stuffed his mouth with rags to keep him from crying out. He was sent to a mental hospital, but God was merciful and he was released …but the local police did not give him a residence permit for the monastery, and ordered him to leave Pochaev… The Antichrist forbids sermons in the churches.[2]

Another passage read:

> The Orthodox Church is in great danger. The Antichrists may well convert the Orthodox Church into heresy. Antichrist will think nothing of changing the symbols of the faith… Our true pastors, the monks of the Pochaev Monastery, in spite of the terrible mockery by Antichrist, have not, and will not, abandon their monastery. They strengthen the weak faith of us, sinful and unworthy servants of the Lord, by their courage and patience. Like sunshine they warm us with their prayers.[3]

The content of the documents went far beyond the local region of Pochaev and began to encompass an all-Soviet perspective. One appeal describes the maltreatment of children in Minsk (capital of the Belorussian SSR):

> The mockery has gone so far that the *oblast* [regional] representative [of the Council for the Affairs of the Russian Orthodox Church], Lavrienko, stands next to the door of Minsk Cathedral spying on children. If he finds any in the cathedral, he tells the verger, and this servant of Antichrist collars the children and knocks their head against the wall.[4]

Another region of Ukraine recounted a worse event:

> This summer [1963] on a holy day, the priest of the city of Gorny in the Mogilev *oblast* was conducting the liturgy; during it the godless ones shouted 'fire'; the people were frightened and ran in panic. Five people were trampled to death; fifteen were seriously hurt and are now in hospital; the priest, who is guiltless, is now on trial.[5]

---

2 Bourdeaux, *Opium of the People* (1965), p. 219.
3 Ibid., p. 220.
4 Ibid., p. 218.
5 Ibid., p. 220.

Already I was becoming aware of the concerted efforts of the official representatives of the Russian Orthodox Church to counteract publicity based on such documents. There had been a protest meeting in Paris, criticised by Metropolitan Nikodim, who had now replaced Metropolitan Nikolai as chief spokesman for the Foreign Relations Department of the Russian Orthodox Church. Nikodim deplored the Paris meeting, saying that such campaigns 'increase international tension… and the participants are not well informed about the life of our Church… and speak in erroneous generalisations.'[6]

Here, then, is the nub of a ferocious debate which would last for the next two decades, and in which Keston College was destined to play a leading role from the first. These events came together to clarify in my mind how forceful the last chapter of my book should be. There was an accumulation of hard evidence about the Khrushchev persecution of religion which was beyond contradiction.

The final three pages of Chapter VIII of *Opium* set out the beginnings of an agenda which would become clearer as my work developed. It is worth quoting from them at some length, because they illustrate how far my thinking had developed by 1964:

> Some take the attitude that any publicity about the real state of affairs in the Soviet Union is likely to make the situation for Christians very much worse. This may have been true in Stalin's time, but it is emphatically not so today. There has been every sign in the last few years that Khrushchev's Russia is sensitive to world opinion…
>
> The persecution which is at present trying to eradicate organised religion in the USSR is the greatest stain on the record of a nation which has many admirable qualities and infinite potential… The Soviet Government would like to have a phantom Church – one which has no members at all within the USSR, but which has powerful international connections which can be used to support Soviet strategy. We must make it known that we see through this and are not impressed.[7]

In Stalin's day, persecution meant death. Now, under Khrushchev, it took milder forms, which could still ruin lives. Churches were being closed, so the leaders of underground groups – whether Orthodox, Protestants or Catholics – could be imprisoned. Bishops were brought to court under false accusations of stealing money, donated by the faithful, designated for the Church. All forms of religious education – except for two Orthodox seminaries – were illegal. If you worshipped God as a young person, the doors to higher education were closed to you. All males had to serve in the Army; conscientious objectors were imprisoned, often without charge. Recruits known to be Christians received beatings. Believers who refused to renounce their faith were

---

6   Ibid., p. 221.
7   Ibid. pp. 231–33.

sometimes incarcerated and forcibly given injections. Some Baptist believers produced literature on improvised printing presses – one of the worst crimes.

In this book I refer to all the above as 'persecution'.

Moving On

The lacuna between final submission of the manuscript to the printer and its publication was an unsettling time, full of uncertainty, yet encompassing interesting new experiences. The scholarship to spend six weeks in Israel seemed to be the logical cut-off point to end our life in Enfield, because in those days the idea of study leave was not on the agenda. Graham felt I should leave, but a travelling scholarship was not a new job and I had a wife and infant daughter to support.

Before leaving for Israel I had answered an advert in the *Church Times* for a chaplain at Aiglon College in the mountains near Lake Geneva in the Suisse Romande and been appointed on the basis of an interview in London.

Israel was the second stage in my over-packed summer. My successful application was to carry out an unusual project. I was to track down immigrants from Russia and write about their contribution to building the State of Israel. I had many intriguing meetings with people I found fascinating and utterly congenial, long before, of course, a major new wave of emigration from the USSR began in the 1970s. This was a decade before Russian Jews were expelled or granted exit permits, but I had the feeling that this might come, reinforced by conversations in Israel with people who expressed the view that their country needed the reinforcements that such a change would provide. I exercised some speculation in a long report designed as a pamphlet, which the Association declined to publish, even though Kenneth Lindsay, the Secretary, received it graciously. Sadly, when I tried to trace it many years later, they could find no record of it. The reason, doubtless, was that my report delved into an area which was too sensitive: relations between Israel and the Soviet Union. I would soon become aware of the growing desire among Soviet Jews to emigrate, something which would develop into a movement, and lead to one of the destabilising factors in the later days of the USSR.

Crossing through the Mandelbaum Gate, I was able at the end to visit the Arab world for the first time: the old city of Jerusalem, then still in Jordanian hands, followed by Damascus and Beirut.

Aiglon College

My first and only experience as a school chaplain was brief, though colourful. Aiglon College was perched high in the mountains and a centre for the education of children of mixed nationalities, with emphasis on skiing and trekking. I should, even then, have learned to fight shy of half-promises not backed up in writing. The original idea, discussed in my conversation in London with John Corlette, the headmaster, was that I would divide my time between teaching Religious Education and introducing Russian to the school. By the time I arrived, the second idea had been dropped, which left me not only disappointed, but under-employed. Nothing else went wrong, but I had the feeling from the first week that we had made a mistake. This grew into a conviction. I re-read my contract carefully and noted that it was initially for a term, then to be renewed for three years. The only solution was to give notice before the end of the probationary term. So I did.

The headquarters of the World Council of Churches were in Geneva, only an hour and a half away by car. I felt that I could not simply walk in, but my attempts to engineer an invitation came to nothing. We did, however, make good use of the half-term weekend. I had heard about Russia Cristiana at Bergamo from their magazine, and I made contact with Fathers Pietro Modesto and Romano Scalfi, who warmly invited us to come down to visit them. This led to an inspirational experience that turned out to be the very beginning of a network of international contacts, which became such a feature of Keston a few years later.

I had never before met anyone who was a kindred spirit in the sense of sharing my intimate knowledge of the Russian scene, and had set out to do something positive. Here was a study centre run by experienced men who had themselves been in Russia recently and seen something of what I had witnessed. They had a network, a magazine and a group of dedicated students who came and went. Fr Modesto also taught at Milan University, not far away. Their headquarters, in Seriate, a village just outside Bergamo, was an old, ramshackle villa, but full of character. An old lady had died and left her villa and its outbuildings to the group. They had no money to renovate it, but abundant space to collect books and documents, publish *Russia Cristiana* and house any passing students and the likes of ourselves. The impression was indelible and these splendid people would remain friends for many years. Fathers Modesto and Scalfi belonged to the Byzantine Rite of the Catholic Church (loyal to Rome, but following the Orthodox form of the liturgy) and had graduated from the Collegium Russicum in Rome, which was, allegedly, preparing a cadre of priests to re-Christianise Russia when this became possible again. This weekend provided a model and an inspiration for what I might one day undertake myself.

I had come to Aiglon direct from Israel, so Gillian had driven the car out with only Karen aboard. My job in Switzerland ended after just the one term. We had amassed no new possessions and just managed to cram everything in for the return journey. Our modest furniture was in store, but we had nowhere to put it, nor did I have a job. These were worrying times, but we had the spirit, not for the last time, to surmount the crisis.

Chapter VIII
Publication

The weeks after early December 1964 were fraught with anxiety. We divided Christmas, as we were so often to do subsequently, between parents-in-law in the Forest of Dean and Cornwall. The welcome in both those homes, as always, was overwhelming. Surrounded by lovely countryside in both places, we could relax just for a week or two, without pressure (and no word of criticism for having given up what, in conventional terms, was a 'good' job).

St Mary's, Charlton Park Lane

The *Church Times* came to the rescue. There was an advertisement offering 'house for duty' in South East London, Charlton to be precise, just east of Greenwich and a mile from 'The Valley', the well-known football ground of Charlton Athletic. We went to meet the vicar of a large urban parish in the heart of the Diocese of Southwark, Fr Bear. He made it clear that I would not have any duties in the parish church itself, but would be running a daughter church. We went up the hill to Charlton Park, a new housing estate of no character, except for a rather attractive new church, four-square and plain inside, but with beautiful stained-glass windows. Fr Bear said that the church had been erected with money from war reparations, awarded after damage done to the parish church by bombing in the war. They had held the money in reserve until the right time, which occurred when the new estate was built and the need for a daughter church became evident.

Attached to the church was a small three-bedroomed bungalow, with an internal door leading rather dramatically directly into the sanctuary of the church. They needed someone to look after the place, an ordained caretaker, to hold Sunday services and possibly one in the week, with the hope that this would begin to build up a community. Attendance had, apparently, been sparse since the church opened two years earlier. There was no money to pay the priest-in-charge, nor any suggestion as to how he could make a living. The house itself was exceedingly plain, with a flat roof, hardly, as we were soon to discover, insulated at all. Surrounding the site was a rough lawn with not a flower bed to be seen.

We had to make a quick decision, but in truth there wasn't much choice. Obviously there was scope for initiative, which appealed to me, but we had no friends in the area and it would certainly be lonely. We moved in almost at once, but how would we live? Gillian could always find work as a supply teacher, though this would have to be part-time only, even if she could find a child-minder – all of which she did. Although I had limited teaching experience and no qualifications, I decided to try to go down the same route. My quick exit from Switzerland cannot have been much of a recommendation, but I soon found two one-term supply jobs in immediate succession, teaching RE. One was at Wilson's Grammar School in Camberwell, the other further away. I was happy and fulfilled, and would later look back with some regret on the fact that I never had a permanent teaching job. At Wilson's one of my pupils, Brian Castle, would one day become the Bishop of Tonbridge, so I can claim that at least I didn't put him off religion.

The parish, though, was not as well run as Enfield had been. It soon became clear that the need was for someone far different from myself: principally a person who was there all the time to immerse himself in the community, where there were many older people who did not leave the area daily to go to work. Had there been even a part-time salary, my calling might well have become a commitment. I did not have time properly to get to know the sparse congregation which attended Sunday services. I quickly came to realise that what the area actually needed was not a church, but a social centre. This would have played a positive role and provided a welcoming space where less formal worship could have taken place. There was a tiny room for coffee, but nothing else, not even a vestry (the house had to be used for that). Gillian did start a toddlers' club there, which worked well, and was by far the best social aspect of our life in Charlton.

It soon emerged that there were serious structural problems in the church itself. It had – not to put too fine a point upon it – been jerry-built. It constantly leaked, not only from the roof, but from the frames of the lovely geometric stained-glass windows, causing ugly green copper discolouration down the walls, which abolished any pleasing aesthetic effect that the windows might have inspired. This was a constant worry, as was the impossibility of keeping the house warm. Our heating bills were stratospheric, but even paying up did not prevent the house from becoming glacial about ten minutes after we had switched off the heating.

I tried to do something with the garden, but with no experience of creating one from scratch I failed utterly. Bits of metal and unidentified objects constantly turned up and made digging next to impossible. Later we heard that there had also been subsidence on the site. Eventually, but not long after we had left, we learned that the structure, erected on top of a rubbish dump, had been declared a disaster. The Diocese of Southwark decided to cut its losses and the whole complex, house and church together, had been demolished. I never went back to see what, if anything, replaced it, but the address, 'St Mary's, Charlton Park Lane', would never again exist.

We did our best to overcome the defects of this cold and gloomy home, but outside it we began to develop a new way of life, which involved the continuing stimulus of singing in the Philharmonia Chorus. My part-time teaching salary was not enough to live on, and I heard that Southwark Diocese might have a fund to supplement private study.

These were the days when religion was a topic of public discussion. John Robinson was *the* Bishop of Woolwich whose name was almost daily in the press as the author of

Honest to God. I read the book, sympathised with parts of it and welcomed this breath of fresh air. There have been many other distinguished bishops in that part of the Diocese of Southwark, but no one else who achieved quite that degree of international fame. One might almost say 'notoriety'. I discovered that he was in charge of a fund set up to assist study programmes for the clergy. He invited me to call on him and I immediately found a sympathetic ear. He did not have any special knowledge of communism or Russia, but he was keen to hear of my experiences. He was down-to-earth and entirely delightful. He said the Church should make more use of my experience and he could not have been more encouraging. I received a letter a few days later promising a small grant. This was a stimulus, the first official backing that had ever come my way, and the only sum I would ever receive from the Anglican Church, except for donations from individual parishes, specifically for my Russian work.

Opium for the Public

Publication of *Opium of the People* could not have come at a more auspicious time for my career. Its appearance produced a far stronger reaction than I could have anticipated. The book was well produced by Faber. The price of 30 shillings was reasonable for the time. The advance had been tiny, but their publicity machine moved smoothly into action, producing not only an immediate foreign translation (Portuguese, of all languages, with circulation in Brazil as the object), but also an American edition (Bobbs-Merrill of New York). Most influential of all was the decision of the then-editor of the *Church Times*, the Revd Roger Roberts, to serialise it over three weeks to coincide with publication. This meant that, at least within the confines of the Anglican public, my work immediately became noticed. The fee of ten guineas per extract, of which 25% was to go to the publisher, seems very little now, but to me it was generous.

The initiative of the *Church Times* evolved into a lasting relationship. The next editor, Bernard Palmer, was especially keen to supply his readership with news about developments in the USSR and he later told me that some subscribed principally to receive such information. He also began to commission a stream of book reviews, which gave me the opportunity and stimulus to write about almost every work of significance within my field of interest. They included analyses of Soviet policies and related human rights issues, but extended to literature. Those were the days when *samizdat*, as well as circulating clandestinely in the USSR, began to be translated in the West. The names of Alexander Solzhenitsyn, Nadezhda Mandelstam and others had been unknown until the 1960s, but now I played a small part in publicising them. The BBC expressed interest, both the Home Service and the Russian Service. These were new openings which I had not dreamed of a year earlier.

Although the reviews were predominantly positive, some influential ones expressed negative opinions. An analysis indicates the beginning of a rift over the stance – even the legitimacy – of my work. Those from sources within the Orthodox Church form a special category and come under separate consideration here.

Looking at the bulging file relating to the publication of *Opium of the People* fifty years after the event, I'm amazed at its bulk. There are some private letters, but many reviews which cast light on attitudes to the Soviet Union of the time. They form a historical record of a special kind, so it is worth paying them some detailed attention.

There were about eighty reviews all told, not only in English, but also in foreign languages (and continuing for over a year after publication). There are reviews in Danish, Swedish, Italian, Afrikaans, French, German and even Polish (a London-based paper, of course). I also noted a quirk: my name is misspelt some fifteen times and in almost as many variations.

A good place to start is *The Observer*.[1] Edward Crankshaw, a self-proclaimed agnostic, who enjoyed a deserved reputation as an expert on Soviet affairs, wrote a lengthy review. He called it 'one of the saddest of books, which should be read by all Western Churchmen who are inclined to put their trust in Eastern prelates'. He continued:

> It is desperately fair to the Soviet Government, and much more than fair to the Orthodox hierarchy as it has conducted itself since 1942… Mr Bourdeaux stumbles, gropes, repeats himself; but that is all to the good, reflecting as it does the explorations of a young Anglican priest looking for God in Russia and finding Him in unexpected places – and not finding Him, frequently, where He is said to be.

Not many agnostics, I suggest, could write with such sympathy of the Christian faith in any context.

Arthur Pottersman wrote generously and at length in *The Sun*. He summarised the main themes of the book and gave several direct quotes. *The Times*[2] wrote more briefly (and anonymously):

> His book has the feel of the place; it is perceptive, warm and well written… The last [part] recounts, with much documentation, the story of the bullying of monks, nuns and the lay faithful during the last years of Mr Khrushchev's reign, and tells also of the closing (under every manner of pretext and chicanery) of monasteries and churches.

The *Oxford Mail*[3] review was particularly gratifying:

> The book deals notably with fact. It is tremendously interesting, not least because the author is so obviously on the side of life and speaks with authority. Indeed, the appeal of his book is wider than its title may suggest. His picture of life inside the mighty block of Moscow State University, for instance, is graphic and appalling.

1   *The Observer*, 18 July 1965.
2   *The Times*, 8 July 1965, p. 15.
3   Brian W. Aldiss, *Oxford Mail*, 8 July 1965.

The secular press did not produce many reviews, but *The Scotsman*[4] said that the book 'succeeds in painting a fascinating and vivid picture of the extent of the Church's life and vigour in a hostile environment' and continued:

> The appeal of Michael Bourdeaux's book lies in his first-hand account of interviews, visits to churches and theological seminaries and universities, and in the penetrating depth of his insight. He takes us behind the propaganda machine to glimpse something of the life of a Russian priest, of the piety of the devout, the questionings of the intellectuals and the extent of suffering through physical and mental persecution… His deep love for Russia and her people shines throughout his book… We are left in no doubt as to the resilience of the indestructible faith of millions of Russian Christians today.

The *Church Times* backed up its serialisation by devoting a whole page to the review, of which it is possible to quote only a short section. It begins:

> In the three extracts which we have published from this first-hand testimony to the state of the Christian Churches in the Soviet Union to-day it has only been possible to give a glimpse of the vast amount of ground which Mr Bourdeaux covers in what on any reckoning must be one of the most valuable, as it is certainly one of the most moving, accounts yet to appear of the real conditions of life for the faithful Christian, Orthodox or Baptist, in the heartland of world Communism.
>
> Mr Bourdeaux is careful to avoid emotional judgments…But the effect of a reading of the whole book (and it should emphatically be read in its entirety) must be to bring home to comfortable Christians in the West the full measure of the appalling difficulties with which the clergy and laity in Soviet Russia have to contend…
>
> One thing which this extraordinary book brings out is the extent to which the propaganda of atheism affects the education of children and students… *Opium of the People* should be required reading for Western Churchmen who have been on official visits to the Soviet Union or who propose to pay such visits in future, and for all, too, who have dealings with the Russian Church through the link now happily provided by the Orthodox membership of the World Council of Churches.
>
> [Russian Christians] are not utterly alone in the dark night through which they are passing. Mr Bourdeaux's book shows how great is the darkness, and how great too is the inextinguishable light of Christ in the hearts of those who cling to the faith in him.[5]

---

4   Graham Hardy, *The Scotsman*, 13 November 1965.

5   *Church Times*, 18 June 1965.

The author of this anonymous review was in fact the editor, the Revd Roger Roberts. He later designated it, in the *Methodist Recorder*, as his 'book of the year', as did Douglas Hyde, a convert from communism, in the *Catholic Herald*. Apart from the obvious boost to my morale, Roger Roberts penetrated to the heart of what I was trying to do in my book, written, I must emphasise, in virtual isolation from guidance or even contact with responsible scholars of the subject in other parts of the world.

No other reviewer in a Christian newspaper went remotely as far as this, but the Revd John Pollock, a noted author, issued an 'urgent plea' in the *Church of England Newspaper*[6] for all his readers to purchase this book. The *Catholic Herald*[7] called it 'on the side of life'; *The Tablet*[8] said, 'he is careful not to indulge in facile generalisations … through the raging gale and amid the lies and the half-truths, he managed to distinguish the quiet voice of faith'.

The *Enfield Weekly Herald*[9] reported the first public reference to the future Keston College: 'Michael's ambition is to open a centre for the study of religion under communism throughout the world and to publish details as they happen.'

My very first BBC broadcast – which would pave the way for what must be approaching a hundred interviews over the years and a much closer association in the 2000s, together with some TV work – was on 25 October 1965.[10] The programme was *Ten to Eight*, the slot which is now called 'Thought for the Day'. I spoke, the *Radio Times* reminds me, about 'Olga recalling a Russian peasant'. My memory of this has faded.

Other Reviewers

The Revd Janis Sapiets was a Latvian Lutheran minister who spent the middle of his life in the UK, first as a Church of Scotland minister at Berwick-on-Tweed, and later as a highly respected commentator and religious broadcaster on the BBC World Service. He was trilingual in Latvian, Russian and English, and his radio voice and presentation were beautiful, measured and eventually influential. It was he who later said more about the persecution of Alexander Solzhenitsyn on air than anyone else in those timid days; consequently, when Solzhenitsyn first visited London, it was Janis whom he immediately sought out. Janis gave a 'European Service General News Talk' on the book on 30 July. He had some reservations about the sketchy nature of my history, but concluded:

> These objections do not detract from the value of Mr Bourdeaux's book. His sensitive and sympathetic portrayal of individual Russian Christians, the vivid

6   *Church of England Newspaper*, 30 July 1965.
7   Donald Nicholl, *Catholic Herald*, 9 July 1965.
8   Victor S. Frank, *The Tablet*, 7 August 1965.
9   *Enfield Weekly Herald*, 18 June 1965.
10   *Radio Times*, 23–29 October 1965, p. 30.

account of the recent persecution, and, above all, his passionate sincerity, cannot fail to arouse deep concern in the West for the intolerable sufferings to which Russian Christians have been subjected during the past decades.

Janis soon became a personal friend, an influential adviser to Keston and was on its Council in its early days.

Sir John Lawrence had served as Press Attaché in the British Embassy during the war, and edited *Britansky soyuznik* (British Ally), the only uncensored publication in Russia between Lenin and Gorbachev. In those days he was an agnostic, but he observed the beleaguered Orthodox Church beginning to come out of its shell after years of persecution and its spirituality influenced him. His book, *Russians as People*, showed profound sympathy for those about whom he wrote – and this included Protestants and atheists, as well as the Orthodox. Every visit to the Soviet Union resulted in a diary for private circulation, which invariably provided rare and sympathetic views on what was happening behind the scenes.

Later he became one of the founders of the BBC's European services in the changed political world of the late 1940s. He was a strong voice on Russia in the UK as a founder-member of the Great Britain-USSR Association, which exercised influence in political circles and was financed by the Government. Its *Bulletin* was required reading by all diplomats and politicians remotely interested in the USSR. John became Treasurer, but worked uncomfortably with the Chairman, Sir Fitzroy Maclean, who, he thought, was too soft on communism.[11] In the ecumenical magazine *Frontier*, of which he was founder and editor, John spoke strongly and consistently for church unity. He was an official Anglican observer at the Second Vatican Council. Nationally, he enjoyed the reputation of being perhaps the most influential commentator on the affairs of the Russian Orthodox Church. I had to take special note of what he wrote.

After a brief résumé of the contents of my book he wrote, 'Michael Bordeaux [*sic*] was always persistent and occasionally naïve. How could he expect that the Metropolitan Nicholai [*sic*] would answer questions put by a student when he could not give a proper answer to half the questions put by accredited leaders of sister Churches? The best things in the book are the chance encounters with Christians who have gone through trials that are more than Diocletianic.'

That's all. It was disappointing. About this time elsewhere he wrote: 'So far experience does not suggest that Russian church-people come to ecumenical meetings in order to play politics.'[12] Among many other roles, John had been an adviser to the World Council of Churches, but his judgement on how the Russian Orthodox Church was acting as a new member of the WCC proved to be flawed. Despite expressing no criticism of the Orthodox Church at this time, he was quietly dropped from his advisory

---

11   The GB-USSR Association became the GB-Russia Society after the collapse of communism, but the Government withdrew its funding, which directly abolished payment of its rent in central London; then there was nowhere to house the library, one of the best on the USSR in the UK, and it was dispersed, to the lasting regret of its members.

12   *East-West Digest*, London, Dec. 1965, p. 285.

role. We never discussed this, but the Moscow Patriarchate, now represented on the permanent Geneva staff, possibly persuaded the World Council that knowledgeable advisers were no longer necessary. The Russian Church could now speak for itself.

On more than one occasion he said that there was no substance in communism and it would collapse like a house of cards; he would live to see the end of it – and he did.

The Orthodox View

It is only now, I think, with over fifty years of hindsight and re-reading the reviews of all that time ago, that I fully realise the way in which my work divided the Orthodox community in the West. This is, in part, a reflection of the nature of the Orthodoxy outside the Soviet bloc. There were two jurisdictions, not in communion with each other. The one represented the old emigration, with outposts in Western Europe and Australia, but the headquarters of which was at Jordanville in New York State. Their views were not only hostile to Soviet communism, but also to the Church as represented by the Moscow Patriarchate, which they constantly criticised for its subservience to political power.

The second was far better known in the UK, largely due to the charismatic leadership of Bishop (later Metropolitan) Anthony Bloom, whose theological insight and attractive voice and personality made him an influential figure on the British religious scene. In order to keep open his channel – personal access to Russia, with the entry visa he possessed – he had to be circumspect in what he said about the country, though there is no reason to doubt the sincerity of his allegiance to the Patriarch of Moscow. I maintained good, though slightly distant relations with him. Archpriest Sergei Hackel, whose mother had taught me Russian in Cambridge, became a valued friend. Like Metropolitan Anthony, he belonged to the Moscow jurisdiction. I sought his advice from time to time and we collaborated on a number of projects. Only after the collapse of Soviet power did the two Churches repair the schism and come together in an uneasy partnership.

My views in 1965, and during the work which would soon open out, clearly sat uneasily between the two camps. The most influential 'Orthodox' review of *Opium* was in the journal of the Fellowship of St Alban and St Sergius, a respected publication widely read by the British Orthodox community, consisting mainly of converts.

Fr Basil Minchin, then Secretary of the Council of the Fellowship of St Alban and St Sergius, the Anglican-Orthodox society on whose council I was already serving, was here reviewing my original article in *The Observer*, as well as *Opium of the People*. He wrote in *Sobornost*, the society's journal:

> He approaches his mission with admirable objectivity in so far as he is not prejudiced against Communism and likes Russians but, in the opinion of this reviewer, is having to overcome an attitude of mind stemming from English Puritanism… Fr Bourdeaux is temperamentally more in sympathy with the direct crusade. He opened his crusade (so far as the writer knows) about five

years ago with an article in *The Observer* soon after his return from a year of study at Moscow University. This article was read with some indignation in Fellowship circles because he denigrated the Orthodox in comparison with the Baptists because they seemed to him to meet the challenge of the atheist state more directly. This seemed not only unfair to the Orthodox but factually improbable, as direct criticism of the regime by anybody would undoubtedly have brought down wide-scale imprisonments and general persecution upon that body.

Since the days of that article Fr Bourdeaux has grown strikingly in his understanding and sympathy for the Orthodox mentality, and we are pleased to have him as an active member of the Fellowship Council.[13]

It was perceptive of Fr Minchin, who by now knew me personally, to point out that I was 'growing' in my understanding of Orthodoxy. This was certainly true and would develop substantially as I was more able to respond to my calling.

By contrast, my old mentor, Professor Nicolas Zernov, wrote a short but gracious review, illustrating that there could be praise as well as criticism from the Orthodox community. His only caution is that I failed to give weight to the strength of the laity in the story of the survival of the Orthodox Church. He praises 'the authenticity of [the] material' and calls it 'indispensable to those who do not want to close their eyes to the complex and baffling reality of the world in which we live at present'.[14] Modestly, but understandably, he does not mention his own role in stimulating the writing of the book or supplying the first of the Pochaev documents.

The Political Vice

Inevitably, *Opium of the People* attracted political comments. It was published in 1965, a time of uncertainty in East–West relations. Nikita Khrushchev had only just been deposed by darker forces at the end of the previous year and the succession, now known as the 'Brezhnev regime' and later criticised as the years of *zastoi* (stagnation), was yet to reveal its hand.

I had recently met the Revd Paul Oestreicher, when he invited me to become a member of EWRAC, the East–West Relations Advisory Committee to the British Council of Churches, and by extension to all member churches in the UK (this excluded the Roman Catholic Church). Paul was the first – and only – person employed by the British churches to work full time on East–West relations. To be effective in this he assembled a small but influential group which for the next quarter of a century would actively seek to develop contacts with the churches which lived under the communist regimes of Eastern Europe.

13   *Sobornost*, Winter–Spring, 1966, pp. 145–6.
14   *Church Quarterly Review*, vol. 167, April–June 1966, pp. 252–3.

In his review Paul exposed the political controversy which was to dog me throughout the activist years of the future Keston College. I describe the cleavage between the two different viewpoints in the following pages.

Paul was always an excellent communicator. Before publishing the review in the *Bulletin of the Great Britain-USSR Association*[15] he sent me a handwritten note accompanying the proof, with a PS: 'I hope I've been really fair.' It's a long review, covering three tightly printed columns.

Paul states that the book 'does not present a great deal of information not readily available elsewhere' (he does not say where), but calls it an 'important and significant book'. He continues: 'It is *primarily* an intensely subjective book. Therein lies both its strength and its weakness.' I agree with this, though with the caveat (about which I wrote to him) that it could hardly have been any other, in view of the intensity of the experiences which I had undergone in Russia. When that period of my life began, there was not a single book I could draw on or compare with what I had lived through.

Paul criticises me for not writing anything on Marxism-Leninism. 'If the writer had the same sympathy for Marxists as for Christians, this would be a more helpful book, because it would enable the reader to better understand the *spiritual* roots which even now are the causes of persecution of Christians in the Soviet Union.' Here we begin to diverge. He seems to be claiming that the persecution was – at least to some extent – the fault of the persecuted. Is he referring to the presumed misdeeds of the Church before the Revolution? This is far from clear. Whatever the clouded history, it in no way justified the persecution which, after all, had persisted from 1917, with only relatively short periods of lesser intensity. It is true that a study of Marxism was not my forte. Even if it had been, my views were coloured by the experience of living in a 'Marxist' society. I had, in fact, originally written a lengthy passage on Christianity and Marxism, but Faber had advised excluding this, as it was outside the scheme of the book.

Most serious of all are the several passages where Paul, in measured terms, considers whether the book would actually cause harm by strengthening the anti-communist cause: 'It will not help Christians in Russia if it hardens Christians outside in their anti-Soviet attitudes.' Despite the qualifying 'if', it seems clear that he fears that such attitudes would be reinforced. Oh dear! In those days holding openly anti-communist views in intellectual circles was considered to be virtually a crime, although we did not go as far as McCarthyism in the US. This masks the key question: how far must truth be suppressed in order to help attitudes which readers might or might not possess? I countered this by writing: 'The correct attitude is surely to present the case for the underdog (did not Christ always do exactly this?)… I never cease to be amazed at the way our press reflects the case for *the official Soviet view*.' I continued by claiming that journalists, with the occasional exception, seem not in general to put the case for the persecuted Christian minority. Therefore I *had* to write from a polemical position at

---

15   London, pp. 2 and 4.

this point. My argument against Soviet communism was not only that it tried to beat people into conformism, but that it was anti-democratic and imposed on the people from above.[16]

The main section of Paul's review concludes thus: 'Had its compassion been even wider, it would have been a better book still. It is a must for the sentimentalists who believe only the Soviet version about Russia. The book will on the other hand, tend to harden the hearts of those whose religion is anti-Communism. But they will be wrong if they conclude the author is of their ilk.'

This conclusion neatly summarises Paul's attempt to be fair, and he was always honest in the expression of his views, excluding me in the last sentence from any charge of being a professional anti-communist, even if the book, in his opinion, provided fodder for those who were.

I continued to work with Paul for the next 25 years as a member of EWRAC. There was always tension right up to the day in 1989 when the committee was precipitately disbanded, but we were always more than civil and openly honest with each other, both in agreements and disagreements. I gained much from learning to work with people from whom I differed.

As events unravelled, the Christian political attitudes to the work I was developing hardened considerably. An undated document,[17] a 'Memorandum on Keston College' which Paul wrote for the BCC East-West Relations Advisory Committee', starkly reveals this. It is in response to a letter written by the Bishop of St Andrews (Scottish Episcopal Church), which is not appended, but to which Oestreicher responds in detail. Here is the second paragraph.

> Bishop Hare Duke articulates the worries of many liberal Christians who feel that Keston, whether intentionally or not, is part of the syndrome that today describes itself in America as the 'moral majority': instinctively anti-communist, an obstacle to East West reconciliation and an ally of all those who oppose détente. They feel it is a respectable version of Underground Evangelism and the Wurmbrand organisation. They regard its objective scholarship as cover for activity that is anything but objective. They also instinctively feel that Keston is incompatible with genuine ecumenism.

Before referring to Paul's reply I should clarify that Underground Evangelism and the Wurmbrand organisation were established in the 1960s as missionary movements setting out to support the Persecuted Church and smuggle Bibles and commentaries. In order to do so, they filled their fund-raising appeals with information about the persecution, sometimes citing Keston as the source. However, it was prone to the wildest exaggeration and generalisation and often the 'information' thus circulated did not even specify which country was under review, thus failing to build up any

---

16   Letter, Keston Archive, Baylor University.

17   In the author's private archive.

true picture of what was developing. Curiously, both were based in the same part of California; they secured financial support by addressing the same evangelical (often fundamentalist) constituency, principally in the US, but also with branches worldwide. Inevitably they clashed and eventually took out a court case against each other, which was then dropped because the leaders could see that continuing a legal case would discredit both parties. I knew the founders of each, Joe Bass and Richard Wurmbrand, who vied with each other in their unsuccessful attempts to recruit Keston to their cause.

Paul responds by saying to the bishop,

> I believe this to be a false analysis. But it cannot lightly be dismissed as fantasy. Impressions held by well-meaning people who also care deeply for the right to believe – everywhere – are not occasioned by mere left-wing or liberal reflexes. If an institution is misunderstood that institution must accept part of the blame.
>
> Keston is inseparable from its founder and director, Michael Bourdeaux. He is a colleague whose sincerity, integrity and single-mindedness are – for me – beyond question. He is a deeply devoted ecumenist with a special love for all the Christians of Russia. And he is a good scholar. With it, he is, in my opinion, markedly unpolitical, at times naively so. He is not always aware of the political implications of what he – and what his staff – say and do.

I regard this response to the bishop as being honest (it goes without saying) and also mainly accurate, although flattering in some ways. Did the Hare Dukes of this world actually read what Keston was publishing? Oestreicher continues: 'Yes, Keston documents and publishes human rights abuses in the sphere of religion. That is a necessary part of the ecumenical spectrum. It is a necessary service to the church in Britain and elsewhere. And it is truthful.' He continues by citing instances of persecution in the USSR which Keston had recently publicised. These should be set beside the personalities in South Africa and Latin America who achieve so much publicity and support. To show his solidarity with this work, Paul allowed his name to go forward for successful nomination to membership of Keston's Council.

Paul's memorandum continues to develop the outlines of the controversy which would almost daily impinge on Keston's work. The following is a summary:

1. Its information service shows imbalance in its reporting.
2. The 'richness of Christian life in Russia, Lithuania and other republics' is 'obscured by Keston in its eagerness to let no abuse go'. The reason for this is that good news does not sell. Its journal *Religion in Communist Lands* does contain good news, but this is mostly ignored.
3. 'The greatest single reason for the imbalances to be found in Keston's staff' – the 'prejudiced anti-communist attitudes complained of... There is no real Christian socialist on the staff with a genuine appreciation of the problems of Communism and the creative Christian witness in a socialist society.'

4. No such people – Paul excepted – serve on its Council. 'And I believe, under
   the able chairmanship of Sir John Lawrence, its weaknesses are reparable.'

I hope that, whatever view one takes of how far these criticisms are justified, they
will be judged against the actual work of Keston. On the negative side, I have to state
that Paul's 'liberal' constituency was not much influenced by what he wrote. Indeed,
attitudes considerably hardened as time went on. Ensuing chapters will give examples
of this. He concluded his document with the following words that ring with his own
sincerity:

> Keston, in my view, deserves the help of the churches and the whole Ecumenical
> Movement. I do not only mean money. I mean critical solidarity. Keston at its best
> is invaluable. But even Keston at its worst has none of the paranoid attitudes of
> its distant relatives on the far right. It falls well within the spectrum of the total
> witness of the *ecumene*, the people of God, worldwide.

Whatever its defects, *Opium of the People* had launched my career. The varied reactions
to it were a warning that the political path of Keston College would never be easy.
For better or worse my name was now before the public. At the same time I read of
William C. Fletcher and it is to him that the next chapter of my life belongs.

Chapter IX
Geneva

Following the publication of *Opium of the People,* the USA enters the picture in the persons of Paul Anderson and Bill Fletcher. Paul was already into his seventies when I first met him in 1965, but he was incredibly tough and resilient. He died in 1985 aged 91, falling off a roof that he was repairing. There was about his white hair and spare frame an aura of unworldliness, which belied his travels and ability to be in interesting places at key times. He was the only person I ever met who had seen Lenin: he was present in the Smolny Convent in Petrograd when Lenin declared the Revolution. His was a stand-alone book in the Second World War, *People, Church and State in Modern Russia,*[1] containing valuable documentation and charitable towards the Soviet Union. Paul was not a crypto-communist, but, as an Episcopalian, he respected and loved the Russian Orthodox Church. For a decade it remained the only book on its subject and, twenty years after he had written it, people were still quoting it as authoritative. He was a keen observer and accurately recorded his experiences in Russia.

After leaving Russia, Paul represented the Russian Student Christian Movement in Paris. As Stalinism and the politics of the Cold War had prevented his continuing to live in the Soviet Union, Paul later worked in New York, where he was the long-term adviser on the USSR to the National Council of Churches (NCC), the ecumenical movement closely associated with the World Council of Churches (though self-governing and independent of Geneva's policies).

It was a time of change in the NCC. Not only was Paul growing older: the emphasis was shifting notably to the Third World, leaving any consideration of human rights and religious liberty in the Soviet bloc to one side. However, Paul, for the time, continued as co-editor with the Revd Blahoslav Hruby, a Czech émigré, of *Religion in Communist Dominated Areas,* which bore the imprint and address of the NCC (475 Riverside Drive, New York, NY 10027, where it long continued). It was well presented and included illustrations and anti-religious cartoons from the Soviet or Czech press. When I first saw it, I immediately recognised Hruby as a kindred spirit. I was not at the time aware that, because of the change of emphasis in the NCC, it was losing financial support for its continuation. As I was later to discover, it had 'teeth' and reported the atheist campaign in the communist countries, engaging with controversial issues. This, though, led to an increasingly uneasy relationship with the NCC.

The World Council of Churches was then circulating a cyclostyled publication, *Current Developments in the Eastern European Churches* (from the 'Desk for Documentation Concerning Eastern European Churches'). This published its last number in 1967,

---

1   London, 1944.

and then was itself abolished, doubtless due to the growing influence of the official representatives of the Russian Orthodox Church, now permanently working in the Geneva headquarters.

There were two other low-key publications in the 1960s. *Religious Digest (Information about the churches and religion in the USSR, China and Eastern Europe and the communist attitude to religion)* appeared anonymously, ceasing in 1966. It was widely believed to have emanated from the Foreign Office. *Religion and Church in the Communist Orbit*[2] was printed in English in the Netherlands and it appeared between 1964 and 1970.

William C. Fletcher

Late in 1965 I received a telephone call from Bill Fletcher, inviting me to meet him at a London hotel. He introduced himself by saying that he was a scholar and researcher on religion in the USSR, a Baptist by faith, but with a research interest in Russian Orthodoxy. He had written a book on the 1920s, highlighting the compromise the Church had been forced to make with the Soviet regime at that time, *A Study in Survival: The Church in Russia 1927–1943*.[3]

He began to recount how he had just established a centre 'for an in-depth study of the ongoing religious situation in the Soviet Union and the rest of the Soviet bloc' – matching my own ideas and expressed in words virtually identical to my own thoughts.

My reaction was almost one of disbelief, so close were his ideas to mine, but an invitation to join his team soon followed, as Paul Anderson had recommended me. Bill was in the process of establishing this, he said. His study centre would consist of eight researchers, one for each of the major countries of the Soviet bloc. They would all be paid for half-time work, on the assumption that they would already be established scholars working at universities. He made no allowances for the fact that my responsibility, the Soviet Union, was many times the size of even the largest of the non-Soviet countries (Poland) and, with its diversity of languages and peoples, it would inevitably entail much more work. The words 'full-time work for half pay' floated across my consciousness, but they did not weigh heavily. For the first time I would receive a small regular salary for working in my own area.

The team had to read the official press of their designated country, locate, translate and evaluate any articles on atheism, religion or the Church. The USSR, unlike the other countries, had many periodicals which carried detailed articles devoted to the philosophy of atheism and a justification of Party policy. Bill Fletcher would order these via the Munich agents, Kubon and Sagner, and they started to arrive regularly.

There were several odd features about the set-up, though. The first, which Bill explained laboriously, was that the name of his outfit would conceal the real purpose of the work. The name he chose was not only clumsy, but almost unpronounceable:

2   INTERDOC, The Hague, van Stolkweg 10.
3   SPCK, London, 1965.

Centre de Recherches et d'Étude des Institutions Religieuses. Throughout the time I worked for it, I never heard anyone use its name in full: it was always the 'Centre de Recherches' or CRE for short. The other researchers included, Bernhard Wilhelm (Deputy Director) – East Germany, Tamas Aczel – Hungary, Blaho Hruby – Czechoslovakia and Marin Pundeff – Bulgaria. Bill's plan called for an annual conference in Geneva (actually in the adjacent suburb of Versoix, on the north side of the lake). The team would discuss developments from a comparative viewpoint. This prospect sounded even more exciting than the work itself, and over the next three years I visited Geneva four times for these conferences.

There was a puzzle. By this time, as my study for *Opium* had shown, *samizdat* was beginning to flow in full spate. I had been introduced to the Orthodox protest in the most compelling way, and the comprehensive letters from Fathers Nikolai Eshliman and Gleb Yakunin had recently come into the public domain. The first Baptist documents reached me, followed by *samizdat* from Lithuanian Catholics, the Jewish community and others. Bill, however, said he was not going to handle *samizdat*. If I were to do this, it would be in private and he would not refer to such documents. From the first I considered this questionable. *Samizdat* and the Soviet press were, after all, different aspects of the same topic, and press articles could be used as cross-references to the *samizdat,* and even prove its authenticity.

There was, therefore, some tension in the air from the day I started, but I was ready to work as though my life depended on it, and the next three years were to be one of my most productive periods. Just when I had formulated my ideas (I was now 32) and was about to start tackling the funding problem of establishing my own organisation, someone appeared on the scene who had a ready-made budget. I could do no other than put my own ideas on hold and begin the work.

Bill knew how to use his sources and produced several valuable contributions to our field. Five years older than me, he was self-confident and could talk persuasively, but he was not attuned to European culture. At his best he was supportive and companionable. I trusted him and felt we were setting out on a venture together.

The sources of his financial support were obscure, although he used to name two backers, of whom I had never heard ('warhorses of the ecumenical movement,' he said they were). None of our team ever met them. His lifestyle was comfortable and he sometimes described himself as 'the last of the big spenders'. The Versoix offices were efficiently run two Germans: Dr Bernhard Wilhelm, Director of Research, and Bill's personal research assistant Sylvia Stöcker. Mme Jauslin was the English secretary.

Bill authorised me to do some travelling in the UK in order to publicise the work of the Centre de Recherches. I enjoyed the freedom of movement, especially the conferences related to the work, and I began to build up my international contacts.

In retrospect, though it was not a worry at the time, the existence of the Centre de Recherches just down the road from the World Council of Churches was not only surprising: it now seems to have been confrontational. If the plan of the financial backers was to set up a counterweight to the WCC, now coming increasingly under the influence of the Russian members of its permanent secretariat, the location was ill judged and we never met any of our neighbours. Perhaps London would have been better, with immediate access to the British press and its ability to influence world opinion.

Bill's own scholarly reputation was growing at this time. *A Study in Survival* was well reviewed. Edward Rogers, writing in the *Methodist Recorder*, stated: 'A cool scholarship prevails, cautious in judgement, and giving little hint of the bloodshed and anguish of those years… Dr Fletcher has written a definitive book for the ecclesiastical historian.'[4]

Bill's work in Geneva had begun in 1965, six months before this review appeared, and I was already on the staff in December 1965 (his first request for a translation is dated 29 December) and I did not therefore have to return to teaching after Christmas. We agreed to disagree over the question of *samizdat*, but I would never change my view that his cyclostyled periodical (yet another) could have achieved much more. This began to appear, modestly entitled *Translations*, renamed *Research Materials on Religion in Eastern Europe* in March 1967. There was no analysis, not even a context, except for the bald reference to the publication and date, no commentary and no listing of new books, unless they happened to be propaganda works published in the Soviet bloc.

The discipline of daily reading of the Soviet press and frequently translating from it was valuable to me. For some time I had been reading three leading Soviet publications, the atheist *Nauka i religiya* ('Science and Religion'), the only Orthodox publication, *Zhurnal Moskovskoi Patriarkhii* ('Journal of the Moscow Patriarchate') and the Baptist *Bratsky Vestnik* ('Fraternal Herald'). Now I would not only do this more systematically, but also write full summaries of each issue, and translate anything which seemed to me of significance. I would send these to Bill Fletcher and copies of all this work are in the Keston archive. To these we added a further twenty or so newspapers and journals such as *Novy mir* ('New World'), *Voprosy filosofii* ('Questions of Philosophy') and *Nauka i zhizn* ('Science and Life'). Fortunately the anti-religious content of all these was sparse, so I did not have to spend time evaluating hundreds of articles. I soon, too, became expert at quickly scanning the official *Pravda* and *Izvestiya*, as well as some provincial newspapers.

Usually, but not invariably, the translations were commissioned by Bill, Bernie Wilhelm or Sylvia Stöcker, and there are dozens of letters in the files with lists of their requests (mostly addressed 'Dear Mike', which I seem still to have been in those days). The published coverage was accurate on all the countries as far as it went, but could be termed turgid at best. Persecution was now a topic reported in the British press, and our coverage from Geneva was not likely to attract many new readers. There is no record of the number of copies printed, but there was no subscription, and it went to the central offices of various denominations worldwide.

---

4   *Methodist Recorder*, 17 February 1966.

What was Bill trying to avoid? Presumably he was afraid of being engulfed by the political conflicts which were already beginning to affect my work. This was unlikely, as his scholarly credentials were well established by his first book. With such a formidable team of researchers, an authoritative periodical would certainly have enhanced his reputation. What he produced could almost have come from a group of automatons. There must have been something else, too. Rumours grew that the Centre de Recherches must be funded by the CIA, a damning association in those paranoid days. If true, there was never any proof, nor for that matter did Bill ever find any convincing way of refuting the gossip. If it were true and the CIA had hoped to counteract the growing leftism in the World Council of Churches, the failure was total. I raised the question of funding in our sparse communications towards the end of his life, but he revealed no secrets.

The atmosphere in the conferences which Bill convened was always positive. A warm understanding and feeling of common cause prevailed and we came to know each other well. Tamas Aczel, who taught at the University of Massachusetts, was an émigré of the 1956 vintage, and was a fund of jokes (and bitterness) about communist rule in his country. Blaho Hruby was knowledgeable about Eastern Europe as a whole. I learned a great deal from him about Czechoslovakia, a country with which I always felt a special affinity, mainly because of its music. Bernie Wilhelm, rumoured to be the CIA minder, was saturnine, but good-humoured. Sylvia Stöcker was supremely efficient and invariably cheerful.

I went to these conferences in Geneva in January 1966, June and September 1967 and September 1968. I always returned from them refreshed and enlightened. I had never before been in such company and knew that, at last, I had broken out of the isolation which encompassed me during the whole period up to the publication of *Opium of the People.*

There was tension, though, in the background. The Moscow Patriarchate, on an official level, had done Stalin's bidding since its establishment towards the end of the war; its successive Patriarchs, Sergi and Alexi I, often appeared as spokesmen for Soviet policies. Alexi launched an extraordinary attack against me in a letter he sent to Michael Ramsey, Archbishop of Canterbury. Dated 15 March 1966, he wrote a bitter criticism of the *Church Times* for having published the extracts from *Opium:*

> The subject matter of these extracts, consisting of accounts of the author's conversations with people he met by chance during his stay in our country, portrays in a distorted manner our country's attitude to freedom of conscience; it falsifies and misrepresents the position of religion and church life in the USSR.

The implication was that the *Church Times* was an official publication of the Church of England (which it is not) and that the Archbishop should have exercised censorship (which, he assured me, when he invited me to see him, he would not have done under any circumstances). His Grace and I agreed that the letter should remain confidential, but then, to our astonishment, the *Journal of the Moscow Patriarchate* published it later in the year.[5]

Bill Fletcher was far from pleased at this. To me it proved that my work had accurately reported my experiences. To Bill it demonstrated that I was 'dangerous' and likely always to be caught up in confrontation, highlighting the work in Geneva in a way he did not welcome. This episode apparently defined the opinion the Patriarchate held of me and this never seems to have changed, even up to the present day.

However, the early stages of my new work developed positively. Bill organised a conference at Riverdale, just north of New York City, a gracious mansion which housed us for four days, 19–23 May 1966, and this was my first trip (via Iceland!) across the Atlantic. Here I was able to meet, for the first time, a group of North American scholars, who were not only well informed, but also excellent company. For me, this was an entry into another new world. The leading lights were all young and personable: Richard (Dick) Marshall, teaching at a Canadian university, Thomas (Tom) Bird and Andrew (Andy) Blane, both teaching in New York City. I was bowled over by their warmth and the extent of their knowledge. I was convinced that here was a group who were certain to relaunch the tradition of American scholarship which Paul Anderson (who was also present) had carried virtually single-handed for so long.

Samizdat

Reading the Soviet press was the least exciting part of my work, even though this continued to be the only function for which I was paid. Trickles of *samizdat* which had filtered through to the West in 1964–5 had suddenly become a spate. Much of this quickly found its way to me. Assessing it began to fill all the available space in my timetable. The stories of oppression, clearly affecting all religious groups, jumped dramatically from the pages, handwritten or reproduced on primitive, homemade equipment. Here was a cry *de profundis* – and I was already committed to be the 'voice' of the persecuted. But how could I possibly do this when the Geneva publication would not touch the documents?

Bill Fletcher privately made an occasional assessment of these and did circulate them to a handful of key individuals. On 10 November 1967 he wrote both to Paul Oestreicher, in his capacity as Associate Secretary of the International Department of the British Council of Churches, and to U Thant, then Secretary General of the United Nations in Geneva, and in fact the addressee of two documents he had just received.

These were the first known to me of what would become a flood over the next twenty years of letters from the Council of Relatives of Prisoners of the Evangelical Christians-Baptists in the USSR, dated 15 June and 15 August 1967. Bill translated them for the recipients.

---

5   November 1966, English text in full in Bourdeaux, *Opium of the People* (second edn., London, 1977), p. 248.

He included a long letter to Paul Oestreicher. The text abundantly testifies to Bill's knowledge and his sympathy for the authors, who were, after all, Baptists like himself. He writes that 'we' had translated the first of the two letters. He stated that he had no knowledge of how the August letter came out of the USSR, nor could he guarantee its provenance. However, 'the June letter was given to a Western tourist by laymen in the Moscow Baptist Church. Thus we have full knowledge that it did actually originate in the USSR… and can be confident that it is genuine and not a forgery concocted in the West…

'We have done a partial analysis of the second list [of Baptist prisoners]. I am enclosing a graph on which we plotted the number of prisoners convicted at each year of age at time of conviction. We have also totalled the number of recipients of each classification of prison sentences. A number of these names have been confirmed by independent sources (the Soviet press): Mike Bourdeaux can give you particulars.'

I was certain at the time that Bill and I could have worked effectively together on these and future documents, but it was not to be.

Religious Ferment in Russia

The only way ahead was to begin to write a book to cover the new information contained in the documents. Faber would have published and were keen to do so, but they wanted me to combine the Baptist and Orthodox documents in one volume. I considered this carefully and discussed it with various advisers, but it seemed impossible. They were two parallel but different stories. Macmillan agreed to publish two separate volumes. I quickly decided that the Baptist story must come first. It had the clearer outlines, more organised material and therefore potentially greater impact, even though it concerned the fringes of Russian society rather than the heartland of Orthodoxy. On consultation with Dr Kelly of St Edmund Hall, it also appeared that I could fulfil the non-residential conditions of submitting this for an Oxford Bachelor of Divinity degree.

Over the late 1960s I worked on the hundreds of pages of Baptist *samizdat,* analysing and translating as much of it as I could. There were lists of some two hundred prisoners, many with family details, numbers of semi-starving children (because there was no social security), photographs (transcripts of their trials would shortly follow, but too late for publication in this volume), personal statements of faith, detailed studies of the internal statutes of the officially sanctioned All-Union Council of Evangelical Christians-Baptists (AUCECB) and of the Soviet laws on religion – and much else.

Evaluation of these documents was my challenge. The information was detailed and it would prove to be accurate. I could sometimes cross-reference them to names, places and dates which appeared in my reading of the Soviet press, something which Bill mentioned in his letter to Paul Oestreicher.

I could see that the Baptist authors were demanding that the State should not interfere in the internal affairs of their church. For the first time, some sort of concerted opposition to persecution was emerging. The trial of the authors Andrei Sinyavsky and Yuli Daniel took place in February 1966 and caused widespread resentment in the Soviet Union, leading to a more concerted protest. Alexander Ginzburg documented the trial in his *White Book*, widely circulated in *samizdat*. Those who had compiled it were discovered and themselves brought to trial, causing in its turn more demonstrations. The typist, Vera Lashkova, was arrested on 17 January 1967 and, as subsequently emerged, she became an Orthodox believer in Moscow's Lefortovo Prison, a phenomenon of which Keston College would discover many examples over the next two decades.[6]

I never felt comfortable with the term 'dissident' for these brave and selfless people, and sometimes used the word 'democrat', even if it did not always suit the context. It would take many years before this usage was fully accepted (if it ever was), but this proto-democracy contributed substantially to Gorbachev's introduction of *perestroika* and the resulting eventual collapse of the Soviet Union. The Baptist contribution to this was by far the most concentrated and organised in that period and also the most widespread. Awareness of this human rights issue was already beginning to develop in the West, especially with the rise of Amnesty International from its low-key foundation in 1961. I supplied it with its first-ever list of Soviet prisoners of conscience, which I had received from the Baptists. Meanwhile the protests of these believers were increasing in intensity.

May 16th 1966 was a day of glorious spring sunshine in Moscow. Crowds of visitors from all over the Soviet Union were strolling about its central streets, but those who were beginning to congregate on *Staraya Ploshchad'* (Old Square) outside the offices of the Central Committee of the Communist Party were different. Some five hundred people assembled in an orderly manner. Most did not know each other, as they were elected delegates from 130 towns and cities, representing virtually every one of the fifteen republics, from Brest in Belorussia on the Polish border to Vladivostok in the Far East.

They came to hand over a letter to Leonid Brezhnev, Chairman of the Central Committee. They were allowed to leave their document with a receptionist, but that was not enough for them: they demanded to see someone in authority. There was no response. They waited overnight, their numbers being swollen by members of the local Baptist church in Moscow. Next morning detachments of the KGB arrived to form a ring around the demonstrators, so that they could not talk to casual passers-by. At noon on the second day an official came out to summon ten leaders inside, ordering the rest to disperse. No one moved, but they prayed together. Empty buses drew up and suddenly an assault began. The militia drove the demonstrators with truncheons into the buses, which moved off as soon as they were full, with those inside still singing and praying.

---

6   Janice Broun, 'Trials of a Typist', *Frontier* (Journal of Keston Institute, Oxford), 9, Summer 2005, pp. 39–41.

The ten inside were arrested. Interrogations began. The KGB discovered that they now held in their custody some of the Baptist leaders who had long been on their wanted list. Three days later two more, Pastors Georgi Vins and Mikhail Khorev, walked into the building to demand to know what had happened to those inside. Vins would not be at liberty again for three years. Peaceful demonstrations outside the building continued for several days.[7]

The documents handed in at the Central Committee building contained, in essence, one simple request: the right of these people to self-determination, to appoint their own pastors without interference from the state authorities, to educate their children in their own faith and to establish new churches where and when they wished. There had been many such appeals in the previous five years, but they had brought no result.

No one had recounted the post-1945 history of the Protestants in the Soviet Union, the creation of the All-Union Council of Evangelical Christians and Baptists, an action which at the time had seemed a liberal measure, but which turned out to be Stalin's way of controlling all the Protestants by shoe-horning them into one body which was under the closest scrutiny of the secret police.

Opium placed a rudimentary account of Khrushchev's persecution before the public. *Religious Ferment in Russia: Protestant Opposition to Soviet Policy*[8] showed a different aspect of this and in far greater detail. This was possible because of the astonishing accuracy of the documents. The thrust of the book was as follows.

In 1960 the Government's Council for the Affairs of Religious Cults, which set out to control all aspects of religious life (except for that of the Orthodox Church, which at that time had its own separate body) imposed a new set of regulations on the AUCECB in Moscow. Their acceptance of these 'New Statutes', supplemented by a 'Letter of Instructions', under threat of increased persecution, caused grief to the whole Baptist community (and the schism persists to this day).

The AUCECB presented these new regulations as their own, but it was obvious from the outset that *force majeure* lay behind them. The texts were not officially published, but became known only through the efforts of those who opposed them. I included them in an appendix.[9]

To summarise a complicated issue, the New Statutes were almost exclusively concerned with control over local church life and not at all with the provision of spiritual guidance. The AUCECB was assuming an authority which did not reside in any of its founding or subsequent documents. Senior presbyters were to be the main line of communication between the AUCECB and local congregations – but the communication appeared to be one-way, with no parallel channel back to the centre. There were restrictions on where and when services of worship were to be held, who should preach and even say prayers. A choir could now perform only in its own

---

7   For a fuller account see Michael Bourdeaux, *Faith on Trial in Russia* (Harper & Row Ltd, London, 1971), pp. 9–22.

8   Macmillan, London, 1969.

9   Ibid., pp. 190–210.

church, never on invitation from a neighbouring one. All musical instruments were to be banned from church, with the exception of organ or harmonium.

The most controversial provision was that only those congregations which had gained registration from the State were to be recognised by the AUCECB. This would disenfranchise the hundreds, possibly thousands, of congregations which had been refused registration or which, on principle, refused to apply for it. Registration also entailed the imposition of a pastor from above, as elections for such appointments were already banned.

The Letter of Instructions to senior presbyters went further. Paragraph 5 read:

> Zealous proselytisation in our communities must definitely cease… and an effort must be made to reduce the baptism of young people between the ages of 18 and 30 to a minimum.[10]

The extent to which these regulations were state-imposed is illustrated by what happened a year later (1961), when an irregularly constituted 'Synod of Bishops' did the same, *mutatis mutandis*, for the Orthodox Church.

Opposition rapidly emerged in the Baptist community, which was spread thinly but widely throughout the republics of the Soviet Union. Initially an 'Action Group' emerged, which called for an all-union congress to review these regulations. As the 'initiators' of this demand, they were dubbed *Initsiativniki*, a name which caught on, and as they came overwhelmingly from the unregistered congregations, the name became more or less synonymous with illegal communities. Their eventual official title became the Council of Evangelical-Christian and Baptist Churches.

The leaders of this movement were Alexei Prokofiev, Gennadi Kryuchkov and Georgi Vins, of whom the last became best known not only because of his tireless activity, but also because of his ability to organise and communicate with the outside world even under conditions of utmost duress. However, it was Prokofiev who at first attracted most attention in the atheist press, so much so that some sources called the movement the *Prokofievtsy*.

The legal expertise of Vins and Kryuchkov (whether aided in secret by qualified lawyers or not) was another step forward in the evolution of understanding of what a law-governed state should be. The document that they wrote on 14 April 1965 to Leonid Brezhnev, in his capacity as President of the Commission on the Constitution, was epoch-making. Never before had there been any such expert analysis of Soviet law and it remains a unique document to this day. The closest comparison is with the letters circulated by Fathers Gleb Yakunin and Nikolai Eshliman in November of the same year.[11] The Baptist initiative, however, is more detailed in its study of the law

---

10   Ibid., p. 20.

11   Bourdeaux, *Gorbachev, Glasnost and the Gospel* (Lubrecht & Cramer Ltd, London, 1990), pp. 7–8.

itself.[12] This is a summary of what the authors presented to those who were in the process of drafting a new Soviet Constitution:

> The laws affecting religious activity are both imprecise and ambiguous. Some may look all right on paper, but in practice they are an instrument of persecution. As they now stand, they deny Lenin's original ideal of the separation of Church and State and the right of people to propagate their faith, as well as to practise it themselves. The 'freedom of conscience' guarantee in the constitution has twice been modified to make it deliberately ineffective, indeed, to give protection to those very people who wish to deny the principle. The main instrument of oppression is the complicated religious law of 1929, which dates, pointedly enough, from the time when Stalin was preparing to initiate the greatest purge in history. This law must be repealed and the original sense of the constitution restored.[13]

Alongside the account of the persecution was the reaction to it. Vins emerged at this time not only as a pastor, with deep care for his scattered people, but also as a poet. Among other works, he sent a long poem – a philippic rather than an irenicon – to Alexander Karev, General Secretary of the AUCECB. With Kryuchkov as co-author, he initiated a remarkable series of *samizdat* publications, dozens of which are preserved at Baylor University in the Keston archive. *Bratsky listok* ('Fraternal Leaflet') was the main title, but there was a flood, too, of appeals, lists of prisoners and even New Testaments and other scripture portions.

Bratsky listok demonstrated an intense pastoral concern for everyone who had in any way helped with the work of the *Initsiativniki* – or 'Reform' – Baptists, but it was the defence of prisoners which attracted most publicity and, after what they considered the failure of the official congress of 1963, the main focus of the work became a battle with the authorities to grant Baptists their right of religious liberty according to the Soviet Constitution. (The actual words of the Constitution at this time guaranteed the 'right to religious worship', as opposed to 'religious liberty', and the two were far from synonymous.) The Reform Baptists were shocked at the murder of Nikolai Khmara, a recent convert to the faith. He had been sentenced to three years in prison and his death was reported in stark detail, complete with grim photographs of his corpse.[14]

The first All-Union Conference of Baptist Prisoners' Relatives, which opened in conditions of secrecy six weeks later, seems to have been a direct response to the murder of Khmara. This was a significant step in the development of civic consciousness, since never before had there been such an organisation defending prisoners anywhere in the

12   Bourdeaux, *Religious Ferment in Russia*, pp. 105–13.

13   This is my own summary, as quoted in Bourdeaux, *Faith on Trial in Russia*, p. 99.

14   Ibid., pp. 96–7.

communist bloc.[15] At this point Lidia Vins, Georgi's mother, emerged as a character as formidable as her son, taking on the organisation of this group until her own arrest.

This first conference in 1964 gathered information on 155 prisoners, publicising as many relevant personal details as they could. The documents also listed the articles of the penal code under which they had been arrested and the length of their sentences. By the time of the second conference in July 1964 this number had increased to 197, excluding five who had died in prison or under investigation. Their dependants were listed – the children could starve as far as the State was concerned, because it provided no support for the relatives of prisoners. These documents provided a range of new information about the Soviet prison-camp system, including the precise location of many camps.[16] The initiators of this campaign soon found themselves in prison, because they publicised their own names, but others were always ready to step into their shoes and there was no interruption in the systematic gathering of news.

The press reactions to *Religious Ferment in Russia* were far less numerous than they had been to *Opium of the People*. As it was to be submitted as my thesis for Oxford University the style was not popular. However, publication of this work sparked an incident and a review which would have no parallel with my future books.

Pastor Mikhail Zhidkov was one of the officials of the All-Union Council senior enough to be entrusted, not least by the KGB, with a solo visit to London. He had previously been given permission to study at the Baptist seminary in Bristol; he completed a course, improved his English and returned to Moscow and, among other duties, 'welcomed' foreign visitors to his church (that is, shielded them from any meaningful contact with the congregation). I had met him there on several occasions. This visit was for 'consultations' with British Baptist leaders and I was invited for a private meeting at Baptist Church House in Kingsway, central London.

Someone, perhaps from Macmillan, the publisher, had sent him a copy of *Religious Ferment in Russia* and our conversation was about little else. He made it clear that my work was far from welcome in Moscow Baptist circles. I had made their own situation more difficult and had acted unfairly by concentrating on the persecution of the unregistered *Initsiativniki* Baptists, while failing to acknowledge the positive achievements of the registered congregations under the AUCECB. I acknowledged that I might have shed more light on positives in the official church, but they sent me no information beyond the stilted reports in their publication, *Bratsky vestnik*. I continued by emphasising how brilliantly and bravely the unregistered Baptists had organised themselves, under the noses of the KGB, to communicate with their own followers in the USSR and with the outside world. Further, they made a persuasive case for themselves, which my book acknowledged.

---

15   Many Western journalists mistakenly reported that the first organisation defending prisoners of conscience in a communist country emerged in Czechoslovakia during the Prague Spring of 1968.

16   Bourdeaux, *Faith on Trial in Russia*, pp. 97–8.

We parted on friendly terms, but a few weeks later the *Baptist Times* published a sharply critical review of the book, headed 'The inhuman treatment – of Christians. Injustice and savagery are exposed in this book – but the book itself is unfair'.[17] The review, by the editor, the Revd Walter Bottoms, continued: 'It would be serious if this book persuaded Western readers to cheer one side and condemn the other.' The sub-text of this lengthy review was a barely concealed attack on my integrity – bias, in other words. He acknowledges the evidence of the brutality which the police were inflicting on the unregistered Baptists, but argues that I was wrong to focus so much on the schism between the registered and unregistered Baptists. He continues: 'Mr Bourdeaux has marshalled his account round a thesis… Unhappily, in presenting his material as he has Mr Bourdeaux appears to be doing the communists' job for them.'

I was taken aback by the tone of this long review and scrutinised it carefully. Embedded in the text was a statement which aroused my suspicions. 'He omits part of some quotations that do not suit his theme.' Walter Bottoms, on his own admission to me later, knew no Russian, so how could he have made this statement based on the contents of Russian texts? Of course, every reviewer has a right to his own opinion and to express it. But my suspicion was that this particular statement could only have originated with Mikhail Zhidkov in the conversations he had had during his recent visit to London. Could not other allegations in the review have also been dictated, or at least suggested, by Zhidkov?

For better or worse, this review shaped Keston's future relations with the British Baptist community – and by extension with the wider circles of the European Baptist Federation – in its earliest days. This episode also illustrates the effectiveness of what was clearly an attempt by the KGB to influence Western opinion against my work.

At the same time articles attacking me began to appear in the Soviet press. Most notable was 'Latter-Day Apostles of the Baptist Church in Anti-Soviet Speculation', which had appeared in *Science and Religion* at the end of 1969,[18] after the publication of *Religious Ferment in Russia*. It always struck me that, in a curious way, such articles achieved the opposite of their intention, because they opened up a perspective, albeit a false one, of the work we were doing to people who otherwise would have known nothing about us. Georgi Vins later told me that he first came across my name, and that of Keston, when he was given access to the prison library where Soviet publications were on display. Not all the 'facts' were falsified, either. Ilya Brazhnik's article began:

> About ten years ago Michael Bourdeaux, a graduate of an Oxford theological college and a British subject, spent a year at Moscow University. Soon after his departure from Moscow, he began to publicize vigorously the situation of religion in our country, and he was later among the professional anti-communists working at the so-called 'Centre de Recherches et d'Etude des Institutions Religieuses' (Geneva, Switzerland). Bulky volumes on religion in our country

---

17   *Baptist Times*, London, 15 February 1968.
18   *Nauka i religiya*, December 1969, pp. 54–57.

issued forth from Bourdeaux's pen; *The Observer* and other newspapers have been opening their pages to him to assess this question, and he speaks on BBC programmes.[19]

So far, so accurate, and a testimony to the record-keeping of the KGB. Brazhnik continued by referring to *Religious Ferment in Russia* and my work on the separatist *Initsiativniki* Baptists. What I allegedly refused to acknowledge was a general decline in religious belief, as a result of the advances of science. He criticised me for not (he supposes!) having read *Honest to God,* in which John Robinson 'casts doubt on all the basic tenets of Christianity in order to bring it up to the contemporary level of science'. He did not know that Bishop Robinson had significantly encouraged my work and encouraged it practically in its early days.

Brazhnik continued by claiming that the *Initsiativniki* were a dwindling minority, guilty of enforced illegal indoctrination of children. He went on:

> The real reason for Bourdeaux's interest in the Initsiativniki is solely this: he likes the fact that they speak out against the laws of the Soviet State and misrepresent its policy in religious matters. And Bourdeaux willingly supports them, so as to drum up mistrust in the West towards our country... There is no doubt that Bourdeaux's writings do not bring honour to the church which has nurtured him, nor to the college within whose walls he was educated. But we are not personally concerned with the question of whether they bear legal or moral responsibility for such activities. Bourdeaux's scribbles reflect a definite direction in the arsenal of imperialist propaganda, poisoning the minds of people in the West with the venom of anti-Soviet ideas.[20]

In this first broadside against me in the secular Soviet press I might have expected something more pointed, but with it I truly felt that I had arrived on the KGB list of active targets, at the same time as my work was beginning to be known around the world – and this was in the same year that, unknown to Mr Brazhnik, Keston College was founded.

St Bernard's Seminary

On the basis of the advance I had received from Macmillan, I was able to employ an assistant for the first time. Xenia Howard-Johnston, a recent Oxford graduate in Russian and bi-lingual in French, came to work with me on the recommendation of Professor Nicolas Zernov. We worked well together and she rapidly became indispensable. The teamwork of Keston, in a very real sense, began before its founding with Xenia's arrival

---

19   English translation of the complete text in Michael Bourdeaux, *Faith on Trial in Russia* (London, 1971), pp. 182–9.

20   Ibid.

in 1967. She has supported the work throughout her life, co-founding its journal and becoming Chairman of the Council in 2002 and continuing to the present.

Domestically, there had been changes. Charlton parish acquired a new rector, John Southgate. He inspected the parish buildings and came to see me when he was on an exploratory visit. I was shocked a few days later to receive a letter in which he wrote that, on his forthcoming appointment, he would require me to vacate St Mary's House in favour of a full-time priest. I was dismayed both at the prospect of the resulting insecurity, but also because he had acted illegally. He should not have written that letter until after his installation in the parish. His own career, though, was on the up. He went on to become Archdeacon of York. We met again a few years later in Australia and mended fences. I told him the truth: his action had forced Gillian and me to look for a house and we managed to raise a mortgage for a pleasant three-bedroom house in Chislehurst, cheap because it was on a main road (13 Red Hill), but reflecting the better economic situation of a more secure job. Unbeknown to him at the time, Fr Southgate had forced me to take a step which turned out to be advantageous, a true 'blessing in disguise', setting my first foot on the property ladder at the age of 32. In June 1967, our son Mark was born.

All this time I continued in a low-key association with Bill Fletcher. Although he had been helpful in passing on some of the documents, he was clearly uncomfortable with the outcome. Apart from publication of these by someone identified with his work, the controversy generated between the Baptist community and me was not something he welcomed. Relations had become strained by the end of 1968. Then I received, out of the blue, an invitation from Bishop Fulton Sheen, well known in America from his regular TV appearances, which gave him a substantial popular following. Knowledge of my work, apparently, was beginning to spread on the other side of the Atlantic.

Bishop Fulton Sheen enjoyed less popularity with the Vatican and other American bishops, having been moved from New York City to Rochester, NY, some 400 miles north, on the shores of Lake Ontario. He was, however, fully in tune with the spirit of Vatican II and invited me to come to teach for a term as a visiting professor at his diocesan seminary. Taking two bold ecumenical initiatives with one stroke – I would be the only non-Catholic on the staff – he organised this as a shared appointment with the Protestant Colgate-Rochester Seminary close by.

Xenia found a new job as research assistant to Professor Leonard Schapiro at the London School of Economics and Political Science. Before taking up the appointment in America, Gillian, the children and I spent a month in Montego Bay, Jamaica, where I ran a parish for the only time in my life.

Before beginning my teaching, I left on a lecture tour, designed to precede the beginning of the new term. This took in Illinois (Wheaton and Chicago), Michigan (Ann Arbor and Berrien Springs) and Indiana (South Bend). The reception everywhere was positive and began to elevate my hopes that eventually my work would receive financial support from the USA.

The welcome at St Bernard's Seminary was warm and positive in every way. Bishop Sheen was kind and considerate: he had discovered that Gillian was a pianist and installed a piano in our flat, which was just up the road towards Lake Ontario from the seminary. Karen, now five, but still below the normal starting school age of six in the USA, attended a 'public' (state) school, on the grounds that she had already begun her education and we rapidly discovered that she spoke 'American' at school and English at home.

I felt like a fully integrated staff member from the first day. It was a fine opportunity to organise my material into two lectures a week and the students showed a genuine interest in a part of the world which was completely unknown to them. I tried to cover the evolution of Soviet religious policy from 1917 until the present, bringing in the full story, such as I knew it at the time, of the evolution of a religious opposition.

There was a problem, though. The spring of 1969 saw the beginning of widespread unrest on university campuses throughout the USA. Not even theological seminaries, Colgate-Rochester included, escaped this. Students occupied the building and barred access to the staff and faculty. There were no such problems at St Bernard's. Bishop Sheen and the staff could not possibly entertain revolt among their own students and stepping over the traces would certainly have entailed a bar to ordination to the priesthood, such was Catholic discipline. The situation was not resolved during the whole of my time in New York State and I never gave a single lecture at Colgate-Rochester, nor did any of their students respond to the invitation to attend mine at the Catholic seminary.

St Bernard's provided us with a car, so we were able to enjoy the area, particularly as the weather improved in April. Deep snow and a frozen lake gave way to a warm, green spring. We drove to the Adirondacks, Boston, Vermont, Washington DC and Erie, Pennsylvania. During the mid-term break I was able to visit California for the first time and lecture in San Francisco and Los Angeles. The whole stay gave me experience of American life, which would stand me in good stead for the future.

Just before the end of our time in Rochester, Bill Fletcher appeared in our flat. I had continued to work for him in the same capacity now as his other collaborators: doing a full-time university job and earning some extra salary by continuing to review the Soviet press.

However, Bill's conversation ended with a bombshell. We entertained him before he announced that my contract was at an end. There was not even a period of notice to be worked. 'You've now established yourself as a scholar, so you don't need me anymore,' he said, oblivious of the fact that I would shortly be going back to England, once again to face the prospect of no job. He said that my place on the Geneva team would be taken over by a Canadian-Ukrainian scholar from Ottawa, Bohdan Bociurkiw. I had never heard of him, but he and his wife would quickly become close friends, when he came to the LSE on a sabbatical. I was in awe of his model scholarship, concealing the passion he felt personally over the Soviet treatment of his homeland of Western Ukraine and the Greek Catholic Church to which he belonged. He had been born in

Lviv and had experienced the liquidation in 1946 of his Church by the communists, overseen by none other than Nikita Khrushchev, who had been in charge of Ukraine at the time.

Bohdan's tenure with Bill Fletcher was not to be a long one: by the end of 1969 the Centre de Recherches had collapsed. Bohdan supposed that the financial backing had simply been withdrawn. Bill's work did not seem to have influenced attitudes towards the churches in the Soviet Union. His personal scholarship had increased through his own publications and he soon established himself as Professor of History at the University of Kansas at Lawrence. I never met him again, although we did correspond towards the end of his life.

I left Rochester with a commendation from Bishop Sheen. On 1 April 1969 he wrote:

> The day is passed when the only ones who are interested in Communism are those who are for it or against it. We have now reached a plateau in the academic world where Communism and religion should be studied factually, scientifically and technically… I have never met anyone who has the thorough knowledge of Communism in relation to religion more than your good self. This knowledge you have not kept to yourself and to your files, but have disseminated it through books which are revered by scholars. While teaching in our Seminary you have also endeared yourself to all who have come in contact with you, and though we would be losing much in your taking another post, we feel that it is imperative for the sake of scholarship and academic excellence in this particular field. A projected center, as the one envisaged, would benefit not only England, but would have a great value for the American churches. Though it is very evident that the National Council of Churches and the Institute of Jewish Affairs would be interested, I should very much like to add that the Episcopal Conference of the United States, that is to say, all of the bishops of the country, would also have a very vital interest in this important subject.[21]

We arrived home jobless at the end of May 1969. Nothing could have provided a greater stimulus to our starting immediately to establish a British study centre, where I would develop my own ideas and give primacy to *samizdat*.

---

21   Private letter in Keston archive.

Chapter X
Domestic Beginnings

Xenia Howard-Johnston and I had established a kind of 'proto-Keston' in the Bill Fletcher years, working from my Chislehurst home at 13 Red Hill. We resumed our work together after my return from Rochester, New York, in May 1969 and an exciting new project began when we received the astonishing transcript of the trial of Aida Skripnikova in Leningrad. This naive young girl simply wanted to share her Baptist faith with others and distributed Bible verses hand-written on postcards while standing on a street corner. This led to her trial from 11–15 July 1968. We received a transcript of it on bedsheets – literally – cut up into twenty-two numbered narrow strips, each covered with faultless script in ball-point pen, recording all the main speeches and interrogations. The plan had been to give this to someone who could smuggle it out of the Soviet Union, wrapped around the body – and this succeeded. Some Finnish friends entrusted me with this precious document and to this day it is one of the most important items in Keston's collection. Xenia and I managed to assemble enough supplementary information to turn it into a book, *Aida of Leningrad*.[1] Years later several Keston staff, including Malcolm Walker, the archivist, were able to visit Aida in St Petersburg, and befriend her. Her faith was unshaken by her experiences. I first met her briefly in 1993 and I reflect now on how much trust was placed in us to be vouchsafed with this treasure; and I am confident that publication of the book helped her avoid another prison term.

The Founding Group

I soon built up a triumvirate of the most remarkable and faithful advisers, experienced, precise and offering a rare quality of friendship as well.

Sir John Lawrence had revised his somewhat equivocal view of my work. He was a wise man, mild in manner but clear in his judgements, not least in his public condemnation of communism, for which he was often ridiculed. On more than one occasion he said that there was no substance to it and it would collapse like a house of cards; he would live to see the end of it – and he did.

According to one of his diaries, on 29 August 1969 he had a conversation with an official representative of the Moscow Patriarchate, Fr Livery Voronov, at Chevetogne, the Catholic monastery in Belgium where the Eastern Rite is celebrated alongside the Latin. John summarised his impressions thus, after a difficult hour walking around the garden:

---

1   Gateway Outreach, London, 1972.

He thinks I exaggerate the decline of Marxism as an ideology… I am never sure on these occasions how far they are deliberately twisting, how far they genuinely do not know things that we know, and how far they do not dare to face squarely the implications of what they do know. I only know that they are under appalling and subtle pressure to put a good face on things. The moral choices before them are brimming over with ambiguity, whatever they do. I make no judgment on people. I do, however, reserve my judgment of facts. I have not gained or kept my faith in a concentration camp. It is easier for me to weigh facts objectively but they have depths of faith and of experience which I do not have.[2]

With private means, he was able to devote his professional life to study of Russia and the passionate promotion of ecumenism. He became chairman of the lay house of the Church Assembly, the most senior position a layman could hold in the days before the introduction of synodical government, and he was an observer in Rome at the Second Vatican Council. He was the natural candidate to become the first Chairman of 'Keston' and without his influence, both internally and externally, it could not have got off the ground. His diplomatic moderation persuaded many people of the seriousness of the enterprise.

Very different, but passionate and equally well informed, was Leonard Schapiro, Professor of Political Science at the LSE. Of Latvian Jewish origin, he knew his Marxism better than any politician or theoretician in the Soviet Union. He was convinced that our approach was sufficiently academic to be able to hold its own in any university company. He did not live to see the collapse of communism. In my tribute to him at the memorial meeting after his death in 1983, I said:

It was a professional association at the beginning. I came to appreciate Leonard as a man of utter integrity, moved by compassion as well as the desire to be factual and accurate about this study… Never once did I hear him offer a word of advice that was not measured, to the point and, in its quiet way, usually galvanising all of us to action… One of his last public acts was to deliver a deeply impressive speech on religious liberty at the annual meeting of Keston College on 15 October, just over two weeks before his death. He held an audience of 200 spellbound – and we are privileged to have this preserved on tape.[3]

Leonard's academic works focused on a dispassionate, but clinical, demolition of the ideology of communism. It was Leonard who gave me my first British academic appointment: a fellowship at the Centre for International Studies at the LSE, to begin in the October after I returned from Rochester. There was no funding for this, but the status conferred was inestimable. I was able to use the LSE as a secure and stimulating base. This was the first academic appointment for the UK in the field of communism and religion.

---

2   'Note of Conversation at Chevetogne', carbon copy in Keston Archive.
3   'Michael Bourdeaux's tribute to Leonard Schapiro' in Keston Archive.

Peter Reddaway had followed in my footsteps at Moscow University, but his time there ended prematurely when he was expelled. The resulting publicity in the press, with a photograph, was the first time I had heard of him, but when we met we immediately found that we had many ideals in common, a fairly traditional Anglican faith, love of sport, music and travel, and our houses were not that far apart to the south of London. We became close family friends, spending time together and discussing just about everything.

Peter was a disciple of Leonard and worked with him at the LSE – indeed, it was through him that I first met Leonard. He was the most activist of us, often pushing us to undertake new projects and openly to challenge the political attitudes which surrounded us. We were still in the period where the backlash from McCarthyism predominated in many circles. Any misdeed in the area of human rights by the Soviets could, allegedly, be paralleled by something the Americans had done. The British focus was very much on the injustice of the apartheid system in South Africa. Our collective calling was to defend religious liberty in the Soviet Union, which immediately put us at odds with those who asked why we were not doing something about apartheid in South Africa.

We decided to found a new study centre. We had a common mind on what needed to be done and we all contributed ideas on how to do it. The work would be grounded in scholarship and integrity towards our sources, whatever their provenance. Thus we would be faithful to the 'voice' of those who were silenced. Important, too, was to evaluate the controlled and censored opinions of those under constraint who spoke for the official churches from within the system. We would also evaluate official atheist sources.

As we were preparing to launch this work, there was an influx of new information from believers, some of whom wrote about religious liberty, but others provided convincing testimony that a religious revival was under way. From the pages of the official *Journal of the Moscow Patriarchate* the censored voice of the Church came across loudly. The result was *Patriarch and Prophets: Persecution of the Russian Orthodox Church Today.*[4]

Although very far from being a popular work – or for that matter easily readable – it did illustrate the variety of new voices, all of which were virtually unknown to readers in the West. I could well have broken up these passages with commentary, but I preferred to let Russian believers speak at length for themselves. There were new prophets, I maintained, calling for their voice to be heard and for new concessions. Meanwhile, the 'Patriarchs' made compromises in the hope of winning through to better times. After a short introduction concentrating on the legal position of the Church, I printed three hundred pages of selected documents from among the spate of *samizdat* texts. I divided them into themed chapters: Outline of the Atheist Campaign, Persecution of the Clergy, Suppression of the Monasteries and Seminaries, Destruction

---

4   Macmillan, London, 1969.

of Parish Life, the Ordinary Believer and the Legal Dimension. I presented many authors new to our public, such as the Christian mathematician and teacher from Kirov, Boris Talantov, who documented the persecution in the north of Russia, and I ended by devoting separate chapters to two of them, Anatoli Levitin (a lay teacher) and Fr Vsevolod Shpiller, a Moscow parish priest, who broke out of the norms to illustrate how caring the Church could be, even when deprived of its social activities by the authorities.

Patriarch and Prophets is still a resource for information about these people, whose names remain largely unknown to the Western world. It is relevant even today, because most of the issues raised have never been fully debated, let alone resolved. Nearly three decades after the collapse of communism, the Moscow Patriarchate remains largely politically subservient to the secular state. These names, which it has passed over, represent a period of heroic opposition to communist control. But today the Patriarchate points to the Stalin persecution as the period when it was excluded from society and almost annihilated, while Khrushchev, who tried for a shorter time to do the same, is ignored. In the last months before the foundation of the new 'Centre' this book became a kind of exemplar of what the work might achieve.

The Centre for the Study of Religion and Communism

The last ten years had had many lonely moments, but I was never to feel isolated again. The first practical imperative was to establish this new work as a registered charity, essential for any fund-raising, before we could begin what was then, years before the introduction of Gift Aid, the cumbersome process of securing promises for long-term support by seven-year covenant.

We also had to have a name. After much deliberation we chose 'Centre for the Study of Religion and Communism'. This was far from ideal, but we could not think of anything better. Choosing a name which incorporated the name of Russia or the Soviet Union was impossible, because it would be geographically too limiting. Also, in the climate of the time, we had to avoid any name which carried even the slightest hint of an anti-communist stance. 'Centre'? This was vague, but we had no premises. 'Study'? We agreed on this easily; it was to be the hallmark of the work undertaken and would qualify us for registration as an educational charity under the Department of Education and Science. 'Religion and Communism'? 'Religion under Communism' ran it close, but we felt, possibly wrongly, that this carried a tinge of ideological bias. The name we chose was too long and some wrongly understood it as a place where we would study the relationship between Marxism and religion (or 'Christian–Marxist dialogue', to use the watchword of the day). When the chance of changing the name to 'Keston College' arose later, we adopted it avidly and 'Keston' has remained indissolubly associated with the work to this day.

I have always dated the beginning as 1969, because that was when intensive discussions began. It would be 24 September 1970 before the founding Memorandum and Articles of Association were passed and we began legally to exist, with valuable charitable status conferred in a new field of study. Our charter specifically precluded us from involvement in political activity, though supplying information to all and sundry would be at the heart of our work. We have never once been challenged over the legitimacy of these activities under the laws governing charitable work in the UK. Accusations soon flew about that our funding came from the CIA, even from the South African security BOSS. From the outset we had established our integrity so firmly that we were never even offered subventions from such sources.

According to our Articles education came right at the beginning. Our first objectives were:

> To promote the advancement of education in religion, the history of religion, including religious beliefs and practices... To promote and encourage the study of and research into religion, religious beliefs and religious practices in Communist States or States which have been Communist or present or former Totalitarian States (whether in Europe, Asia or elsewhere) and the relationship between different religions...

Behind the legal jargon lay a robust concept. We did not need to change the wording after the collapse of communism. There was further mention of publishing, providing scholarships for students, acquiring premises, and co-operating with like-minded institutions. The objectives which we failed to achieve for four decades were making this work a formal part of a university, but we fully achieved this in 2007 at Baylor University in Texas.

The Council

Apart from the founders, there was further distinguished support among the first members of the Council.[5] A small group of us met, informally, for a 'pre-inaugural' meeting of the Council on 30 June 1970, chaired by Sir John Lawrence at his Chelsea house. Most of the discussion was on aims and objects, fund-raising and the appointment of patrons. There was then a long review of publications being considered or under way, a full agenda for an organisation which was in its earliest days.

At our official inaugural meeting on 24 September 1970 we discussed possible patrons. The Archbishop of Canterbury, Michael Ramsey, had expressed willingness to stand, conditional on his not being alone. He soon formally agreed, which was a boon

---

5   Founding-members included: Geoffrey Goodwin, Montague Burton Professor of International Relations at the LSE, the Revd Janis Sapiets (BBC), Canon David Paton, head of the Missionary and Evangelical Council of the Church of England, the Revd John Arnold, an outstanding ecumenist, who eventually became Dean of Rochester and then Dean of Durham. Before the end of the year the Revd Alan Booth (Christian Aid), Fr (later Metropolitan) Kallistos Ware and Alexander Lieven (BBC) also joined the Council. In 1971 Patrick Rodger, Bishop of Manchester, joined and became one of our most active supporters. He and John Arnold resigned in 1972, but Roger Hayden, who would eventually replace John Lawrence as Chairman, Victor Hayward who advised on China, and the Revd Bernard Tidball (Bible Society), who would later become Deputy Director, all diversified and strengthened the Council.

to the status of our project. Negotiating the current stormy political and ecclesiastical waters was an exercise in diplomacy, which we successfully navigated. Before the end of 1970 Cardinal König of Vienna had agreed, as had the Chief Rabbi, Lord (as he later became) Jakobovits. Other early patrons were Professor Georges Florovsky, the Orthodox theologian, Lord MacLeod of Fuinary (Church of Scotland) and Professor Gordon Rupp (Methodist).

Before long the burden on the Council, with its essential frequent meetings in these early stages, was felt to be excessive, so we appointed a smaller executive committee at the end of 1973, to deal with essential business between Council meetings, which would now be twice a year.

Fund-raising

Peter Fahy joined our staff for a short time to undertake the essential task of fund-raising and Dennis Atkins succeeded him. Neither found it easy: we had no natural constituency, as we might have done had we been a denominational organisation. Dennis worked out of a small office, with a secretary, at the Church Missionary Society headquarters in Waterloo Road, just south of the Thames.

The Revd Stuart Harris, of the European Christian Mission, did us a signal favour by allowing us to use his mailing list for a one-time appeal to help build up our support base, which soon grew to the thousand mark and then to 3,000 early in 1971 (our target was £6,000). Alongside this we set a financial target of £100,000 by the end of 1972. A real breakthrough came in the form of an anonymous interest-free loan of £5,000, intended to be ours in perpetuity and to become legally ours on the death of the donor. This later proved to be Ms Beryl Eeman, a British citizen who lived and worked for the Greek Orthodox Church at the headquarters of the World Council of Churches in Geneva. We came to know her well, as she often stayed overnight in the Bourdeaux household in Chislehurst, breaking her car journey from Switzerland to London.

Dennis worked consistently and well, but a cash-flow problem rapidly overtook him. In April 1972 I had to announce that there was no money to pay the salaries at the end of the month and it looked as if the appeal would fail. We would have to try to negotiate a bank loan against the security of the covenanted promises. Barclays Bank, Chislehurst, refused to do this and all staff barring myself were told that they would have to leave at the end of the month. In the end, however, this was unnecessary and enough money came in over the next two weeks to pay the salaries. We had surmounted the first of innumerable financial crises over which I presided during the next three decades. Then there was a dramatic upturn in our fortunes.

In July 1972 I renewed a contact which I had first made in Rome several years earlier. Fr Werenfried van Straaten, founder and head of the Catholic agency, Aid to the Church in Need, was one of the most decisive people I ever met. In Rome he was becoming impatient with Italian bureaucracy and he moved his organisation to Königstein, in what was then West Germany. As a young man he joined the Norbertine abbey of Tongerlo in Belgium. At the end of the war, he threw himself almost single-handedly into relief work for the myriads of displaced people in the Low Countries and became known as the 'Bacon Priest', a name he took up in his autobiography.

As a man who moved hearts and fed bodies, his attention soon turned to the oppressed people of Eastern Europe, arousing controversy as a staunch anti-communist. Sending aid to Russia was beyond the political spectrum, but on our first meeting he appreciated that we had access to information which he did not. He promised us annual support of $5,000, soon to be increased, in return for regular reports on situations of concern to his own organisation. Thus was forged a friendship, later mediated through his influential niece Antonia Willemsen, which persisted to the end of the communist years. In recognition of this, Fr Martin Gosling, part-time Director of ACN in the UK, became a member of our Council.

ACN's grant was soon followed by financial support from a range of mainly European Protestant missions and the forging of friendships with their directors, which became one of the marks of our work in its pre-1989 heyday. With annual consultative and private meetings we established a true fellowship. By the end of the year we reached the target of £100,000. Included in this, thanks to the persuasion of Alan Booth, was a small grant from the World Council of Churches.

Over the next two decades we kept within the budget for the core work, but there was not sufficient to pay realistic salaries. Those who joined us – and there were many over the years – did so as a labour of love, but most could not consider it as a permanent career.

A Busy Life

Today, in retirement, I have reflected many times on how I managed to juggle so many activities in my life at this time. I continued to produce books and articles, I travelled the country, and indeed the world, as a lecturer, during which time I was also constantly trying to broaden the constituency and to raise funds for Keston. I had consultations with church leaders and politicians and – perhaps less efficiently– ran the day-to-day affairs of Keston.

In addition to family commitments, my hobbies provided a welcome change of focus. Playing tennis continued actively until 1972, when I broke my leg. By the time I was fully recovered I was nearly forty and the best of my playing days were over: but the hiatus led me to start on an umpiring career which became an absorbing hobby right up to my retirement in 2000. Membership of the Philharmonia Chorus was a demanding experience of music-making to a professional standard – often two nights a week – for thirty years, shared with Gillian for the first seventeen of them.

I went to deliver the Dawson Lectures on Church and State at Baylor University immediately after coming out of hospital in February 1972 and with my leg still in plaster. This, as it turned out, was a more than fortuitous occasion, for it was to lead, many years later, to a permanent association with this distinguished university.

We were able to invite a range of visitors to share their expertise with us and I devoted considerable time to them. Dr Gerhard Simon, a German scholar, came in July 1972, followed by Paul Anderson two months later. He underlined the importance of our work at a time of what he called a 'growing pro-Soviet' mood in church circles on his side of the Atlantic. In April 1971 we had invited Tom Bird to become our official representative in the USA, prior to beginning the process of registration as a tax-exempt organisation there. In October 1973 his colleague, Andrew Blane, attended a Council meeting and took this discussion forward with enthusiasm.

Most important of all, during this year we began to develop a relationship with the Mennonite Central Committee, which proposed to send to us Walter Sawatsky, a young Canadian scholar of great energy and enthusiasm, on a long-term assignment, for which they would bear all the costs. I met him for an informal interview in December 1973 and he attended a session of our executive committee, following which we appointed him to our staff for three years. During this time he undertook a research programme on the Soviet Evangelicals, which led to the eventual publication of what became the standard study of the subject.[6]

Throughout the 1970s I maintained a busy schedule of lectures in various countries, always in consultation with the Council and maintaining strict guidelines to prevent being drawn into political controversy. Most challenging was a three-week visit to Southern Rhodesia and South Africa (March–April 1973). In the latter, controversy over apartheid was raging. The focus of one strand of opposition to it was the South African Council of Churches, made up of several bodies, including mainstream Anglicans, but of course excluding the Dutch Reformed Church, which supported the minority government. SACC leaders believed they were being maligned, including accusations that they were pro-communist. Ignorance about the situation of believers in the USSR was almost complete, so my invitation was to be a contribution to setting the record straight and to report on my research as accurately as I could. My brief was to stick to the known facts and demonstrate the truth about religious persecution in a part of the world, about which there was virtually no objective reporting.

En route to South Africa, Ian Smith, then Prime Minister of Southern Rhodesia, invited me for a private interview in Salisbury (later Harare). This was difficult, but it set the tone for some of the meetings I had in South Africa. Smith looked at an early issue of *Religion in Communist Lands* and saw the name of Archbishop Michael Ramsey, listed as one of our patrons. 'He is a man of known communist sympathies,' said Smith, claiming that this proved where our loyalties lay. My time in Salisbury was mercifully short, but soon after I found myself talking to John Vorster, Prime Minister of South Africa, in similar terms.

However, the South African Council of Churches proved to be marvellous hosts. My itinerary covered many major centres of the country, with lectures at several universities and sermons in key cities. It was a sharp learning experience, carried

6   *The Soviet Evangelicals since World War II* (Herald Press, Kitchener, Ont., 1981).

out under the watchful eye (which did not disguise its presence) of government agents. I presented many facts about the Persecuted Church and it was remarkable how universal and instantaneous was the sympathy which my black audiences and congregations expressed. The SACC showed me the worst conditions under which the oppressed people lived, and preaching in the township of Soweto was an unforgettable experience. In Cape Town I stayed at Bishopscourt, at the foot of the Table Mountain, with the Anglican Archbishop, Robert Selby Taylor, who led me, point by point, through the problems South Africa faced: a remarkable man whose memory deserves to be better remembered. His successor, Desmond Tutu, became a world figure, but his later career stood on the shoulders of Archbishop Taylor, a man of integrity and clear vision.

Looking for a Home

In the very early days of the Centre we rented a shabby three-roomed office in nearby Sidcup. This was convenient, but too small. We soon discussed buying 'permanent' accommodation, to give the work the security it needed.

Gillian and I had lived in Chislehurst for five years since leaving Charlton in 1966. From our domestic point of view, with a growing family, it would be preferable to move from a main road to a quieter location. Property prices in the London suburbs had not yet reached the stratosphere.

Our search led us to Lubbock Road and to a house called 'Bishops Down' (we later simplified this to 'Bishopsdown'). It was of Victorian red brick and had been converted and reconverted several times in the past. The site sloped steeply, with surrounding trees (outside the boundaries of the property), which made it seem almost rural. When we first saw it, there were two flats, up and down, each consisting of six rooms, the top flat including a small room on the second floor.

The owner was an eccentric lady who lived alone, with the top floor unoccupied at this time. Mrs Kipping claimed to be Cornish, though I never saw nor heard any evidence of this. As we later discovered, she had laid carpets in the lower part of the back garden so she could walk around and keep clean shoes, but with the passage of time these pathways had eventually acquired a thin overlay of soil which soon degenerated into a slide of liquid mud when it rained.

After a period of tortuous negotiations, which our Council encouraged me to pursue, a price of £17,000 was agreed. This was later increased by £500 and we could just afford to raise a mortgage, with our existing house quickly attracting satisfactory offers.

We had to apply to the Bromley Council for planning permission to use living space as offices, which was refused in April 1971, causing a hold-up on our side. This was eventually overcome by stating that we would continue residential use by installing at least two tenants, who would 'work from home' and the legal obstacle was overcome.

After Mrs Kipping had said yes and no several times, we eventually moved in November 1971 and '34 Lubbock Road, Chislehurst' became the 'permanent' address of the Centre, with the rental income helping me to keep up my mortgage obligations.

At first this was a brilliant arrangement and the accommodation suited the work as it then was, with various secretaries and research assistants occupying the residential part of the upstairs. Moira Blacklaws and Sally Carter, both graduates in Russian, seemed particularly happy there in 1973, living rent-free in part-return for work during Moira's first year out of university; Sally enjoyed a gap-year before going up to Oxford.

However, no one in 1971 could possibly have predicted the rate of expansion over the next two years. Almost every day brought new demands. The financial crisis of April 1972 notwithstanding, we not only envisaged expansion, but were forced into it by the demands of the sheer volume of material without our making any particular efforts to acquire it. We had either to expand the staff beyond the legal limits imposed by our occupancy of Bishopsdown or to fail to cope with the work in hand.

Public support was increasing. Already in Bishopsdown days a defining tradition of our work evolved: our annual AGMs, which eventually became open days, were attended by as many as two hundred people and were noticed even in the national press. The first was in the Methodist Church in Chislehurst on 5 January 1973; the second was a year later at the CMS residential centre, Foxbury, also in Chislehurst.

At the second, Christopher Cviic and Lucjan Blit were elected to the Council, bringing Yugoslavia and Poland closer to our orbit. In these early days I would always give a long (too long?) speech, surveying not only our work, but religious developments in the Soviet Union, alongside the response of Western bodies such as the World Council of Churches.

Less than a year after moving to Bishopsdown I was already beginning to look for a new solution. In September 1972 I met the Vicar of Keston, just south of Bromley, and he told me about his redundant Church of England school, after which I paid my first visit to Keston Common.

The school was in an isolated though pleasing location, in the middle of the Green Belt, surrounded by woods and with only one other building, the village hall, in the vicinity. Three linked ponds nearby were fed at the top by a spring, reputed to have supplied the army of Julius Caesar. A short walk away was something of deep symbolism: the 'Wilberforce Oak', beneath which William Pitt the Younger and William Wilberforce resolved to end slavery in Britain in 1787.

The school itself was a typical Victorian construction dating from the 1880s, after the passing of the Education Act in 1870. It had three vast classrooms with ceilings as high as a two-storey house. Separate was a wartime Nissen hut behind, where the pupils ate and which, in later years, was in use as an extra classroom. There was a portacabin, formerly serving as a staff room, opposite the front door bordering on Keston Common. Now there was a new modern school some distance away, nearer the centre of population, rendering the original Keston Primary School redundant. The external aspect was not unpleasing: grey brick and two gables. The second building, to the right, looking from the road, was a house built as residential accommodation and still occupied by the retired headteacher and his wife. In front there was a small garden with mature trees of fir and laburnum. To the left was the wide expanse of a playing field, common land, but well maintained and in use still by the school. It merged attractively into the woods. Every émigré Russian who subsequently visited at the right time of year remarked on the prodigality of mushrooms: they felt at home.

Negotiations with the Education Department of Rochester Diocese, owners of the property, were of necessity somewhat bureaucratic, because the statutes stated that the sale could not be discounted. However, the price was extremely reasonable, because the old school could be released only for educational purposes and the house had a sitting tenant. The diocese asked for £35,000; we offered £32,500, which was accepted after negotiations, which meant that we had immediately to launch on a new fund-raising campaign.[7]

We had nothing like the money to complete the purchase, but we secured a bank loan against the security of our covenanted promises. Before the purchase could be finalised, we also had to apply for planning permission for change of use. More remarkably, the issue was solved by the offer of a loan of £21,290 from the Rochester Diocesan Board of Education, no less, a truly remarkable example of practical help by the Church of England. We were still waiting for planning permission when the Council met on 15 July 1974, but we were in breach of the planning laws at Bishopsdown, too so we moved at once. The premises had deteriorated since the school became empty.

A new chapter in the history of the 'Centre' immediately opened. There was structural work to do to make Keston School even remotely suitable for occupation, but we had the will, Gillian's organisational capacity and many volunteers. 'Keston College' immediately suggested itself as the new name. In the old sense of the word a 'college' was a collegium of scholars doing the same work.

On 11 January 1975 we held the first of our popular and successful open days in the adjacent village hall, offering our supporters the opportunity of viewing our new premises, still little improved from their original primitive state. Professor John Dunlop (Hoover Institution, Stanford University, California) galvanised the meeting with a superb lecture on 'The Russian Orthodox Church and Nationalism'. Keston was beginning to provide public events which were unique. The venue and programme grew in popularity by the year. At subsequent AGMs, a popular feature was a forum in the afternoon. The audience, including journalists, asked a wide range of questions to our panel of experts.

My father, still active in his bakery business, sent up freshly baked pasties on the overnight train from Cornwall, which I met at Paddington station in the morning, and brought to Keston. Some people claimed to attend the AGMs just for this and I often reflected subsequently that, had my father been more entrepreneurial, he could have become a pasty millionaire, beating the well-known companies to the starting line.

---

7   Council Minutes, 2 October 1973, p. 1.

There would be sixteen of these open days at Keston, each generating its own brand of excitement and unity of purpose, despite occasional and inevitable controversy. The move to Keston School had provided an identity and a perspective which was to shape our work up to 1991.

Chapter XI
The Founding of Keston College

My earliest memory of work at Keston is a picture in my mind's eye of Sally Carter, a gap-year student, balanced high on a stepladder, with a dripping long-handled brush in her hands, cleaning years of grime off the walls, while Moira Blacklaws was below with a brush and pan.

The Old School

When those in charge of the old school knew that, for the children, its days were numbered, not only did maintenance virtually cease, but cleaning as well. It felt as though we were removing generations of filth, much of it created by smoking flues from the old solid-fuel heating system. What we had not anticipated, though, was that these ancient installations, probably a hundred years old, would be ripped out, nor on whose authority this was done. In the hot weather when we moved, we didn't at first take too much notice of the threat of the cold hanging over our heads, but as autumn turned to winter we began to break every regulation of the time regarding health and safety. We received donations of portable electric fires and convector heaters of various ages. There is a photograph of me, sitting at a desk in a massive, but virtually empty room wearing my Russian *shapka* and a winter coat.

In July 1974 the name 'Keston College' appeared for the first time in the records and the Council voted to introduce it officially, alongside the original name of 'Centre for the Study of Religion and Communism', which was to be retained in brackets.

Relays of people, some volunteers, worked beyond the call of duty to make the place habitable. In February 1975 we installed up-to-date convector heaters. Without such communal spirit Keston could never have survived the early days after the move, despite the big advance in recognition for our work which came with the adoption of the new name.

When we moved we had raised almost nothing of the purchase price: we had to borrow almost the whole sum, so we were £29,500 in debt and repayments to the Diocese of Rochester at 15% were draining away any new money we raised. This sounds today as if we were the victims of extortion, but this is not so: such were interest rates in the mid-1970s.

Not for the last time we discussed launching a 'Save Keston' campaign. Yet we survived that dreadful winter and the spring brought signs of improvement, as our morale rose with the burgeoning greenery which so bountifully surrounded us.

At the time of our move we redefined our aims and published them. The Council, united behind our efforts as always, decided that no fundamental change was necessary and a sense of purpose motivated all of us. What we were doing had grown naturally out of the needs and we described our present work and future goals thus.

Keston College:

1. Does research and provides information. The breadth of this work must increase to include a fuller study of individual countries.
2. Trains young people, provides facilities for study and human resources for the future.
3. Helps to unify the work of present organisations, bringing them to understand each other better.
4. Sponsors days of prayer.
5. Broadcasts, both to the West and to Russia.
6. Does indirect relief work, by means of providing literature and publicity in English.[1]

The statement went on to say that we were not involved in publishing in Russian, nor in direct relief work, nor in organising or participating in demonstrations (which would have put a question mark against our charitable status).

Gradually, as our list of contacts grew, so did our resources. Our Catholic friends, Aid to the Church in Need, increased their support. A substantial contribution came from the Billy Graham Evangelistic Association, almost out of the blue, as we did not have strong personal links with them and I had not met any of their senior people, except Leighton Ford, Billy Graham's brother-in-law. He must have been the motivating force behind this bounty, though, as he had demonstrated a warm sympathy for the Russian Baptists and an appreciation of how we had highlighted their plight.

Then in May 1975 we heard that an application I had made to the Ford Foundation for a grant had been successful. Although they promised only half of the requested sum, this was a great boost, particularly as their policy was against giving grants for religious causes. Our application was for $30, 000 to do a tripartite study of Catholics in the Russian Republic, Ukraine and Lithuania, involving Professor Dennis Dunn (Southwest Texas State University), Professor Bohdan Bociurkiw (Carleton University, Ottawa) and myself respectively. For me, this was the beginning of what was to become a lifetime of devotion to Lithuania. Dennis Dunn and his wife came to live in the now-vacant top flat at Bishopsdown for a time and Bohdan Bociurkiw came temporarily to the LSE in London. Eventually this grant produced no less than three books and put Catholics in the USSR on the map in a way they had never been before.

Marite Sapiets, a new staff member, worked with me, as she could read Lithuanian and commissioned and edited excellent translations from Lithuanian *samizdat* from the small community in London. The result was *Land of Crosses*.[2] This work helped

---

1   Council minutes, 15 July 1974, p. 2.

2   Michael Bourdeaux, *Land of Crosses: The Struggle for Religious Freedom in Lithuania, 1939-1978* (Augustine Publishing Company, Chulmleigh, 1979).

cement our relations with Aid to the Church in Need, which bought up 5,000 copies of the Lithuanian book for their supporters.

Marite was the daughter of Janis, our Council member. Her family was Latvian by origin and she was fluent also in Russian, which she had studied at university. Her lasting legacy to Keston is her fine translation of another Russian spiritual classic, *The Unknown Homeland*.[3] Being trilingual, she added immensely to the breadth of our work. Sadly, she suffered from ill health and died in her forties, soon after Keston moved to Oxford.

We also began to look for Jewish and Muslim support, highlighting the work we were doing on behalf of their oppressed fellow believers in the Soviet Union. Good relations existed with the Jewish community from the very beginning, though there were never any significant Jewish donations. The Muslims were wary of the presence of the Chief Rabbi among our patrons and never used our resources or supported the work, though our files on Soviet Central Asia began to grow, mainly through careful reading of the Soviet press. Many years later, our Moscow team began to produce new information on Islam, not available elsewhere, in its volumes of an encyclopaedia on religion in Russia today.

Gaining Influence

Keston College was not an international – or national – institution in the 1970s in the way in which its contemporary Amnesty International was. It did, however, rapidly gain a reputation at home and abroad among those who most directly needed its work. For some time I had been building up a relationship with two like-minded institutes in Switzerland and the Netherlands.

Glaube in der 2 Welt (G2W, Faith in the Second World, Zurich) had no relationship to Bill Fletcher's earlier Swiss-based work. I had met Pastor Eugen Voss in St Moritz on 2 March 1970, while I was still, in a sense, evolving my own ideas for CSRC. Rarely in my life has there been such an extraordinary meeting of minds. Eugen was pastor of a Reformed parish there, but was looking for a change. As we walked on a swept, but snow-lined path in the hills above the resort, the countryside glowed in light of sensational clarity. Our ideas evolved with equal definition and it soon became obvious that Eugen wanted to found an organisation which would undertake in the German language what we were just beginning to do in English. Over the next twenty years I would visit him six times for conferences which he organised, not to mention many meetings in other places to which we were both invited.

It is remarkable that this serious, slowly spoken, gentle man and I agreed on all our views, right up to the time when he retired when the Soviet Union collapsed. Trilingual, with a Russian mother, he was suited to the work in every way, including carrying with him the loyalty of his Swiss Reformed constituency. We agreed on a general plan of action, but, just as importantly, support from the Swiss Church meant

---

3   Mowbray, Oxford, 1978.

that there was no rivalry in fund-raising, either. To this he later added support from West Germany. His publication, of the same name as his institute, was similar to our *Religion in Communist Lands* and we regularly exchanged information and sources. As Keston did, he began collecting *samizdat* and his judgement of its importance coincided with mine.

Soon to join us was Professor Hans Hebly, a Dutch ecumenical scholar, head of the Inter-University Institute for Missiology and Ecumenism, Utrecht, a fully fledged and funded research centre, but he had the freedom to adopt new initiatives. He did not aim to produce the kind of original research which Eugen at G2W and Keston were publishing, but he reprinted some of our best work in Dutch and also used his influence in ecumenical circles to widen our sphere of acceptance. We called a joint conference for the three institutes 30 September to 3 October 1974 and together we began to have an impact on the ecumenical scene which none of us could have achieved individually.

As early as September 1973 Ane van der Bijl (Brother Andrew, as he was universally known) had invited various Protestant missions to meet in conditions of considerable secrecy at Noordwijk, Holland. Already a leader of striking personality and influence, a fine preacher and author of the controversial book, *God's Smuggler*,[4] Andrew was probably the only person who could have drawn together such a disparate group of people.

Although each of them was protective of its own interests, Andrew established a remarkable missionary fellowship among them. The leaders of these groups had a common goal: supporting their fellow believers or spreading the Gospel in the Soviet Union and other countries of the bloc. Andrew's aim was to avoid duplication, of which there had already been unfortunate examples (for instance, translations of the same scriptural texts by different agencies into the same language). In drawing these missions together, these conferences succeeded beyond expectation and the potential rivalry between the groups was dissipated by the fellowship which developed.

The venues revolved around the Scandinavian countries, the Netherlands and West Germany. There was no secretariat, each main mission in turn organising the local annual conference it hosted. There were no minutes, decisions merely being noted by those committed to act upon them. The hosting mission organised an agenda, but no papers were ever circulated. The bond of secrecy was meticulously upheld and there was never any subversion or infiltration, right up to the time when the decision was taken to disband, owing to the free access to these countries which was now possible following the collapse of communism in the Soviet bloc and the easier access to the USSR under Gorbachev.

My role, later shared by Jane Ellis, was to recount to the delegates what was happening on the ground in the Soviet Union. The missions were especially anxious to hear about developments in the Russian Orthodox Church, about which they knew

---

4   New American Library, New York, 1967.

very little. Even on the Protestant scene, what they knew was often localised and coming to them through a limited number of contacts.

Through my regular attendance I was able to forge wonderful friendships, though it remains one of my regrets that after 1990 it was impossible to maintain these links in the same way.

Among this group were Ingemar Martinsson (Ljus i Oster – 'Light in the East' in Sweden), Gulbrand Overbye and Lasse Traedal (Misjon bak Jernteppet – 'Mission Behind the Iron Curtain', Oslo), Hans-Kristian Neerskov (Danish European Mission, Copenhagen), the Finnish Lutheran Mission (Helsinki), Bernd Dyck (Licht im Osten – 'Light in the East', Korntal, near Stuttgart) and of course Brother Andrew himself, with Open Doors in Holland and many branches elsewhere. From the USA the most influential was Peter Deyneka, Jr., of the Slavic Gospel Association, whom I already knew and with whom, and with his wife Anita, I established an enduring friendship. In my personal roll of honour, every one of the above is a hero of the Cold War, without ever once having used any weapon beyond that of Christian commitment.

Keston by the mid-1970s was already being seen and used as a resource by the media. Articles were appearing occasionally in the national press and regularly in the *Church Times,* as a result of following up the original invitation from the Revd. Roger Roberts. His successor, Bernard Palmer and I were in regular happy communication.

The Archbishop of Westminster, Cardinal Heenan, agreed to be a patron at the end of 1974, which began an association with the Catholic Church. At the same time *The Tablet* and the *Catholic Herald* began to publish information based on our work.

In response to an article of mine published on 21 February 1975, Joanna Nash, a member of the ACN board, wrote to the Catholic press:

> For too long Mr Bourdeaux and others like him have battled on almost alone, attempting to point out the plight of those whose freedom to preach, teach and worship is restricted under a regime in which the secret police, the prison camp and the 'special mental hospital' reign supreme… We need more prayers for our persecuted brethren; we need more pressure on our Government to take note of the realities of what is going on in Russia; we need constant and determined pressure on the World Council of Churches; and, perhaps most of all, we need firm guidance in this matter by our own church leaders.[5]

There were frequent radio interviews, too, as well as occasional appearances on TV. The *Sunday* programme early on a Sunday morning on BBC Radio 4 was a new attempt to cover developments in religious life in a world context. From its early days, the producers found Keston College to be a source of reliable news. The only problem was that they were primarily interested in controversy: that is, information about the latest arrests or criticisms of church leaders. These were invariably interview slots lasting

---

5   Letter, Keston Archive, Baylor University.

five minutes or less. There was never an opportunity to build up a more complete picture in a documentary or scripted contribution.

I first met Archbishop Donald Coggan in Sweden in July 1968, while he was still at York, where he was a delegate to the Uppsala General Assembly of the World Council of Churches. We spent the inside of a day together, being guided around the ancient town of Sigtuna by the Revd Sydney Linton, who was to become a lifelong supporter of Keston, and was the Anglican Church's most lively ecumenical contact with Sweden, speaking the language and marrying a Swede. In his gentle way, Archbishop Coggan expressed a warm friendship. While at Lambeth he visited Keston to open a new part of our building. During his time in office, communication was regular, even if at one remove, because Canon Michael Moore, head of the Council on Foreign Relations at Lambeth, reported our Council meetings back to him, so our work was closely observed by the Church of England at the highest level until 1980. However, early in his primacy Archbishop Robert Runcie asked Michael Moore to vacate his post and this degree of communication between Keston and Lambeth did not continue.

There was one Anglican archiepiscopal visit to the Soviet Union which stands out. Donald Coggan, who became a patron on his accession to the throne of Canterbury, had clearly done his homework and when he visited Moscow and Kiev in 1978 he caused a 'scandal'. He was informed about Georgi Vins and, when he was in Kiev, he asked to be taken to his church. At that time the Soviets refused to recognise it, so it was unregistered, even though it had a building in which there were regular services. His hosts, with the greatest reluctance, took him there, in the company of the Revd John Arnold, his interpreter and adviser. The Archbishop asked to see Pastor Vins himself and there is a recording of the exchange.

'He is not here,' came the reply from an official accompanying the group.

'No, I thought not: that's because he's in exile.'

'No, he's not in exile.'

'What do you mean? Where is he?'

'It is not exile. It is a place where he should live.'[6]

Without doubt, such interventions by Western Church leaders, rare though they were, had their effect. Many prisoners attested to a positive outcome: their situation improved, both in diet and in treatment in prison, when they were the subject of a campaign.

Archbishop Coggan visited Keston to dedicate the building. He also did another signal service for Keston. Archdeacon John Youens had recently resigned as Chaplain General to the British Forces and, still in full vigour, was looking for a new challenge. The Archbishop set up a meeting with John and me and we immediately saw eye to eye. John joined our Council and became an active Vice Chairman. His charming manner endeared him to everyone, but he was also tough and clear thinking in his relations with the staff, who often benefited from his wise counsel, especially where

6   Tape in Keston Archive.

personal relations were concerned. He would remain with us until he had a stroke in 1986 which deprived him of speech – a servant to Keston in its heyday whose contribution could never be replaced. We renamed our reading room the 'Youens Library'.

By 1975 politicians were beginning to take notice of Keston's work. While I was on holiday in the Scilly Isles in the summer of that year, the Anglican Chaplain, the Revd Trevor McCabe, an old friend from Wycliffe Hall days, invited Gillian and me to a private dinner where the only other guests were Harold and Mary Wilson. It was, of course, Trevor's initiative, but it would not have happened unless the Prime Minister had wished to spend several hours in our company, in the middle of one of his holiday breaks in his own house just up the road from the chaplaincy.

Harold Wilson was always proud of the fact that he had visited the Soviet Union many times before becoming PM, usually heading a trade delegation. Human rights did not feature high on his priority list, but he must have been keen to hear my views in a relaxed atmosphere. He asked me to put all that I was saying into writing and I later highlighted the names of Georgi Vins and Petras Plumpa, a Catholic activist, and the plight of the Lithuanian people. In his reply the Prime Minister said that he would keep all this in mind and bring up these names with the Soviets, if the opportunity arose. I do not know whether he ever did, but I'm certain that this pleasant development led to my name being on a list at Number 10 and later, when David Owen became Foreign Minister, he invited me in to the Foreign Office for a day-long consultation on human rights in the Soviet bloc. This was the beginning of a long association with the Labour Government and then with the Conservative Government of Mrs Thatcher. It is notable that such occasions remained at a higher level than they did with religious bodies. We also had many friends among the Liberals (later the Lib Dems), including such respected politicians as David Alton and David Steel. Keston, from the outset, was proud of its association with all the main political parties.

Publications

With the increased flow of information in the early 1970s, the question quickly arose as to how we could most effectively handle this. The publication of books had up to now provided the answer, but they could never spread information quickly enough, even though publishers were approaching us to commission new titles.

Even before the Centre for the Study of Religion and Communism came into existence, there had been a fledgling documentation service, which I compiled while still in America. At this stage I had a helpful colleague, who had a career at Exeter University. Peter Scorer was a member of the Orthodox Church and later became a deacon. I had kept a private mailing list, which had grown to about one hundred names and in November 1968 the first *Documentation Service on Religion in the USSR* appeared, circulated by Peter. A letter signed by Sir John Lawrence, Peter Reddaway,

Peter Scorer and me accompanied it. We requested £1, for what we hoped would be four to six issues a year.

The aims of our publishing programme were therefore well in place before there was an organisation to promote them. It is no surprise, therefore, to read in the Council minutes for 1971 that the publication of a journal was at or near the top of its agenda in all its early meetings. Various memos and discussions rehearsed arguments on how 'popular' or how 'academic' the envisaged publication should be.

On 2 May 1972 the Council agreed to bring out a dummy issue of a journal, but it took until the beginning of 1973, while we were still at Bishopsdown, before the first issue of *Religion in Communist Lands* (*RCL*) appeared. The editor was Xenia Howard-Johnston, now working part-time, whose earlier experience of collaborating with me and then with Leonard Schapiro made her the perfect candidate to inaugurate this exacting project. She initially planned six issues a year of about forty pages. We sent out 9,000 free copies, in response to which we had received about 1,000 subscriptions by the time the second issue went out. We would need to achieve about three times this number to make *RCL* permanently viable.

Looking 45 years later at the olive-green cover of the early issues, I am still filled with pride. The editorial work by Xenia (now Dennen) was of the highest quality and the world of Soviet studies had never seen anything like it before.

Inside the cover there was a page of impressive names: the patrons and Council of Management. As well as listing these, we had an international board of reference. Our editorial board turned out to be extraordinary: the most relaxed forum we ever had for a considered exchange of opinions.

> It is not – and a journal devoted to education could never become – a 'record of persecution'. It intends to cover all aspects of religious life, putting the persecutions and pressures in perspective, while emphasising positive features, particularly the spiritual rebirth which seems to be occurring in church life in so many Communist lands. The scope will not be confined to the Christian faith. The task of the CSRC is to cover all aspects of religious and spiritual life and the journal will reflect this.[7]

In view of more recent history, not least the way in which the name of Keston continues to be honoured in the Republic of Lithuania, it is symbolic that the first item of issue No.1 was 'Recent Events in the Lithuanian Catholic Church', by Kathleen Matchett.[8] By this time we had established a strong link with the Lithuanian Catholic Priests Association in New York, They had their own channels for procuring documents from their country, but believed that more effective publicity could be gained by forwarding them to us for publication. Lithuania had been part of the Russian Empire in the nineteenth century, gained its freedom after the Revolution, but lost it again during

---

7   *RCL*, No. 1, 1973, p. 1.
8   *RCL*, No.1, 1973, pp. 9–11.

and after the Second World War, first to the Soviet Union, then to the Nazis, and finally to the Soviets again. From the outset, then, *RCL* told the story of an oppressed people, who, with dignity and commitment to the Catholic Church, strove for freedom of religion and even, at times, for independence.

Kathleen Matchett noted that 'the trickle of documents has become a stream' and that the first two issues of the *samizdat 'Chronicle of the Lithuanian Catholic Church'* had just appeared.

The second article brought my book on the Russian Baptists up to date by printing an article by Katharine Murray on 'The Council of Baptist Prisoners, Relatives' 1964–72', followed by my book review of Joshua Rothenberg's *The Jewish Religion in the Soviet Union*. The issue fulfilled its initial promise of referring to official sources. There was an extract from the government newspaper, *Pravda*, on atheist education and a passage from the censored *Journal of the Moscow Patriarchate* on St Tikhon of Zadonsk. The Russian Baptists were also given an official say, with our reprinting of their recent Christmas message.

The second issue of *RCL* broadened the perspective, with articles by Christopher Cviic on Yugoslavia and Victor Hayward on China. The list of new Baptist prisoners filled eight pages. This was the first feature to cause controversy: Fr Michael Moore said it would make relations with the Soviets more difficult, though once more there was a message from the official Baptist leadership, reprinted from their journal, *Bratsky vestnik* ('Fraternal Herald').

Before the end of the year articles appeared on the Romanian Orthodox Church, Church and State in Poland, East Germany, Buddhism (the trial of the doomed scholar Bidiya Dandaron), Christian–Marxist dialogue, Baptists in Romania, atheism in Estonia, German Lutherans in the Soviet Union and much else. The scope was broadening with each issue.

It seems to me that, over these early issues, and continuing through to the collapse of communism, between 1989 and 1991, *RCL* managed, to a surprising extent, to be both academic and populist. This was due not only to skilful editorial work, but also brilliant back-up by the staff. Most of all, though, it was the material itself: the succession of stories of bravery, Christian witness in the face of persecution, conversion to the faith (including the Jewish faith) in prison and so much else. Those who accused us of bias, of concentrating only on the 'negative' side of Soviet and East European society, must have had their eyes closed. Those issues contain a treasure trove of spiritual witness, of human stories, of historical events, which, even today, open a perspective on the history of the declining years of communism which does not even begin to be reflected elsewhere and which is yet accessible to non-Russian speakers.

Communicating Information: A Constant Challenge

However dramatic or full of intrinsic interest were the materials we were gathering, even before Keston fully expanded to cover the other countries of the Soviet bloc, it was never easy to persuade others to share our enthusiasm. I think the Christian public in the UK had no tradition of interest in our area of work. This did gradually build up over the years, but slowly. How could we persuade people to read and act on information which we ourselves found utterly absorbing?

After the enthusiasm engendered by the launch of *Religion in Communist Lands*, there was no clamour to renew the subscriptions in the second year, which I found dispiriting after what I knew to be the solid achievement in 1973. Should we become more popular? This was a perennial question, often discussed but never satisfactorily answered.

We could not keep up with the wealth of new information coming to hand, yet we had to reduce the print-run of *RCL*, as well as its frequency. We held a meeting on 11 April 1975 devoted solely to discussing the future of the journal. This was the first time that Mrs Stella Alexander came to one of our policy meetings. A Quaker with a degree in English from Oxford University, she had a meticulous eye and offered to compile an index for the issues to date and she continued this for a number of years. She was also travelling frequently to Yugoslavia, struggling (as she said) to learn Serbo-Croat, and she brought a new Balkan perspective to our deliberations, though not everyone agreed with her positive assessment of Marshall Tito.

Peter Reddaway wanted *RCL* to become bigger and more academic, so that universities would take it seriously. In addition we would have needed something more popular.

Therefore we invited David Kelly, a persuasive Irishman (not perhaps quite persuasive enough, it turned out), a man with journalistic flair, to join us. In October 1975 he began looking at our publicity and responded to a request to launch a popular magazine or newspaper. He produced a dummy issue in tabloid form, which the Council thought brilliant, but the response to it was negligible and a bright idea languished unfulfilled. Eventually the Information Department circulated our articles to the press. Later, we started *The Right to Believe*, a popular newsletter, to go out free to everyone on our mailing list.

Expansion: New Staff

Despite recurring financial difficulties, the 1970s witnessed an expansion of our work beyond any expectation that I had had when we began in 1969. As there were so few existing experts on the subject – and these were widely scattered around the world – it soon became obvious that Keston College, among much else, would also need to become a training centre where young people could come and learn about a subject that was not being taught at universities. We had no formal courses or lectures on site, but young people came, some as volunteers, others on a minimal salary, to learn about the subject by being pitched directly into the work itself. Some were quiet, some outgoing, others eccentric, but all were brilliant in their own way and contributed immeasurably to mark Keston with an indelible stamp. It is impossible to mention

Bourdeaux Bakery, c. 1935. My father, Richard, second from left with his mother, Anne Carah.

Truro School Choir, 1950s.

Michael, right,
Cornwall Junior Tennis
Champion 1952.

Jimmy Connors, Centre Court,
Wimbledon, 1970s,
with Michael as line judge.
© *The Times*

RAF Hednesford, gym drill, 1952.

Joint Services School for Linguists, on parade at Foxton Hall, near Cambridge, 1953.

Soviet atheist posters

'Religion is the opium of the people'

'Keep our children safe from priests' claws'

'"There is no God!" Yuri Gagarin's
mission accomplished!'

'It is a sacred duty of honest people
to save children from church
obscurantism'

Destruction of central Moscow church, St Peter and St Paul, where Michael met the two Ukrainian women, 1964.

Most rural churches were converted to use for agricultural purposes.

Michael holds Aida Skripnikova's
trial transcript; with Gillian, 1970.

Gillian with Karen and Mark, 1968.

Nijole Sadunaite demonstrates for Lithuanian independence, February 1989.

Fr Alexander Men' in his study.

Alexander Ogorodnikov, founder of the Christian Seminar, holds the Chronicle of Current Events.

Peter Reddaway, co-founder of Keston College, with Andrei Sakharov, 1988.

Pope John Paul II at Fr Jerzy's grave, 1987.

Fr Jerzy Popiełuszko, c.1983.

Fr Dmitri Dudko before his
recantation.

Valeri Barinov, rock musician, in a secret
recording studio.

Fr Gleb Yakunin, late 1980s, after return from
8 years in prison.

Georgi Vins and Jane Ellis,
at Keston in 1980.

Irina Ratushinskaya, poet, later imprisoned
in notorious Mordovian labour camp.

Alexander Solzhenitsyn with Archbishop Robert
Runcie after the Templeton Prize in 1983.

Keston staff

Grazyna Sikorska

Alexander Tomsky

Michael Rowe

Keston staff

Alyona Kojevnikov

Mavis Perris

Marite Sapiets with Michael

Xenia Dennen with Sir John Lawrence

The early days of Keston College

Philip Walters and Michael

Philip Walters with Sir John Lawrence

Michael unveils Keston plaque in 50th anniversary year, June 2019.

Sergei Filatov and Xenia Dennen, Novo-Tikhvinsky Convent icon studio, with community leader, Ekaterinburg, January 2008.

Sergei and Xenia outside a Buddhist temple in Buryatia, July 2009.

Sergei and Xenia with Fr Shul'gin and Martha and Mary lay sisters in Novokuznetsk, November 2013.

Michael on a field trip to
Yakutsk, July 1999

Lara Clare's christening in 1990, with, from left to right: me, Lorna, daughter Karen, my mother Lillian, son Mark, my father Richard. Our son Adrian and the daughter of a friend are in the foreground.

Lorna and Michael with grandson, Oliver, February 2019.

Baylor team 2019: Kathy Hillman, Larisa Seago and Julie deGraffenreid.

all of them here, because such a roster would be unreadable, but this list picks out just a few of them.

Kathy Matchett, a gifted linguist, very quiet in personality and with a soft-spoken Belfast accent, was well organised and produced excellent work still visible today in the calibre of our archived *Documentation Service* and other early publications. She left to join Brother Andrew's Open Doors in May 1974, but was elected to the Keston Council the next year.

Another young person who appeared in 1975 was Alan Scarfe. On a visit to speak at my old college, St Edmund Hall, I went out with him for a meal beforehand. Alan, who was from Yorkshire, was reading theology, but still seeking a direction in his life. He asked whether there might be an opening for him at Keston. I replied, 'No, not unless you know a relevant language.' Alan asked what might be easy and I replied, that with his knowledge of French, Romanian might be possible. He took this to heart and subsequently applied for a British Council scholarship to spend a year as an exchange student at the Orthodox theological institute in Bucharest. This was to change his life in more ways than one, because it was there that he met and later married an American, Donna, who was on student scholarship to study dance.

On his return, he joined Keston and gradually established himself as an expert on Protestants, as well as the dominant Romanian Orthodox Church. At this time Ceauşescu was persuading the world that his brand of communism protected believers, while the exact opposite was happening. Alan saw through this and proved the contrary, both meeting persecuted believers and collecting a wealth of *samizdat*. This was a new field for Keston, albeit a controversial one because of the strength of communist propaganda. Alan exposed these double standards and brought a new dimension to Keston's work. We had rocked the boat again!

Alan later moved permanently to America, for a time becoming Keston's representative in the USA. Later he was ordained into the Episcopal Church and eventually he became Bishop of Iowa.

Mavis Perris began to help me, too, first as a volunteer, having met us through the children at St Nicholas Primary School, Chislehurst, then full-time as my personal assistant, one of the steadiest, most reliable people with whom I worked. She had previously worked as a secretary at the highest level in company boardrooms and was correct in all her dealings with staff, but with the warmest heart. She became a friend and help to the family, as well as bringing the highest professional standard to Keston's administration. After the move to Oxford in 1992 she worked for Aid to the Church in Need for many years. She died in 2018.

Sandy Oestreich, an American Evangelical, joined us and, with her warm open personality and deep faith, made an impact. Under the influence of her committed Christian faith, she inaugurated a short daily prayer for those who wished to attend at eleven in the mornings. She teamed up with Victoria Watts at the end of 1975 to form a publicity department. Despite contrasting personalities, they formed a close friendship. Victoria, too, was an effective communicator and used her acting experience to form a 'Keston Road Show'. In their spare time they wrote scripts developed from *samizdat* documents. They staged these performances in church halls and reached a new audience. Their thespian efforts added another new dimension. Later, she and Alan Scarfe, established a Romanian Aid Fund.

The staff list for 1974 records eighteen people regularly involved, eight full-time, five part-time, four part-time unpaid, and one, Walter Sawatsky, full-time, but paid by the Mennonites. I was on record at the time – in a report to the Council – as working an average of 54 hours a week and I know that the staff were similarly dedicated. We shared an overriding sense of purpose, which the number of volunteers underlined.

A senior person who came as a volunteer and whom we saw for a day most weeks was Shura (never known by her full name of Alexandra) Kolarz, the widow of Walter, who became a trusted adviser and family friend. She made her way to Keston across London from Maida Vale, where she lived, took the suburban train to Bromley South and then a bus to Keston. She never asked for a lift and never failed to appear when she promised to come. Shura was Russian and a Catholic and a career archivist for the Trades Union Congress. She now brought her superb organisational expertise to the formation of a system for our archive. She saved us from chaos, as voluminous materials began to flow into Keston, and her basic system persisted until the Archive moved to Baylor University in 2007.

Some more senior people appeared on the scene. George Patterson (not to be confused with a later Oxford University observer on our Council of almost the same name) had a reputation as a China specialist and for a short time he was 'Director of Asian Studies'. In this role he went to Australia and New Zealand for us on a lecture tour, as interest in our work was growing rapidly there. But controversy dogged his visit. Although he undoubtedly knew a great deal about the Church in China, he kept digressing into political byways, often attracting criticism during his tour.

George wrote an article for the *New Zealand Herald*, which Sir John Lawrence and Peter Reddaway found too political in content. Leonard Schapiro 'expressed profound disagreement' with it. The Council minutes record that I 'apologised for an error of judgement in sending him to Australia and New Zealand'.[9] There was no row about this on the Council, but I had learned another lesson and this was my most chastening experience as Director to date. I would never become involved in China or its politics, much as I wanted to see Keston develop work on Asia. Sir John's letter to George followed two days after the Council meeting, inviting him to leave in terms of exquisite politeness and also giving an insight into the political minefields which Keston was negotiating at the time:

> I think you must certainly realize that the Council has some difficulties about the association of Keston College with any definite political viewpoint, especially if it is polemically expressed. Religion is our subject. We are bound by the expression of our aims and objects which has been accepted by the Charity Commissioners.

---

9   4 June 1975, p. 2.

For this reason, a discussion of politics without putting religious questions right in the centre of the picture and giving most of the space to them is outside our terms of reference. Since CSRC was inaugurated, we have been at pains to establish it as a non-political research organisation. As is your right, you have very definite, strongly held views about the political situation in Asia.

You stated on 4th June that you want to be more politically involved in the future. The Council understands and respects this desire, but feels that the only way to give freedom to express your political views without causing embarrassment to Keston College is to terminate your association with Keston College as Director of Asian Studies.

George's visit to Australia and New Zealand had followed mine in March–April 1974, where I found a lively interest in our work, which would lead to the establishment of several local committees set up to promote what we were doing, spread the factual information which they received from us, and develop local ways of persuading people to become involved. These committees existed with great vigour (though little financial support found its way to us) until the Australian ones all decided to discontinue their work after the collapse of the Soviet bloc in 1989.

My visits to America continued. There were many invitations to speak, but negligible financial support. This problem applied to a lesser extent in the UK. We were non-political and non-denominational. Many potential supporters held back because, either they would have liked to see us join the anti-communist crusade, or to be an evangelical mission, a superior Bible-smuggling organisation. This is how the press sometimes mistakenly portrayed us. Standing back from either type of involvement, we cut ourselves off from potential political or denominational support. Over many subsequent visits to the USA I was to discover the hard truth: that in a very real sense our integrity was our worst enemy.

St Norbert's

As the only non-Catholic on the British board (or any other national board, for that matter) of Aid to the Church In Need (ACN), I was touched by the confidence which the young Dutch administrator of ACN, Antonia Willemsen, showed in me. Ton, as everyone called her, flew to London to talk to me and empowered me to look for a successor for Fr Gosling, who had gone abroad. We soon found a remarkable woman, Sister Catherine Shakespeare, who no longer wore the habit and had been released from residence in her convent to take up outside work, but still kept to her vows. She held the fort as secretary, while we looked for a new Director. Before long we appointed Philip Vickers, who had had a business career, but was looking for a change.

The hunt was also on to find permanent premises for an organisation which, in the UK (as opposed to Germany and the Catholic countries of Western Europe) was not fulfilling its financial potential. Philip and I talked and the idea evolved of housing the staff of ACN, just Philip and Sister Catherine, in the old canteen at Keston. In order to maintain independence of the two organisations, we called the canteen 'St Norbert's' and a short but happy period of close association began. ACN paid for some subdivisions of the large space inside the canteen and the work of both organisations proceeded happily side by side.

The KGB

With the higher profile of Keston and the heyday of Leonid Brezhnev's period of 'stagnation', as Mikhail Gorbachev was later euphemistically to call it, inevitably the KGB began to watch us carefully. I was never aware of any personal intimidation following the failed attempt to recruit me in 1959, but I was naturally a little worried about my family. Also, the Keston building was out of sight of any habitation, other than the former headmaster's adjacent house. This provided a strong reason why we did not try to sell it separately, which we could have done, but we preferred to have someone whom we would nominate living there.

Further, to have installed high-level security would have cost money, which we did not have, and no kind of fencing would have been acceptable on aesthetic grounds: planning permission would not have been forthcoming. We had a beautiful site and felt obliged to improve it, both inside and out, in any way we could.

The only violation of our premises came during these early years. Intruders smashed a window and disabled the burglar alarm, which must have gone off unheard for some time in the middle of the night. They had gained access to the filing cabinets, even breaking open a heavy-duty fireproof one with a crowbar. Papers were strewn all over the place and it took us two days to clear up and re-file the documents which had been disturbed. Yet, as far as we could discover, nothing was missing. The police attributed this to common burglars looking for money, and that was why there was so much attention to the security cabinet. We were never so sure. The KGB would have had ample time to photograph any documents they wanted before leaving them in disarray. Nothing, however, was proved, but suspicions remained. Even if it were the KGB, it is doubtful whether they found much they didn't know already. We always prided ourselves that we were an 'open society', with no secret arm, and that we operated within the law. The most they could have gained was a copy of the mailing list. I feared afterwards that my 1959–60 diary had been a casualty, because I forgot about it at the time and did not see it again for years, but it eventually re-surfaced.

Were we later infiltrated? Many people thought so, but despite the fact that suspicions once, in the 1980s, fell on a young man who was with us for a short time, nothing was ever proved.

However, a vigorous verbal campaign against Keston and me was now well under way. This was partly in so-called 'briefings' given to church delegations and even individual visitors to the Soviet Union. The KGB, through its compromised Christian spokesmen, warned visitors against collaboration with Keston.

Chapter XII
Keston's Heyday

My last visit to Moscow had been in August 1964, after which I was on a blacklist. I applied for visas most years, especially to visit Soviet Central Asia, where I had never been, but the answer was always no. Then came the new enterprise of 'Thomson Winter Holidays', which led to my receiving visas for visits to the Soviet Union again three times, every other year from 1975 to 1979. These were the years of the Helsinki Accords and maybe the Soviet authorities wanted to prove that they were open to allowing 'free movement of people' to illustrate that they meant to fulfil their obligations. Perhaps, more likely, the Soviet Union needed the hard currency from tourists, who might have been turned against such visits if there were widespread visa refusals.

Moscow Again

The trip was short, five days in February 1975, a dull itinerary for anyone who had lived in Moscow. It was memorable, however, for being my last trip to Russia with Gillian. We visited Moscow only and kept entirely within the group, determined to avoid any whiff of controversy. I also hoped to safeguard future visas by not pushing the boundaries on this occasion, even while I was under attack in the Soviet press. Our minimal contact with the Church was a group visit to the Holy Trinity Monastery at Zagorsk. Even to visit familiar places, such as the Kremlin and the Tretyakov Gallery, after a long absence provided a stimulus for future work and to speak Russian again in its proper context was also a joy.

Gillian

Over the next two years we concentrated on the increasing demands of a growing family, holidays at my parents' home in Cornwall, the Philharmonia Chorus and the fulfilling possibilities of foreign lecture tours, but the scene was soon clouded by Gillian's illness in 1977, with her death a year later.

Gillian had been the very essence of goodness and energy in everything connected with the early days at Keston, smoothing over dozens of mini-crises and ensuring that all our affairs were kept in order in the days before there was a proper administration.

It was on one of our trips abroad, to sing with the Philharmonia Chorus in the great Roman theatre at Orange in Provence, that Gillian had a premonition that all was not well. On our return she discovered that she had cancer. The treatment was long drawn out, but unsuccessful, a time, it goes without saying, of emotional difficulty for all of us, not least the children, who were eleven and fifteen when she died.

Gillian's funeral, in Christ Church, Lubbock Road, almost next door to where we were living, was an occasion still vivid in my memory. Members of the Philharmonia Chorus came and sang unforgettably, ending with 'In Paradisum' from Fauré's *Requiem*.

The active social life Gillian had led was reflected in the support we received from a wonderful circle of Chislehurst friends, mostly parents from our children's school, St Nicholas. Mavis Perris was always on hand to help. Friends from the choir also rallied round, but most of all it was the parents who kept us going. Gillian's mother, Ethel Davies, was a tower of strength amidst her grief, as was Norma Ashworth, Gillian's younger sister and only sibling. My mother also helped practically, by her frequent and extended visits from Cornwall. They sustained me and enabled me to keep Keston going at a time when it was developing fast, but needed strong leadership. They helped me concentrate on my work as well as on Karen and Mark, who needed more than I could give them.

Before long a team from Johns Hopkins University, Baltimore, contacted me. There was evidence that a number of people, much higher than the statistical norm, in Spaso House, Moscow, the US Ambassador's residence, had been afflicted with cancer. Would I co-operate with the investigation? I replied yes and gave permission for them to access Gillian's medical records. I never heard any more, but the 2018 biography of Llewellyn Thompson by his daughters, Jenny and Sherry Thompson, raises the issue again. The university had received a large grant to investigate whether some kind of electromagnetic surveillance had affected the health of those who had regularly passed through it. The investigation closed without a conclusion, but the question remains open as to whether Gillian was an unwitting victim of the Cold War.[1]

Russia 1977

My caution in 1975 seemed to work, because a visa was forthcoming two years later for a much more ambitious and daring trip, but in the safe company of Sir John Lawrence. This, too, was a Thomson Winter Holiday, but it included Leningrad and Kiev, with Moscow at the end. The main purpose was to try to make contact with the Vins family in Kiev. Georgi was well into his second prison sentence at the time. We had received his autobiographical manuscript and we wanted the family's permission to publish it. We gave our assurance that, after expenses, the royalties would be retained for him.

We had success beyond our hopes in our mission. We had the address of the unregistered but accessible church which Georgi had founded. Someone there told us where the family lived, but while we were on the premises something unforgettable happened. We were taken through a trapdoor, down into a cellar, where we joined the 'underground church', literally, for the only time in my life. A 'Sunday school' lesson

---

1   Jenny Thompson and Sherry Thompson, *The Kremlinologist* (Johns Hopkins University Press, Baltimore, Maryland, 2018), pp. 181 and 441.

was in progress on a week-day evening and we were welcomed with great warmth by the teacher, who instructed us to tell the whole world what was going on here.

On leaving the lesson, we assured ourselves as best we could that we were not being followed and on the bus we found ourselves with Georgi's eldest daughter, alone, who accompanied us to her mother's house. The conversation was warm and to the point. Nadezhda Vins agreed to our requests in detail and was delighted to hear our proposal about the financial aspect.

Mission accomplished, but problems subsequently arose. We went ahead with publication and Jane Ellis, a new staff member, translated, edited and conflated what were originally two separate manuscripts, under the title, *Three Generations of Suffering*, which was a publishing success.[2]

However, the waters were muddied because Richard Wurmbrand acquired a bootleg copy and went ahead with his own version. After Georgi was released from prison unexpectedly in April 1979 and sent to America he subsequently visited Keston and expressed displeasure at the agreement and wanted the book to be withdrawn from circulation. It was not that we had done anything wrong, but he was dissatisfied with his own manuscripts, having written them under conditions of duress when he could not have access to all his sources. We consulted with Edward England, the publisher, and with great reluctance, we concluded that the honourable course of action would be to accede to Georgi's request. The 'improved' version of which he talked failed to see the light of day, so everyone was a loser.

A further note of sadness came many years later, in April 2002, when Walter Sawatsky took me to visit the now-widowed Nadezhda in Indiana, the only time I saw her in exile. She was a sad, lonely figure, who said she could not remember our visit of 25 years earlier, which had taken place in cloak-and-dagger circumstances. Walter Sawatsky took me to her husband's grave, which was nearby. Nadezhda died soon afterwards.

My third visit was my first to Siberia. Another 'Winter Holiday' took me to Irkutsk and Lake Baikal in March 1979. This time I was bold enough to take some Christian books for designated friends in Moscow. Although we changed planes there on the way out, there was no chance to leave the airport and deliver my cargo. I did telephone my friends, who invited me to celebrate my forty-fifth birthday with them on 19 March, when we were due to make an overnight stopover on the return journey.

So my books successfully reached Siberia, but they had to remain in my room while our group had the experience of walking on the glass-clear waters of the lake and seeing fish frozen in the ice many feet below. On the return journey to Irkutsk there was a scheduled stop. I wandered off to the nearby village church and was immediately greeted by the priest, who begged me for *dukhovnaya pishcha* (spiritual

---

2   Georgi Vins, *Three Generations of Suffering* (Hodder & Stoughton, London, 1976), translated and with introduction by Jane Ellis. There were four translations into foreign languages.

food). I thought of the books in my hotel room. What could I do? How could I let down my Moscow friends?

Instinctively I felt compelled to act. I agreed to meet him at a designated place later that evening. I had a few Russian Bibles and commentaries. I gave him all I had and experienced gratitude such as I have rarely known in my life. But even more unexpected events, two of them, were still to come.

Our next destination was Ulan-Bator, Mongolia, for three days. I had thought of this as an internal border crossing, though, of course, Mongolia was technically an independent country. At the Mongolian customs every suitcase was opened and even the few books for personal reading that I had left were confiscated. My Christian literature would have disappeared to the last volume, if it had still been with me. In Ulan-Bator I called on the British Ambassador, Julian Hartland-Swann, an old acquaintance. He was delighted at the rare appearance of a British traveller and took me to the peasants' market, where every personal possession seemed to be on sale in the desperate attempt to stave off the privations of a brutal winter.

The second event was that, when we returned to Irkutsk, we were taken to a hotel, instead of changing planes and continuing to Moscow, as per schedule. Apparently Moscow's airports were snowed in by a heavy storm and we had to wait. At the hotel we were told there was no permission to leave it. I objected, calling this restriction ridiculous, and led a charge on to the street for an impromptu walk, followed by the other tourists. Permission was granted *post factum*. We waited and eventually had to spend the night in Irkutsk. When we finally reached Moscow, there was just time to change planes and continue to London. Had my precious books been still with me, they would have ended up in the UK, where they had originated.

A significant year for me personally was 1979. Lorna Waterton applied to work with us on hearing an enthusiastic account of Keston from Sally Carter while they were studying in Russia together. Then, by chance during a conference of Open Doors (she was actually attending something else in the same building), someone said, 'You must apply for a job at Keston College'. Later in the year she joined us and showed an immediate empathy with our work, as well as bringing some fresh perspectives from her recent summer in Leningrad. We were married in September 1979 and spent our honeymoon in Poland. The atmosphere was highly charged, following Pope John Paul II's first return visit. There was a palpable sense that change was imminent and we had extraordinary conversations with many Polish intellectuals. We spent our last few days walking in the pristine Tatra mountains.

A Great Team

The first fifteen years or so that we were at Keston College saw the formation of an outstanding team of talented, mainly young, people. They all contributed in their own unique way to the rapid development of our work. It was still funded entirely by small donations from private individuals, supplemented by some modest grants from a few British trusts and foundations, as well as our 'mission' friends (no other major American gift followed the grant from the Ford Foundation).

One can hardly over-estimate the contribution which Jane Ellis made to Keston during these middle years. She came from an evangelical background, but in a few years became a leading expert on developments within the Russian Orthodox Church.

Early on she got to grips with some of the most important documents in Keston's collection, translating and editing *An Early Soviet Saint: The Life of Father Zacharia*, a martyr of the Stalin era who died in 1936.[3] Her study of the Russian Orthodox Church is today quoted as an authoritative source more than thirty years after its publication.[4] This book has no rival as a record of the situation of the Russian Orthodox Church in the last years before Gorbachev's era and the resulting changes. She became the second editor, after Xenia, of *Religion in Communist Lands*.

Jane managed, also, to visit Moscow frequently and it was there, probably, that she felt most at home. She met virtually all the outstanding figures who played a role independent of the Moscow Patriarchate, not least Fr Alexander Men' whom I never managed to meet myself. These contacts were invaluable when she established Keston's Moscow office in the early years of Gorbachev's *perestroika*.

Jane was a fine presenter. In this capacity she visited Australia and New Zealand, where loyalty to her as a person and trust in her judgement rapidly developed. She frequently presented papers at academic conferences in various countries and she was always in demand as a lecturer in the UK.

Peter Reddaway had suggested that the relief agencies aiming to help Russian believers were not always well informed and their aid was not sufficiently targeted. He wanted to see an organisation parallel to and close to Keston, which would benefit from our expertise. We conferred and suggested that Jane might be the person to set this up and she started it on a small scale (unpaid) before she joined the Keston staff. On 27 February 1975 Jane wrote a long memo for circulation to the Council, including these words:

> ARC [Aid to the Russian Church] came into being in August 1973 with the specific purpose of sending direct relief to Orthodox Christians in the Soviet Union. Several parcels were sent through channels made available by recent émigrés. New channels have been opened up by my recent visits to Moscow. The sending of relief may now be divided into two areas of activity: first, sending parcels of clothing through the post. This work is expanding. Secondly, provision of Bibles and Christian literature. My Moscow friends say that while clothing is needed and welcome, the primary need is for books. Clearly, religious books can be taken in only by tourists, and the development of this will be the next key stage in ARC's development.[5]

---

3   Mowbrays, London and Oxford, 1976.

4   *The Russian Orthodox Church: A Contemporary History* (Croom Helm, London and Sydney, 1986).

5   Letter in Keston Archive.

Jane continued by saying that another activity could be sending Christmas cards to Baptist prisoners and their relatives. Although ARC had been involved in organising demonstrations, Jane felt that now others could generate these campaigns, based on Keston's information. She had also been asked by friends in Moscow to produce a newssheet in Russian, which was specifically excluded from Keston's initiatives for the political reasons of the time. There was even a possibility of reproducing *samizdat* book-length texts for secret distribution in Russia. Her request was to rent office space at Keston for developing this activity, which would be administratively easy for her, as she was now a full-time member of Keston staff.

The Council agreed to this as a practical solution to ARC's problems and so it continued for a while, before its staff began to increase and they needed their own separate office. Today this lives on in 'ChildAid', still based in Bromley, which continues work in several parts of the former Soviet Union where needs are great but forgotten, such as Moldova.

Jane had a great vision, both for Keston and for ARC, and she developed leadership qualities. Alas, she developed health problems in her late thirties and died prematurely, aged 47 in 1998 in Oxford. However, having been a leading expert on the Russian Orthodox Church for many years, she left a strong legacy in her own publications, as well as in ARC.

Philip Walters was one of Keston's longest-serving members of staff, joining in 1979 and becoming Head of Research. I first met him in Cambridge, when he was an undergraduate and I went there to lecture. Subsequently he spent a year as a volunteer in Cambodia. For his doctorate in London he worked on the Russian Christian philosophers in the period leading up to the Revolution. His academic background earned him the respect of all. With gifted powers of analysis and a meticulous eye for detail in his editing of others' work, he soon came to play an invaluable role in the ever-larger array of publications. He eventually became editor of *Religion, State and Society*, the successor to *Religion in Communist Lands* (in essence the same publication, but with a new title). Philip delivered impressive lectures, always illustrating a great breadth of reading and insight. His book, *Light Through the Curtain*,[6] is a treasure-trove of spiritual insight, in which he chose excerpts from the *samizdat* writing of a whole range of Eastern European authors. Philip was committed to ecumenism and took over the work of the East–West Relations Advisory Committee from the British Council of Churches after its funding was withdrawn in 1989.

Michael Rowe had worked at the University of Glasgow on Soviet research and was another fluent Russian speaker, joining us in April 1977. His particular field was the Russian Evangelicals and his work at Keston followed that of Walter Sawatsky. Again, in the Keston tradition, his marshalling of facts was impeccable and, on any given day, he would know exactly, according to our records, how many religious prisoners there were in the Soviet Union. He could quote names, prison addresses and articles

---

6   Lion Publishing, Tring, 1985.

of the Soviet Penal Code with instant recall. His further strength was in the regular booklets he produced, five editions in all, listing the details of prisoners which we recorded, as well as a stream of articles for our publications. Towards the end of his time with us he produced an authoritative book on the Russian Evangelicals[7] and his working archive is a permanent legacy of his contribution which the Keston Archive preserves at Baylor University.

Keston's influence began penetrating the world at large with greater vigour and insistence from 1978 with the arrival of Alyona Kojevnikov. Alyona was born of Russian parents in Yugoslavia, where her family found itself living after the fall of the White Army. She was about a year old when they joined the ranks of the hundreds of thousands of dispossessed wandering around Europe with no idea of what would be their ultimate fate. Alyona's earliest memories are of the refugee camp in the American sector of occupied Germany. The family eventually emigrated to Australia in 1950 when she was six years old. She trained as a journalist and previously followed a distinguished career with Radio Liberty in Munich, where she also frequently worked as an interpreter at international conferences. Her linguistic facility was an asset at Keston, both in the telephone conversations with the Soviet Union, which were becoming more frequent and important, but also in her ability to absorb the contents of some new piece of *samizdat* almost instantaneously.

Alyona set up and for several years was in charge of an Information Department, which became almost overnight the most influential section of our work. She chased up journalists and urged them to write more stories about Russia based on our information. Most important of all, she reinvigorated *Keston News Service*, which she despatched regularly by telex, fax and mail, interspersed with on-the-day press releases – or even a telephone call to the BBC – when news of high importance broke.

Alyona's role became high profile, most outstandingly with the release of Irina Ratushinskaya in 1987. Over the years, though, due to her acumen, there were dozens of occasions when Keston was first with the news of an arrest of a leading dissident or release of a prisoner in the Soviet Union. Knowledge of our work increased rapidly worldwide as a result of Alyona's tireless commitment and she managed to combine this, one day a week, with writing and recording a religious news programme to Russia on the BBC, so she was an essential contributor there, too.

Sometimes the 'Left' criticised Alyona for being too one-sided. She made no secret of the fact that she was anti-communist, but to an almost superhuman degree, dealing daily with 'breaking news', she virtually never made a mistake. She would often publish supplementary information, but only occasionally corrections, which were essentially updates when new information became available. What her critics could not stomach was the fact that her work, taken as a whole, was a devastating indictment of the Soviet performance on human rights. She rarely made predictions, but she,

---

7   *Russian Resurrection: Strength in Suffering – A History of Russia's Evangelical Church* (Marshall Pickering, London, 1994).

as certainly as Sir John Lawrence, and indeed myself, was totally confident that the system would eventually fail. In 1990 she asserted her Russian citizenship (under the law of the time) and moved to Moscow to set up from scratch, as its Chief, the first official bureau of Radio Liberty.

Alyona's considerable energies also led her to doubling up as senior librarian. She was joined by Malcolm Walker in May 1980. Keston could scarcely have survived as a viable research institute without his steady hard work over the next 30 years. Malcolm built up a comprehensive knowledge of what the Archive and library contained and – a priceless asset – could find even the most recondite materials when times became more difficult. Most valuable of all, though, was his endless patience and dedication to the needs of the researchers who visited the Archive from all over the world to carry out their personal research.

The only firebrand we ever had at Keston was Alex Tomsky. Alex, a convert to traditional Catholicism from a Jewish background, came to the UK at sixteen, after his parents left Czechoslovakia at the time of the Soviet invasion of 1968. Alex was tri-lingual, being equally fluent in the two languages of his parents, his Czech father and Polish mother. He joined us in the late seventies and left to live permanently in Czechoslovakia in 1989. He was an expert on Marxism, using this in his frequent confrontations with the Left.

Alex believed with passion that communism was doomed and he carried out all his work in that conviction, from which he never wavered. Frequently I had to pick up the pieces and try to restore relations with respected writers in the media, such as, for example, the commentator on Soviet affairs in *The Observer*, Neal Ascherson. Gradually I became aware of other work, which he carried out in a kind of double life. For example, he organised a book export business, not for profit, aiming to support underground intellectuals.

While he was at Keston, however, he was either reacting to events of world-shaking importance in Poland, or standing outside his room in the corridor impressing other staff with his views. He expressed these, too, in a series of brilliant, galvanising lectures, but he never put it all together in monograph form, so his legacy is a series of coruscating articles for our publications on the rising opposition to communism in Catholic circles in Poland and Czechoslovakia.

Despite the conflicts and the question marks raised about Keston's impartiality, Alex's contribution was immeasurable. His great moment came with the election of Karol Wojtyła as Pope John Paul II in 1978. That news, which stunned the world, not least the Kremlin, was initially greeted in the West with incomprehension. Nobody knew who this man was: on St Peter's Square the assembled crowd did not initially even recognise the name. Alex knew the new Pope's background and could produce an immediate character-sketch of the man and what he stood for. Alex already had worldwide contacts with journalists and his briefings filled the world media outlets, radio, TV and newspapers, for days. This was one of Keston's finest moments.

Alex Tomsky could claim, with justification, that he was in at the death of communism. It would be Keston's contention, even today, that there was no single factor which contributed more to the collapse of the system than this election. The Pope's first return visit to Poland in the summer of 1979 led directly to the founding of Solidarity, the independent Christian trade-union movement. Its suppression followed, with the imposition of martial law. This resulted, in 1989, in the Round-Table Conference, leading to power-sharing with communism and its inevitable demise. The Pope never directly intervened politically, but his influence in the collapse of communism was there for the world to see.

Alex was later joined by Grazyna Sikorska, who took over some of his workload. Born in Poland, but resident in London, she had a winning personality and was highly organised. She produced two books of great merit. The first was an account of the life, preaching and martyrdom of Fr Jerzy Popiełuszko, the 'Apostle of Solidarity'.[8] Translated into Polish, Grazyna's was the first book on this fearless young priest and when I visited his grave in Warsaw in April 1993, nine years after his murder, hers was still the only full biography on display. Grazyna went on to write a biography of Fr Franciszek Blachnicki, a much-loved priest in the life of the Polish Church in the Solidarity period, who founded the 'Light and Life' movement.[9] She received a commendation from Pope John Paul II, whose message appears as the Foreword. Grazyna was a writer of clarity and style, both in English and Polish.

This book is designated as 'Keston College Book Number 28', a reminder that Keston had begun to number the books with various publishers that its researchers were producing and which culminated with my book on Gorbachev in 1990, No. 31. This informal series, to which almost every researcher contributed in one way or another, is another lasting testimony to the quality of the 'contemporary history' which Keston scholars produced. These books are abundant evidence of the contribution Keston made to the Russian Orthodox Church in rescuing some of its lost heritage.

A Unique Archive: Lithuania

The work that this team produced is preserved not only in the series of Keston Books, but even more fully in the unending stream of articles which they wrote for our publications. Vying with this as their most important contribution to the church history of the second half of the twentieth century is the assembly of *samizdat* documents, press cuttings, analyses, briefing papers, travellers' tales (often with critical notes appended) and much else preserved in the Archive.

At one time we had 21 members of staff on our payroll, who, if we included part-time volunteers, could read 19 languages between them. Some of the latter covered areas for which we could not possibly have hired professional staff. For example, Nicki Crane, who often visited Albania, learned the language and began to contribute

---

8   Grazyna Sikorska, *A Martyr for the Truth: Jerzy Popiełuszko* (Fount Paperbacks, London, 1985).

9   Grazyna Sikorska, *Light and Life: Renewal in Poland* (Collins, London, 1989).

information to the Archive. No country of the Soviet bloc was left uncovered. We lived on the edge, expanding the staff in preference to building up a financial reserve. Perhaps this contributed to the sense of dedication and commitment which was palpably present among the Keston team. In their work they veered between dogged persistence in pursuit of the truth and occasional flashes of brilliance.

The weakness was Asia, both Soviet Central Asia and China's satellites. We never managed to bring in anyone who knew the Turkic languages of that swathe of Soviet territory. Occasionally we published articles which shed light on the area when the world at large ignored it.

The responsible way in which we had handled our Baptist documents from the outset must have encouraged the Lithuanian Catholic Priests' Association in New York to contact us and ask whether we might do the same for the information they were receiving. Before long we established a regular channel of communication, which also protected us from any need to set up one ourselves directly with Lithuania. With Fr Casimir Pugevičius and his assistant, Ms Ginte Damusis, we forged a productive relationship. However much I sympathised with the desire of the Lithuanian people to be free, if anyone then had told me that this young lady would, in just over a decade, become ambassador of an independent Lithuania to Vienna, I would have laughed in scorn.

In *Land of Crosses* (1979) I concentrated entirely on the religious, as opposed to the political, situation, though I knew from the earliest stages that the two were indivisible. In every one of the twelve chapters I developed Keston's policy of 'being the voice' of those who had no other sounding-board for their views. More than half of the text was devoted to extracts from the documents themselves, particularly their main *samizdat* voice. Far from being clandestine, it tried to put the Lithuanian case urgently before the forum of world public opinion. In Chapter XIII ('Conclusion') I wrote:

> Although this book has concentrated on the affairs of a tiny nation, tucked away in a corner of Europe difficult of access because of political barriers, speaking an ancient language known to scarcely anyone not born into a Lithuanian family, it is about people who have a message for the world. More, they are upholding principles of personal liberty, freedom of conscience and of speech which are not only utterly valid in themselves, but should also be dear to the 'liberal' human-rights conscience of the democratic nations. The fact that their case is not better known is a comment on the selectivity of that conscience.[10]

That was a plea which seemed to have gone unheeded at the time (not unexpectedly). There were hardly any reviews, the publisher, as well as the nation, being small and little known. Frequently our journalists would deal out the insult of calling Lithuanian sportsmen (basketball players, for instance) 'Russians'. The Foreign Office, which

10   Bourdeaux, *Land of Crosses*, p. 323.

did not officially recognise the legitimacy of the Soviet occupation, refused to let its ambassadors visit the republic, so knew little about it.

While I was in the later stages of writing, news came through of the election of the Polish Pope. I could not include a full consideration of the possible consequences for Lithuania, but it was already becoming clear in my mind that a combination of religious revival and nationalism could possibly be a detonator for an eventual explosion in the Soviet Union's republics. Before long I would be forecasting this with confidence, but I never, in my wildest dreams, imagined that a political upheaval would take place with only a minimum of bloodshed, nor that I would one day visit Lithuania as a guest of the President.

Keston's Worldwide Ministry

Keston's objectives and influence were becoming international. According to my records, during Keston's heyday I travelled abroad 94 times on behalf of the work, these visits taking me to all continents except South America.

By 1981 I needed a break from the day-to-day work of Keston. Two invitations came my way, one to lecture at a summer school at Fuller Theological Seminary, Pasadena, California, and a second to spend a term as Shelby C. Davis Visiting Professor in Soviet Studies at Wellesley College, Massachusetts. I found both of these teaching opportunities rewarding, though later I felt regret that I could not spend more of my life in contact with students. I learned how to present and pare down the multi-faceted material on all aspects of contemporary religion which I had at my fingertips as a result of the work I had now been doing for sixteen years. Both Fuller and Wellesley College treated Lorna and me so well that we left with the happiest memories of life in an American university.

In 1985 I had the opportunity of working for a month in East Africa under a church-to-church programme put in place by the Church Missionary Society. My brief in Kenya, Zambia and Zimbabwe was to bring to local theological colleges and other educational institutes something of the life of Russian believers. It was a unique and rewarding experience with a spontaneous response everywhere that I visited.

During later trips to the USA a few people emerged who became committed supporters of Keston and helped set up and maintain a branch of our work there, registered as a tax-exempt organisation. Myrna Grant, who taught at Wheaton College, became a popular author on Russian Christians. She had achieved special success with her children's books in the 'Ivan' series, in the 1970s, one of which she dedicated to my son, Mark, when he was eight.[11]

Peter and Anita Deyneka, of the Slavic Gospel Association, whom I saw occasionally at the secret East European Missions conferences, became wonderful friends. Later they set up 'Peter Deyneka Ministries' and my contact with them over many years showed just how closely Keston and I could collaborate with an American evangelical

---

11   Myrna Grant, *Ivan and the Secret in the Suitcase* (Tyndale House Publishers, Wheaton, Illinois, 1975).

mission. They both demonstrated a clear vision and sensitivity to other Christian traditions.

Dr Kent Hill emerged as a fine writer and university teacher on Russian church affairs, a man of impeccable judgement in an America which did not take easily to the defence of religious liberty in the Soviet Union. Competent in Russian, Kent lived in Moscow with his family for a period soon after the collapse of the Soviet Union and taught church/state relations at Moscow State University. A close friend of Keston since the late 1970s, Kent utilised its archival materials in his book on religion in Russia.[12] In 1992, he became President of Eastern Nazarene College in Massachusetts. Nine years later, Kent was selected to lead the U.S. Agency for International Development's Bureau for Europe and Eurasia. For many years, Kent advised Keston on all aspects of its work in America.

I made five visits to Australasia, with extensive internal travel and a heavy lecturing schedule. Our state committees were flourishing and they arranged many interesting and challenging meetings. The most important opportunity was to deliver the Moorhouse Lectures in Melbourne, which resulted in another book, *Ten Growing Soviet Churches*.[13] In New Zealand our most vigorous ally was the Revd Ray Oppenheim, an American, who was a fount of knowledge about Russia. He had been the first Episcopal Chaplain in Moscow, but his time in the Soviet Union had ended in tragedy. Ray's wife died in a car crash and he was left with two broken legs. He recovered, but retained a suspicion that the KGB may have been involved. A lorry had come straight out of a side street, directly into his path, while he was driving on a completely clear road.

Ray had been given to understand that he would, on return, take over the role that Paul Anderson had created at the National Council of Churches, New York, but they withdrew from this, doubtless as a result of the growing ecumenical determination not to employ non-Russian experts in their dealings with the Soviet Union. Ray abandoned this career path, relinquished his US passport to become a New Zealand citizen, and became an expert on cricket, rugby and the local wines. His love of Russia, however, persisted. He advised the New Zealand Government on Soviet affairs. For Keston, he chaired our committee, wrote articles, did broadcasts and organised lectures. He was one of the most stimulating companions I had and a great friend. He invited me to come to New Zealand to lecture in 2002. I knew by this time that he was terminally ill. He died before my arrival, aged 59. It was then my privilege to speak at his memorial service.

---

12   Kent R. Hill, *The Soviet Union on the Brink: An Inside Look at Christianity and Glasnost* (Multnomah Press, Portland, Oregon, 1991).

13   Marc Europe, Northampton, 1987.

Mrs Thatcher and Other Politicians

Keston's international profile reached its peak in the early 1980s: Mrs Thatcher at Chequers, the Centre for Policy Studies, the Templeton Prize, private lunch with the Queen – all these events came in quick succession.

Since the first invitation to the Foreign and Commonwealth Office under David Owen in 1977, my contacts with diplomats had grown. The Helsinki Accords of 1975, with their subsequent review conferences, had made provision for NGOs (non-governmental organisations) to play a full part in the monitoring of human rights. The FCO focused on this and invited Keston on numerous occasions to take part in briefings. One especially interesting day conference was an occasion when all the British ambassadors from Eastern Europe were assembled and I had the opportunity of presenting my perspectives to them. This was a far cry from the 1960s, when the 'Bourdeaux view' was not welcome in the Foreign Office.

Then, in the summer of 1983, there was a summons from Downing Street itself. Could I write a briefing paper for Mrs Thatcher on human rights and religious liberty in the Soviet Union? This would be put together with short papers from seven other academic experts who would be invited to Chequers to present these to the Prime Minister in person. Professor Michael Kaser, later to be Chairman of Keston after it moved to Oxford, would co-ordinate the contributions and stitch them into a 'seamless garment'; we would have to present our sections, but not read them, as the PM and her officials would already have done so. We spent the previous night (7 September 1983) at the Spread Eagle Hotel in Thame, Oxfordshire.

There was an instantaneous meeting of minds over the dinner, when we discussed Soviet politics, military matters, economics, international diplomacy and much else. The common factor among us was that – as Mrs Thatcher would soon point out – not one of us was a journalist. We were all noted, she said, for having devoted our lives to our subject of expertise. Two cars came to collect us the next morning and take us the short distance to Chequers.

On the day of our arrival at Thame there had been a disaster: a Korean airliner had been shot down over Siberia, with a loss of all on board. The Soviets were alleging that the plane had been on a spying mission; everyone else was saying that this typified Soviet paranoia and disregard of human life. Mrs Thatcher began her introduction by saying that this disaster must not dominate our thinking: we must act as though the incident had not taken place. This was difficult and inevitably sharpened the atmosphere, but the PM went on to tell us that she had been learning about Soviet affairs during her first period in office; now, re-elected in 1983, she wished to embark on a programme which would bring about change. She was working with President Reagan on a new approach to international affairs.

Mrs Thatcher said that she wanted us to put our viewpoints forcibly, so that there would be no ambiguity. 'I want you to present me with an agenda for change,' she said. 'If you don't force me to disagree with you, you will have failed!'

The atmosphere round the table was electric, despite the laid-back presence of Sir Geoffrey Howe, Foreign Minister, alongside his advisers, including Lord Armstrong, Cabinet Secretary, and several others.

During our initial presentations Professor Archie Brown (St Antony's College, Oxford) said that change in Kremlin political circles was inevitable and that this would happen soon. In running through the list of those who might replace the current gerontocracy, he mentioned the name of Mikhail Gorbachev, to Mrs Thatcher an unknown figure. Before long, still with no international profile, he was in the UK with a delegation from the Supreme Soviet and the PM invited him to Chequers, the beginning of a series of events which would change the world. When Konstantin Chernenko died in 1985, she flew to Moscow for the funeral. While she was there Gorbachev was named as his successor and Mrs Thatcher, building on her existing relationship with him, was the first foreign leader to meet him in private. Indeed, no other Western leaders were present in Moscow.

Mrs Thatcher asked me what my specific advice would be. I said that, when there were high-level visits to countries of the communist bloc, they should take into account the 'dissidents', whom I preferred to call democrats. This should not short-change the endless meetings with communist officials, but other meetings, probably involving more junior officials, should take place as well.

So it was that, some time later, when Sir Geoffrey Howe visited Prague, one of his officials ducked out of an official dinner and went instead to call, unannounced, on Vaclav Havel, who had recently been released from prison and was under house arrest. Assuming this was an official part of the visit, Havel's minders allowed the diplomat access, Britain therefore becoming the first country to recognise the leader of the unofficial opposition. Soon after, a similar visit to Poland led to meetings with the Solidarity leaders, many of whom had recently been in prison.

We broke off for lunch, a formal sit-down affair, and I was surprised to find myself sitting next to Mrs Thatcher. She asked a stream of questions about my personal experiences in the Soviet Union. She said I had become a member of this group because she had often heard me on the radio on the *Sunday* programme. I later heard that I was the only person the PM had asked for by name and that I (so I was told) replaced someone else who was on the original list.

This led to a close relationship with Mrs Thatcher. I received numerous subsequent invitations to Chequers and No.10. One notable occasion was a reception for Vice-President Bush, Sr., at Chequers, during which the PM asked me to deliver a specific briefing to Mr Bush, as he was about to go to Moscow.

I also became a member of the sub-group on Eastern Europe of the Centre for Policy Studies under the chairmanship of George Urban, the distinguished Hungarian émigré commentator on East-European affairs, whose incisive mind ensured that our discussions were animated and to the point. Any recommendations we made would be forwarded to Downing Street.

This period culminated, astonishingly close to the collapse of the communist regimes in Eastern Europe, in my being invited to be an official FCO representative at what turned out to be the last Helsinki review conference, over a whole month in June 1989. Although all the communist officials were stony faced, we were all aware of the imminence of major change. I would later reflect that, in a way more influential than I could ever have imagined, Keston had played a role in the collapse of communism. Perhaps, most of all, it was our encouragement to the believers of Eastern Europe which was effective. We had 'been their voice'. It was this which received recognition in 1984 in a totally unexpected way.

The Templeton Prize

On 4 February 1984 I was at a conference centre, Hydepark, near Doorn, in Holland. A telephone call came through and a message was delivered: 'A Mr Forker called and he will telephone you later.' I thought nothing more of it. Two days later I was back at my desk at Keston and at 1 p.m. my phone rang. 'Michael Bourdeaux? This is Wilbert Forker here. Are you sitting down? I'm going to rearrange your schedule for the next few months. You have won the Templeton Prize for 1984.'

This was impossible: a joke it had to be. The Templeton Prize was for 'Progress in Religion' in those days, not for personal qualities or holiness! However, every March, I had admired the prize, as another well-known name was added to the roster: Mother Teresa of Calcutta was the first; the list also included Billy Graham and Dame Cicely Saunders. I couldn't possibly be in such company. But there was another factor which made it impossible.

The previous year there had been great excitement when the prize was awarded to Alexander Solzhenitsyn. Archbishop Runcie had invited me to dinner with him at Lambeth Palace and for the first time I was on the guest list for the prize giving, too. Now I expressed my disbelief on the phone. Solzhenitsyn's win last year had surely disqualified for years anyone else whose interest was in religion in Russia. 'On the contrary,' Wilbert Forker replied. 'Each year is a one-off and candidates are considered entirely on their merits, without reference to anyone who's previously won it. We want you to come to New York next month for the announcement, the Duke of Edinburgh will make the presentation in May at Buckingham Palace, you will lecture at the Guildhall, where there will be a reception, and then later in the year we would like you to come to the Bahamas as a guest of John Templeton himself. By the way, the prize is worth £140,000 and the money will belong to you personally, not to Keston College. You will, of course, keep all this confidential until the announcement in New York.'

Keep it confidential? In front of a highly motivated staff who were sensitive to atmosphere? Caroline Andrews, my personal assistant at the time, caught me, on the rebound, virtually speechless. Lorna was there and said I must confirm all this by ringing back, which I did. There was no mistake. Caroline immediately had to start rearranging my timetable and booking the flight to New York. How could she cover up the truth while she cancelled several speaking engagements? Noel Doubleday, our Development Director, had to replace me at an important public meeting. Confidentiality had to be broken. Mavis Perris, the Keston secretary, made everything happen at the right time and in order. I couldn't suddenly start cancelling arrangements without her knowledge.

However, this tiny group kept it all admirably secret until the day appointed and approved by Wilbert Forker for the staff to be told: 24 February. Champagne and a buffet had appeared on a table in the library before the old school bell, still in existence, summoned the staff. Caroline wrote of the staff's puzzlement: 'Was the Pope coming to Keston? Had a millionaire bequeathed his fortune to the work? It was Anne Walters who finally identified the reason for the celebration. The staff were elated by the wonderful news and there was great excitement.'

A letter had already arrived from Nassau, confirming the arrangements in some detail. I was to arrive in New York on 27 February and stay at the United Nations Plaza Hotel for two nights. The award ceremony and associated events would be on 14–15 May and the visit to the Bahamas was still to be arranged.

On the TWA flight out (not business class!) I ordered myself a half-bottle of champagne. Wilbert Forker met me at the airport and gave me a full briefing, but this was followed by a completely free day on 28 February to cope with jetlag. On the 29th, however (it was a leap year), the New York events came so thick and fast that it was difficult to keep a clear head.

In some ways it was a strange day. It is not only with hindsight that I felt that there was something low-key about the tone of the events. They followed what was by now a well-worn pattern and the various hosts had been expecting someone much more high profile.

First there was a press conference at the Church Centre of the United Nations at 11 a.m. This was not particularly well attended and, of the American press, only the *New York Times* ran any sort of story. They summarised my statement in one sentence: there had been 'an absolute decline in the degree to which religious liberty is permitted' in the Soviet Union, a summary so bland as to be almost meaningless, and continuing by saying that 'Keston College Center [is] not a college in the usual sense, [but] monitors religious developments in communist countries.' The rest of the article named the others on the platform and that was it.

I was to discover later that the press as a whole, not least in the UK, were cool towards the Templeton Prize. They felt that John Templeton's claims that he had designated it as a 'Nobel Prize' in religion, as there was not one, were self-promoting and unhelpful. In more recent years the prize has received greater acceptance, and therefore more publicity, in the press.

Even stranger was the tone of some of the speeches. One has to remember that at this time the ecumenical movement worldwide was deeply involved in some kind of 'reconciliation' with the Soviet Union, however one-sided this was. I have already quoted some of the divisive effects of this, but for the moment it is enough to mention

Claire Randall, the General Secretary of the World Council of Churches, who spoke. Sadly, there seems to be no record of what she said and I did not have a copy even at the time. She mentioned me in her introductory sentence and followed this by speaking for some ten minutes about how wonderful was the National Council of Churches' policy towards Moscow, paving the way for a new world order, in which the evil of capitalism would disappear. It occurred to me at the time how deeply distasteful it must have been for her to be there and how the award to me went against just about everything she stood for. The other speakers offered genuine congratulations, but not one seemed to be properly informed about the work of Keston and none of them followed up by expressing any particular interest. They were Archbishop Iakovos, Primate of the Greek Orthodox Church in America, Bishop Joseph O'Keefe, acting administrator of the Roman Catholic Archdiocese of New York, and (with some warmth) Rabbi Arthur Schneier, of the Appeal of Conscience Foundation.

We all crossed the road to the UN building, where there was a lunch for the speakers, with five or six other people. Afterwards, before leaving for my plane, I had a few hours spare and decided to call at 475 Riverside Drive, the headquarters of the National Council of Churches, where I imagined I still had some friends. Paul Anderson was no longer there, Blaho Hruby was genuinely away, but I found the room where the 'East European Desk' was situated to be entirely empty. A secretary in an adjacent room said that they had all been called away on urgent business. I later discovered that their absence was 'diplomatic', in order to avoid an embarrassing conversation. I'm not sure that we had a single new enquiry about Keston's work as a result of this visit to New York.

The reaction to the news in the UK was more genuinely enthusiastic. When it came to the time of the actual award, Lord Coggan, the now-retired Archbishop of Canterbury, attended, but few other church leaders. In the *Sunday Times*[14] John Whale made much of the Templeton's description of me in their briefing pack as 'a mild, soft-spoken, ruddy-cheeked baker's son from a remote mining region in south-west England'. Well, at least the 'baker's son' was accurate. Whale continued by saying that I had won the prize not for my 'ruddy cheeks, but for starting and running the Centre for the Study of Religion and Communism, which now operates from a disused Church-of-England primary school in a Kentish wood'. All this did make me think how provincial and distant from the establishment I was. The dear old *Camborne and Redruth Packet* was obviously totally genuine when its big headline stated, 'Top prize for baker's son'.

Paul Oestreicher wrote a strange letter. He congratulated me on my achievement, which he said was well merited. However, I was 'blind in one eye'. What I could not see with the other was the enormous achievement of socialism. He signed himself 'Your friend, partially sighted – in both eyes'.

---

14   4 March 1984.

There were some notable absences among the tributes, for example, the BBC Radio 4 *Sunday* programme, for which I had done so much work over the previous decade. I might have expected that *The Observer*, too, would have had something to say. *The Times*, however, printed two splendid articles, the first, a long one, appeared on what happened to be my fiftieth birthday.[15] This was an anonymous survey of the areas covered by our work, concluding, in reference to Russian believers, 'For people such as these, publicity and support in the West are the main hope. The award of the Templeton Foundation Prize for 1984 to Mr Michael Bourdeaux, the founder and director of Keston College, who has done so much to help believers in the Soviet bloc, is a welcome acknowledgement of the importance of the work undertaken by him and his colleagues.'

A feature article, also anonymous, with photograph, followed a month later.[16] It concluded: 'Keston just watches and witnesses it all, passing on its knowledge to those who want to know. And occasionally the post brings a letter from some communist land with nothing more to say than, "Thank God for Keston College".'

Perhaps, though, it was the reaction of the *Church Times* which gave me the greatest satisfaction. As mentioned previously, Bernard Palmer had constantly championed our work. Now he wrote:

> Normally, when a man is ordained into the ministry of the Church of England, he can expect to serve a parish or (if his talents for leadership are exceptional) a diocese; but it is the Church's privilege to offer men with unusual vocations unusual opportunities to follow them. They may become monks or missionaries, chaplains or national secretaries, teachers or charity organisers – or something more unusual.
>
> This week the warm congratulations due to the Rev. Michael Bourdeaux on the prestigious award of the Templeton Prize for Progress in Religion must be largely personal, for he is very much an individual who has had the courage to carve out the work of his life in response to his own vision of duty; but the congratulations – in which the *Church Times* is especially proud to share, as he has for many years been one of our own valued contributors – may rightly be accompanied by thanksgiving that it has proved possible to release this exceptionably able and talented priest in his call to conduct and organise studies of religion under Communism.
>
> Under his leadership, and fired by his example, Keston College has become world-famous for the quality of its accurate information and independent, forthright comment. In a field where careless research can do great damage, a commentary both truthful and sensitive has been sustained since 1970; and there is plenty of hard evidence that such publicity has deterred persecution – not perhaps as often as all Christians or other lovers of freedom would wish, but

---

15   19 March 1984.

16   'Beacon in a twilight world', 21 April 1984.

still often enough to make these researches and deliberately timed revelations of far more than academic interest.[17]

Tributes from friends, former teachers and public figures flooded in. I must mention Ella Veale, my primary school teacher at Praze, who wrote 45 years after having taught me and who I had thought was dead: 'I am so glad to have been connected with you in those early days and I would like to feel that in some small way I may have been able to help you.' That she surely did and few tributes were more moving.

Dr J. N. D. Kelly, formerly my tutor and now retired as Principal of St Edmund Hall, wrote to say, 'It's the most exciting, and encouraging, news I've heard for years.' Archbishop Runcie expressed a 'whoop of joy'. I received other letters from Cardinal Basil Hume, Sir Immanuel Jakobovits, the Chief Rabbi, and my MP, Roger Sims, backed by a Cornish MP, David Mudd, who put down a supportive motion in the House on 25 April. Alexander Solzhenitsyn, writing in Russian from Cavendish, Vermont, underlined that this award once again drew attention to the 'barbaric persecution of religion in the communist countries'.

Mrs Thatcher personally signed her letter: 'Under your Directorship, the scrupulous fairness and accuracy of Keston College's studies and bulletins about religious life in communist countries has become a by-word. Your reports give us all profound food for thought. They reveal starkly how great is the darkness which descends upon human societies when governments attempt, by force, to extinguish their citizens' religious aspirations and beliefs... Indeed, the light of this costly Christian witness, which your Bulletins record so vividly, is a sharp challenge to us in the West.'[18]

In April, Keston held a reception in London at which Mrs Thatcher was the principal speaker. She drew attention to the role played by the staff of Keston, without whom there would have been no award. I constantly reiterated at press conferences and in personal conversation that the prize should have gone to the whole staff of Keston (as the Nobel Peace Prize sometimes goes to an organisation), for without their integrity and hard work I could not even have begun to achieve such status for what we did. Even more deserving, though, was the bravery of persecuted believers in the communist world and I put this passionately at the end of my acceptance speech on 15 May: 'In the very truest sense, the Templeton Prize has been awarded not to me nor to Keston College, but to believers under communism. Theirs is the '"progress in religion". The prize goes especially to those who have sacrificed liberty – and some even life itself – for their faith. It is for them that I speak.'[19]

If I had the retrospective power to change those words, thirty-five years after the event, I would not wish to alter a syllable.

How did the prize come my way? How did I even make the short-list from among the approximately three thousand nominations that Wilbert Forker said he had

17 *Church Times* editorial, 2 March 1984.
18 Keston Archive.
19 *The Templeton Prize 1984* (Lismore Press, Grand Cayman, 1984) pages not numbered.

received? The process is, of course, secret, but the initial selection must be done at the Templeton office. Then a refined number of dossiers go to the judges. Their names are published and I know that I was fortunate that two of the eight would have known my work and been certain supporters. They were Lord Coggan and Bishop Michael Mann, the Dean of Windsor. I later 'overheard' one or two confidences. The former Archbishop much later told me that, in the pre-final vote, the final short-list had been reduced to two. The judges never actually met: it was, rather strangely, all done by correspondence. Before the final vote, each had to write in support of one or the other and Lord Coggan said he had never expressed himself with more urgency in his life. American Senator, Orrin Grant Hatch, from Utah, had also warmly supported me, whispered Wilbert Forker, but I never found out who had come second in the voting, nor how the others had voted. They included Sir Lynden O. Pindling, Prime Minister of the Bahamas, the Grand Duchess Josephine of Luxembourg, and Mrs Anwar Sadat, widow of the recently murdered President of Egypt. The Templeton officials always went for big names and I sometimes wondered how much time these illustrious people had to go through the dossiers. However, come to a decision in my favour they did and I was shortly to be the possessor of £140,000.

Claridge's Hotel was the hub of the events of 14 and 15 May and it was there that Lorna and I stayed for two nights, along with the Templeton Prize officials and many of their friends, who make the journey annually from the United States to be present for the occasion. It was here that I first met John – later Sir John – Templeton, donor of the prize. He was eligible to use the title, because he had British citizenship and a Bahamian passport. I was assured that he did not interfere in the judging process of the prize which he had so lavishly endowed. He specifically stated on many occasions that it was deliberately intended to be larger than the Nobel Prize, because religion was the greatest of all subjects. Indeed, I found myself in the *Guinness Book of Records* the next year as the holder of, in financial terms, the world's most valuable prize.

There was a reception at the House of Lords on 14 May, followed the next morning by a press conference at Claridge's chaired by Jenny Robertson, who had written a book about our work. In an informal style she had described the mission of Keston and some of the characters on the staff who, at that time, were driving our work forward and expanding its horizons.[20]

After lunch we went to Buckingham Palace, where the Duke of Edinburgh received us in the Chinese Drawing Room. It was rather a shame that there was no invitation to either of my children or to my parents to accompany us. How my father would have loved it when, at the very beginning, Wilbert Forker introduced the 'informal' occasion rather stiffly by saying that 'Michael Bourdeaux is the first Englishman to be awarded the Templeton Prize'. The Duke broke in, 'He's not English, you know, he's Cornish'. My father would have gone up to the Duke and slapped him on the back if he had been

---

20   *Be Our Voice: The Story of Michael Bourdeaux and Keston College* (Darton, Longman and Todd, London, 1984).

there. There had been a *Scots*man as one of my eleven predecessors (Professor Thomas Torrance in 1978) and an English *lady*, (Dame Cicely Saunders, in 1981).

The Duke then addressed Lorna in mock solemnity, handing over the cheque for £140,000: 'Don't spend it all on the housekeeping, Lorna!' Everyone present enjoyed the informality of the occasion, which was such a contrast to the solemnity of the public event.

On presentation of the cheque, I became rich beyond comprehension, but only for a day. Donald Sly, the Keston treasurer, had organised a new account in a Mayfair bank. After the Palace, I met Donald and together we paid the cheque in and made the Bishopsdown Trust a reality. I set up Bishopsdown as a family trust which would enable me, as Chairman, to direct donations to three causes which were central in my life. First would be Keston College, or anything connected with religion in Eastern Europe of which the trustees approved; second, music, especially local or amateur music, with choral singing highlighted; thirdly, disabled sport – I wanted to give some disadvantaged people the opportunity of participating in competitive sport, as I had gained such enjoyment from active participation over my whole life.

Later, in difficult times, the 50% of the accrued capital which I handed over to the administration of Keston was a lifeline and it helped support the ongoing research work in Russia in the twenty-first century. The other half, with the chairmanship now passed to my son Adrian, still supports disabled sport, as well as musical events mainly in Oxford, but also in Cornwall. We have given away money to all these causes over the years, but the invested capital has grown and both the funds flourish.

The limousine which had taken us to the Palace in the rain conveyed us on to the Guildhall. The weather had not deterred some nine hundred people from attending: teachers from the past, colleagues, friends, family, politicians, some church leaders and – most important of all – a swathe of Keston supporters, whom I was able to thank in person for their wonderful contribution over fifteen years to Keston's work.

The text of my speech, lasting much longer than the 25 minutes which Wilbert had originally requested, was published in full. It was not only a résumé of my life's work and guiding philosophy: it was also, uniquely for me, because I did not much indulge in prophecy, a manifesto for the future. With passion, I tried to demolish some of the nostrums of the time. The first was the phrase 'the Soviet people'. I said: 'The phrase itself is a misnomer. When I look at the complex ethnic map of the Soviet Union I see Lithuanians, I see Jews, I see Ukrainians and Armenians, yes, I see a myriad of Muslims and of Russians. I don't see "Soviets" and when I hear some such phrases as "the aspirations of the Soviet people" I know that we're in the realm of "newspeak".'[21] I expect that this phrase came to mind because we were in the middle of 1984. I was, however, bold enough to suggest, for the first time in my life publicly, that the days of the Soviet Union were numbered.

---

21   *The Templeton Prize* (Scottish Academic Press, Edinburgh, 1988).

I was already beginning to formulate my conviction that a combination of religion and nationalism might bring down the Soviet system: 'I see an empire in the process of decay, because there's no binding loyalty which will keep it together. The Red Army, not Marxism-Leninism, provides its cement. Sixty years, many purges and a world war on from the death of Lenin, the subject peoples retain their individuality, they retain their hopes. They still identify themselves not just by language and a few attractive folk dances. Religion strikes the deepest chord of all in the hearts of the people who will never accept Moscow domination along with enforced atheism.'[22]

The visit to the Bahamas, which followed in October, was the culmination of the ceremonies themselves. I was officially the guest of John Templeton and his wife at Lyford Cay, though Lorna and I stayed in a hotel in Nassau. I preached in the Anglican cathedral, where the dean received me expansively, with the words that I was 'old enough to use the prize wisely, but young enough to enjoy it'. He made me reflect on the fact that I was the youngest to have received the prize, and I believe, 35 years later, that I still am. There was a succession of receptions. The first was hosted by the Prime Minister (who had been a Templeton judge); then the Governor-General invited us to the mansion once occupied by King Edward VIII during the war, to keep him away from international affairs after his abdication. We managed to take a short holiday, before returning to give a lecture at Chatham House two days later.

That's another story, though. The British Airways plane had to make an emergency landing in Bermuda and we were 'guests' of the airline for 24 hours, with a beautiful hotel and a lovely island tour thrown in. I failed to make the lecture, though, and Philip Walters kindly gave it from a written text in my absence. I suppose this was the penalty for taking on too much.

After all this, life would never be quite the same again.

---

22   Ibid.

Chapter XIII
Ecumenical Relations

While still at St Albans, Bishop Robert Runcie had visited Keston. Unknown to us, he had already accepted the invitation to succeed Donald Coggan and was clearly anxious to form a personal impression of our work. Later, just after he had taken up office, he telephoned me at home for a lengthy discussion, though there was never a follow-up to this. Before his consecration, he had criticised the Soviet Union for its invasion of Afghanistan, which made his personal relations with the Moscow Patriarchate difficult, subservient as it was to the regime. Although he was drawn to the Orthodox Church, these relations never recovered. In 1983 he invited me to a private dinner at Lambeth Palace with Alexander Solzhenitsyn. After his retirement he wrote me a letter, saying that he hoped to be able to support us more openly now that he had left Lambeth. I never fully understood the rationale of this, but he was as good as his word and gave the most delightful introduction to my BBC Radio 4 broadcast based on the worship of the Russian Orthodox Church in Smolensk on the last Sunday of 1999, marking the Millennium. This turned out to be one of the last public statements he made before his death.

'*Michael Bourdeaux – u Vas plokhoi image!*' 'Michael Bourdeaux – you have a bad image.' The visiting bishop from the Moscow Patriarchate used the English word 'image' for effect and pronounced it with an ingratiating smile. He was in Canterbury for the enthronement of George Carey as Archbishop in April 1991. Meeting him at the reception, I had hoped for a different tone, perhaps one even recognising the contribution Keston had made to defending the Russian Orthodox Church during the persecution of the previous decades. I was shocked that the 'image' generated by the KGB persisted into better times. Perhaps the bishop had passed on a quiet word of disapproval to Lambeth Palace; perhaps not. However, this was a warning that, even in new times, we would not be party to the innermost circle of Anglican policy-making when relations with Russia were concerned.

Reviewing my relations with the Anglican Church in retrospect, I feel that, despite the infrequency of meetings with Lambeth Palace, grass-roots contacts with my own Church were more than positive. During the formative years of Keston I had many invitations from around the country to speak. Invariably I was warmly received at all levels and often the bishop would be involved. Then, much later, honours were bestowed: an honorary canonry at Rochester Cathedral from Bishop Michael Nazir-Ali in 1990 and a Lambeth Doctorate of Divinity from Archbishop George Carey in 1996, both of which meant a great deal to me personally. Once Dr Carey did invite me to Lambeth for a briefing before he went to Poland. After a short but lively and most useful conversation, he turned to his then-adviser on foreign relations, Canon Stephen Platten, and said, 'We really must make more use of Michael'. I thought to myself, 'More use? Lambeth has hardly ever made any use of me at all.'

Curiously enough, I spent more time talking to Roman Catholic leaders than to Anglicans. I once had a private and productive lunch with Cardinal Heenan, then Archbishop of Westminster, and his adviser, Monsignor George Leonard, who alerted me to a fund at their disposal which, under conditions of secrecy, could support Keston. This contribution, to the tune of some £10,000, continued for many years and was one of the props which helped us develop our work. Subsequently there were occasional useful meetings with his successor, Cardinal Basil Hume. When he visited Ethiopia in 1984 and saw the famine, he reported on it in the national press. I was caught unprepared during a radio interview on another topic, but I knew that General Mengistu's agricultural policies were partly responsible for this disaster and I said so. Cardinal Hume was furious with me, because he thought I had undermined him. However, before long we patched up our relations.

On my visits to Rome I was received by senior officials, including Cardinal Casaroli, Secretary of State, who guided policy on Eastern Europe. Rome, in those days, was home to heroic anti-communist bishops, all of whom had, in one way or another, opposed the atheist policies of the new regimes. News about our work had circulated in the Vatican and my meetings with exiled figures, confessors of the faith, were personally inspiring. Cardinal Slipyj and Archbishop Beran applauded the ideas I had for the future work of Keston, as Cardinal Mindszenty did the emerging organisation.

The World Council of Churches

In my day, as a theological student, the goal of Christian unity pervaded my thoughts and my early motivation in building up my relations with the Russians was ecumenical. Indeed, this ideal has never left me and I am infinitely saddened that my lifetime has seen so very little progress towards unity. Now I feel we are further away from unity with the Orthodox Church than when I was ordained in 1960. However, my contacts with the ecumenical movement were constant, as Keston's work developed. Although the lines often crossed, it is easier to follow the narrative if I separate them and begin with the World Council of Churches (WCC), then follow this with my work for the British Council of Churches (BCC). The negatives in the first often explain reservations I had about the second.

My own attitude to the WCC was coloured by the lack of support that the great ecumenist, Fr Gleb Yakunin, received from Geneva. After serving a ten-year ban from exercising his priesthood by the head of his own Church for systematically exposing the Soviet persecution of religion in the Khrushchev era, he renewed his ecumenical work with an even more focused initiative: he prepared a report for the Fifth General Assembly of the WCC in Nairobi (1975). His subsequent arrest and imprisonment, followed by the events surrounding the Sixth General Assembly in Vancouver (1983), motivated me to study the whole issue and present my observations in public. This I did at a lecture prepared for Chatham House in 1984 and later published.[1] It is on this that I base much of this subsequent report.

From its foundation until 1961, the Moscow Patriarchate and the Soviet Press represented the World Council of Churches more or less as a Protestant agency, reflecting American values. Then there was a *volte-face* in 1961, leading to admission of the Russian Orthodox Church (and subsequently other Soviet churches) to the WCC at its Third General Assembly in New Delhi in 1961. I had been on the periphery of this move at one point, when I had my encounter with the Revd Francis House in Moscow at Christmas, 1959. The Soviet regime obviously encouraged this, because it perceived that there would be political gain if the Russian Orthodox Church could influence policy. It is in this light that subsequent WCC policies must be evaluated.

Reverting to the Fourth General Assembly of the WCC in Uppsala (1968), I quote Canon Bernard Pawley, who wrote a report for the *Church Times*. Besides criticising the way in which the Programme to Combat Racism was introduced, he stated:

'The most controversial and, to my mind, the most disastrous decision of the Assembly was a unilateral request to the USA to stop the bombing of military targets in Vietnam. An attempt to link this with the condemnation of the infiltration of the South by armed guerrillas was defeated. So the old dark shadow of appeasement fell over the Assembly – there will have been joy in the Kremlin that night.'[2]

Keston, therefore, was born into this atmosphere of conflict on ecumenical issues and, as I have previously described, passionate attitudes came to the surface.

Although religious liberty and human rights in the Soviet Union had become a cause of Christian concern in the West by 1975, the Nairobi Assembly did not have any consideration of this on its agenda. However, in the first days, events quickly veered out of the control of the bureaucrats who oversaw such matters. There was a daily newspaper, *Target*, produced by local Kenyan Christians, which was designated for the period of the meeting as the record of events for delegates. On the third day they published an 'Appeal to the Delegates of the Fifth Assembly of the World Council of Churches' which had arrived on the editorial desk. So the unlisted item of the agenda which was already in some people's minds became the universal talking point. The authors were Fr Gleb Yakunin and a layman, Lev Regelson, a physicist. It was a long and passionate appeal for ecumenical help for believers and presented a practical plan. They made the following suggestions: information on persecution, the need for prayer, establishing personal contact, framing an ecumenical response, publicising the need for Christian literature in the USSR – these were the key points the authors raised.[3]

---

1   *Religion in Communist Lands*, No.1, 1985, pp. 4–27.

2   *Church Times*, London, quoted in *RCL*, No. 1, 1985.

3   *RCL*, No. 1, 1984.

The response from the delegates of the Moscow Patriarchate was swift and sure-footed in the misinformation it presented. Metropolitan Yuvenali, leader of the delegation, wrote: 'We note that the first of the signatories, the priest Gleb Yakunin, has been in conflict with his own church authorities for some time, while the other, a layman, Lev Regelson, is known for his anti-ecumenism.'[4] After questioning the credentials of the authors, the Metropolitan made no attempt to respond to the substance of the letter, but emphasised 'the ever-increasing development of democratic principles' in the USSR which gave great hope for the future.

Whether or not there would be any formal discussion of these issues, which everyone was discussing behind the scenes, remained an open question until two days before the end of the Assembly, when there was to be a debate on the Helsinki Accords, which had been signed earlier in the year and which included provision for the monitoring of human rights within the confines of the nations which had assented to them.

A Swiss delegate, Dr Jacques Rossel, proposed an addition to the motion for that debate: 'The WCC is concerned about restrictions to religious liberty, particularly in the USSR...'[5] The Revd (subsequently Bishop) Richard Holloway, of the Episcopal Church of Scotland, seconded the motion, and, in an atmosphere of great tension, the Soviet delegation opposed it. The proposal was put to the vote and carried on a show of hands by a huge majority – the only time in the history of the WCC that there was such a resolution.

The chairman of the session was the British Baptist leader, Dr Ernest Payne, who adjourned the session for a 'tea interval'. One can only imagine the fraught discussions over the refreshments. He came back to claim to the Assembly that the motion had been out of order and that it should be referred back to the Resolutions Committee – which duly happened, though the consequences were still not predictable.

Such was the emotion which was being generated that a debate was announced, to take place outside the official agenda, but still part of the proceedings, necessarily, because of time constraints, late in the evening and of course with no proper documentation. Eventually out of this came a substitute motion which now referred to 'alleged infringements of religious liberty', but which excluded any reference to the Soviet Union. Next morning Rossel and Holloway offered to withdraw their amendment in favour of one obligating the General Secretary of the WCC to present a report on the implementation of the Helsinki Accords to the next meeting of the Central Committee of the WCC in August 1976.

Keston College was now a participant in the story of the unfolding events. We had had nothing to do with the furnishing of the Yakunin-Regelson document to *Target*. Reports of what had happened reached back to Fr Gleb and he wrote to Dr Philip Potter, the General Secretary, firmly believing that he now had the ecumenical

---

4   Ibid.

5   Ibid.

movement behind him: 'We are confident that the WCC, guided by the spirit of Nairobi, will prove worthy of its assignment and will study the problem of religious discrimination today with the necessary seriousness and objectivity.'[6]

Events were soon to unfold which would be far removed from the hopes and expectations which the Nairobi events had aroused, both in Moscow and in the West. Yakunin and Regelson were by this time actively preparing the next step in their campaign. They founded a 'Christian Committee for the Defence of Believers' Rights', which was fully ecumenical in its aims and which encompassed support of religious liberty for the non-Christian religions as well. Over the next three years they sent documents to Keston College, consisting of no fewer than 417 separate texts, comprising 1,302 pages, and there may have been others which did not find their way to the West. There was *samizdat* supporting Baptists, Pentecostals, Adventists and Catholics, as well as Jews. The whole enterprise, on any evaluation, was one of the outstanding ecumenical activities of the twentieth century.

The main action of Dr Philip Potter, General Secretary of the WCC, was to consult further with the Moscow Patriarchate. He did not take into account that the very act of writing a letter asking how far the Soviet Union was fulfilling its Helsinki obligations would put the Patriarchate in an impossible position. It had either to lie to the WCC or find itself under renewed pressure from the Kremlin for failing to suppress the train of events. Some senior figures in the WCC did, however, appreciate the dangers of the web of intrigue in which the organisation was now enmeshed.

For the first time I was summoned to Geneva, via Hans Hebly and his WCC connections in the secretariat, for a consultation in March 1976. So secret was the meeting that we convened, not at the headquarters of the WCC, but at the railway station. Our hosts met us there and, in order to avoid the eyes of the Russian staff, we crossed the road to the nearest hotel. Eugen Voss joined us. We were asked not to take notes, so I do not know the identities of the two or three who attended from the WCC.

The substance of the consultation, however, would soon go on record, because the WCC was secretly asking for documentation, but it would be co-authored by Keston, G2W and Hans Hebly, and attributed to them and not the WCC. There was little time to compile this, because the consultation at which the documentation had to be presented, a direct follow-up to Nairobi, was scheduled for 24–28 July in Montreux, Switzerland. We managed to fulfil our task and the resulting documentation was one of Keston's most influential publications.[7] Its hundred pages could hardly have been comprehensive, given the time constraint, but it did cover established ground, focussing on the last decade. An essay by Hans Hebly illustrated how great was the WCC's concern for religious liberty in earlier days and how that ideal had become dimmed. Also available for the Montreux meeting was the much more comprehensive

---

6   *RCL, No.* 1, 1985.

7   *Religious Liberty in the Soviet Union: WCC & USSR – A Post-Nairobi Documentation*, published in English and German by the three institutes together.

record, covering all the relevant countries of Europe, *Discretion and Valour* (see later in this chapter for an account of this pioneering ecumenical initiative).

However, the Montreux report excluded the names of the authors of the study, so its impact suffered from their non-availability to answer questions. It is one thing to have a lengthy report in your hands: quite another to hear persuasive advocacy from a participant. In fact, the sole British representative at the meeting was Paul Oestreicher. The star of the event, however, was Alexei Buyevsky, my old acquaintance from Moscow in 1959–60, still the arch lay bureaucrat of the Moscow Patriarchate and subsequently exposed as a KGB agent. Buyevsky's outstanding initiative was to call upon the ecumenical movement not to co-operate with the three institutes which had supplied the documentation or any similar group of experts in the future. Paul did object to this, but the matter was never put to the vote and Buyevsky's proposal seems to have become policy from then on.

Despite Mr Buyevsky's strictures, the Central Committee of the WCC did set up a Human Rights Advisory Group and resolved to strengthen the work of the Commission of the Churches on International Affairs (CCIA), a body formally independent of the WCC, but with premises in the same Geneva building. The former met in Copenhagen in October 1979 and advocated co-operation with existing human rights groups, but the *in situ* bureaucracy of the CCIA was obviously destined to play a more influential role in the follow-up to Nairobi. In charge of it was Dr Leopoldo Niilus, who seemed to me a shadowy figure who came from Latin America, but whose name reveals Estonian origins. He suddenly emerged on the scene, a man whose origins were mysterious and qualifications unstated.

The Advisory Group's recommendations led to the recruiting of a Swiss pastor, Dr Theo Tschuy, whose main working experience had been in South America. His mandate was to initiate a five-year programme, conditional upon the churches supplying the funding. Events were proceeding slowly in Geneva (it was now four years since Nairobi), but in Moscow there was a serious setback. Fr Gleb Yakunin was arrested on 1 November 1979 and Lev Regelson two months later. Fr Gleb would not see freedom again for eight years and Regelson was subjected to such pressures that he renounced his human rights activities.

It was Keston which conveyed this information to Dr Niilus. In return, we received by telex one of the most astonishing communications from an official body which I have ever read and I must quote it in full:

1. Presently no immediate action contemplated.
2. Contacts maintained with concerned member churches.
3. Strengthening of longstanding ecumenical human rights endeavours mandated by WCC Fifth Assembly an outcome of 1971 Central Committee and 1974 St Pölten Consultation reflecting alarming developments worldwide and not generated by individual cases or single countries.

Regards
Leopoldo J. Niilus, Director International Affairs WCC.[8]

Subsequently the WCC did raise Fr Gleb Yakunin's case privately with the Moscow Patriarchate and in public almost a year later, when it circulated a forthright letter from Konrad Raiser, by then Acting General Secretary of the WCC, to Metropolitan Yuvenali. However, it did not convey any details to the member churches of Fr Yakunin's life history and his record of bravery in defence of religious liberty.

By this time the 'spirit of Nairobi' had more or less evaporated and the tendency now was to look forward to the Sixth General Assembly, due to take place in Vancouver in 1983. Dr Tschuy evolved a plan of dividing Europe for consideration into two bands, north and south, which seemed to many of us a devious procedure for diverting attention away from East–West issues, but it did begin some case work, not least on Fr Yakunin himself. Tschuy's brief was, however, to report to the Conference of European Churches, a body nominally independent of the WCC itself, and so he would have no *locus standi* at the Vancouver Assembly.

Instead, an astonishing document appeared, *Human Rights on the Ecumenical Agenda*, by Erich Weingärtner, an employee of the CCIA, and therefore under the authority of Leopoldo Niilus. Even now, thirty-five years later, the member churches of the WCC should demand an investigation of what occurred in that office in the early 1980s, for the publication, following the telex from Niilus quoted above, could have been penned, not in the Moscow Patriarchate, but in the offices of the Soviet Council for Religious Affairs. Time has not softened my reaction to this publication, which I recount in greater detail in the pages of *Religion in Communist Lands*.[9] This article caused my rift with Geneva, because I could no longer, in all conscience, refrain from setting out my views on all the developments since Nairobi. The WCC may have long since regarded me as an outsider, but up to that point I had refrained from publicly criticising WCC policies.

In six separate passages Weingärtner implied that there was something dishonourable in the motivation of those in the West who defended religious liberty and human rights in Eastern Europe. After the Second World War many Christians in the West 'propitiated for their sins of omission during fascist rule by turning to a fervent comment on the religious liberty of their sister churches in Eastern Europe,' which contributed to the Cold War. They indulged in 'pious denunciations from a safe distance' which 'are not only ineffective ... but mask a certain hypocrisy.'

In a scarcely veiled reference to Keston College he continued:

> In fact, 'complainants' to the WCC are rarely the victims themselves, but very often special interest groups whose human rights motivations stem from political programmes in opposition to particular ideologies or governments.

---

8   *RCL*, No. 1, 1985.
9   Ibid..

These groups may wish to trap the WCC into actions in support of their political programmes, using human rights violations as the bait... Rumours of the [Soviet] infringements have reached western Christians in an exaggerated and sometimes distorted form, provoking inappropriate reactions which complicate the resolution of internal church problems.[10]

Weingärtner continued by proposing a conspiracy theory which, apparently, held that the 'misinformation' supplied by such groups was finding funding from the South African regime. There followed a long exposition of how inspired the Eastern churches were to promote 'group rights' over 'individual rights' (surely a Marxist concept if ever there was one). Disregarding St Paul's words on the Church as the Body of Christ, he continued by stating that member churches must be responsible for the implementation of human rights in their own area and not be concerned about what was happening elsewhere. Weingärtner laid the blame for the sufferings of the Russian Orthodox Church on its complicity with the policies of the Tsarist regime in the distant past. He continued: 'Communism has guaranteed employment, food, shelter, education, medical care and social security... Soviet society is evolving in the direction of an extension of democratic principles.'[11]

Such was the voice of a pro-Soviet advocate. Weingärtner's booklet was not debated at the General Assembly itself, but it represented an attitude of the time. Thus it was that what I had earlier called 'Nairobi: a door opened' was now succeeded by 'Vancouver: a door closed'. There were no other general briefing documents to set beside Weingärtner's.

There was one cynical Soviet 'preparation' for Vancouver. The Moscow authorities sent a priest to Fr Yakunin in prison to give him communion and a Bible just before the opening of the Sixth Assembly. Developments in Canada were not without their significance, however. By now Dr David Russell was the chief representative of the British Baptists, as General Secretary of the Union, and he raised the ongoing issue of Christian prisoners in a short but telling speech. Outside of the formal sessions, the Archbishop of Canterbury, Dr Robert Runcie, brought up the name of Deacon Rusak, in a press conference and a BBC radio broadcast. Keston had received information about Rusak, who was being threatened with imprisonment because he was trying to write a history of the Russian Church since the Revolution. A Russian representative countered Archbishop Runcie's statement by saying that no notice should be taken of him. He was unbalanced, having been 'kicked in the head by a horse when a child'.[12]

Christian Solidarity International, an emerging group, set up a 'Yakunin Hearing' during the Assembly. They had booked a room on the university campus where the

10   Ibid.
11   Ibid.
12   The *Daily Telegraph*, London, 12 August 1983, p. 12.

Assembly was being held, but inexplicably the booking was cancelled, so it had to be held at a remote venue, making it impossible for many delegates to attend.

In a summary of these events written up for my Chatham House lecture in 1984, I put forward these conclusions:

> It is not too much to say that Geneva policy has misled the worldwide membership of the WCC on the real situation of Soviet believers. If the aim of this was to alleviate the lot of the persecuted, it has failed... Beneath the superstructure of collaboration with the [Soviet] regime there is a 'confessing church', as there was in Nazi Germany... [Under a new policy] there would be aid for the persecuted 'morally, materially and politically', in the WCC's own phrase... The World Psychiatric Association in the late 1970s, in response to strong persuasion, put great pressure on the Soviets. They withdrew from the Association, but there was immediately less psychiatric abuse in the Soviet Union.[13]

After Philip Walters had read my text at Chatham House, the only intervention was from Paul Oestreicher. He read a statement from the WCC. This acknowledged the 'important research of Keston College... but seriously distorts WCC policy and methodology, in particular in the treatment of *Human Rights on the Ecumenical Agenda* by Erich Weingärtner.'[14]

So an occasion, which could have produced a significant debate, was blunted and the WCC, maintaining its position, went unchallenged except in the lecture text itself.

There was a sequel. The Revd Roger Williamson, Executive Secretary for Peace and Human Rights at the British Council of Churches, wrote an item for the *Ecumenical Press Service*, in which he called for a dialogue between Keston and the WCC. In response to this the BCC called a 24-hour residential consultation to deal with the issues I had raised and other related questions. This met in London on 20–21 February 1985, but in the event the prospective WCC delegation boycotted the conference, as did a representative from the NCC in New York. I was of course there, but no serious discussion of the substance of my lecture took place.

A month later Eugen Voss, Hans Hebly and I were offered sponsorship to call a conference in Stuttgart and invite ecumenical representatives to take part. In the event we were mostly preaching to the converted, but I took a back seat, as it transpired that the promised German financial sponsorship was threatened with withdrawal if Keston were represented as a key player in the proceedings. Bishop Held, highly influential in German Protestant circles, was Chairman of the Central Committee of the WCC at the time and may have had something to do with this. In the event, he did attend, but for the first evening only. All this was a little strange, as the work of Keston was virtually unknown in the German-speaking world.

---

13   *RCL*, No. 1, 1985.
14   Bourdeaux, incorporated in unpublished MS, Keston Archive.

I had also received a surprising invitation from Bruce Rigdon, an influential figure in the National Council of Churches (New York) known for his positive views on the Russian Church, to lecture at the NCC summer school in 1985, but a subsequent letter cancelled this invitation.

The British Council of Churches held a second consultation in London on 24 June 1985, attended (surprisingly) by Erich Weingärtner, Theo van Boven (Netherlands) and the Revd Jaroslav Ondra, deposed secretary of the Christian Peace Conference (CPC) from Prague. Again, the subject matter of my lecture was discussed only in generalities and Weingärtner, who was brave to attend, took very little part in it. The conclusion was that Keston representatives should be invited to pay a formal visit to the WCC, but in the event this never took place.

After Dr Emilio Castro was appointed General Secretary of the WCC in late 1985, he telephoned me on 8 November, expressing appreciation of my work. I wrote a follow-up, as I did to Dr Ninan Koshy, Weingärtner's new superior at the CCIA, but there was no response. Roger Williamson wrote a document for circulation within the BCC. He left on one side the substance of my lecture, but stated that my analogies, especially with the World Psychiatric Association, were misplaced.

Dr Theo Buss, Editor of the *Ecumenical Press Service*, was one of the few Geneva officials to join directly in the dialogue, but his article was published in French only, never translated into English and, indeed, I did not even know about it until months after its publication in Paris. It was a single page only, accusing me of 'falsifying [my] facts [and] falling into the snare of elementary anti-communism'.[15] It was not worthy of a reply and neither did it receive one.

On a completely different level was a contribution by Professor Nicolas Lossky, of the Moscow jurisdiction of the Russian Orthodox Church, who taught at the Russian Theological Institute (St Serge) in Paris. He upheld the quality of the information provided by Keston College. He indicated that it was the very objectivity of its work which motivated the Soviet regime to represent it as an especially dangerous enemy. He went on to underline the central role of Fr Gleb Yakunin in the movement for religious liberty in the Soviet Union. He continued: 'Fr Bourdeaux is unquestionably right when he states the WCC policy *vis-à-vis* attacks on human dignity in Eastern Europe has largely failed.'[16] He ends with precisely the kind of original contribution to the debate which I had hoped to elicit from many others when I decided on the subject for my Chatham House lecture:

> It seems to me that, in the present state of affairs, the only valid attitude for the World Council to take would be to admit publicly, before the whole world, that, for the time being the three hundred or so member-churches of the Council are able to speak on the attack on human dignity, as a body, only in a one-sided way

---

15   *L'Actualité religieuse*, No.18, 15 December 1984, pp. 44–45.

16   *Service Orthodoxe de Presse*, No.96, Courbevoie, March 1985, pp.10–14..

and that, consequently, they are *unable* conscientiously *to pronounce on them at all.'*[17]

Here I would have been content to rest my case, but the afore-mentioned Dr Tschuy wrote controversially in September 1985, reflecting on the work of the three institutes. His words were all too reminiscent, in a milder form, of those of Erich Weingärtner. Commenting on the information we were publishing, he wrote:

> The problem was whether this information was really objective or whether it fitted too much into a certain political patterns... It was noted that certain 'specialised' organisations would on occasion initiate regular campaigns which seemed to be designated to embarrass either the World Council of Churches or our Programme ... Neither were we in a position to explain in public certain circumstances that had been shared with us in confidence, and which would often shed a very different light on a case.[18]

Thus the results of painstaking research are dismissed because they do not tally with information from 'secret sources', which cannot be divulged. One wonders whether one of those sources was the Vice-Chairman of the Soviet Government's Council on Religious Affairs, Pyotr Makartsev, who paid an unprecedented visit to Geneva on 7 December 1984, only five weeks after my Chatham House lecture. He claimed, in familiar terms, that Soviet laws guaranteed that Soviet citizens could worship free of interference from the secular authorities and that his Council was established to monitor observance of these laws.[19]

Dr Emilio Castro potentially opened up a whole new area of possible progress when he visited Moscow in September 1985, where he had forthright conversations with Soviet officialdom on several levels. According to one source, he requested that religious prisoners should be released and that the legislation on religion should be liberalised.[20]

This was the fraught context in which the BCC delegation to Moscow was to take place. At this point, however, the debate between Keston and the ecumenical movement came to a halt for a startling reason: Mikhail Sergeyevich Gorbachev's new policies of *glasnost* and *perestroika* came into force, under which the official representatives of the Soviet churches soon spoke out with a new voice or abandoned the scene altogether.

---

17   Ibid.

18   Theo Tschuy, *An Ecumenical Experiment in Human Rights* (Geneva, 1985), pp. 19–20.

19   Michael Bourdeaux, unpublished MS, p. 35.

20   *Service Orthodoxe de Press*, No.102, November 1985, p. 11.

The British Council of Churches

It was as a member of the East–West Relations Committee of the British Council of Churches (EWRAC), which Paul Oestreicher led for a quarter of a century, that I met him regularly. Churches were invited to nominate their own members of this committee, but Paul invited others also (I was one). This resulted in the enlisting of a number of Quakers, members of a tradition for which he had great respect: indeed, he professed to be a Quaker as well as an Anglican. They enjoyed the deserved reputation of being peacemakers, though this did not always go alongside in-depth study of the realities of life under communist domination. However, I found them ready to listen and several became friends of Keston.

My reaction was always to keep close to the facts and never, unless unduly provoked, to enter into arguments for and against communism as a political system. My personal experiences in Moscow, not paralleled by any other church people with whom I came into contact, led me to the conviction, which I have often expressed here, that communism was a system rotten to the core, not least in its one-sided and relentless war against religion. For better or worse, I was labelled as a cold warrior. Often in our BCC discussions there was only one other whose views came close to mine and that was Sir John Lawrence.

The BCC was closely allied to the World Council of Churches, but was not subservient to it and it had its own independent viewpoint, which it quite often expressed. It did not have any direct input into the structure of the WCC, so was not party to the appointment of Russian Orthodox officials to positions of authority after 1961.

A controversial issue in the WCC, after its General Assembly at Uppsala in 1968, was its Programme to Combat Racism. I frequently expressed opinions about it within the confines of EWRAC. I maintained that the idea of the programme was positive, but the concept must be applied worldwide, not just in Africa and the USA, to which its criticisms seemed to be solely directed. Needless to say, the Russian participation in the Geneva administration prevented any discussion of the USSR from even being considered.

My experiences had taught me that Russians were the dominant race in the country. Republics like Lithuania or Turkmenistan might have a national as the titular head of the Communist Party in the region, but there was always a Russian in the number two position or close enough to the seat of power to ensure that no expression of nationalism would ever surface – and any rumblings below the surface would be repressed by the threat of the KGB. My strongest case, however, was the treatment of the Jews. Eventually Christian voices in high places did support their emigration campaign, but that was much later and it never amounted to a demand that the Jewish community should be granted equal rights to develop their traditions in the parts of the Soviet Union where their representation was strong. The continuing colonialism of the Soviet Union in its subjugation of the conquered nations of the Soviet bloc was then absolute, at a time when colonial rule in Africa had mainly ended, but racism was still endemic in South Africa and Rhodesia. In the USA the civil rights movement was gathering pace and was already gaining considerable publicity, even, on occasion, leading to violence. The argument about the Programme to Combat Racism also raised the question of whether the abundant funds poured into the programme were, in some instances, being diverted to pay for arms.

Another issue predominant at the time was the Holocaust. While the world, rightly, paid unlimited tribute to its victims, similar weight was not being given to those, far greater in number, who perished in the Gulags. Dietrich Bonhoeffer's prayers are often read in church and his testimony quoted, but conversely it is only rarely that anyone cites the equally impressive testimonies of Christian martyrs in Russia.

In the Vatican there was a debate under Pope Paul VI about *'Ostpolitik'*. The belief prevailed that communism was here to stay, therefore the emphasis must be on building relations with the regimes of the communist bloc, which were permanent. This led to a new emphasis on patient diplomatic negotiation, with the Catholic side more being prepared than previously to negotiate with the communist regimes over the appointment of bishops, for example. This applied particularly to Hungary and Czechoslovakia, the Church in Poland taking a stronger stand against the imposition of secular authority.

One constant debate, already mentioned in passing, was whether publicising abuses of human rights in the communist countries was 'rocking the boat' (a phrase so often used), which meant that supporting the cause of the persecuted would turn governments against them with more ferocity and one would harm the very cause one wished to support. Any representations, the argument continued, must be done quietly and through diplomatic channels. In Eastern Europe many were crying out for public support, a plea which fell almost invariably on deaf ears. This was not an argument which would persuade Amnesty International to keep silence.

All these issues surfaced with some regularity in EWRAC. Presiding over them with a firm hand was the Revd (later Dean) John Arnold, a Russian speaker and long-time adviser to the Anglican Church on Soviet affairs. He conducted debates with diplomacy and insisted that all sides of a question should be heard. In my experience, no comparable group existed in any other country, so such frequent and lively discussions did not take place elsewhere. The admirable and oft-expressed aim of EWRAC was to keep open channels of communication with the churches of Eastern Europe, insofar as communist governments permitted this. In one way or another, when the substance of our deliberations were communicated, local church groups learned much from and contributed to EWRAC.

Discretion and Valour

In the earliest days of Keston there had been informal discussions between Peter Reddaway, Leonard Schapiro, Sir John Lawrence and me which led to a consideration of the WCC's agenda: to inform its members of the life of the churches, particularly in those areas where information was hard to come by. The British Council of Churches was well placed to fill this vacuum, as EWRAC commanded wide expertise.

In 1971 Sir John Lawrence and I presented to EWRAC a proposal for a establishing a working party which would eventually produce a report. To our satisfaction, Paul Oestreicher strongly supported the idea; it was accepted and the new group met many times from 4 October 1971 and then throughout 1972–3, with publication following in 1974.

In order to produce such a work there were three essentials: selection of a working party which included expertise on all the relevant countries; a chairman who would guide the whole process; and a rapporteur who would weld the disparate material into a readable whole. In all three tasks we were singularly fortunate. London at that time was the world centre for research on religion in the communist countries, not only because of the presence of Keston College, but because there were many other experts, too. We considered it within our brief to call for occasional contributions and advice from other countries also; the published introduction lists twelve people by name.

The British members who met regularly (usually once a month, 26 times in all) provided the backbone of the work. They included several well-informed people who had knowledge, but were not members of EWRAC, especially Catholics, who did not join the BCC. Among the sixteen members listed, the names of Lucian Blit (Poland), Peter Hebblethwaite (Catholic journalist), Peter Reddaway (LSE), Janis Sapiets (BBC) and Alex Shillinglaw (Church of Scotland) stand out. There were of course some changes during the course of these two years of hard work, but the *esprit de corps* was reflected in the excellent attendance record. The Russian Orthodox priest, Fr Sergei Hackel, contributed positively, but was not listed for diplomatic reasons.

The choice of a moderator was controversial. Sir John Lawrence was the obvious choice, with his lifelong experience, mature judgement and the respect he commanded across the denominations. His views on communism were also well known. His nomination was opposed by Dr Ernest Payne, former General Secretary of the Baptist Union and a President of the World Council of Churches, who probably feared that John would pay too much attention to the 'dissident' Baptists in the USSR and too little to the role of their registered counterparts. However, Dr Payne was outvoted and eventually made his peace with the group, coming into it as an eventual replacement for the Revd Walter Bottoms, Editor of the *Baptist Times*.

It was an inspired suggestion to invite the Revd Trevor Beeson to write up the reports and weld the whole enterprise together. He had been a parish priest in Ware, Hertfordshire, and a journalist, writing on European affairs for the (now-defunct) *Christian Century*. Trevor had a limitless capacity for work, combined with an eye for detail, and the ability to highlight the major issues. Throughout he wrote and rewrote other people's work, invariably turning the whole into a product of his readable and jargon-free style. Through his rewriting, *Discretion and Valour* reads like an original book by a single author. Trevor's achievement was considerable and this probably led to his appointment to a canonry of Westminster Abbey, and as Chaplain to the House of Commons.

Trevor – on his own admission – did not claim any special knowledge of Eastern Europe, but this quickly became evident as an advantage. He did not accept humbug from anyone and quickly edited out the political agendas which appeared in some of the early draft submissions by individual members. He made his own contribution to Chapter 1, 'Communism, Religion and the Churches'. Regarding the communist bloc in Eastern Europe, he wrote: 'A form of Communism was imposed upon people who found both the doctrine and the practice unacceptable.'[21] This was far from being the universal view of the members of the working party. There were some who did think that communism, by and large, was accepted by the hundreds of millions of people who lived under it in Europe, even though they had no choice. These words, which are so obviously true from the perspective of the twenty-first century, were controversial in the 1970s.

Sir John Lawrence's Foreword gives an account of just how painstaking and time-consuming the work was:

> The memoranda prepared for the group have been first submitted to searching scrutiny by us and have sometimes been totally rewritten before being accepted as raw material on which Mr Beeson could work... The material for each chapter has thus been before the working group several times... We have had to deal with a number of contentious and delicate matters, but in the end we have always been able to reach agreement about how each such matter should be treated.[22]

What were these 'contentious and delicate matters'? There were far too many to set out here. The one which most sticks in my mind is not the disagreements we had with senior Baptists in the UK over 'registered' and 'unregistered' Baptists and Evangelicals in Russia. The facts, I think, were irrefutable and there was no attempt to downplay the repression which was occurring at that moment in the Soviet Union. The sharpest disagreement was over the person of Cardinal Mindszenty, who had recently been brought to Rome from his long years of confinement in the American Embassy in Budapest. Pope Paul VI relieved him of his post (from which he had long since been absent) in early 1974, one of the latest dates mentioned in the book. Some people in the working party felt he was a figure of the past and Paul Oestreicher successfully argued against inclusion of his rallying speech to the Hungarian people during his few days of liberty before the Soviet invasion of Hungary in 1956. Our published text reads, 'Mindszenty fought the advance of Communism in Hungary with little awareness of the social issues at stake in the country.' I'm now sorry that I did not oppose that sentence more strongly and insist on the inclusion of Mindszenty's broadcast text.

---

21 *Discretion and Valour,* revised edn (Collins Fount Paperbacks, London, 1982), p. 20.

22 Ibid., p. 11.

He did, after all, as one of the great prophets of the twentieth century, show acute awareness of the reality involved. The 'social issue' was the question of whether communism was bringing an advance to Hungary, which of course Mindszenty opposed with heart and soul, sacrificing decades of liberty to stand in opposition to the new regime. This text was slightly modified in the second edition.[23]

Overall, our intensive work, resulting in 348 closely packed but readable pages, was an ecumenical landmark. Paul presented it to the General Assembly of the British Council of Churches. In this he omitted – perhaps understandably – any reference to Keston College. Not only had we ignited the initial spark, but we had contributed the backbone of the work on the USSR, which comprises more than one-third of the total text. In my own life there would never be an 'ecumenical' achievement to rival it.

The introductory section omitted to state clearly that this work took place within the confines of the British Council of Churches. Diplomacy presumably denied a clear statement of its purpose: that it was designed to set a new agenda for the Ecumenical Movement. Participants in the discussions were listed, but without reference as to how they came together.

It was a disappointment that presentation of the book did not lead to a full discussion of its contents. We had hoped that after two years of work *Discretion and Valour* would influence WCC policy. It failed to have an impact on ecumenical attitudes worldwide. Significantly – though the reasons for this are obscure – the book was not published in America until much later and there were no foreign-language translations.

The title, I always thought, was pointed and should have helped to promote the book. The first chapter notes its literary origin. In *Henry IV, Part* I, Falstaff says: 'The better part of valour is discretion; in the which better part I have saved my life.'[24] When we discussed the title, one of us suggested 'Discretion or Valour', but John Arnold immediately 'corrected' this to 'Discretion and Valour'. The title, to my way of thinking, exactly expressed the bi-polar path which the churches of Eastern Europe could follow: some moving forward in a process of tortuous negotiation with an atheist regime (Catholics in Poland), others treading the path of suffering (unregistered Baptists in the Soviet Union). Playing such an active role in the preparation of *Discretion and Valour* was one of the highlights in my early career. Though 26 long meetings may have seemed a grind to many, to me it was a process of acquiring diplomacy and immeasurably enhancing the sum of my knowledge, which was far from extensive about such countries as Poland, Romania and East Germany (the GDR) before the work began. Much of this learning came from watching at close quarters Sir John Lawrence exercise his skills in achieving what he wanted by patient persuasion rather than using a bludgeon. The process set out an agenda for me: how to broaden Keston's coverage to bring in other parts of the communist bloc.

---

23   Ibid., pp. 276–8.

24   Ibid., p. 25.

Christian Aid

In January 1981 my phone rang and I heard the voice of Bernard Palmer, Editor of the *Church Times*, saying something like, 'Michael, did you know about the attack on Keston by Christian Aid?' I could hardly take in what Bernard was saying. This episode illustrates just how much hostility there was to Keston in certain quarters. My documents on the case fill a box, but I must summarise briefly in order not to let one episode overbalance the ecumenical work I had now been doing for many years.

The book, by Derrick Knight, was entitled *Beyond the Pale: The Christian Political Fringe*. [25] On the back cover he is described as 'currently researcher and writer in the Information Department of Christian Aid'. Chapter 4 of the book is entitled 'Private Research and the New Right'. In his introduction to this chapter Knight wrote: 'The revelations about the sort of secret contacts made by the former South African Department of Information, exposure by journalists of links between the South African Bureau of State Security (BOSS) and military police with high-ranking members of similar Western organisations, should make us ever more sensitive. Can anyone be trusted to be what they seem?... Organizations involved in academic research are not immune and there are a number which should be assessed.'[26]

The first organisation to come under the cosh was Keston, to which he devoted two and a half pages. The implication was that Keston acted as a pawn of the South African government which bolstered its anti-communist stance by quoting information from Western organisations critical of communist regimes. Knight drew the inference that Keston was funded by BOSS.

The Keston Council took immediate legal action, which was reported in both *The Times* and *The Guardian*.[27] Leonard Schapiro pressed us to claim exemplary damages. The Associate Director of Christian Aid, Martin Bax, wrote: 'I believe it has been made quite clear to you, and to some members of your Council, that Christian Aid did not commission, publish or distribute the book and takes no responsibility for it at all.'[28]

Such a clearly mendacious statement did not help the cause of Christian Aid. The publishers, it emerged, had distributed the book worldwide, but the Information Department of Christian Aid was the last word on the back cover. Apologies followed. Leonard Schapiro opposed the reluctant Council decision not to press for damages. The book was officially withdrawn and all our legal costs recovered. We asked how one could withdraw a book already sent around the world. A revised version followed the next year, and Knight was listed again as a researcher for Christian Aid.

---

25   Kogan Page, 1981.

26   Ibid., p. 66.

27   *The Guardian*, 30 January 1981.

28   Letter on file, dated 12 March 1981.

EWRAC discussions continue

Keston's relations with EWRAC were not harmed by the Christian Aid scandal, which speaks strongly for the degree of trust that we had established over recent years. Discussions continued vigorously after the publication of *Discretion and Valour*. I had, for example, constant disagreements with the Quaker, Eva Pinthus, who seemed to think that the East German regime had discovered the recipe for the salvation of souls. In 1981, when the twentieth anniversary of the building of the Berlin Wall was being 'celebrated', there was a strong body of opinion which felt that it was 'necessary' in order to safeguard the 'integrity' of the East German regime. No one ever revealed the all-pervasive grip of the Stasi, the *Staatssicherheit* or secret police, and we were never fully informed about the numbers of political prisoners (though Paul did sometimes petition for their release in person with the high-ranking East German officials whom he occasionally met on his travels). Nor did we know about the immensely comprehensive work of the Stasi, but to be fair, neither did anybody else know the true extent of the reach of its tentacles. We did hear from time to time of acts of heroism within the Lutheran (EKD) Church. John Arnold's wife's brother was a clergyman in East Germany, so he was a source of information, while he also needed to be diplomatic in order to safeguard his family.

With so many interested people as members of EWRAC, discussions of the GDR were always lively. The Revd Ian Harker, Chaplain of Newcastle University, represented a viewpoint shared by one or two members of EWRAC on the GDR. His report on an extended visit to East Germany was presented to us in 1981. His summary of impressions read in part:

> There has been a decisive break with pre-1945, and it takes a long time to realise that the effort to build a society for Workers and Farmers is genuine and not just rhetoric. Coming from the West, one is still slightly incredulous that a whole economy or society can be aimed in this direction. There has been a revolution... The standard of living seems to be higher on average than in Britain, with less extremes.[29]

Re-reading these words 37 years later, one is still surprised that such a document was considered worthy of serious discussion by a well-informed body, but usually our debates were based on more substantive reports.

Another argument which constantly arose was over the concept of 'equivalence'. This meant, roughly, that every sin of Soviet communism could be equated with some malpractice of the USA. One of the main proponents of this idea was the Revd Roger Williamson, who was an official at Church House, the Anglican administrative centre in Westminster. The idea seemed preposterous to me, having lived in both the USSR and the USA.

---

29   'GDR Visit October/December 1980: Some Impressions', by Ian Harker, 23 March 1981, circulated to EWRAC for meeting on 27 March 1981.

Sometimes, though not in that committee, I was questioned as to why Keston was concentrating on the Soviet Union, while 'far worse' horrors had been perpetrated by American troops in Vietnam and, currently, by the apartheid regime in South Africa. In response, I said that my calling was to enlighten public opinion about the real conditions under which Soviet believers lived.

Czechoslovakia was always a thorny problem for EWRAC and we devoted much time to its affairs. Professor Josef Hromadka, a Czech Protestant theologian, against all the odds, established a 'Christian Peace Conference' in Prague in 1958, using as his cover the magic slogan of 'peace', which was then on the lips of every Soviet propagandist. The movement flourished and gradually became an important forum for East–West encounter. The CPC (as it became known) was, not surprisingly, politically suspect from the beginning, considering that it was at first financed from the East and that Professor Hromadka himself had his critics on the grounds of alleged collaboration with a harsh regime. Nevertheless, in the early days of EWRAC the CPC was steadily gaining acceptance. Although the British churches were never formally members, many individuals attended on their own initiative and regional groups in the West counterbalanced the full membership exercised by the churches in the East. The British regional group provided several people who became members of various committees. In its very early days the Quaker, German-born theologian, Richard Ullman, 'represented' Britain on the CPC executive committee. Incidentally, it was he who provided the initial stimulus for the establishment of EWRAC, which, for a considerable time could exist only because of generous Quaker funding. David Paton, Paul Oestreicher and a lawyer, Irene Jacoby, all held office in the CPC at various times and we spent many hours listening to accounts of their comings and goings.

The CPC received criticism in the UK and elsewhere as a fellow-travelling organisation, yet overall I felt that it commanded more pluses than minuses within the necessary political limits of its existence. As the WCC had by the mid-1960s abrogated any responsibility, the CPC might have become a forum for the discussion of vital issues in East–West relations. There was no other arena to equal it. The Quakers did good work in bringing the CPC to the attention of so many British Christians. In those difficult days, the Quakers almost alone alerted British Christians to the need to use any possible means of keeping contact with Christians in the East. In April 1966 I attended, for the only time, one of these big international assemblies of the CPC in Germany (at Chiemsee in Bavaria). This was at my own initiative and was financed by Bill Fletcher's funds at the Centre de Recherches. Not all governments of the Soviet bloc exercised the same absolute control over the selection of delegates as did the Soviet Union itself; in other words, these meetings offered some scope for genuine encounters and were not purely propagandistic exercises. However, 1968 saw a fundamental change.

The true value of the CPC came into the open only after its virtual destruction. The Soviet invasion of Czechoslovakia, the brutal end of the Prague Spring in August 1968, saw the end of the CPC in its original form. If it had been carrying out the fine pro-Soviet propaganda job its critics often accused it of doing, it is inconceivable that the new Czech regime would have annihilated its original structure and personnel. This traumatic event of 1968 caused endless debate within EWRAC, too. Indeed, Czechoslovakia had dominated our discussions throughout the year since Alexander Dubček had become General Secretary of the Communist Party. Paul and several others repeatedly claimed that Dubček's 'socialism with a human face' represented their ideal of the way society should develop, with all its repercussions for the West, too. Therefore the crushing of the Czech initiative was a body blow for those who hoped the changes were permanent. The treatment of the CPC unfolded a classic Soviet scenario. In the words of *Discretion and Valour*:

> After the events of August 1968 the then leadership of the CPC obviously had no future. Warsaw Pact conformity was firmly stamped on the movement by Metropolitan Nikodim and Bishop Bartha. The Czech General Secretary, Dr Jaroslav Ondra, was in effect dismissed. Heartbroken, Hromadka resigned. Nearly all the leading members of the CPC from the West were in effect barred from making any further creative contribution. The old statutes of the movement were largely ignored and a new 'normalised' CPC emerged.'[30]

Professor Hromadka died soon afterwards. Many wrote the CPC's obituary alongside his, but this was premature. Its rebirth as an unmasked agent of Soviet policy saw it use its new financial support to entrap many Third World church leaders in its web. Desperate for their own increased contacts and without the money to travel extensively, these men and women were served platefuls of propaganda and unwittingly swallowed many spoonfuls of the gruel.

One valuable and constant activity of EWRAC was sending delegations to Eastern Europe or receiving their counterparts when they came to the UK. Much of our time was spent on these activities, which of course entailed hearing detailed reports of these visits after they had taken place. For financial reasons, there was much more West to East activity than vice versa, so unfortunately I did not often meet the personnel involved from the Soviet bloc.

During the 25 years that I spent as a member of EWRAC, I was not invited to participate in any of these delegations. Obviously, my value on the committee was felt to be more as a back-room adviser than as a front-line ecumenist. I often reflected on this lack of face-to-face contact with many people in the East, from meetings with whom I could have greatly benefited. I perforce had to accept what Bill Fletcher had once said to me: 'Diplomacy and research are two completely different functions. If you engage in the latter, you will never be accepted in the ranks of those who engage in the former.' That certainly turned out to be true in my own career, except in the brief period before the collapse of communism when I was used in both capacities by the Foreign Office.

---

30   *Discretion and Valour*, 1974 edn (Fontana), p. 334.

The comings and goings of delegations to and from the Soviet Union were reciprocal. There had been an 'ecumenical' delegation from the Soviet churches, to which the BCC prepared a return event in Russia, to take place in 1986. Paul knew that selection of delegates would be controversial, though the major denominations were supposed to nominate their own representation. 1985 marked Gorbachev's accession to power, but it took a year for his reforms to start in any serious way. I had been refused Soviet visas since 1979 and thought that there was a chance – just a chance – that the decision might now be reversed.

At several EWRAC meetings during 1985 the forthcoming delegation was discussed, with its many ramifications, but there was no mention of my name as a possible interpreter and adviser, to represent the BCC itself. Keston's Council met on 19 September, by which time we were in possession of the draft list of participants. The unanimous view was that my name should be included.

There was a tense meeting of EWRAC on 23 September, at which I questioned why Keston had been excluded from an occasion where its expertise could have been of service to the majority of the delegates, who did not speak Russian. Some claimed that Keston was not a church and therefore had no rights in this, to which I replied that being a staff adviser was a different role. I tried to find a way in which the issue could be properly discussed.

The subsequent minute of the meeting, written by Paul, stated that 'the member churches had nominated delegates and then a delegation had been suggested which took into account regional and denominational balances as well as considerations such as age, sex, etc. Some members of the Committee expressed the view that there should be more delegates with a profound knowledge of the USSR. The BCC staff were asked to consider representatives who might meet this need. Paul agreed to put this to the Executive Committee.'[31]

At the meeting of 23 September 1985 we were not told that the Executive Committee was going to meet in just a week's time (30 September), giving virtually no time for proper consultation. I subsequently rang the EWRAC office and a secretary told me that there had been 'no change' in the composition of the delegation. However, Paul himself told me in a telephone call on 14 October that the list had not yet been finalised, because he said he was 'thinking' of asking Mrs Xenia Dennen to become a delegate. This was the last I heard of such a proposal until her name appeared (incorrectly described as 'BCC staff') on a list prepared for the EWRAC meeting of 5 December.

At a heads-of-department meeting at Keston on 3 December we all felt that the whole affair was bad, both for Keston and the BCC, and Philip Walters was particularly decisive in putting forward this view. I put together some notes on what I might say at the next EWRAC meeting, read them out loud to myself and then rehearsed them to the heads of department on the morning of 5 December. They were unanimous in their view that I should present Keston's case later in the day.

---

31   Document in Keston Archive.

When I looked round at those who were present I almost changed my mind. Of the members who had most strongly supported my case at the previous meeting – Sir John Lawrence, Chris Cviic and my old school colleague, Peter Stephens – not one was there. Out of fifteen in the room I could count about nine who were possibly unsympathetic to my views and – embarrassingly, for they should surely not have been present during this conversation – two guests from West Germany.

I had intended only to make a statement and then to allow the meeting to pass to other business, but to my amazement, such were the emotions stirred that the discussion continued for the next hour and a half. It emerged – I think to the astonishment of all in the room – that Paul had already given the provisional list of delegates to Fr Oliver McTernan, a Catholic priest who was close to the work of EWRAC, and he had taken it to Moscow, asking Metropolitan Filaret (head of the Department of Foreign Relations at the Patriarchate) whether it was acceptable and whether he could confirm and finalise the dates. Filaret, it later emerged, had close connections with the KGB and enjoyed a chequered career (which later led him to quit Moscow's jurisdiction in order to join the break-away Kiev Patriarchate). He was also on record as having publicly denounced Keston to the British press when he led the original delegation to the UK. Whatever his status at the time, it was an error of judgement to request his imprimatur on the composition of a British delegation.

After a lapse of over thirty years, these controversies may seem to be trivial, but in fact they were symptomatic of the deep divisions of opinion which governed all discussions of human rights and religious liberty in the communist bloc.

The final list contained fifteen names besides three staff members. There were three Russian speakers, but Paul said that the emphasis was on people who could benefit from the experience. At that stage I made my intervention. I said that, *de facto*, the BCC was casting a vote of no confidence in the work of Keston and we were firmly placed on the sidelines. Yet we were constantly in personal touch with church officials in the Soviet Union. Most recently two Moscow Baptist leaders, at a conference in Croydon, had met me on three consecutive days, even cutting sessions of the conference to do so. They wanted my help in publicising the Baptist cause. Many ordinary believers now knew of the work of Keston. I concluded with some strong words:

> The very fact of selecting the delegation has let [the Soviets] off the hook. Why should we do their censorship for them? They already know that they can manipulate the ecumenical movement. They always thought they had more trouble with the British. Now they realise they can do it after all.[32]

I concluded by referring to the central role which Keston had played in the research for *Discretion and Valour*. The resulting discussion was difficult. John Arnold said he had been misreading the signals. Peter Jarman (Quaker) said, 'An error of judgement has taken place and Michael Bourdeaux's name should have been included.' Oestreicher

32   Document in Keston Archive.

said that he had seen the signals and this led to his current suggestion: that Xenia Dennen's name should be a late addition to the list.

Elizabeth Salter (Quaker): 'Is Michael saying that without his presence the delegation would be manipulated?' to which I replied, 'No, I'm not saying that, even though there have been some most unfortunate examples in recent years. My main point, if I had to choose one, is that a whole month of briefing cannot replace, for people without the background, the advice of a real expert on the spot. Somebody whose whole life has been spent studying these issues will know instinctively what is going on and will be able to guide the delegation in crucial moments in a way than cannot possibly happen from the sidelines.'[33]

Pete Peery: 'The frankness of Michael's approach has helped considerably. It is right that we should be aware of danger ahead of time. Last year the NCC in the USA came in for rough press criticism because it failed to anticipate the difficulties which would be incurred by sending its own delegation (who were a self-selected group of 260 people).'

Pastor Patkai (Hungarian member of EWRAC): 'Presumably the delegation will be trying to get inside the real situation and Keston is uniquely equipped to help in the process. The BCC should have requested its help at an earlier stage. If we are too diplomatic we fail. Represent yourselves as you are. Be open and honest. I was threatened in a similar way with the Lutheran World Federation's meetings in Hungary last year. I was told I would not get a visa and it would not be advisable to include me in the party. In the end I was included, I got my visa and I received the most wonderful welcome from my fellow countrymen.'

John Arnold said to me, 'You should not feel aggrieved at not being invited to join delegations … You are part of our home team.'

Following many high-octane interventions, Pastor Patkai put a resolution to reconsider the list and Stella Alexander seconded this. However, no vote was put and the matter was referred to the Standing Committee. The two people who, because of their official positions on EWRAC (chairperson and secretary), Elizabeth Salter and Paul, were empowered to do this had already made their views known, so I did not expect any outcome other than the possible inclusion of Xenia Dennen.

On 22 December Paul sent to me a handwritten letter, in which he said: 'To have included your name would have meant to put the whole project at risk … Your presentation actually made me wonder whether I'd made a great mistake. When I suggested this to some of the key people it became clear to me that even had EWRAC unanimously suggested you should go, this advice would have been rejected by the Executive Committee.'[34]

There is much more detail in the Keston Archive, which records how the affair continued up to the departure of the delegation itself. Xenia Dennen's name was

---

33   Unpublished notes written up immediately after the meeting, Keston Archive.
34   Keston Archive.

included as a member, so my interventions had had some effect. However, fate intervened in the most unexpected way. Just before the group was due to leave, the Chernobyl explosion occurred and Kiev was on the itinerary. Foreign Office advice was that no woman of childbearing age should go to Ukraine. She had little alternative but to accept the advice and so withdrew.

As events unfolded in 1986, there were already signs that Gorbachev was introducing new policies. Anatoli Shcharansky, the Jewish activist and dissident, had been released from prison and sent to the West on 11 February 1986. Surprisingly, the records of the delegation's visit do not contain any reference to this, nor do they suggest that there was any in-depth discussion with the Soviet hosts on whether this was a portent of significant change (as it turned out to be).

The reports which the delegation brought back were discussed at the EWRAC meeting on 1 July (when I was away on holiday, but Philip Walters represented Keston at it). The participants, Philip wrote, agreed that there had been an 'atmosphere of trust [in which] it had been possible to discuss difficult issues such as registration, dissidents etc.' He continued:

> Bychkov [General Secretary of the Baptist Union] made an attack on Keston College and Paul Oestreicher defended us as part of the British religious scene. His defence however made it clear that he and others disagreed with the alleged concentration by Keston College on persecution, and he did not draw attention to the range of our publications and breadth of our coverage.[35]

The Revd David Coffey (President-elect of the Baptist Union) expressed disappointment that there were so few Baptist contacts and he was distressed at the negative attitude of Russian Baptist leaders to political prisoners of their own faith. He commended Keston for illuminating the plight of the families of prisoners, some of whom he had visited.

Communism in Europe collapsed, bringing these controversies abruptly to an end. EWRAC's greatest moment should have been after 1989, when new possibilities opened up, but unfortunately a reassessment of the BCC's activities by the Archbishop of York, John Habgood, led to the abolition of EWRAC in that form. If such activities were to continue, individual churches would have to pay their share of the costs. There was no longer a permanent secretariat and no money to invite or send delegations. Just at the time when EWRAC might have operated with greatest effect, its abolition told us overnight how much we had lost. The minutes and records of its activities are held in Westcott House, Cambridge, and study of them would provide material for many a thesis.

In Geneva itself the WCC rapidly lost the influence it had commanded before the end of communism in Europe. Its international profile diminished, particularly after the Russian Orthodox Church no longer needed a forum in which it could publicise its views and discontinued its active involvement.

---

35   Keston Archive.

I received an official invitation to attend a conference in Geneva from 12–15 September 1991. We met at the Ecumenical Institute at Bossey, adjacent to the WCC headquarters. During the course of that meeting, a long-standing Romanian Orthodox representative on the Central Committee, Professor Dumitru Staniloae, came up to me and said (in precisely these words), 'Michael, you were right all along – and you are still right now.' This conference was supposed to be an appraisal of what had gone wrong, but its discussions, unprepared as they were, never saw publication and the member-churches since have not insisted on a full evaluation of Geneva's policies during the key years, 1961–91.

This was the end of Keston's involvement with the WCC. We established that we could be committed to ecumenism, but at the same time rectify, to the best of our ability, misleading information which had emanated from it. Had EWRAC lived on, we would undoubtedly have continued to play a positive role in that aspect of British church life.

Chapter XIV

Baptists and Other 'Evangelicals': Countering 'Disinformation'

There are at least eight themes interwoven in this chapter and the only perspective from which it is possible to keep them in view is that of Keston's or my personal involvement in them. During the late 1960s and over the next decade I had dealings, many of them convoluted and plagued by controversy, with the Baptist World Alliance (BWA, Washington DC), the Baptist Union (London), the Bible Society, the Russian Reform Baptists *(Initsiativniki)*, the All-Union Council of Evangelical Christians-Baptists (Moscow), the Christian Mission to the Communist World (Richard Wurmbrand), Underground Evangelism (Joe Bass) and Open Doors (Brother Andrew). Much of the material contained here comes from notes taken on conversations which had to remain secret at the time, but which can now be revealed.

Russian Documents and the Baptist World Alliance

In Tsarist days the fledgling Russian Baptist movement received more than a sympathetic ear from the USA: practical help was forthcoming in abundance, which makes one wonder why, in the time of great need from 1960–85 there was not a more defined and practical policy from a body with a massive membership (some 30 million in the USA alone). The Russians sent delegates to the first-ever Baptist World Congress in 1905 and the evangelist Ivan Prokhanov spoke of the persecution under the Tsarist regime. The second congress in 1911 raised no less than $66,000 in a morning for the building of a seminary in Russia.[1] In 1925, just after the death of Lenin, Prokhanov visited America again and secured the production of 175,000 volumes of Christian literature, including Bibles.[2] This was a time of enormous growth for Russian Baptists, but it was not long before the rise of Stalinism saw both the closing of the window of religious liberty, which Baptists had enjoyed, and the rupture of contacts with foreign countries. Echoing the Macedonian Christians of the *Acts of the Apostles*, Pavel Ivanov-Klyshnikov spoke at the Fourth Baptist World Congress (1928) and challenged those present to 'Come over and help us', but there could be no practical response to this.[3]

In reaction, as it were, to the condemnation of communism in subsequent Baptist congresses, the sole permitted publication of the Russian Baptists proclaimed in 1947:

---

1   Rebecca V. Strode, 'The Role of Baptists in Soviet Foreign Policy', *Survey*, London, No.1, 1985, p. 146.

2   Ibid., pp. 148–9.

3   Ibid., p. 149.

Not only do the Russian Baptists not consider communism to be an obstacle to evangelism, but they also fully contend that its socio-economic principles do not contradict the teaching of our Lord Jesus Christ.'[4]

It was not until 1954 that the first official small Baptist delegation went to Moscow, led by Dr F. Townley Lord, President of the Baptist World Alliance and minister of Bloomsbury Baptist Church in central London, and Dr Ernest Payne, General Secretary of the Baptist Union of Great Britain and Ireland. The following year, ten Soviet Baptists were able to come as delegates to the Ninth World Congress in London, two of whom were hosted by the Archbishop of Canterbury at Lambeth Palace. These were the years of Khrushchev's 'thaw', during which there was a cautious exploration of the new possibilities of contact. This was a short-lived period, however, supplanted by harsh victimisation, which coincided with Khrushchev's last five years in office (1959–64). This had a disastrous effect on the internal life of the Baptists and Evangelicals in Russia, both those registered by the authorities under the aegis of the All-Union Council of Evangelical Christians-Baptists (AUCECB) and those whom the state refused to register or who, on principle, would not apply for it.[5]

Persecution of the Baptists was universal throughout the USSR, though it varied in intensity from region to region. Leaders and activists in the unregistered churches faced show trials and imprisonment; families of prisoners were victimised; prosecution for teaching religion intensified (unlike the Orthodox Church, they were not permitted any seminary); production or circulation of religious literature was an offence, with secret printing presses being destroyed when discovered.

Though the registered church (under the AUCECB) avoided this comprehensive onslaught, it was at the cost of intimidation, adherence to the anti-religious legislation, state interference in the appointment of pastors, censorship of the one permitted publication, *Bratsky Vestnik* ('Fraternal Herald') and the presence of KGB appointees to some senior administrative positions. The leaders were a group of frightened and compliant people, but it was with them that Western Baptist leaders perforce had fellowship.

The immediate consequence of this renewed attack, including the disastrous imposition by the Soviet atheist authorities of new regulations restricting evangelism and much else, was not only a schism within the Baptist community, but also the rise of the most determined opposition to the new policy by the unregistered – and therefore more heavily disadvantaged – communities. They began systematically to send documents out of the Soviet Union detailing their plight.

---

4   *Bratsky Vestnik* (Fraternal Herald), Moscow, 4, 1947, p. 7 (cited in English in translation in Walter Sawatsky, *Soviet Evangelicals since World War II* (Herald Press, Ontario, 1981), p. 121).

5   See Michael Bourdeaux, *Religious Ferment in Russia* (Macmillan, London, 1968), *passim*.

Baptist Documents Reach the West

One of the documents in Keston's Archive, originally confidential, sheds light on how contacts were made. Denton Lotz, a young American Baptist, who would one day become General Secretary of the Baptist World Alliance (1988–2007) was in Moscow on a Russian-language course. He met a young Baptist and built up his trust. Subsequently a second man joined them as they walked into a wood. Lotz continues:

> [One] told of secret schools where believers instruct their children in the name of the Lord. He told of punishment that was given to those who taught and were discovered. He was only 27 years old and had already spent five years in prison for his Lord … The stranger took out of his pocket three letters. One was for the United Nations … They wanted me to mail these letters when I got back home. Personally, I became quite frightened. I had visions of prison and of being caught at the border … I said definitely, 'No'… I kept making excuses.[6]

The Russians shed tears and implored Denton Lotz to take at least one letter, saying that this was not for themselves, but for 300,000 Christians. There was a list of 250 pastors imprisoned for their faith. Lotz eventually agreed, took one letter only and secreted it in his room, where it stayed for the last two weeks of his course. Eventually, after much prayer and thought for the children he was helping, he brought it out and it became one of the body of documents which, by then, were beginning to reach the West in abundance.

Mikhail Zhidkov

Mikhail Zhidkov, the 'foreign minister' of the Moscow Baptist Church, as previously recounted, visited the Baptist Union headquarters in London in 1968. On this visit he stated that the AUCECB was trying to be reconciled with the unregistered Baptists. He also made many statements attacking their integrity, which I knew to be untrue and attempted to counter, for example, the claim that they were deliberately seeking martyrdom and creating a bad impression by vaunting their suffering. If they kept the law, all would be well (a claim which was to resurface dozens of times, not least in the mouths of Western visitors, over the next twenty years).

Zhidkov asked me why I had not called at the AUCECB headquarters in Moscow to find out the real situation, to which I replied that I had been denied a Soviet visa since 1964 and I had not known about the Reform Baptists then. Dr Ronald Goulding, General Secretary of the European Baptist Federation, was present at the conversation and claimed that the timing of my forthcoming book on the Baptists was unfortunate, because the persecution was easing and my work might exacerbate the situation. I replied that I was only giving a voice to those who could not appear on a public platform and make a case for themselves. Zhidkov said that moves for reconciliation were progressing well, which I questioned, wondering how this could possibly be

---

6   Denton Lotz, 'How the August 1967 Baptist Documents Arrived in the West' (undated), unpublished document, Keston Archive.

when all the leaders of the unregistered churches were in prison. I repeated insistently that my purpose was not to take sides (except against the Soviet opponents of religion), but to illuminate objectively a dark corner, about which abundant misinformation had already been published.

Dr Goulding, too, made an effort to inform Keston of what he knew. After he had visited the triennial Baptist Congress in Moscow, 9–11 December 1969, he deposited with us an extensive confidential report on what he had seen and heard. (It was difficult to verify because of the many errors in Russian names.)

Tokyo

A fraught year for my dealings with the Russian Baptists was 1970. I received an invitation from Radio Liberty (Munich) to go to Tokyo in the middle of July to report the Twelfth Baptist World Congress. Independently of that, the Revd Roger Hayden, a British delegate, approached me to ask advice about the keynote speech he was to give there on religious liberty. Roger, who would subsequently become Chairman of Keston, wanted to be better informed and was disturbed by ongoing reports of persecution. He was determined to grasp this opportunity, but wanted to be absolutely sure of his facts. His eventual text, which he showed me, was excellent, covering Albania, China and India, as well as the Soviet Union.

It is difficult, in retrospect, to underline how important such events seemed at the time. It is only too easy to represent them as jamborees for participants. They were much more than this. In a world of travel bans on Russian Christians (and many others from the communist bloc), an opportunity to pass through the curtain and have fellowship with their Western counterparts was unmissable. Delegations were permitted exit permits, but the credentials of each individual were vetted by the authorities; delegates had to report back and their activities were carefully monitored by a KGB operative who, wearing a cloak of sincerity, had to monitor their activities. The delegates were tightly held in a vice and the end result had to be a gain for Soviet propaganda. It was in this fraught atmosphere that Roger Hayden prepared his paper.

We deliberately had not planned to meet in Tokyo before his speech, but I received a call in my room from Roger asking me to see him urgently. He was clearly in some distress. The Russian delegation, he said, had vetoed the section of his paper which concerned them. Roger had submitted it for duplication, ready for distribution the next morning, just before the speech itself. The BWA officials, unwisely, had shown it to the Russians and there was immediate consternation, to put it mildly. The organisers of the congress summoned Roger for a meeting with the Russians.

At this point in the evening, Roger called for me to be at the meeting and the Russian delegation could do little other than agree to my presence during the discussion. However, as I was not a delegate, I remained silent and promised not to report what I was hearing. Roger said the text could not be changed, as hundreds of copies had been duplicated and were ready for distribution next morning. The Russians invited him to scrap the text, saying that to present it would make the situation for them and their fellow believers back home disastrously worse. Several times the Russians mentioned my name as the perpetrator of falsified information, yet they did not dispute that there were about 170 Reform Baptist prisoners at the time and this was mentioned in the text.

The arguments were protracted and went on well into the night. Eventually the Russians persuaded Roger to omit the Russian section of his paper, against the promise that when they returned they would take a new initiative with the Soviet Government to try to persuade the authorities to release the prisoners, claiming that secret diplomacy would be far more effective than a public bludgeon. It was, however, far too late for Roger to rewrite the text. The best that could be done was to use scissors and paste, cutting out the title, printing a new one, and omitting the whole section on Russia. Secretaries were summoned and the operation performed in the small hours. The result was an obvious codge – anyone could see that the printed text had been subjected to crude surgery.

Roger delivered his expurgated text, but not one delegate or journalist raised the question of why the text looked as it did. Nor did anyone ask why there was no reference to the Soviet Union, when the world's press had been reporting on discrimination against believers for months.

If the Soviet delegation did make their promised approach to the Kremlin, nothing came of it. The *Baptist Times* subsequently published the unexpurgated text, but even then no one raised the question of why it differed from what had been distributed in Tokyo.[7]

This uncomfortable experience deepened Roger's commitment to religious liberty and he retained a lifelong interest in the East European scene. He became an important figure in the Baptist denomination, a leading church historian and Superintendent of the Western Area of the Baptist Union.

Mikhail Zhidkov Again

In 1970 I received another invitation to a meeting at Baptist Church House in London with Mikhail Zhidkov, but this time accompanied by a new face, Alexei Bychkov, the new General Secretary of AUCECB. He, at the relatively young age of 42, promised a new approach. I hoped that this would herald a more constructive relationship with those who reported the truth about Soviet reality. He was personable and talked immediately of his personal problems in bringing up his children in the faith. Indeed, his daughter of 19 had abandoned it; his son, a year younger, was a believer, but was unable to go to church.[8]

---

7   *Baptist Times*, 1970.

8   'Notes on Conversation between Michael Bourdeaux, Alexei Mikhailovich Bychkov and Mikhail Zhidkov, Baptist House, 22 September 1970, 3-5 p.m. and telephone conversation, 23 September', marked 'strictly confidential' and here reported for the first time.

I have no doubt that this opening of the conversation was engineered in order to produce a good impression, but I also have no reason to believe that it was not sincere. It was Zhidkov himself who had called this meeting and I suspected that he must have a reason for doing so. This soon became evident. He wanted – possibly at the request of the KGB – to find out what he could about the work of the Centre for the Study of Religion and Communism, just beginning at that time, beyond what he could glean from printed sources. I was open with him and told him we had no secrets. I listed the names of our patrons and Council of Management, emphasising how this guaranteed the integrity of our work, stressing that there would have been a quick comeback if we ever fell below the highest standards. Of course, the staff of the Centre was very small at the time and there was little to say about them – but their names, too, could be gleaned from what we published. Zhidkov did say that our objective approach worried the Soviet authorities more than the emotive appeals of Pastor Richard Wurmbrand, which were attracting publicity at the time.

Wurmbrand had published *Tortured for Christ* at almost the same time as my *Opium*. A Romanian convert from Judaism, he had suffered long imprisonment, before a group of Norwegian evangelicals secured his emigration, and his body bore the marks of torture. His book immediately saw translations into many languages, which preceded his invitations worldwide. His emotional, charismatic addresses, attacking communism head-on, attracted support and his appearances led to the establishment of missions worldwide, under the title in the UK, 'Jesus to the Communist World'. I met Richard early on, was impressed by his personality, but less so by his lack of attention to detail. In talking of 'millions' of Christian prisoners, he did not differentiate among the countries he was describing.

At our meeting Mikhail Zhidkov told me that, as members of a delegation, they were permitted each to take back fifty Russian Bibles to Moscow, but Dr Goulding had told them he did not have any. I said I could help at once. I telephoned the Revd Stuart Harris, Director of the European Christian Mission, which had an association with Wurmbrand, and arranged for them to be delivered the next day. After this had happened, I received a telephone call from Zhidkov, saying that the Bibles were unacceptable, as they 'came from Wurmbrand'. I said this was untrue. ECM had existed long before 'Jesus to the Communist World' and the two organisations were separate. Zhidkov insisted that they were 'Wurmbrand's Bibles'. I replied that a Bible was a Bible and that his allegation was untrue in any case, because they had not been printed by his organisation. I defended the reputation of Stuart Harris with some vigour. They did eventually decide to take the Bibles, as they were urgently needed for the students on a biblical correspondence course which AUCECB was just beginning, a concession recently granted.

We talked about a controversial figure, Dmitri Krasnenkov, who had been a student at Spurgeon's College in London and whom I had invited to my parents' house in Cornwall for a weekend in 1958. We had had hours of conversations, I said, during which I tried to calm his nerves and allay his suspicions that he was being constantly watched. We stood alone on the cliffs at Land's End without a soul in sight, but a fishing boat passed by. *'Eto patrulnaya,'* he said – 'It's a patrol boat.' I wasn't sure whether he thought it was spying on him or stopping the Cornish from emigrating illegally. After Dmitri's return to Moscow he disappeared from the scene and I heard that he had denied his faith. Zhidkov told me that Dmitri had been excommunicated by the Baptist authorities for extolling the virtues of drinking and smoking. I said that he certainly had not picked up any of this in my parents' house, suspecting that the real cause of the trouble might have been his contact with me. Zhidkov denied this and said that I was welcome to talk to any Soviet Baptist students at any time and in any place.

The conversation ended with a rather coarse observation from Zhidkov. He said, 'If you look around the streets of London, you'll see many different fashions, the mini-skirts, the maxi. Choose the midi, Michael, choose the midi …' Then (in a corny American accent), 'Cool off, boy, cool off.'

On the street outside and while Zhidkov was detained inside, Bychkov, who had said little earlier, conveyed apologies from the Russian delegation for the way they had treated me in Tokyo.

World Reactions

Over the years I had many conversations with senior Western Baptists and it might be useful here to record some impressions.

In 1966 Dr Josef Nordenhaug (born in Norway and working in America), who served as General Secretary of the Baptist World Alliance from 1960–69, visited Moscow and what he reported to his constituency became more or less the accepted mantra for a generation. His conversation with the AUCECB officials persuaded him that the complaints of the Reform Baptists were unjustified, being motivated in some instances by a personal ambition for leadership and bringing trouble upon themselves. While many of the Reform Baptists had well-motivated Christian convictions, he averred, 'There are others who major on separatism… A few have a craving for being martyrs on a limited scale and deliberately seek to be arrested.'[9]

Had Dr Nordenhaug been able to meet the Reform Baptists in person, he might have reflected on his use of the term 'limited', when two hundred of the most active pastors and laity were in prison, when some registered congregations had been thrown out of their buildings and countless unregistered ones assaulted by the police almost daily. A few believers had met their deaths at the hands of their persecutors: the murder of Nikolai Khmara had taken place two years before Nordenhaug's visit to Moscow.

Dr Ernest Payne, to some extent, shared these attitudes, though he never expressed them so strongly in public. His outlook was conditioned by the personal friendships he had made with Russian Baptist leaders on his first visit to Moscow. He found it

---

9   Josef Nordenhaug, *The Baptists in the USSR* (Washington DC, 1966), pp. 7–8.

difficult to comprehend the deep split in the ranks of Baptist faithful in the 1960s. He also believed that all Russian Baptists should obey the existing law.

One result of all that had happened was that Dr David Russell, when he took over the reins of General Secretary of the Baptist Union from Dr Ernest Payne in 1967, applied himself to these contentious matters with the utmost seriousness. We developed a relationship of trust which enabled us to pass on specific cases to him. Many times on visits to the Soviet Union he raised individual cases, based on information which we had sent him.

I experienced something of the prevalent American attitude among senior Baptists when I visited Adolph Klaupiks, of Latvian origin, at his home in Philadelphia in 1971. Klaupiks served on the BWA staff from 1947, initially dealing with correspondence concerning the resettlement of displaced persons, of whom he had been one, but from 1961 until his retirement in 1968 he had the title of Relief Co-ordinator. He told me that on his travels in the Soviet Union representatives of the Reform Baptists had often approached him and he did agree to take their appeals back with him, which, as he was on official visits, he could presumably do without too many problems. He had acquired a drawer full of documents. As I had already published some of these, he obviously felt free to show them to me, though he did not allow me to hold them in my hands, so I could not check whether there were any which were unknown to us.

I asked Mr Klaupiks whether he had passed on these texts to the people to whom they were addressed (for example, the United Nations) and he declined to comment on this. We had what I must describe as an unsatisfactory conversation and I detected no depth of sympathy for the Reform Baptists, some of whom he knew personally. Our meeting did not last long.

I was genuinely puzzled during Keston's early years about the lack of reaction worldwide to the plight of the Russian Baptists. I could clearly see the systematic pressure by the state, the mental terror brought on the official leadership of the Church, the savagery of the treatment of the unregistered Baptists, yet in the midst of it all there was evidence of heroism and devotion to the faith, the like of which had only rarely been seen in history. The Reform Baptists had no substantial theological dispute with their registered counterparts, but the essential controversy was whether state interference in the administrative aspect of church life should be resisted. To put it simply: the registered Baptists allowed their children to wear the red neckerchief of the atheistic Young Pioneers; the unregistered did not.

Emigration

From the early 1970s the Soviet regime began to make a significant concession. There had been a German community in Russia since the days of Catherine the Great. They preserved their own language within their communities, but had undergone severe disruption of their lives and deportation from their Volga-region homelands during the

Second World War. Some subsequently returned, but in the 1970s they were still spread widely in the regions of their banishment, where others had settled permanently. Among them were believers of several different traditions, Baptists, Mennonites and Catholics. At the same time as many Jews began to petition the Soviet Government for the right to emigrate, the Soviet Germans did the same, and with growing success during the 1970s. There was a financial deal: the West German authorities paid a ransom to the Soviet Government to secure each person who emigrated. It was no easy task for the Bonn Government to resettle them. They wanted to preserve their own communities without integrating into West German society. They found it uncongenial because of what they considered to be its moral laxity and failure to impose standards on the younger generation. Many of them established their own community in Neuwied, on the Rhine near Koblenz.

In one particularly productive and informative meeting with a group of Russian-German Baptists in Oslo in December 1973 I gained many new insights which had not been possible from the documents which I had been reading and translating. Their families in the Soviet Union, sometimes comprising fifteen children, parents and grandparents, formed the basic unit of their congregations. They insisted on teaching the faith to their children, in church as well as at home. This ensured that they received repeated refusals in their regular attempts (at least twice a year) to register, and thus to live within the law. The authorities replied that they would grant registration only if the congregations renounced special prayer services, kept children away from church, gave up helping the old and sick in state institutions, renounced the right to elect their own leaders and restricted their pastor from visiting neighbouring villages to preach.

While none of this was new to me, it was stunning to hear it from such brave figures as Arnold Rose, himself one of fifteen children, and Johann Jundt, who had become a Christian in 1957, after abandoning life as a drunkard and active atheist who had himself mocked and persecuted believers. The humanity, dedication and zeal which shone in their eyes and resounded in the passionate speech of these people reinforced my conviction that they could on no account be considered fanatics and that they had qualities which would be admired by the vast majority of Christians in the West. One point which they emphasised and which was new to me was how good relations in the USSR often were with the local registered Baptist communities. They felt sorry for the pastors who were under the thumb of the atheist authorities and who were forced to keep unacceptable regulations. The unregistered Baptists often welcomed the children of families from registered congregations who were sent to them for religious instruction. Iosif Bondarenko, one of their heroic evangelists, had even once preached to a great welcome in a registered Orthodox church in Riga, having donned a cassock for the occasion. I asked what, in their view, was the single most striking characteristic of the Reform Baptists and they answered, 'Prayer for every member of the congregation and organised relief for the sick and for families whose bread-winner was in prison for the faith. We are like the Christians of the Acts of the Apostles who organised relief for the Jerusalem Christians..

Expulsion: Georgi Vins

Following Sir John Lawrence's and my visit to Nadezhda Vins in Kiev, as described earlier, eighteen months later (28 April 1979) the phone rang in the middle of the night. A voice announced itself as an official of the State Department in Washington DC. 'We have to tell you that Georgi Vins has just been expelled by the Soviet authorities. He's on a plane now to New York and we need you to come over at once to help us to debrief him.' I rang back to ensure that I was not the victim of a joke or provocation, but shortly afterwards I was on my way by taxi from Chislehurst to Heathrow Airport.

My instructions were to report to the UN Plaza Hotel in Manhattan. To my astonishment, when I walked into the room where Vins was that evening, there were four other 'dissidents' with him, all of whom had been exchanged in a deal for seven people held in US gaols as Soviet spies. Among them was Eduard Kuznetsov, who was a Jewish dissident, editor of the *samizdat* journal *Syntaxis*, who had been sentenced to death after being convicted of taking part in a plot to hijack an aeroplane – this subsequently commuted to fifteen years in prison. All were well known to me by name. It was, of course, an astonishing experience. The Soviets were high on adrenaline, though physically exhausted after their ordeal. Their prison-camp commandants had sent them peremptorily to Moscow, where they were fed, shaved, issued with civilian clothes and bundled on an aeroplane without so much as an explanation of where they were going. Not surprisingly, they were disorientated. Out on the balcony of the room where we met, they looked at the lights of Manhattan and could not express their emotions. It was difficult to know where to start and try to have a coherent conversation. At least this first night there was no formal debriefing.

Pastor Vins already had an American minder, who became a good friend: Dr Olin Robison, President of Middlebury College, Vermont, a Baptist in touch with Soviet affairs and host to a renowned Russian summer school at his college. He had evidently played a leading role in persuading the US administration to put Vins's name on the exchange list.

We quickly moved to Washington DC, where a formal reception at the State Department awaited Vins. President Jimmy Carter, a Baptist himself, had a private conversation with him, Olin and an interpreter. Sadly, I was not permitted to meet the President and had to await the outcome of the meeting while in the next room. Many years later I met the retired President in Oxford, but he had no recollection of the event.

It had fallen to Olin's lot to arrange for Vins's onward passage. His plan was to take us both to Middlebury College, where we could discuss detailed arrangements for the future. I stayed there for several days, trying to get to know a man who had spent so many of his recent years in prison. It was not that easy. However, he quickly began to express his own clear ideas. Predominant was his determination to align himself with the Soviet Germans who had recently emigrated and whom he trusted more than his American rescuers. I quickly discerned the iron will which had brought him through his ordeals. In him the KGB had found a worthy opponent with a stronger will than they. Some of his colleagues arrived from Germany and took over his timetable.

I had left by the time Vins returned to Washington DC. Now the Baptist World Alliance had arranged a proper welcome for him and the immediate outcome was remarkable. He addressed a conference in May 1979 of thirty leading BWA officials, including David Russell and Robert Denny, who was now its General Secretary. Vins received, according to one who was present, 'a hero's welcome, complete with photographs, applause and congratulations'.[10] He moved on to Houston, Texas, where the Southern Baptist Convention gave him a similar welcome. Both groups, apparently, offered him platforms in their own churches and financial support.

Sadly, however, these initiatives, which promised so much, came to nothing long-lasting. There were clearly problems on both sides. Although the time was right for healing the rift between the Reform Baptists and the BWA, the psychological problems were too great. Vins, on his part, trusted no one except those who had been through the crucible of suffering with him in the Soviet Union. The BWA had too long a record of criticism of the Reform Baptists, but one can understand their frustration at the lack of immediate response from Vins, now accompanied by his émigré advisers.

Vins requested the BWA to invite his co-leader, Pastor Gennadi Kryuchkov, still in the Soviet Union and on the run from the KGB, to address the next World Congress in Toronto in 1980. The aim, of course, was to protect Kryuchkov, rather than to expect his physical presence. But after months of silence, the BWA leadership eventually declined, on the spurious grounds that the Reform Baptists were not affiliated to the movement, so Vins could not appear either. The BWA attempted a compromise: Vins could attend, but without the right to speak. But Vins was not a man of compromise. He requested the right to speak on behalf of the 'persecuted church': he would not criticise the AUCECB, but would confine himself to describing the conditions under which the Reform Baptists lived. Alexei Bychkov was consulted, but, not surprisingly, protested at this suggestion and no invitation followed. Eventually Vins sponsored a small parallel conference in Toronto, called the 'Voice of the Persecuted Church'. It did present the facts, but naturally this led to a further deterioration of his relations with American Baptist officialdom.

I have already mentioned Georgi Vins's visit to Keston and his request for us to withdraw his *Three Generations of Suffering*, to which we acceded. Fortunately, the later part of our meeting was more satisfactory. He began to look at our archives and gradually his emotion and admiration took over. He physically shed tears when he saw his own original signature and those of his trusted friends on some of the documents in our possession. He had seen them many years before, between his two periods of imprisonment, but he thought all copies had been confiscated by the KGB. Now here they were again and he could hold them in his hands.

---

10   Strode, op. cit., p. 155.

Pastor Vins and I kept in touch and I was eventually able to write an obituary for *The Guardian* when he died several years later.[11]

Billy Graham

The BWA was far from being the only American Protestant organisation which was interested in the Soviet Union during those years. The Billy Graham Evangelistic Association commanded worldwide attention and support. It had been known for some time that Billy Graham, a Southern Baptist pastor who had close associations with the BWA, had once visited Moscow privately and expressed to the AUCECB leaders his wish to come back and preach.

As conditions in the USSR imperceptibly eased, at least as far as foreign visitors were concerned, it became known that Billy Graham planned to preach in several communist countries. He was already well known by reputation in Russia and translations of some of his books had circulated clandestinely. When Iosif Bondarenko led an audacious and successful evangelistic campaign he acquired the nickname, 'the Billy Graham of the Ukraine'. In 1982 and 1984 the opportunity opened up for the American evangelist himself to become the 'Billy Graham of the Soviet Union.' For Graham, these were opportunities which, a few years before, would have been beyond the wildest dream. The visits eventually took place, but they were never free of controversy and did not quite fulfil the great hopes placed in them.

The Soviet Union, in the early 1980s, was still alive with various officially sponsored 'peace initiatives'. The authorities hoped that any visiting church dignitaries from the West whom they could influence would, at least by passive implication, endorse Soviet foreign policy. So it was that in 1982 Billy Graham appeared at a conference sponsored by the Moscow Patriarchate entitled, 'Religious Workers for Saving the Sacred Gift of Life from Nuclear Catastrophe'.

The announcement that Billy Graham would be one of the main speakers naturally aroused worldwide interest, both because he was known for having been close to a succession of American presidents and also, of course, because evangelistic rallies of his type were anathema to Soviet atheism. In the event, his speech did not in any sense endorse Soviet policies or the unilateralist view of nuclear disarmament. He was clearly addressing governments worldwide, not just the Kremlin:

'Talk about peace must never become a substitute for actions that will lead to peace... We should urge all governments to respect the rights of religious believers as outlined in the UN Universal Declaration of Human Rights.'[12]

Prior negotiations had granted him the right to preach as well, which he did both in the Baptist church and the Orthodox cathedral, attended by large crowds. Yet there was trouble. The Billy Graham Evangelistic Association claimed that this was caused by

11   *The Guardian*, London, 22 January 1998, p. 16.

12   Billy Graham, *Approaching Hoofbeats* (Hodder & Stoughton, London, 1984), p. 142. The book prints the whole text of his Moscow speech.

journalists, to whom he spoke while hurrying between meetings, and that they had tried to create an incident out of nothing. There is no transcript of what Graham said, but he should certainly have been prepared to field questions about the situation of Baptists in the Soviet Union. He apparently said that there was 'a measure' of religious freedom in the USSR and, according to one newspaper, he continued: 'It would seem to me that in the churches I visited – and there are thousands of them – services are allowed to go on freely'.[13]

There was obviously some mis-reporting here, as Graham cannot have claimed to have visted thousands of churches, but he meant that he had visited some of the thousands of Baptist churches. He also referred disparagingly to the existence of a 'state church' in some countries, such as England, while comparing this to a preferable system, such as that in the Soviet Union, where there is separation of church and state. Whatever his actual words, he certainly conveyed the impression that he was agreeably surprised by the degree of freedom of religion which he found.

Soviet publications, of course, were ready to distort what he said and use it for their own purposes. The atheist flagship journal, *Nauka i religia* ('Science and Religion'), put it thus:

'As far as Billy Graham himself was concerned, he has stressed that during his time in Moscow he was 'unable to discover evidence of any kind of religious persecution'. 'Naturally', he remarked, 'there are differences in religious practice in the USA and the USSR, but this does not mean that there is no religious liberty in the Soviet Union. My own observations in Moscow indicate that there is complete freedom of religion."[14]

Doubtless, this statement contains distortion, but one is nevertheless surprised that Billy Graham's team of advisers did not prepare a careful statement on the topic which he could have read out at any appropriate time. To have called simply for prayer for the oppressed would have defused the whole controversy at the outset. Billy Graham was clearly being guarded and was presumably hoping to establish his credentials in preparation for a longer visit. Yet he had witnessed a demonstration, albeit a minor one, in Moscow's only Baptist church, when a group of Reform Baptists suspended a banner in English from the balcony, calling for the release of prisoners. His hosts would certainly have underplayed this.

There was no other public incident of note during this official visit, but there was a private one which became public later when Graham called on the 'Siberian Seven'. They were a group of Pentecostals immured for four years in a single basement room of the American Embassy. They had taken refuge there following their invasion of the embassy compound, demanding that the Americans petition for registration for the Pentecostals, who were outlawed as a denomination. It reflects credit on Billy Graham that he went to see the group, but Timothy Chmykhalov, one of their number,

13   *International Herald Tribune* (Paris), 22 June 1982.

14   *Nauka i religia*, Moscow, 10, 1982, pp. 3 ff. quoted as part of an interview the journal had with Vladimir Kuroyedov, Chairman of the Council for Religious Affairs.

subsequently wrote that Graham's advisers had visited them ahead of the meeting and sworn them to secrecy. Chmykhalov, then aged twenty, had spent virtually the whole of his young life either victimised at school or, for four years, confined to a small area of the embassy, so he was a little surprised to hear Billy Graham say, 'I came to preach, not to get involved with any political issues' and he claimed that of the many visitors they were freely permitted to receive, this was 'the most strange, the most disappointing visit … in my basement home'.[15]

News of Graham's subsequent visit in 1984 quickly spread nationwide among Baptists and they flocked to Moscow. At the last minute before his sermon in the Moscow Baptist church, there was a sudden change of schedule. The original plan was to preach to the Orthodox in the morning of 9 May and to the Baptists in the evening. Now the Baptist sermon would be at 9 a.m., followed immediately by the visit to the Orthodox cathedral. The reason for this is self-evident and Billy Graham's advisers should have refused. The Soviets would almost certainly have yielded, in order to prevent a row.

In the event, Graham's team accepted the change, with predictable consequences. Although there had never been an official announcement of the sermon, when people arrived, some from afar, they found that it had already taken place. Now, however, there was an excuse to rush the preacher to his next destination, saying that his second hosts would be mortally offended if he should be late. This precluded the original intention Graham had: to walk freely among the great crowd which he thought would gather outside the church. The Revd Ilya Orlov rushed him into his car and it took off at speed. The police had blocked off the street in which the church was situated, but many more people had massed in the adjacent one. There was not even an opportunity to greet them. Billy Graham later, at a meeting described below, told me that, when he arrived at the cathedral, he was much earlier than expected and they kept him waiting – and standing uncomfortably – for a considerable length of time before formally introducing him to the congregation. He told me that his only thought at that time was that he needed to go to the bathroom!

Some controversy in the Western press followed Graham's return from the USSR. Had he encountered the realities? It was, therefore, a surprise and a unique opportunity when I received a telephone call from Billy Graham in person, inviting me to come to Paris to meet him. I flew out on 6 October 1982 and, after staying overnight, went early to his hotel.

His first words were, 'Michael, what went wrong?' It could not have been a warmer or more friendly conversation, lasting unbroken for some six or seven hours, with no advisers present and no notes taken. We did not even go for lunch, which was served in his room. I was deeply impressed with Billy Graham's sincerity and he treated me as a friend from the very first – not a hint of wariness or mistrust. I was soon convinced

---

15   Timothy Chmykhalov, *Release* (Marshall, London), 1984, pp. 114–6.

that Graham was deeply aware that not all had been well with the visit, doubtless due in part to the inadequate briefing he had had before leaving.

I was able – indeed he encouraged me – to state my concerns with complete openness. As outlined above, I spoke of his lack of preparation in handling the inevitable questions from the press corps, his manipulation by the KGB over the time of the sermon in the Baptist church and the omission of any occasion when he could simply shake the hands of the people who gathered on the streets to see him. At the same time I commended what he had said in his difficult speech at the earlier peace conference. He said he wished he could have had this conversation before going, to which I replied that I was available as an adviser any time.

At the end he warmly invited me to stay with him ('any time') at his home in Montreat, North Carolina, and I said I would work it into my next visit to America, if possible. Sadly, no occasion arose in 1983 and then the situation changed dramatically.

Something odd happened. Following our Paris meeting, Keston had indeed been fully in contact with the Billy Graham Evangelistic Association in the months leading up to his long-planned next visit to the Soviet Union, but three weeks before his departure we received a strange telex from Dr Alexander Haraszti, one of his staff, who seemed to be the key person in setting up this visit. Haraszti ordered us to break off contact immediately and not to be in touch in any way until after the trip was over. Was Haraszti aware of our Paris meeting? I never found out.

In the weeks following Billy Graham's latest visit, I spoke to dozens of people whom I would regard as experts on the Soviet Union, both in the secular and religious fields. Not a single one of these has been even moderately happy with its overall outcome.

Billy Graham and a team of ten staff next visited Leningrad, Tallinn, Novosibirsk and Moscow, in that order, from 9–21 September 1984 (during which time I was personally too involved with events following the Templeton Prize award to pay a great deal of personal attention to the visit). Obviously the Soviet authorities were satisfied with the way Billy Graham had conducted himself on the previous occasion and especially with its fall-out in the Western press. Now there had been much more time for preparation, for the setting of objectives and almost two weeks in the Soviet Union to fulfil them. There were far more preaching opportunities than either he or his staff can have expected initially.

In this overall assessment, I pay attention both to the subsequent booklet and the official film distributed by the Billy Graham Evangelistic Association, as well as to one of the contemporary press reports. One highly regarded American publication quoted Billy Graham as having said:

'So some groups get extremely fanatical and they do things they think are right when actually they are breaking Soviet law and they get into trouble. But you can go to church. They're building seven new Baptist churches in Moscow… Under Leonid

Brezhnev there was a period of great relaxation toward the churches, also under Andropov to a great degree.'[16]

It is impossible to discover how accurate was this quotation, fallacious as it is in every single sentence, but there was no refutation in the official book of the visit.

The official volume, *Billy Graham in the Soviet Union,* published more than a year after this visit, provides the opportunity to check the organisation's own assessment of the achievements of the visit, free of glosses and possible misinterpretations by the press.[17]

The book consists of 96 pages, with much of the space devoted to lavish illustrations. To the general reader, unfamiliar with conditions then prevailing in the USSR, it gives the impression of an evangelist enjoying unfettered progress through the country, with opportunities to preach the gospel unhindered. Everywhere he met the utmost cordiality and enjoyed lavish hospitality: there are no less than thirteen photographs showing tables laden with food and drink (non-alcoholic, of course). In the accompanying film there are segments, especially about the 'hero-city' Leningrad, which might have come straight from an official Soviet travelogue.

There are a few passages in the text of the book, however, which indicate that not all was quite as it seemed on the surface, but they are scattered and do not amount to an exposé of Soviet reality. Walter Smyth, a senior member of Billy Graham's staff, does state that in the Soviet Union 'religious belief is not encouraged'.[18] Even at this time, 1984, we should remind ourselves, teaching of religion to anyone under the age of eighteen was punishable by imprisonment and there were indeed many under sentence at that very moment. However, Billy Graham believes 'because he has been reliably told – that there is a certain amount of oppression, and in some areas of the Soviet Union suppression of religious freedom.'[19] The subsequent text gives no indication of the nature of this repression. One has to go right through to p. 79 to read Billy Graham's reference in his address to the Baptist 'Jubilee Seminar' to the 'active persecution that you have endured' and to the very end (p. 92) to read that, in meeting Soviet political leaders, he said: 'Such issues as religious freedom and the imprisonment of unregistered believers are of real concern to American Christians and Jews.' These statements, at least, seem to counterbalance the probable inaccuracy of the quoted press report.

This last sentence is followed by these words: 'Nevertheless officially recognized Soviet churches enjoy religious liberties today on a scale which they have not known for decades.' Billy Graham appears, at this moment, to have believed that there had been a recent overall improvement and this is probably the same point which he

16   *USA Today,* 15 May 1985.

17   Bob Terrell, *Billy Graham in the Soviet Union* (Billy Graham Evangelistic Association, Minneapolis, 1985).

18   Ibid., p. 5.

19   Ibid., p. 9.

made to the American reporter. Leonid Brezhnev, in his last years, acted outside the law to suppress any voice calling for greater religious liberty or for a real separation of church and state. Andropov, it is known, entertained a crusading zeal to suppress dissent by every illegal means.[20] Billy Graham is further officially quoted as saying:

> Many churches are open and active and are allowed to carry out their work on church premises so long as they are registered as the law requires. At the same time, the Soviet Union does not allow churches to be a rallying point for what it considers to be anti-Soviet activities. Congregations that refuse to register run into difficulties and may face definite opposition from their government.'[21]

It was as though my Paris meeting with Billy Graham had not taken place. I had emphasised that he needed only to read some of the documents in the Keston Archive to learn that some evangelical congregations had repeatedly applied for registration, but had been refused. Others would not apply, because to do so made them promise to keep laws (such as agreeing not to instruct their children in the faith) which contradicted their own conscience. Graham's statement repeats virtually every myth the Soviet government of the day wanted to propagate: if you keep the law you are safe. The truth is that registration itself was used as an act of control and suppression. The book is silent on this.

The book refers in summary to a conversation lasting almost two hours which Billy Graham had with Boris Ponomarev, a member of the Politburo, during which he raised the issue of 'human and religious rights repeatedly'.[22] There was clearly an agenda to improve the lot of the ordinary believers, but this comes out as a minor theme only in the overall assessment of the visit. There is a misleading statement on the printing of Bibles,[23] but this is nothing beside the claim that 'nine of his books have been printed in the Russian language and are circulating there'.[24] Any reader would assume that this meant that they had been officially printed and circulated, whereas the reality is that they were produced elsewhere and brought into the USSR only in minute quantities (possibly copied and further circulated as *tamizdat* – literature produced outside the country and circulated clandestinely inside). There have been many reports of such Western volumes having been confiscated during house searches or raids on churches by the KGB. Similarly, 'cassette tapes of Mr Graham's messages would later be distributed in many parts of the Soviet Union'.[25] Indeed they were – but clandestinely – and there is a report of Christians in Estonia having been in trouble for distributing a videotape of one of his messages.

---

20   See Christopher Andrew and Vasili Mitrokhin, *The Mitrokhin Archive* (Penguin, London, 2014), pp. 651–7

21   Terrell, op. cit., p. 93.

22   Ibid., p. 82.

23   Ibid., p. 9.

24   Ibid., p. 92.

25   Ibid., p. 76.

Perhaps it would be better not to refer to the more quirky statements, yet some of them are irresistible, particularly those referring to his time in Estonia. 'Estonians relish caviar with Pepsi Cola',[26] which may or may not be true, but it masks the fact that at that time caviar was virtually unobtainable except by the *nomenklatura* and for the purpose of entertaining foreign visitors. The Orthodox cathedral in Tallinn may or may not be 'beautiful',[27] but it was built in the nineteenth century and was then a *Russian* Orthodox church, symbolising for many Tsarist imperialism of the time (since then the persecuted Estonian Orthodox Church has re-established itself as an independent entity).

The film of the visit, in a powerful sequence, shows young people in Novosibirsk struggling to hear Billy Graham through the open windows of the Novosibirsk Baptist Church, but it is strange to see a picture (p. 86) of Richard Owen, then Moscow correspondent of *The Times*, and his wife in church, allegedly representing the younger generation. Anyone can make mistakes, but the fact remains that the Billy Graham Evangelistic Association had used this photograph a year earlier for the same purpose. Keston pointed out the error then, but it slipped in for a second time.

Before the earlier visit of 1982 Dr Haraszti visited the Soviet Union five times in five months. Then before the next trip there were twelve preparatory visits to Moscow, some involving more than one person.[28] On the latter occasion ten aides accompanied him. No one would expect such secret negotiations to go on public record, but they must have been incredibly detailed and some of what transpired would make interesting reading. Perhaps sometime one of the participants might write a frank memoir. Billy Graham, with his world reputation, was of course a special case, but one might note that several other American preachers (Jimmy Swaggart, for example) visited the Soviet Union even before the advent of *glasnost* with nothing like the elaborate preparations. Billy Graham's essential message in his preaching was: 'Jesus Christ… is willing to come into your heart, into your family, into your great country, and change your hearts.'[29] Perhaps he was aware that he was, incidentally, addressing a posse of KGB assessors, but the majority were already Christians and many had suffered for it. 'A high percentage [*of listeners*] indicated their desire to follow Christ as Lord and Saviour'[30] states the booklet.

We at Keston were deluged with queries for months after this visit, some asking such questions as, 'It's not really as bad in the Soviet Union as we've been told, is it?' We thought we should try to put the record straight and wrote to the Billy Graham Evangelistic Association, expressing some disappointment at the lack of follow up to my Paris meeting with Billy Graham two years earlier. After all, in a very real sense, these

---

26   Ibid., p. 8.

27   Ibid., p. 37.

28   Ibid., p. 6.

29   Ibid., p. 25.

30   Ibid., p. 5.

visits had aroused some doubts about our documentation of persecution in the Soviet Union, so we had no alternative but to try to clarify what Billy Graham really believed. Dr Walter Smyth wrote an unequivocal reply to my letter, here quoted for the first time:

> Let me assure you that Mr Graham has a definite and deep concern for those who are being oppressed and persecuted because of their faith, no matter where they are found. He is the first to admit that his trips to Eastern Europe have been far too brief for him to claim to be an expert on the problems of the churches in that part of the world. [What of the numerous preparatory visits by his staff?] In addition, though he has wanted to meet with representatives of unregistered churches, this had not been possible except in a few instances. At the same time, however, I want to assure you he is not naïve about those who are involved in unregistered churches, or are otherwise involved in activities which are interpreted as illegal by their governments. Before each trip he has been thoroughly briefed on the situation in each country. In fact, during his 1984 trip to the Soviet Union we had with us copies of Keston College's list of religious prisoners and information in it was used as a resource when Mr Graham discussed specific cases with ranking authorities… Hence, the opportunity to express concerns about religious liberty to these men is not to be taken lightly.

Bible Smuggling and Conflict

With the arrival in the West of Pastor Richard Wurmbrand and the publication of Brother Andrew's *God's Smuggler*, Bible smuggling became a headline issue in the Christian press. Ill-informed reporters sometimes placed Keston alongside the Bible-smuggling organisations. We queried the word 'smuggling', because the Bible itself had not been declared illegal in any European country except Albania. The Bible Society rightly negotiated for the official printing of Bibles, which occasionally occurred in various places in inadequate quantities. It went beyond its brief, however, in criticising those who tried to find alternative ways of satisfying the limitless hunger for the scriptures of those deprived of them. The Wurmbrand organisation condemned the reservations of the Bible Society out of hand, while we attempted to keep out of the conflict.

There was, of course, a wide divergence of opinions within the various Bible Societies, national and international, but some roundly condemned 'Bible smuggling', claiming – at the most extreme – that this work actively harmed the process of patient negotiation which alone could satisfy the needs of believers living under communism. In fact, this policy of negotiation did have its tangible benefits, but they applied much more readily to some countries (Poland, the GDR) than to others. Almost excluded was the Soviet Union, where the needs were especially acute. Without 'smuggling' there would have been very few Bibles in circulation until import became possible during the Gorbachev period. Some Bibles – in sporadic fashion – were printed there, but there were few official imports over the first seventy years of communism. In fact, various groups printed Bibles on clandestine presses with some success. They were always prepared to suffer for this – and some did – but the results from primitive methods were amazing. The Keston Archive has an example of a Gospel printed so small that it could be secreted in the palm of one's hand.

Keston's Archive also has a fine report[31] which shows how positive the Bible Society work could be at its best. There is no sense of false optimism there. However, other ecumenical agencies, for example, the World Council of Churches, took the offensive against the 'smugglers' and raised the temperature. The *Ecumenical Press Service* (Geneva) published such a document in 1978.[32] The title was 'LWF Executive attacks "Bible Smugglers",'. Here are some extracts:

> Dr Paul Hansen of the Lutheran World Federation's department of church cooperation has attacked certain 'East Missions' in the USA, West Germany, Switzerland, Sweden, Norway and Holland as being responsible for smuggling Bibles into Eastern European countries and illegally importing into the USSR roubles bought at cheap rates in the West.
>
> 'The people who illegally take Bibles into the Soviet Union regard themselves as "God's Smugglers"' said Dr Hansen. These people should realize that the vast majority of people in the USSR do not understand this. 'They look upon the "smugglers" with disgust, as a kind of criminal, and this attitude is immediately directed also towards those Christians who have contact with the "smugglers" and unfortunately in many cases also towards Christians as a whole.'

To my certain knowledge (from the mission conferences I attended), smuggling illegal currency never formed part of their work. Why would they do this? Further, by introducing this here, Hansen irrevocably muddies the discussion of the main issue – the import and local printing of Bibles. He goes on to claim that this activity has exacerbated persecution in the Soviet Union. Keston has documents from believers claiming the exact opposite: that these imports forced the Government occasionally to relieve the pressure and grant licences for official printing. In a pre-echo of what Weingärtner was later to claim, Hansen continued:

> Anyone in the Democratic Republic of Germany, Poland, Czechoslovakia, Hungary and Yugoslavia who really wanted a Bible could get one. 'To smuggle Bibles into these countries is a demonstration, not a necessity', he said. He attacked those who only painted a grim picture of life in socialist Eastern Europe. He said ... 'For every story about congregations which come together secretly in the woods, we can tell about thousands of others which gather in their church buildings, with state permission, and whose members are just as committed and faithful believers as are those in the forest.'

---

31   Confidential file, 'Report on visits to USSR and CSSR [Czechoslovakia], Nov.1970, from the Revd S. Smaadahl, UBS [United Bible Societies] Secretary – Consultant for Europe'.

32   No.14, 18 May 1978, Keston Archive.

Such intemperate words lumped together undifferentiated reports of Underground Evangelism, Christian Mission to the Communist World, the fine missions who attended the secret conferences and, by implication, Keston itself. The question one would have wanted to ask Dr Hansen at this point was whether he had travelled in Siberia attempting to contact his own scattered, persecuted and *de facto* illegal Lutheran congregations which had barely survived the communist onslaught. It is a pity that he had not taken to heart a previous official Bible Society report which stated:

> In all Baptist churches we were asked for Scriptures. The Baptist leaders admitted openly the great need for Bibles and expressed their gratitude for the attempts being made to send the Bible into Russia... We were urged to back all good attempts to send Bibles into Russia.[33]

There is no hint here of criticism of the 'smugglers', nor does this report use the word. The whole issue was bedevilled by a lack of transparency, even of open, honest debate and resolution came only with the advent of Gorbachev.

Conflict

Conflict arose in many different contexts. On one notorious occasion I went to Copenhagen for what was called a 'Sakharov Hearing', which the Danish organisers were taking extremely seriously (at parliamentary level). On 17 October 1975 journalists were present from several countries, ready to hear a succession of witnesses testify on Soviet abuses of human rights. The Danish administrators had chosen them carefully, men and women who would speak principally from their personal experiences. In addition, there was a jury, consisting of legal, academic and government experts. One famous name on the panel was Simon Wiesenthal, then in his heyday as a hunter of Nazi criminals who had disappeared. I was there, as I thought, to guide the jury on the facts of religious persecution, if there should be any dispute. The jury had assembled the previous day, spending much of it briefing each other on the approach we would take with various witnesses in the questions we had the right to ask. We planned to write a report immediately afterwards and that would need careful thought and timing, too. Our Danish chairman was meticulous in setting the agenda and he constantly stressed the need for objectivity, particularly if the Soviet Embassy responded to the request to send a witness.

On the morning of the first day of the hearing proper, I was already sitting in my seat, watching a large crowd assemble on the floor of the hall in front of us. I was just settling down to what promised to be a fascinating and revealing day, in view of the imposing roster of recent Soviet émigrés who were listed to appear as witnesses. At that moment, just before the official opening, someone came up to the platform and took his place on one of the jury seats. I immediately recognised him, but I don't think anyone else did. It was Michael Wurmbrand, Richard's son.

---

33   Smaadahl, loc.cit., pp. 3 and 5.

I was astounded and quietly asked him by what right he was sitting there. He replied that he was a member of the jury, to which I replied that he couldn't be, as we had worked all the previous day on our approach to the event, setting ourselves rules and guidelines. He immediately began blustering and turned to the chairman of the jury, who said, 'Mr Wurmbrand can stay: his organisation has helped to finance this event.'

This was the only occasion in my life when I was sitting on a platform that I was so upset that I had to leave my place. I walked out, saying quietly to the chairman that I would return if Mr Wurmbrand vacated his place. Even though the audience, still assembling, could not have heard what I had said, they realised that something serious had happened. The journalists were out of the hall after me in a flash. I tried to explain to them the careful preparatory work that the jury had done the previous day and that my objection was on the principle that no one should join the panel without participating in these preliminaries.

By this time it was obvious that the hearing would not start on time. The journalists summoned Michael Wurmbrand out of the hall, but I had said all I needed to and did not wait around to hear him. I went back to my hotel, which was close by. After an hour or so an emissary came round and said Michael Wurmbrand had left, so would I come back? I did and the hearing started mid-morning.

Sadly, but predictably, the next day the Danish newspapers concentrated more on the row than on what they had heard from the witness box. It transpired, at least according to a leading Danish newspaper, that Michael Wurmbrand had called me a communist in answer to a question from one of the journalists. He said this because I was allegedly downplaying the number of Christian prisoners in the USSR and thus helping the KGB in their disinformation campaign. This was clearly libellous and I immediately consulted one of the Danish lawyers on the panel. He confirmed that the accusation was serious and should not go unchallenged. The Danish libel laws, he said, were similar to the British: the paper was guilty, for to repeat a libel is to commit a libel. He offered to accompany me to see the editor of the paper as soon as the Sakharov hearing ended.

The editor immediately offered a full apology and published a retraction the next day, with some good publicity about Keston's work, so I took no further action. The lawyer advised that it was useless to pursue Michael Wurmbrand, as he was not Danish and had now left the country.

This episode reveals how fraught was the situation in the 1970s. In a sense, we were lucky to escape so lightly. As mentioned earlier, there was a dispute between the Wurmbrands (Christian Mission to the Communist World, CMCW) and a new rival organisation set up by Joe Bass (Underground Evangelism, UE). This was bitter and continued for more than a decade. The trigger of the dispute is lost in the mists of visceral hatred. In general, though, the cause was clear.

They were both raising millions to further their mission, which majored on 'Bible smuggling'. Each side needed speakers who could galvanise their audiences into supporting the respective organisations. For CMCW this was easy. Richard was one of the biggest personalities, perhaps the most impressive, I have ever heard on a public platform or in a pulpit. He held his audiences worldwide (USA, South Africa, Scandinavia, the Far East, Australia) with a torrent of rhetoric which, sadly, sometimes went beyond the evidence of the known facts.

UE had no such natural advantage. Joe Bass was pleasant and urbane to talk to, but wasn't in the same league as a speaker, so he needed people he could promote as platform presenters. One such was David Hathaway, a British evangelist who was imprisoned in Czechoslovakia for 'smuggling' Bibles. Harold Wilson personally negotiated for his release. The resulting book, *Czech Mate*, provided something of what UE needed, but not enough. Hathaway, too, proved to be less stable in his personal life than Bass had expected. Someone else was needed.

This man appeared in the person of Sergei Kourdakov. In 1972 Bass reported a sensational event: the defection from the Soviet Union of a young communist who had organised brutal raids in the Soviet Far East (Kamchatka Peninsula) against Evangelical Christians, breaking up their secret meetings and injuring participants. Kourdakov had since defected and proclaimed that he was now a believer. This Pauline conversion must have seemed too good to be true to UE – and so it soon proved to be. Catapulted into a public ministry and occupying pulpits in America almost before he had read the Bible, he died just sixteen months after his defection. UE could not claim him as a martyr (though they made a half-hearted attempt to say that the KGB was responsible for his murder). The facts, though, seemed to point in another direction. His body was found in a Californian hotel with a girl with whom he had apparently run away. Her testimony to the police claimed that, in order to impress her, he had been playing Russian roulette with a revolver, which had gone off by accident.

This whole story could well have been a fabrication, but I had no means of discerning the truth when I was asked my opinion by a reputable publisher, Marshall, Morgan and Scott (London). They sent me a manuscript, *Sergei*, which purported to be an edited transcript of a series of tapes which he had made, recounting the persecution he had led, with his conversion following soon after. Joe Bass had earlier sent me a very short section of one tape and I was satisfied that the transcription was accurate relating to the portion which I had heard, so I did recommend the book for publication, but with reservations.[34] I should probably not have done so.

Sergei's dramatic appearance in the West, immediate ascent of every Evangelical platform and rapid descent to a sordid end (confirmed by the local police) is an affair which should now be clarified after 46 years, but I know of no attempt to do so. My feeling at the time – after all, Sergei had undisputedly gone in secret to a hotel room with a girl – was that he had been elevated and pushed far too quickly by UE, having to testify to his new faith before he had been properly instructed in it. If the KGB had been involved, one would have expected the final chapter of *Sergei* to have made a

---

34   Report dated 4 June 1973, 'confidential' file, Keston Archive.

far stronger case: an accusation against the whole Soviet system. That the book was published without this account of his demise seems to indicate that, basically, the local police were correct. Whatever the truth of a thoroughly unpleasant business, UE was bereft of its most outstanding spokesman almost before he had begun his new career.

There are still unresolved questions about Sergei Kourdakov. I saw a photo of his passport, in which his surname is spelt with the first 'o', a most unusual combination in Russian. One would have expected 'Kurdakov'. This is strange and was never explained. All this was relevant to Keston not least because, wherever I went in 1972–3, even before his death, the question, 'What do you think of Sergei Kourdakov?' constantly confronted me.

Many details of the life of Soviet Evangelicals in the 1970s and 80s, obscured by constant obfuscation by the religious surveillance arm of the KGB, remain unclear. However, the Keston record contains enough and has published the evidence to set out the essential facts in the existence of the life of believers of the time.

Chapter XV
Perestroika and the Collapse of Communism

George Orwell had endowed 1984 as a year with weighty symbolism. It was also a year when Keston could, perhaps for the first time, look back on its achievements: its coverage, its accuracy and the number of people it employed. It was ready to be amongst the first to embrace profound change.

Looking to Eastern Europe, we were certain that something fundamental was occurring – a democratic movement which seemed less susceptible to being terrorised into submission than what had happened in Hungary in 1956 or Czechoslovakia in 1968. The Soviet authorities had deported Alexander Solzhenitsyn, exiled Andrei Sakharov to house arrest without trial in Gorky (Nizhni Novgorod) and imprisoned the leading Jewish activist, Anatoli Shcharansky. Nevertheless, decades of repression had not silenced the voice of Lithuania, expressed especially through its activists in the Roman Catholic Church. The Russian Baptist *Initsiativniki* continued their vigorous campaign to live their lives free of State interference.

There were stirrings, to put it mildly, within the largest underground community: the Ukrainian 'Greek-Catholics'. Towards the end of the Second World War, an extensive area of Ukraine had fallen, for the first time, under communist domination. The majority church owed allegiance to Rome but belonged to the Byzantine (Eastern-Rite) tradition. The new communist power seized their churches and transferred them to the Moscow Patriarchate. The church was outlawed, all its property confiscated and the Greek-Catholic university abolished. The bishops and clergy who resisted were imprisoned and many did not survive. However, the Greek-Catholics continued as an underground church, deeply concealed, but eventually coming more into the open.

Kronid Lubarsky had been an astrophysicist who studied meteors and space biology, before giving this up to edit the *Chronicle of Current Events* in Moscow. Despite suffering imprisonment and constant interrogation, this *samizdat* journal set out to be comprehensive in its coverage of human rights, informing the world, through copies which were smuggled out, of the rise of independent thinking and of society's growing resistance to KGB control.

But something of much greater – indeed, explosive – force was gathering next door in Poland, which had a long and occasionally porous frontier with Lithuania, Belarus (as it now is) and Ukraine. Cardinal Karol Wojtyła, as previously recounted, was elected Pope on 16 October 1978. When he returned to Poland in the summer of 1979, the people realised their own strength. Literally millions turned out to see or hear him and he influenced almost the whole population. The authorities had no idea how to counteract this and the Catholic trade union, *Solidarność* (Solidarity) received support in the shipyards, with frequent celebration of the mass on site. Even after the military crackdown and the imprisonment of twelve Solidarity ringleaders, it became increasingly obvious that the Warsaw Government was failing to provide any competent answer to the workers' demands.

Fr Jerzy Popiełuszko, a young priest, called for a new society in his sermons and his brutal, bungled murder by the police on 18 October 1984 provided the world with one of its highest-profile martyrs since the political executions of the 1950s. His funeral on 3 November saw tens of thousands on the street again, demonstrating to the nation that the spirit engendered during 1979 was still alive and that General Jaruzelski's regime, backed by Moscow, had no answer to popular demands. The BBC and Radio Free Europe/Radio Liberty broadcasts were daily making the Polish example widely known and these newscasts were not falling on deaf ears.

Unrest was already affecting several countries of the Soviet bloc when Konstantin Chernenko died in March 1985. Now it was time for Soviet citizens, and especially the Communist Party, to take stock, too. Leonid Brezhnev had been in power for almost twenty years, a period which brought the USSR to the brink of economic catastrophe and which became known as the years of 'stagnation'. Then the Central Committee twice sidestepped the issue of reform, by electing two ailing, aged men, Yuri Andropov then Konstantin Chernenko, in quick succession. The speed with which Mikhail Sergeyevich Gorbachev was elected as the new General Secretary of the Communist Party testifies to the frustration which even such a hide-bound group of men was experiencing. They chose a much younger man (he was 54), whose rise from the southern provinces had been recent. His task was to reform the economy: they got something very different.

Mrs Thatcher had forged a relationship, but to begin with few Western observers believed that anything much would change. Russian people approved the rejuvenated image of the Kremlin, but waited to see if there would be new directions of policy.

At first little new happened. It took Gorbachev almost a year for any signs to emerge that there was more than economic reform on the agenda. He had inherited international opprobrium for his country's invasion of Afghanistan six years earlier. Now he tested the waters by travelling abroad. On his agenda were engaging with America and possibly making concessions over arms control. When he travelled outside the Soviet bloc he was confronted by a well-organised campaign by demonstrators demanding the freedom of Anatoli Shcharansky, who had been in prison for eight years (of a 13-year sentence). This campaign soon became a personal irritant and it reduced Gorbachev's stature in Soviet eyes, as well as internationally. His priority was to build up an improved image of the Soviet Union, to demonstrate, in Mrs Thatcher's words, that he was a 'man we can do business with'.

Shcharansky's 'crime' had been, as a young secular Jew, to campaign for the right of Jews to emigrate to Israel. He was engaged to be married to Avital, which must have prompted the KGB to play a trick on him. His marriage arrangements were all in place. The authorities told the couple that they could emigrate the next day. Avital boarded the plane; Anatoli was turned back, arrested and eventually sentenced to thirteen years. In prison he reflected on his heritage and adopted the faith of his ancestors. His fate captured the imagination of the Jewish community worldwide and provided a clear focus for the more general demand for the right to emigrate.

When Gorbachev visited Paris in the autumn of 1985, he was disturbed by these protests. There were people thronging in the streets in welcome, but there were also audible groups shouting, 'Free Shcharansky'. He gave an interview to French TV on 30 September, in which he already began to show some willingness to debate the issue of human rights. Then on 8 February 1986 he spoke to *L'Humanité*, the French Communist newspaper, and went further, though still obviously trying to make several contradictory points at once:

'Soviet Jewry has become the cause of psychological warfare waged against the USSR … I believe that in a civilised society there must be no room at all for anti-Semitism, Zionism or any other manifestations of nationalism, chauvinism or racism. Now for political prisoners. We have none, just as we do not persecute people for their convictions. But any state must protect itself against those who try to subvert it.'[1]

At the time Gorbachev spoke there were at least 400 such political prisoners, judging from Keston's list alone. Three days after these words were published Shcharansky walked free over the Glienicke Bridge between East and West Berlin. He had served more than half of his sentence. This image – a small man, grasping his KGB-issued trousers to hold them up, but denied a belt to hang himself with – conveyed a message to the world: concessions were possible in the face of a determined campaign. His wife, Avital, had reached Israel a decade earlier and was now awaiting him to hear his greeting, 'I'm sorry I'm a little late.'

In Israel, Shcharansky became an influential politician, rising to the post of Deputy Prime Minister, so his subsequent career has been controversial.

Shortly something horrific was to occur: Chernobyl. The explosion of the nuclear plant in northern Ukraine on the night of 25–26 April 1986 was followed by the typical old Soviet style response: first a denial, then a week-long silence. The following Saturday children played on the contaminated streets of Ukrainian towns. But the massive environmental catastrophe could not be long concealed. Men sacrificed their lives in an effort to staunch the escape of deadly material. This event and its dishonest sequel profoundly affected Gorbachev and propelled him forward into his reforming campaign. *Glasnost* ('openness/giving a voice to') and *perestroika* ('restructuring') became the watchwords. Now the Kremlin became aware that nuclear energy, whether for peaceful or offensive uses, was not a panacea for mankind.

Keston proclaimed the genuineness of the new policies and sought to interpret them. Arms reduction was on Gorbachev's agenda for the forthcoming summit. The Reykjavik meeting between Gorbachev and President Ronald Reagan opened on 10 October 1986.

---

1   *L'Humanité*, Paris, 9 February 1986.

In the few hours of hiatus between the departure of the world leaders from their home base and their arrival in Iceland something dramatic happened, which temporarily filled the world's news slots at a time when there was little else to record: a telephone call to Alyona Kojevnikov, head of the Keston information desk, announced that Irina Ratushinskaya was free.

Since the release of Shcharansky, Irina, whose biography appears in more detail later, had become the highest-profile Soviet prisoner. This poet and Christian schoolteacher of only 28 was even more 'innocent' than most Soviet dissidents. She had been arrested for the second time in September 1982 and sentenced six months later to seven years' hard labour, to be followed by five of internal exile, the maximum possible punishment for the 'manufacture and dissemination' of her poems, for which she had been charged. In 1986 her poetry appeared in English translation under the title of one of the poems, *No, I'm Not Afraid.*[2]

Keston College had been a link in the transmission of many of these poems from her prison at Barashevo, three hundred miles south-east of Moscow, and had somehow managed to keep in touch by telephone with her husband, Igor Gerashchenko. Alyona had spoken to him several times. Dick Rogers, Anglican priest and medical doctor, had mounted a celebrated and imaginative campaign on her behalf, incarcerating himself during Lent in a cage in the Birmingham Bullring to simulate her conditions of imprisonment and replicating her diet. To him, as well as to Keston, she undoubtedly owed much of the subsequent course of events. Dick may well have saved her life, as it was known that her health had sharply deteriorated in the 'small zone' which housed her.

Alyona, taking the call, had every connection needed with the media and the BBC's eight o'clock radio bulletin ran the news of her release as its lead item, to be followed shortly by virtually all other news services in the free world.

To some it seemed that this was a deliberate and cynical ploy by Gorbachev to gain world favour at this key time. We at Keston had other questions to ask, though. Could this be the beginning of a real *volte-face* by the Soviet regime, at least on human rights and religious liberty issues?

Two months later Andrei Sakharov was somewhat surprised, in his isolation in Gorky, to hear a knock at his door, followed by the entry of a group of engineers preparing to install a telephone. Such events in the Soviet Union never happened by chance and, sure enough, very soon there was a ring. None other than Mikhail Sergeyevich himself was on the line, inviting Sakharov back to Moscow to participate in his process of *perestroika.*

Glasnost and *perestroika* were now being put into practice. Gorbachev proclaimed on innumerable occasions that communism had taken some wrong turns. Although the basics of Marxism-Leninism were correct, serious reforms were necessary to put the country's development back on course. We asked ourselves whether this was going to

---

2   Bloodaxe Books Ltd, Newcastle upon Tyne, 1986.

affect the root of anti-religious policy and the view among our staff was that it would. There were dissenting voices in other places, but Keston began to prepare for major changes and, in subsequent months, was often the first to proclaim them. We noted the systematic release of religious prisoners, as our list became shorter.

Keston's critics sometimes claimed that we were being misled and that the changes were superficial. They had ammunition: for example, barely three weeks before Sakharov's return from exile another veteran human rights campaigner, Anatoli Marchenko, author of *My Testimony*, died as a result of a KGB attack on him in his prison at Chistopol, near Kazan. The Jewish community continued to complain, with justification, that the Soviet Union's emigration laws had not been significantly relaxed.

Sakharov's return to Moscow, though, did herald change. Now Gorbachev began to receive a hero's welcome wherever he appeared outside the Soviet bloc. At home, scarcely a day passed without his criticising those who resisted *perestroika*. There was a third buzzword, too: *demokratizatsia*, but in this there was a catch. Democracy, as a concept, is an absolute: you either have free elections or you don't. 'Democratisation' attempted to be a halfway house, but, given the conditions, was a logical impossibility and Gorbachev would later come unstuck by introducing elections which were only partly free. The occupants of some parliamentary seats were nominated by the Communist Party, while others were genuinely elected. General Jaruzelski would try to impose something similar in Poland in 1989 and he failed utterly.

The release of prisoners continued sporadically during 1987, however, and at the end of the year Gorbachev established a 'Public Commission for Humanitarian Questions and Human Rights', popularly known as the Burlatsky Commission, after its chairman, Fyodor Burlatsky. A most approachable and open man, he quickly proved that his new organisation would not be a sham to conceal the continued existence of old policies. He entered into negotiations with Mrs Rosalyn Carter, wife of Jimmy Carter, former US President, who submitted to him names of individual prisoners, on which he acted. Keston played its role in the transmission of some of the names and detailed biographies to the United States. Burlatsky also called for the legalisation of the Ukrainian Greek-Catholic Church a year before this was granted.

Since the signing of the Helsinki Agreement in 1975, all governments, including that of the Soviet Union, had been obligated to monitor human rights and religious liberty. The review conferences became a forum for debating failure to conform, although the governments of the Soviet bloc stoutly defended their own record. After 1985, discussions became more open and pointed.

At the same time Gorbachev was an enthusiastic traveller. During his foreign trips he occasionally scheduled time to talk to church leaders. In Reykjavik Raisa, his wife, visited a Lutheran church while the summit progressed. In Washington Gorbachev responded to an invitation to talk to a circle of church leaders. In London, during a visit lasting less than 48 hours, he met the Archbishop of Canterbury, Robert Runcie, during a private lunch with the Queen. He visited Westminster Abbey, where the choir sang specially for him. I was invited to meet him as a guest at the state banquet in his honour. Raisa visited Christ Church Cathedral during a rushed visit to Oxford. On 1 December 1989, Gorbachev had his most significant meeting of all with a church leader: he visited the Pope (but the outcome of that takes us ahead of our story).

Gorbachev decided to abandon the old nostrum that religion was a regressive force in society, and would die out as communist society developed, a dogma which had held sway since Lenin. This was a step which would have enormous repercussions. In general, he realised that there were tens of millions of believers in the Soviet Union – Muslims, Jews and Buddhists, as well as Protestant and Catholic minorities, vigorously present beside the much larger Russian Orthodox Church. They had failed to succumb to communist 're-education' programmes, so they were unlikely to change now, when the possibility of self-expression was becoming greater by the day. For Gorbachev this was a challenge: *perestroika* was meeting opposition from the old guard and slowing down after an initial surge. Could it be that believers could be incorporated into the process? He turned to the Orthodox Church.

It is one of the coincidences of history – call it the direct intervention of God in human affairs if you like – that at this very time the Church was preparing to celebrate the Millennium of the Baptism of Rus'. It was in 988 that Prince Vladimir of Kiev was baptised at Kherson, an ancient city, now an archaeological site, near present-day Sevastopol in the Crimea on the Black Sea. This was followed by the mass baptism of his people in the River Dnieper.

The timid Moscow Patriarchate, still under the passive leadership of the invalid Patriarch Pimen, had not been in the forefront of demanding changes corresponding to the upheaval Gorbachev was causing in society. There were Christian voices, but they belonged to scattered individual believers who had no common or unified platform. However, the opportunity to meet Gorbachev face to face had to be taken. It is claimed that it was the church leaders themselves who requested a meeting, though this may well have been as a result of an unofficial feeler being put out by the Kremlin.

The Church had abundant reason to be overjoyed at the possibility of a personal meeting. It was not only that believers had been suffering under restraints, now greater, now lesser, for the seventy years since the Revolution of 1917: the timing afforded an unmissable opportunity. The meeting was scheduled for 29 April 1988, a mere five weeks before the celebration of the Orthodox Millennium was due to begin. The very date itself had a certain significance: it was the fify-ninth anniversary of the promulgation of Stalin's law which sealed the fate of religious communities and finally blocked any hopes they might have had of asserting even a modicum of independence from the State. It was also the first face-to-face meeting of a Soviet head of State with a head of the Church since Stalin summoned Metropolitan Sergi to the Kremlin on 4 September 1943, a meeting which promised greater breathing space to the Church. However, the 1929 law had remained in place despite a modification of executive policy.

Gorbachev made a significant speech. He began by admitting mistakes in past policies:

'Not everything has been easy in the sphere of church-state relations. Religious organisations have not been free from being affected by the tragic developments that occurred in the period of the cult of personality.' [3]

Konstantin Kharchev was the Chairman of the Council for Religious Affairs, the body which monitored Christian activity and enforced legal restraints. Under him it had adopted a more liberal stance. Believers were being encouraged to contribute to the *perestroika* process and they would receive a reward for this: no less than a new law on freedom of conscience which would 'reflect the interests of religious organisations'. Gorbachev continued:

> Believers are Soviet people, workers, patriots, and they have the full right to express their convictions with dignity. *Perestroika, demokratizatsia* and *glasnost* concern them as well – in full measure and without any restrictions. This is especially true of ethics and morals, a domain where universal norms and customs are so helpful for our common cause.[4]

Although 'dialogue' between Christians and communists had been widely proclaimed in the West, communist leaders in power had never participated in it. These words, then, were unprecedented from the leader of one of the world's superpowers. One wonders how this dialogue might have developed, had Gorbachev remained longer in office.

First, however, came the response of the Church. The Patriarch's reply put more emphasis on *perestroika* than on God, who was not mentioned, but he did pledge the unconditional support of believers for the 'architect' of the changes. He would pray for the forthcoming summit meeting with President Reagan in Moscow, which was due in May, before the Millennium celebrations opened. He went on to assure Gorbachev that the 'problems' in church life to which he had referred were already on the way to being solved, thanks to the helpful co-operation of the Council for Religious Affairs. The Patriarch did not make a single request of the Government or of the Chairman of the Central Committee in person or of Konstantin Kharchev, though in a supplementary discussion with officials after the main meeting 'specific questions associated with the guaranteeing of the normal performance of the Orthodox Church' were raised, according to the Church's own account. In various speeches to government officials during the imminent Millennium celebrations, Patriarch Pimen emphasised what a profound impression this meeting had made on him.

Gorbachev, for his part, did keep his word regarding a new law. This was duly passed in 1990: it not only abolished Stalin's decree of 1929, but became one of the most liberal in the world. Not all countries have specific laws on religion, but for those that do, this would have become a model, had it remained longer in place.

---

3   Michael Bourdeaux, *Gorbachev, Glasnost and the Gospel* (Hodder & Stoughton, London, 1990), p. 44.

4   *Loc.cit. Gorbachev, Glasnost and the Gospel* contains a fuller account of these events.

Before the new law was passed, however, dramatic events took place in Moscow and virtually throughout the Soviet Union.

The Moscow Patriarchate had long been preparing for the celebration of the Millennium. In the more relaxed atmosphere, invitations were issued to world Christian leaders, but the tone of these events would be low-key. Now, however, the planned series of events suddenly took on a new colour. The State indicated that it would take over the publicity and adopt the events as though they were its own celebration. This was the moment, not the collapse of communism three years later, when active atheism vanished from the scene. The Moscow Patriarchate suddenly realised that it had an opportunity unprecedented in history. It could expand its plans and prepare to be the centre of international focus.

However, even before these celebrations began, the TV cameras of the world focused their attention on the Russian Orthodox Church. This was because President Reagan, on his visit in late May, called at the new headquarters of the Church, the Danilov Monastery.

Strangely out of character (and the reason for this has never been explained) Andropov, during his brief time in power five years earlier, had returned the Danilov Monastery to the Moscow Patriarchate. It was in a ruinous state, having been converted into a juvenile prison, a natural for this owing to the massive wall surrounding the monastic buildings. For several years, therefore, the Patriarchate had been restoring it with the intention of converting the buildings into its main administrative centre. Thousands of believers voluntarily took part in the restoration work. By May 1988 the work was nearly finished and the complex looked superb, despite some areas still being unfinished. Reagan's advisers did a great service to the Russian Church by putting this visit on the agenda and wonderful pictures resulted, which appeared on TV screens around the world. Reagan also met Christian and Jewish activists during his visit.

I had not been to the Soviet Union since 1979, my second involuntary exile of nearly a decade from the subject of my work. Some time earlier the agency Inter-Church Travel had invited me to lead a group to Russia to join Christians in the celebrations. Suddenly we saw that the event was taking on greater importance. We heard that there would be a great gathering of church leaders of all denominations, including such figures as the Archbishop of Canterbury, Dr Billy Graham and Cardinal Willebrands, *de facto* head of the Vatican's foreign relations.

My path to Moscow was not a smooth one, however. I had a visa, issued well beforehand, to visit Moscow, Leningrad and Kiev from 7–17 June, as had all the other members of my party, including Lorna. About two weeks beforehand I received a phone call from the Soviet Embassy saying that my visa had been rescinded.

After urgent telephone calls to Inter-Church Travel, they appointed Lorna as leader in my place, seeing that her visa had not been challenged. A week later, however, a similar call came through, cancelling her visa. We decided, though, that the other members of the party would make the trip under protest and simply put themselves in the hands of the Soviet authorities when they arrived in Moscow.

In a mood of deep depression, Lorna and I began to run down the preparations we had been making for some time. It was, after all, a matter of excitement, needing much planning, that I would be back in Russia after over nine years of absence. One question stood out during our conversations round and about this disappointment: how could it be that Gorbachev's extensive reforms could not solve the visa issue for us? Obviously, the old guard was still in control of this. We were, of course, in touch with the Foreign Office, for which I had been doing some advisory work during the *perestroika* period, but they said, with regret, that they didn't think they could help, especially in such a short time. We decided at Keston that nothing would be lost by going public.

We had many influential friends and there were several mentions in prominent places of what had happened. This was the first negative publicity that the Soviet Union had received in the press for some considerable time. Loudest of all was the BBC Radio 4 news headline item on 6 June, the day Archbishop Runcie was due to leave for Moscow. The announcer prefaced the bulletin with the words: 'Today the Archbishop of Canterbury leaves to join in the Millennium celebrations of the Russian Orthodox Church in Moscow. One person who will not be going with him is the Revd Michael Bourdeaux, whose visa has been refused by the Soviet authorities.' The only slight inaccuracy was that listeners received the impression that I was to have been an official member of his party.

That night we were sitting, discussing events of the day and feeling bitter that we would not be joining our group at Heathrow the next morning. Then the phone rang at 9 p.m. A voice announced: 'Mr Bourdeaux, this is the Soviet Embassy. Your new visas are waiting: you can come and collect them now and leave in the morning.'

Stunned, I wondered how this could possibly happen out of hours (it was midnight in Moscow) and I thought of a Soviet Consulate that constantly showed a shut door to importunate callers. The voice replied that they would open the door at any time and that anyone could come and collect the visas.

As well as sitting for a moment in disbelief, the practicalities immediately began to crowd in on us. Yes, we had valid plane tickets still – but we had a son, Adrian, two years old in bed upstairs and the check-in time for the flight was 6.30 a.m.

The next few hours passed in a fog. My elder son Mark, aged 22, was fortunately living at home, so he departed for the Consulate in London while we set about the task of packing. By the time he had returned, reporting a friendly encounter with the Russians, who seemed to treat him as a welcome caller, we were ready to leave for the airport. By then it was a midsummer dawn and we left with no sleep. Our party greeted us in disbelief.

What had happened? There never was an explanation, though several curious events in the days to come would have the initials 'KGB' scrawled all over them. The timing itself was strange, to say the least. At midnight in Moscow some officials must have been working overtime to sort out the bad publicity spoiling a good event. There has never been a doubt in my mind that the negativity given to the case, especially the BBC's broadcast that morning, must have caused the *volte-face* and some high-level official must have overruled the KGB's decision to negate the visa. Gorbachev was, after all, at the height not only of his *perestroika* campaign, but also of his monumental efforts to upgrade his image and improve the Soviet Union's relations with the West. Were the Russians also wondering if they could use me for their own ends?

We were, unusually, waved through immigration at Sheremetyevo Airport, with a smile and a welcome. In no time we were sitting, exhausted now, in our hotel room in Moscow.

Intending to doze off for a few hours' rest before dinner, I turned on the television. In those days Moscow had only two channels. It was no surprise that the first day's programme led with the arrival of the honoured foreign guests. But then, turning over to Channel 2, we found ourselves watching a feature film about the life of the Russian Orthodox Church, *Khram* ('Church'), which caught the atmosphere of worship with compelling beauty and great reverence. Clearly there had been a fundamental change and never again would the airwaves be filled with raw propaganda against Russian Orthodoxy. Two channels with religious programmes showing simultaneously were an indicator of just how saturated radio, TV and the newspapers would be in their coverage over the next ten days.

Before long, however, the phone rang and another strange conversation took place. A voice said, 'Mr Bourdeaux? I work for the *Novosti* ('News') Press Agency and I would like to meet you.' *Novosti* was notorious as one of the KGB's many arms, so I was wary, but decided to agree to such a meeting – I could always simply fail to turn up if I had a change of mind later.

I thought it all over. It wasn't easy to find a slot in the middle of a busy programme, at all of which, as leader, I had to be present, but I did go to the *Novosti* building, as requested. A Mr Troyanovsky greeted me warmly, introduced me to some colleagues and came quickly to the point. He said (the whole conversation was conducted in Russian) something like: 'Mr Bourdeaux, we live in a new Russia now. We have long respected the work of Keston College as the most reliable conveyor of information about the life of our(!) churches to the West. We have a proposal to make. We would like to collaborate with you and send you regularly our best information, which you can reproduce for your news service.'

In recollecting myself after the initial shock, I was able to find a holding caveat. 'I'm most grateful for your suggestion, but you must understand I'm not a free agent. There must be a proper proposal in writing and I will convey this to my Council of Management, who will take the decision.'

After the exchange of some social niceties, we left it at that. I never heard another word from them, but that was not the end of the story. A week later, after we had visited Leningrad, we flew to Kiev. On arrival the local officials ushered us into the VIP lounge to await our onward transport. On sitting down, I picked up a publication

– in English – bearing the *Novosti* imprint and entitled '*Prisoners of Conscience in the USSR and Their Patrons* by Boris Antonov. There were several copies lying around. I flicked over the pages and there, 'black on white', as the Russians say, was an attack on Keston and me, calling us traitors to the truth. It was not, in itself, anything new, for similar attacks had appeared from time to time in the Soviet press over the previous twenty years, but on this occasion it was in English and I immediately realised that many Western church leaders, including Billy Graham and Cardinal Willebrands, had passed through that lounge earlier in the day. I never discovered whether any of them had picked it up, but the duplicity of the *Novosti* approach to me lay exposed in these pages.

The heading of one section read, 'Spies from Keston College'. Two pages of attack against Keston followed, in which the author accused us of sending a certain David James into Russia as a spy. The passage contained the following:

> James, confiding in his [Russian] girlfriend, admitted that most likely Keston College was gathering information for special services. When he became convinced that Anna would go to Britain with him, he said that she would be received by Michael Bourdeaux and a representative from the intelligence service who would interview her.[5]

This was all in the realm of fantasy, particularly as, to this day, I have never heard the name of David James. My views on *Novosti* were now as entrenched as ever.

In the USSR, events were occurring with a speed almost impossible to follow. On the day of our arrival, 7 June, the Ukrainian Council of Ministers made a conciliatory gesture of more than symbolic significance towards the Orthodox Church: they announced the return to the Church of the great Monastery of the Caves in Kiev, which, in a very real sense, was the cradle of Russian Christianity. Television, I discovered later, made a great showing of the return of the title deeds to Metropolitan Filaret of Kiev. It happens that I had been one of the last foreigners to visit the monastery before its closure in 1961 and I would be one of the first to visit it after its reopening.

There were many impressive public events during the week of celebrations in Moscow, but the central drama was unseen by the general public. This was the *Pomestny sobor* (literally, 'Local Council', but used in Orthodox terminology to mean a 'national' council, as opposed to an 'ecumenical', that is 'all-world', council of the Orthodox Church). Even invited guests were present only at the opening and closing ceremonies, except for foreign representatives of the Russian Orthodox Church, who were official participants. The *sobor* took place in the great monastery of Zagorsk, later to revert to its original name of Sergiev Posad. It ran for four days (6–9 June) and kept most church leaders away from Moscow itself during that time.

To detail its deliberations would take us beyond the confines of this book, but I give a few observations. The Soviet regime had permitted previous *sobors* only to elect

---

5   *Prisoners of Conscience*, Novosti, Moscow, 1988, pp. 36–37.

a new Patriarch (1944 and 1945); then in 1971 a *sobor* elected Patriarch Pimen, who was still in office in 1988. Nefariously, the last also legitimised the controversial new statutes, which had been imposed on the Church by the KGB a decade earlier and which prevented parish priests from participating in the administration of their own parishes, thus facilitating Khrushchev's anti-religious campaign of the early 1960s.

Now, however, the atmosphere was different. State representatives were still illegitimately present, but they played no active role. Debate was relatively open. New statutes, which the young and gifted Archbishop Kirill of Smolensk had drafted, were presented, briefly debated and passed without dissent. Kirill claimed that the Church should consider the new *ustav* (statutes) as the successor to what the *sobor* of 1918 had put in place.

While the *sobor* authorised the canonisation of several martyrs of the past, it was too early to enter into a discussion of those of the Soviet period. Some bishops demanded the opening of new seminaries to cope with the increased demand for priests in the wake of the revival of parishes in so many places. Metropolitan Vladimir of Rostov and Novocherkassk – in a scarcely veiled criticism of his fellow-Metropolitan Pitirim of Volokolamsk, head of the publishing department of the Moscow Patriarchate – was unambiguous in his condemnation of the inadequacy of the current publishing programme. Metropolitan Mefodi of Voronezh could hardly have been more outspoken in his criticism of the Government's punitive taxation policy against the Orthodox Church.

The *sobor* should have lasted for weeks if it were going to tackle the multiplicity of problems in depth, but in this short time a dam had been breached and the Russian Orthodox Church had found an official voice more boldly expressed than at any time since 1918.

Meanwhile, the main events of the Millennium celebrations were proceeding in Moscow and in other places round the Soviet Union. The official opening liturgy had taken place in the Cathedral of the Epiphany, which had been the Patriarchal seat in Moscow since the destruction of the Cathedral of Christ the Saviour fifty years earlier. Various other celebrations took place in different locations and the 1,500 foreign guests followed a programme which took them in bus convoys to see the main sights of Moscow. Our Inter-Church Travel programme took us to Zagorsk on the closing day of the *sobor*. We did not expect to receive any official welcome, as we were only unofficially present at the celebrations. The monastery complex was closed to ordinary Russians, including thousands of pilgrims, but we were permitted inside and had the opportunity of conversation with some of the official participants in the *sobor*, as well as with pilgrims gathering outside the churches.

The concluding act of the Moscow celebrations took place on two consecutive evenings in the Bolshoi Theatre, no less, in the heart of Moscow. The venue, however impressive, was of course hopelessly inadequate to house the tens of thousands of people who had some claim to be there. The closing ceremony took place on Friday 10 June, with Raisa Gorbachev and President (as he then was – formerly the redoubtable foreign minister) Gromyko sitting in the VIP box. It was unprecedented that such high-profile secular figures attended a religious event, which was also televised. A representative of the Moscow Patriarchate had contacted Lorna and me to invite us to the theatre. He could, he said, just find space for us on the first of the two evenings, which was not to be a dress rehearsal.

That evening we sat among a group of nuns in the second row of the stalls. What we saw on stage could truly be described as a symphony of Church and State. After seven decades of persecution the two came together in an astonishing representation of the role of the Russian Orthodox Church in history, movingly, dramatically recounted by the great Soviet actor, Sergei Bondarchuk, with his deep, commanding voice and a stage presence more imposing than one might have imagined possible from his many films. In his readings from the chronicler-monk Nestor, telling the story of the conversion of Rus' to the faith, he seemed to generate as much emotion among his atheist as among his Christian audience. The returning envoys from Constantinople, advising Prince Vladimir to adopt the Byzantine form of Christianity, reported their experience of the liturgy, 'We did not know whether we were in heaven or on earth'. One had the impression that he spoke, too, for the representatives of the Communist Party present.

Then the Bolshoi Chorus and Orchestra combined first to sing to the Church the traditional Russian paean, *Mnogaya leta* ('long life'). This, as the whole event, was broadcast live to the nation on the second evening, to many believers who had had, until recently, to endure the ceaseless propaganda that there was no future for the Christian faith in the Soviet Union. The choir of the Moscow Theological Academy came on stage to join their voices to the general celebrations. Then the heavens opened – literally. I had never known that, high above the stage in this great theatre, there was a set of bells, real bells, mounted as though in a church tower. At the climax of the final scene of Glinka's opera, *A Life for the Tsar* (now accorded its original title, after having been renamed *Ivan Susanin*), a curtain rolled back to reveal the bells, which rang out in a peal of thunder. No one in the theatre, Christian or atheist, could have missed the symbolism: for years the authorities had banned the ringing of church bells, usually even removing them from their stays and throwing them to the ground. Surely this was a pledge of a new beginning for the Church in society.

And so it proved to be, though with many caveats along the way. One member of the Christian intelligentsia said to me later that this was 'vulgar drama without substance'. He was wrong, but his point was worth making. None of us realised that we would soon observe the death of the Soviet Union, to be replaced by a regime which would elevate the Russian Orthodox Church to the highest status.

This was not the end of the events of that week. The official Moscow celebrations concluded with a liturgy in the Danilov Monastery. The great gates swung open, on a cold and windy morning, to receive a more representative crowd of believers than had been able to attend any event previously. It took place in the open air, in the vast enclosure between the two main churches. Six Orthodox patriarchs and an archbishop representing seven different nationalities concelebrated. At the conclusion, one of the most prominent Roman Catholic guests present, Cardinal Glemp of Poland, spoke. He commanded the rapt attention of the huge congregations as he pointed out that this past week had provided incontrovertible proof that God was renewing the faith of His people by sending spiritual strength from above and that the Russian Church could look towards the future with confidence, hope and love. One wonders whether the fate of Fr Jerzy Popiełuszko, murdered less than four years earlier, may have been in his mind. His words, in retrospect, form a sad reflection on what might have been in setting a new Christian agenda for East and West.

During these unforgettable eleven days new experiences followed one another in a crazy procession. Sometimes invitations coincided, making it impossible to do everything I wished – and I had always to bear in mind that I was receiving a free trip as leader of a party which rightly expected to receive due attention from me. I can do no more than list some of the highlights.

On our first evening, our Moscow telephone number having been transmitted by Keston, we received an invitation to visit Fr Gleb Yakunin's flat. His release from a ten-year sentence had come just slightly early the previous year. On receiving us (we had never met face to face), he swept us into the room, where there was a galaxy of some of the great activists of the religious liberty movement: Fr Georgi Edelstein, outspoken supporter of freedom for all religion, Fr Yevgeni Genrikhs, unofficial Catholic chaplain to students in Leningrad, Alexander Ogorodnikov, lay activist and long-time political prisoner, and others. For me, this was 'coming home', a few hours of conversation which deserved to have been spread over months.

Following up this, Alexander Ogorodnikov, who had co-founded a seminar in which young people were encouraged to discuss religion, accompanied us to see his unofficial Millennium exhibition of photographs and documents which formed part of the true, non-propagandistic history of the Russian Church. He took us on to a secret destination where we were to meet a delegation from the banned Ukrainian Greek-Catholic Church. They had come to Moscow to petition Cardinal Willebrands and others to further the cause of legalisation of their church. In an anonymous block of flats, we mounted a dingy staircase and waited in a small room. Then the door to an inner room swung open – and there, in majestic regalia, were several of the leading figures of the 'underground' Ukrainian Greek-Catholic Church: Bishops Pavlo Vasylyk and Fylymon Kurchaba, together with key activists, Fr Mykhailo Havryliv and the layman, Ivan Hel (who had spent seventeen years in labour camps). They begged my assistance in persuading Cardinal Willebrands to meet them. I had no access to him, but found a way of passing on a message and a meeting did take place.

They also gave me an introduction to another redoubtable Ukrainian lay leader, Stepan Khmara. He had sacrificed a career as a dentist to edit *Ukrainsky vysnyk* ('Ukrainian Herald'), a *samizdat* publication which gave full attention to religious affairs, and for which he had served seven years in the notorious Perm-36 labour camp. On his release he devoted himself full time to the campaign to legalise his church. When I met him later in Kiev I was deeply impressed by his single-mindedness and passion, not least in his legitimate claim that the Russian Orthodox Church had elbowed Kiev out of its rightful place as the historical centre of early Eastern Slav Christianity, and therefore as the centre of the Millennium celebrations. Eighteen months later, on 1 December 1989, Gorbachev would visit Rome and meet the Pope: the gift he bore was the lifting of the ban on the Ukrainian Greek-Catholic Church, which, with its strong nationalism, became another key factor in the imminent demise of the USSR.

In Leningrad, which we visited before Kiev, the celebrations continued, but in muted fashion. Tourism was top of the agenda, but again I received a strange telephone call at our hotel. This turned out to be a genuine invitation to do an interview for a late-night TV show. It was the season of the northern 'white nights', so many people would be up during the midnight daylight. The interviewer, on the steps of our hotel, asked me questions about the role of Keston, which I answered directly in Russian. Then came a question about prisoners of conscience. I said how encouraged I had been to meet so many former victims of the system and this made me believe that *perestroika* was here to stay. I continued, *'odnako'* (but) – and mentioned that there were still some in jail, not least many leading Lithuanian activists. At this point, someone felt the conversation had already gone too far and the plug was pulled. The censorship cut me off in mid-sentence. But walking down the Nevsky Prospekt the next day people came up to me, having seen the interrupted programme, and asked, 'What would you have said if they had allowed you to finish the sentence?' My answer led to an impromptu seminar on the wide pavement of the main street in Leningrad.

On returning from Kiev to Moscow on the last day I had one more memorable meeting – with the above-mentioned Konstantin Kharchev. An appointee of Chernenko, he at first appeared to be just one more bureaucrat, who, in the lives of the churches, wielded immense power to intervene in their affairs and to obfuscate the essential issues. However, he had started to get the Gorbachev message of *glasnost* and he invited me to his office in an old building on the inner ring road. I found him true to his reputation: domineering and inconsistent. I had jotted down agenda points. He demanded I should read them out and he would then bark out a single-sentence answer. 'Next point?'

Typical of this conversation was a meeting I reported which had taken place in Kiev the previous day. A group of Baptists from Dneprodzerzhinsk had approached me and solicited my help in their efforts to build a new church, which the authorities had frustrated for years. Kharchev shot back: 'Tell your friends to go ahead and build their church. We'll sort out the permission afterwards.' Soon they would – and this was his not ineffective way of doing business.

Kharchev ended the interview by ordering me to his car, in which he transported me, grandiosely and chauffeur-driven, through central Moscow to a press conference he would address for the foreign dignitaries who had attended the celebrations. Our conversation ended by my inviting him to visit Keston on his forthcoming visit to England, which he duly did five months later in November 1988.

Kharchev's visit to London occasioned a rush of blood to the collective head of the Foreign Office, which put him on the balcony with the Queen Mother for the Remembrance Day celebrations at the Cenotaph. Many of his hosts, in public or reported sessions, brought up Keston's current list of Christian prisoners, which had gone down from the two hundred or so, the total which I had mentioned to him in June 1988. At a press conference he clouded the issue in response to one question, claiming that there were now only six on his list. Most of the rest were criminals, imprisoned as they would be in the UK, Christian or not, for offences such as drug peddling. He went on, as reported in *The Tablet*: 'Tomorrow I'm going to visit Keston College and I will continue discussion of the question with Michael Bourdeaux, who is here in the audience tonight.'

When Kharchev came to Keston the next day he was defensive and unwilling to pursue any agenda item in a spirit of dialogue. Indeed, he claimed to be our 'guest' and said he therefore should not be subjected to any agenda. Instead, we listened to his delivery of a series of monologues. Nevertheless, during Gorbachev's last two years, he became – if not the architect of church *perestroika* – then a faithful executor of what he perceived Gorbachev's policy to be. He then retired into Moscow obscurity, but he had managed to put something of a human face on to the office of 'commissar for religion'. If there should be access to his department's archives in the future, a study of his life and the twists it underwent would make interesting reading.

Reconsidering these events after thirty years, I am even more certain than I was then that 1988 was the turning point in the modern history of religion in Russia. While Gorbachev ended the persecution, he was persuaded of its injustice by the petitions and integrity of those of all traditions whose lot he observed on accession to power. History owes him a greater honour than he is usually accorded.

The unfettered leadership of the Russian Orthodox Church would soon face the opportunity of pursuing a new agenda and transforming itself into a power for good in society. The leadership, however, averted its gaze and began to follow a nationalist agenda.

Chapter XVI
Soviet Retrospective

Over a period of some thirty years – the 1960s to the 1990s – it was my privilege to work on behalf of many believers, Orthodox, Baptists, Catholics and sometimes Jews and Muslims, who were prepared to suffer as a result of their determination to struggle for religious freedom in societies which all, in different ways, restricted it. They have been classified as 'dissidents', though many were trying to persuade various atheist regimes to abide by their own laws. At heart, they were petitioning for democratic reforms, though not many of them would have responded to the label. The fate which they met was various: some suffered imprisonment, even death; others simply received a warning from the police. Only a few could be called martyrs; they were all heroic in their own ways, even if they did nothing more than sign their name on a piece of paper. Compared with martyrs of the twentieth century such as Pastor Dietrich Bonhoeffer and Archbishop Oscar Romero, even figures such as Cardinals Mindszenty and Wyszynski are not frequently quoted in sermons, at least outside their own countries. Many more, such as Fr Gleb Yakunin, Pastor Georgi Vins and Irina Ratushinskaya, achieved temporary recognition, but now the world has mostly forgotten them. An exception might be Fr Alexander Men', whose life and teaching seem to be gaining widespread recognition. There are many others whose names never became known. Keston College, however, to the best of its ability, has attempted to bring to life names which are only otherwise on forgotten lists. Its archive is maintained at Baylor University, and is available for consultation and perhaps, one day, for the evaluation of what it contains by future historians. Their example will, I trust, inspire and enrich the lives of future generations.

Petras Plumpa, a Lithuanian layman and 'nationalist activist', was converted to the faith during a seven-year prison sentence. He left a spiritual legacy in prayer:

> Only the King of Souls knows where we could bring most benefit. If he has sown us in the field of sorrows – let us bloom in sorrow. If he has sown us in solitude, let it be solitude, for the Creator sows even the most beautiful of flowers on inaccessible tracks between mountain paths, and they have their value though nobody sees them. In these days it is impossible for us to live without being seen: only the anguish of the soul can be unseen, and like blossoms it can be constantly plucked and offered to the Saviour.[1]

---

1   Philip Walters and Jane Balengarth, *Light Through the Curtain* (Lion, Tring, 1985), p. 123.

Several dozen Russian believers – Orthodox, Baptist, Catholic, Jewish, Muslim – became iconic for Keston's work in the 1970s and 1980s. During the long years of persecution, we could never, except under the rarest circumstances, meet the people we wrote about personally, but subsequently various staff members were able to do this. My long short-list would include Orthodox priests Fathers Gleb Yakunin, Alexander Men', Georgi Edelstein and Dmitri Dudko; lay people Boris Talantov, Anatoli Levitin-Krasnov, Irina Ratushinskaya, Alexander Ogorodnikov and Viktor Papkov; Baptists, Aida Skripnikova, Pastor Georgi Vins and Valeri Barinov; Latvian Lutheran the Revd Juris Rubenis; Lithuanian Catholics Fr (later Archbishop) Sigitas Tamkevičius and Nijole Sadunaite; Ukrainian Catholic Cardinal Ivan Lubachivsky; the Jewish activist Anatoli Shcharansky, and the Muslim leader Mustafa Dzhemilev. As it happens, I eventually met all but three of these and I would add, in a place of special honour, three Roman Catholic cardinals whom I met in exile in Rome: Beran, Mindszenty and Slipyi. Even sitting in the same room as any of these heroes of the faith was a privilege beyond imagining, but I must pare the list down, choosing them because of the varied interest of their characters and their different affiliations. Some have already appeared in the text, but a more detailed biography is apposite.

Fr Gleb Yakunin

Of all the Russians on whose behalf I responded to the call 'Be our voice', Gleb Yakunin was the one who meant most to me in the personal sense, not least because he was born in the same month and year as I was (March 1934).

His consistent appeal for a new deal for the Russian Orthodox Church and his rejection by the state and then the church authorities for his actions is a sad story. He came from a religious family, but lost his faith after the Second World War, at the age of fifteen, under the influence of communist propaganda in the late 1940s. He became a student of forestry in Irkutsk, Siberia, where he met the young Alexander Men' and shared many ideas with him. Fr Men' became one of Russia's most influential teachers, working often in secret, while Fr Gleb chose the path of open activism.

After Yakunin's temporary break with the Church, he returned to it with renewed zeal. He came to Moscow determined to seek ordination where he found a mentor, Archbishop Leonid of Mozhaisk, who successfully guided his studies. Ordination followed in 1962.

It was the severity of Khrushchev's persecution, especially the closure of churches all around him, which sharpened Fr Gleb's conscience and his determination to start systematically collecting information. Attached to a Moscow church, he met visitors from outlying parts of the Soviet Union and began collating evidence from them. By the end of 1965, working with Fr Nikolai Eshliman, he had enough in his files to compile a long and detailed dossier on the state's intolerable interference in believers' lives. He converted this into two documents: a letter to the Soviet Government and another to Patriarch Alexi, urging him to speak out more boldly in defence of the

Church. It was this which soured his relationship with his own hierarchy and it never recovered.

After more than fifty years it is impossible to reproduce the astonishing impact of these documents. There had never been anything like them from the Orthodox Church, except for, thirty years earlier, a letter from the bishops imprisoned in the island monastery complex, Solovki, in the far north. The Baptists, over the previous three or four years, had attempted something similar and many of them were already in prison as a response. The atheist authorities reacted very differently. Instead of bringing the two priests to trial, they leaned on the Patriarch to act. He banned them from public office for ten years, which injunction they faithfully obeyed. Fr Eshliman withdrew from the scene and died in obscurity. After a decade of serving the Church as a lay helper, Fr Gleb reappeared in a dramatic way as an active ecumenist, intervening by letter in the Nairobi Assembly of the World Council of Churches.

The publication of Fr Gleb's letter, detailing further pressure against believers, gave him a false assurance that he had established a relationship with the world churches. He had set out a draft proposal for co-operation with the WCC and he now believed that he would receive their support. In this he turned out to be sadly misguided. Yet in the USSR, in setting up the Christian Committee for the Defence of Believers' Rights, he became the leader for dozens of prominent Christian (and Jewish) dissidents, who were now becoming increasingly emboldened in defence of their cause. Andrei Sakharov, who would later be summoned by Gorbachev as an adviser on the human rights aspect of *perestroika*, passed to Fr Gleb the many appeals he received on religious issues.

Fr Gleb's position at this time was curiously ambiguous. From contacts and supporters he was receiving a trove of documents from all Christian denominations and from Jews. Yet the Orthodox Church continued to treat him as a pariah. The WCC still ignored him and even when he went to prison there was no call for support for this outstanding ecumenist. It was not until much later that they raised his case privately with the Moscow Patriarchate, to no avail.

His last act before arrest was to throw out an unprecedented challenge to the Patriarchate: believers who wished to evade the straitjacket of state control should deliberately create unregistered – and therefore illegal – parishes. The secret consecration of bishops would lead to the establishment of another structure, parallel to the Moscow Patriarchate, but independent of it.[2]

His inevitable arrest followed on 1 November 1979 and at the trial he was sentenced to ten years. Only this staunched the flood of documents which had been evading Soviet control in 1977–8.[3]

We were able to keep in touch with Fr Gleb at times during his imprisonment. He

---

2   Bourdeaux, *Gorbachev, Glasnost and the Gospel*, p. 9.

3   Jane Ellis (ed.), *Letters from Moscow: Religion and Human Rights in the USSR* (Keston, Kent, 1978).

smuggled a handful of letters out of his camp, one of which asked me personally to intercede for him with the Soviet Government and with world opinion. This was a petition for a Bible, which he did eventually receive (illustrating the effect of publicity). Only the advent of Gorbachev saw his early release after eight years.

Then, in May 1987, he immediately sent an appeal to Gorbachev petitioning for the release of other political prisoners. He publicised this at a press conference for foreign journalists, at which he claimed, 'Church life is not responding today to the principles of democratisation and *glasnost*.'[4]

Reacting, Metropolitans Filaret and Yuvenali held their own press conference, at which the latter expressed his displeasure at Fr Gleb Yakunin's 'negative assessment' of the Russian Orthodox Church and its hierarchy. Only the Moscow Patriarchate, he claimed, could settle such issues, so Yakunin was speaking out of turn. He hinted that a rush to *glasnost* and *perestroika* in the Church could quickly lead to anarchy.[5]

Despite the Kremlin's adoption of new policies, Fr Gleb was destined to remain an outsider. He had gained the freedom to speak openly, but at the cost of increasing hostility from the hierarchy. On 28 April 1987 he appealed to the Holy Synod to reinstate him in the parochial ministry. He had never left the priesthood, but had not been able to work actively as a priest for over twenty years. On 12 May the Synod passed the following resolution:

'In view of the mercy and love of God, Gleb Yakunin is to be reinstated as a priest, but chastened with the following words: "Go, your faith has made you whole, sin no more, lest a worse thing happen to you (John 5:14)."'[6]

Subsequently, Fr Gleb successfully stood for election to the Moscow City Council on a human-rights platform. This, too, displeased the Patriarchate, which issued a decree forbidding clergy to stand in secular elections, even though some of the leading bishops were members of Gorbachev's first semi-elected parliament.

Fr Gleb's status gave him access to state archives, which were briefly open after the collapse of the Soviet Union. He discovered information about the close links of individually named bishops (under pseudonyms, which he identified) with the KGB. He passed this to Keston, where Jane Ellis recorded and translated it.[7]

Fr Gleb's break with the Moscow Patriarchate became inevitable. He never relinquished the priesthood, although he left its jurisdiction. He failed to be re-elected to the Duma and eventually joined the secessionist Kiev Patriarchate, not an entirely happy decision, and later the True Orthodox Church, successor of the underground church of the 1930s. He died on (Western) Christmas Day, 2014.

No one would pretend that Fr Gleb was easy in his personal relations, his voice often adopting a peremptory tone, but he clung to his principles with a fierce determination.

---

4   Bourdeaux, op. cit., p. 96.

5   Bourdeaux, Ibid., pp. 96–7.

6   *Journal of the Moscow Patriarchate*, Moscow, 7 July 1987.

7   'Russian priests gain access to KGB files on Church', *Keston Research News Release*, 14 February 1992.

His contribution to the issues of religious liberty in 1965 and again in 1977–8 stands even today; his uncovering of secrets in the archive grabbed a unique moment. A Church which cannot encompass a man of such stature and integrity is the poorer.

Fr Dmitri Dudko

Though many people at one time spoke of Fr Dmitri Dudko and Fr Gleb Yakunin in one breath, their ministry and eventual fate were widely contrasted.

Dudko was born into a peasant family in the village of Zarbuda, in the Bryansk region. He embraced Christianity after finding a copy of the Bible when all the churches in his region were closed. He lived under Nazi occupation from 1941–3, when a few churches reopened. After liberation he served in the Soviet army. His first arrest was in 1948 for writing a poem criticising the destruction of Russia's holy places and he served eight and a half years before release under the post-Stalin amnesty. The KGB kept a careful watch on him from this time on.

Even though an ex-political prisoner, unusually he was accepted into the Moscow Theological Seminary at Zagorsk. He graduated and began what for several years seemed a fairly conventional, though not ineffective, life as a Moscow parish priest. It was only gradually that he began attracting young people in significant numbers, carrying an aura of saintliness as he did, not only in his looks, but also in the triumph of his faith over his prison experiences. But once the younger generation discovered him word spread and students began flocking to his church.

Dudko answered questions from his crowded Moscow congregation, first in writing, then later face to face. Reconstructed from notes, circulated in *samizdat*, these informal sermons appeared in French in 1975 and two years later in English as *Our Hope*.[8] With subsequent publication in eight other languages, his work reached a wider world audience than that of any other Russian Orthodox priest of the time. Knowledge of Fr Alexander Men''s teaching and writing spread widely only after his death in 1990.

In 1973 Patriarch Pimen bowed to the instructions of the KGB, as his predecessor, Alexi I, had done in the case of Fr Gleb Yakunin, and ordered him to stop preaching his unconventional sermons, which came at the end of the service and did not interrupt the flow of the liturgy. However, he continued his 'conversations' in the privacy of his home.

This further infuriated the KGB. In 1975, on his way by car to visit his mother in the country, he was involved in a road accident, resulting in two broken legs. All his pupils and he himself viewed this as the work of the state security, but his survival only further convinced his students of his saintliness. After his recovery, the Moscow Patriarchate posted him to a more distant parish, Grebnevo, twenty miles from Moscow, to which many travelled to learn from him. In 1977 a virulent press campaign began against him. Fr Dmitri once said that no week of his adult life had passed

---

8   Dmitrii Dudko, *Our Hope* (St Vladimir's Seminary, Crestwood, NY, 1977).

without some direct interference from the Soviet authorities. Clearly, this pressure was already grinding him down before his subsequent arrest.

On 20 June 1980 Fr Dmitri appeared on Soviet television and renounced his activities in a twenty-minute interview, which was reported verbatim in nearly every Soviet newspaper. Before his imprisonment he had been one of Russia's bravest dissidents, yet here he was a broken man. The KGB had clearly prepared the event as a decisive measure, not only against the 'anti-Soviet' activities of the Moscow proto-democrats, such as Fr Gleb, but also against any residual independence within the Russian Orthodox Church. One analyst at the time detected no less than twenty phrases in the confession likely to have been contributed by the KGB at the time they broke him. He also had a beatific look upon his face and it is still disputed whether he was under the influence of drugs at the time he appeared on TV. Nothing can have potentially undermined the morale of his followers more than this catastrophe.

Fr Dmitri's tragedy was not only in his recantation, but in the subsequent direction of his life. With the advent of *perestroika*, he was able not only to write voluminously, but also to publish his work. His political ideals had changed. There was a new note in what he wrote. He became a kind of 'spiritual adviser' to the hard-line nationalist newspaper *Zavtra* ('Tomorrow'). He used this platform to support a return to authoritarianism, arguing that a Stalin- (and later a Putin-) type discipline was the only way to save Russia from the effects of the oligarchs.

Even though Fr Dmitri was now distanced from his former disciples, his earlier influence was not lost, as the lives of hundreds of converts demonstrate. No one reading the words he subsequently vouchsafed to Xan Smiley, then a British correspondent in Moscow, could feel anything other than deepest sympathy with the man whom the KGB broke in 1980. 'I thought that if I didn't agree, I wouldn't live … Compared to the hell that I then brought into my soul, anything – even torture or execution – would have been easier to bear.' He went on to write in *Vybor* ('Choice'): 'I consider my [confession] to have been treacherous, if not before God and the Church, then towards those friends with whom I was walking along the same path and doing the same work.'[9]

His converts included the young Alexander Ogorodnikov, who went on to found the Christian Seminar, a discussion group which, in part, modelled its activities on Dudko's dialogues (and for which many of them were suffering imprisonment at the time of Dudko's confession). Viktor Papkov became Ogorodnikov's collaborator.

Throughout the whole decade of the 1970s, seen from the perspective of Keston's work and growing archive, he was one of the most influential activists in the Russian Orthodox Church. The file on him in our archive is extensive and detailed, including many of his own writings, some unpublished.

---

9   Both quotes are from my obituary of Fr Dmitri Dudko in *The Guardian*, London, 4 August 2004, p. 23.

Soviet Jewry

The public at large never sufficiently realised how much reporting Keston was doing outside the confines of the Christian faith. Our work, from the first day, was committed to the ideals of the UN Declaration on Human Rights and, later, the provisions for religious liberty inscribed in the Helsinki Accords of 1975. These international agreements singled out no individual faith, and indeed their main strength was in their universality. By following this ideal Keston was making a non-interventionist stand on principle and it conformed to my own conviction of what must be the correct approach.

Curiously, I was concerned with Jewish rights in the Soviet Union many years before the question imposed itself as one of urgency on the international agenda. As previously recounted, when I spent my study period in Israel in 1964, I was in daily contact with Jews who had emigrated from Russia. They all had their own stories to tell and I absorbed their words with rapt attention. In my Moscow days I had heard nothing like it, the Jewish community there being so intimidated during Khrushchev's time that they never dared talk to a foreigner. In Jerusalem I heard of the hopes, always dashed before they could be properly expressed, that somewhere, somehow Russia would provide a sanctuary for the residue of East European Jewry which had escaped the Holocaust. Stalin's establishment of the so-called Jewish autonomous region of Birobidjan, in the far east of Siberia, was thin cover for exile and control, not an act of liberation. The 'Doctors' Plot' of the last months of Stalin's life indicated only too clearly his true intentions towards the Jewish community.

By the end of 1964 I had learned something of the real aspirations of Soviet Jewry, but I had gained this knowledge in Israel, not in Moscow. I had speculated, in my unpublished report of the time, about the possible impact on Israel of a future emigration from the Soviet Union.

Three years later the Six-Day War of 1967 caused an upsurge of Jewish pride in the Soviet community. For the first time since the foundation of the State of Israel, Soviet Jewry appreciated the strength of a homeland they had never seen. News of the victory could not be kept from them. Many of them danced the *hora* in the streets.

Still the Western press said almost nothing about the upsurge of Jewish feeling in the USSR. Keston, however, from the early issues of *Religion in Communist Lands*, was reporting regularly on the rise of Jewish 'dissent', which expressed mainly – but not exclusively – a demand for the right to emigrate. Alongside this, though, there was also a clear indication from time to time that Jewish ideals of faith and tradition were far from dead (as the world seemed to believe at the time) and indeed were beginning to revive. Some of those who wanted to emigrate made their demands on religious as well as ethnic grounds. Young people with a secular, indeed atheist, education were beginning to ask questions about the God of the Hebrews and the Torah.

Received Jewish opinion in the West, as well as in Israel, was that the emigration question should be entirely separate, an issue on its own, not linked to either more general questions of human rights or to the revival of Jewish religion within the Soviet Union. It was, therefore, particularly galling for the international Jewish community, not to mention for the Soviets themselves, when Jews seeking to emigrate became implicated in the broader question of human rights. One of our patrons, the Chief Rabbi, Lord Jakobovits (as he later became), was particularly active in seeking our opinion and I discovered that, like me, he did not believe that the emigration question could be dissociated from related issues. He invited me to call on him one day and he opened the conversation by saying, 'Michael, tell me how it is that a Russian atheist Jew can become religious out of nothing.' I cited the case of the Latvian Jewish scientist, Herman Gertsovich Branover, who embraced the faith while fully active in his laboratory work. Branover wanted there to be a space for religious Jews, especially converts to the faith, to develop their beliefs and find sustenance in the availability of literature as well as synagogues for worship. Only if these were not available would emigration become the practical alternative.

Keston was never – and could not have been – part of the 'emigration lobby', though we theoretically supported the right of Jews to emigrate and we had many Jewish friends who gave up part of their lives to support it.

Anatoli Shcharansky made the separation of the emigration and the human rights issue unsustainable. Jewish to the core – and at that time non-religious – in the early 1970s he became one of the foremost activists in the human rights campaign. In this he joined forces with many religious believers, nationalists and other would-be reformers. The power of his young and attractive personality (he was born in 1948) propelled him into a leadership role, yet he was deprived of a career before it had even begun. I have already mentioned the bare bones of it, but it is worth reflecting on the organised Jewish protests which led to his freedom.

The horrified Jewish community worldwide mounted protests on every conceivable platform and in nearly every country of the free world. Once I was unwittingly involved – or almost. In 1980 I was singing a concert with the Philharmonia Chorus in London's Festival Hall with a Russian conductor, Yevgeni Svetlanov. On the programme was the concert suite which Prokofiev extracted from his incidental music to the film, *Alexander Nevsky*. What music could be more nationalistic? The Soviet regime loved it. The programme was being broadcast live. Soon after the start of the work the stage doors behind the choir burst open and a small group of demonstrators ran on to the platform, grabbed the live microphones and shouted 'Free Shcharansky' several times. They managed to continue their protest for a good minute before the BBC switched off the microphones. The demonstrators did not have to be escorted off the stage: they left in orderly fashion. The concert continued, the imperturbable conductor going back to the beginning of the movement as if nothing had happened. Ten minutes later a back-up team stormed on to the platform and the same happened a second time, after which the concert continued to its conclusion. In conformity with BBC policy, the announcer never referred to what had happened, but the whole concert was recorded live. There were no consequences for the demonstrators.

Information began to filter out of Shcharansky's prison camp about his deprivations, but also about his friendships. He had made a Christian friend who taught him how to be a fervent Jew – by reading the Old Testament and learning prayers. The Shcharansky whom the Soviets released in 1985 was not the secular activist of 1976. He was a believer. His visit to Keston (then in Oxford) in 1992 a few years later produced an unforgettable impression on all of us, making us laugh with the warmth of his personality.

Valeri Barinov

The liveliest – and perhaps the most unpredictable – character we ever met was Valeri Barinov. He followed his own rules – or not – according to his whim. He did not conform to our concept of what a dissident should be. He was simply *sui generis.*

It was, in fact, Lorna who first brought him into the picture. She studied Russian in Leningrad in 1977, where she met this unconventional young man at the Baptist Church. He was already an ardent evangelist, 33 years old, married with two daughters, with little formal education (product of an orphanage), but he had an intrepid zeal to spread the gospel and convert young Russia to God through the medium of rock music, having heard a broadcast over the airwaves of Andrew Lloyd Webber's *Jesus Christ Superstar*. Under Soviet conditions it was impossible to rehearse. In Lorna's book about Valeri[10] she recounts two incidents, both connected with his profession as a driver, which typify the man.

An ambulance, red cross painted on the side, was speeding through the streets of Leningrad with a team of doctors inside, on its way to a terrifying accident where a building under construction had collapsed on top of the workmen. Lorna wrote:

> In the few minutes between the call at the depot and arrival at the scene the doctors were anxiously preparing themselves to do their work, but this driver challenged them with the name of God, telling them that he would be watching over them while they tried to save lives. These doctors had probably never heard a sermon before and least expected it while on call, but Valeri Barinov rarely missed an opportunity to present others with a testimony about his belief in God.[11]

We do not know the outcome of this engagement. Very likely the team was too busy to take any notice, but Valeri often mentioned the name of God to the patients themselves whom he transported.

On another occasion he (illegally) borrowed the vehicle one evening to transport a set of drums, amplifiers, three electric guitars and electric organ and other paraphernalia picked up from various locations around Leningrad. He took all this to the local *Lunokhod* ('Moonwalker') youth club. As he started to unload it all, his team

---

10   Lorna Bourdeaux, *Valeri Barinov: The Trumpet Call* (Marshall-Pickering, Basingstoke, Hants., 1985).

11   Ibid., p. 13.

of four others arrived, all in their teens or early twenties. They set up the equipment and began rehearsing their latest – a Paul McCartney number recorded off air with great difficulty. Lorna was one of two English students present. During the first half, Valeri and the group went through the repertoire of old Beatles' songs which they had learned, English lyrics included, accompanying as best they could on their clapped-out equipment.

After a break outside the group returned. To the astonishment of the two English girls, as well as the horde of young Russians present, the evening continued in this way:

> Valeri put his hand in his back pocket and drew out a small, well-thumbed New Testament. 'Before we sing again, I want to read a few verses from God's holy word so that you can think about them in the coming week.' He read from one of Paul's epistles and then gave a short impassioned exposition of the verses. The young people listened with complete attention, unable to take their eyes away from Valeri's face, which was transfigured with joy as he spoke.[12]

Valeri then gave a thumbs-up sign to the musicians and they continued playing as though nothing out of the ordinary had happened.

Valeri's career as an ambulance driver was – inevitably – not long extended, but I thought of him when I was in the Danilov Monastery, Moscow, a former juvenile prison, making a programme for Easter Sunday 2005. I reflected on my surroundings in the following words:

> When I was a student in Moscow in 1959 I walked round the outside wondering what was inside, but found the doors firmly locked and guarded. Someone who did manage to get into one such institution was Valeri Barinov, an Evangelical Christian, also well known in Britain, founder of the Christian rock group, *Trumpet Call*. He was a driver by profession. One day about 30 years ago his assignment was to drive a load of planks to a juvenile prison. When a detail of the young offenders had unloaded them, he stood on top of pile and began to preach the Gospel. They all gathered round and listened intently. The prison governor was enraged and sent the boys packing – but one hid and whispered to Valeri that he wanted to believe in God. Amazingly, Valeri was ordered to return next day – and he brought a copy of St Luke's Gospel for the boy – who appeared at once. The governor saw what happened. He was furious, summoned Valeri to his office where he cursed and swore at him. He ordered Valeri off the premises, but when he got back to the lorry, the young offenders had immobilised it and stolen several vital parts. Valeri threatened to report the governor to his transport HQ. The governor was so frightened, he had to let Valeri stay and talk to the boys for hours until the truck was in working order again.[13]

---

12 Ibid., p. 16.

13 Michael Bourdeaux, 'Orthodox Easter 2005', script, Keston Archive.

Clearly, this could not continue. The authorities arrested and interrogated Valeri on several occasions and once incarcerated him in a psychiatric hospital. On his release he just carried on as before, although work became more and more difficult to obtain. That only increased his opportunities for evangelism, though. He managed, with the help of some friends in Estonia who had access to a studio, to record his group's Christian rock opera, *The Trumpet Call*. He smuggled out the tape to Keston and we passed it on to Seva Novgorodtsev at the BBC Russian Service.

Although Seva had a weekly jazz slot broadcast to the Soviet Union, heavily jammed, the BBC would not have wanted this item played at length. Seva bided his time. Then one day the BBC news correspondents went on a short strike, so during that time there was no news on the airwaves. This affected the foreign broadcasts from Bush House especially. The Russian Service had a blank day, which the Soviet authorities knew about, so they decided to save some money by switching off the jamming equipment. Seva seized the opportunity and played the whole of Valeri's tape. The response was astonishing. He, more or less against the rules, had given Valeri's address, which led to sheaves of letters from all over the Soviet Union arriving at Valeri's flat. They are an astonishing collection, now in the Keston Archive, and showing how Valeri had touched a chord with hundreds of scattered listeners. Some approved. Some did not. But all of them wanted personal contact with Valeri and to know more about his message. Their varied content offers a unique insight into the spiritual lacuna in the minds of Soviet young people in the years just before the advent of Gorbachev.[14]

Eventually Valeri decided he must emigrate, in order to be able to make a career in Christian evangelism through music. We advised him strongly that this would be very difficult. Valeri ignored the advice and tried to cross the Soviet border into Finland, where he was arrested and subsequently imprisoned. However, the huge publicity surrounding his case persuaded people as diverse as Cliff Richard and Sir David Steel to take up his cause. Eventually Mrs Thatcher, in what was now the Gorbachev era, negotiated his release and then emigration. He came to Britain with his wife and daughters, who were by now in their late teens.

As we predicted, he found it impossible to settle. He did not want to build up a 'professional' rock group here. He expected everyone to work for free, as they had to under Soviet conditions. This cost him any possible relationship with the music industry. Those in Christian circles who wanted to help him also found it difficult. He would preach in English, but his constant theme was a series of variations on 'the end is nigh'. Valeri continued to follow his own path and after the collapse of the Soviet Union was able to revisit Russia. His name, though, will always be associated with some of the liveliest pages in our annals. Only the Soviet Union and its repression could produce such a character and the events related to him.

---

14   Lorna Bourdeaux, *Valeri Barinov*, pp. 156–194.

Nijole Sadunaite

Among the many women who hold a hallowed place in the Keston Archive, Nijole Sadunaite is one who stands out, not only because of her bravery, but also because of the person who leaps out before our eyes from the letters she wrote in prison. Our work on behalf of the persecuted church in Lithuania started later than that for the Baptists and the Orthodox, yet by the mid-1970s it was in full flow. From 1972 the *samizdat* included the *Chronicle of the Lithuanian Catholic Church*, which appeared regularly from then until the Gorbachev years, when the attention turned more from the freedom of the Church to the liberation of the whole nation. Often the *Chronicle* was published bilingually, in Russian as well as Lithuanian. When it appeared in the latter only, we had a Lithuanian translator on hand. Major Jonas Mykalous Liudžius was retired and living in Bromley. He had had a sterling wartime career in the British Army, distinguishing himself especially in intelligence matters.

The first issue of *Religion in Communist Lands* accorded Lithuania a place of honour, being the subject of a group of articles.[15] The flow of documents ensured that Lithuanian Catholics were the next subject to fix my attention after the work I had done on the Baptists and the Orthodox and throughout the mid-1970s I was riveted by the volume and calibre of the information we were receiving. Never once did we receive a counterfeit document, designed to lead us into error and ridicule by the KGB: overwhelmingly, the facts in the documents turned out to be accurate from first to last. There was even an exposé of the circulation of what were indeed falsified documents originating from the KGB.

This was to be the beginning of what would become one of the most important strands in the life of Keston's post-communist years. No book of mine was less reviewed or more honoured. Still a captive nation, the country appeared to those who set the agenda in the West as an outpost of the Soviet Union which had long since lost its identity. Yet this book established communications both with Lithuania itself and with broader communities in the USA, following up our regular contact with the Lithuanian Catholic Priests Association in New York, who forwarded many key documents to us after Lithuanian seamen had secreted them out of the Soviet Union.

Within such a cornucopia of material, dozens of names stood out, individuals as notable for their bravery as for the calibre of their faith: Bishop Julijonas Steponavičius, Fr Alfonsas Svarinskas (who would eventually visit Keston), the martyr Fr Juozas Zdebskis, laypeople Petras Plumpa and Virgilijus Jaugelis, who was to die in prison before his thirtieth birthday.

Nijole Sadunaite received more recognition outside the Lithuanian community in exile than anyone else, partly because of her youth, partly because she was female, but perhaps most of all because of the poignancy of her suffering and the means she found of communicating it in the most heart-rending language, especially in a series of letters smuggled out of prison after her sentence in 1975 at the age of 36.

---

15   *RCL*, No. 1, 1974.

A nurse by profession, she devoted almost every minute of her spare time to the cause of editing and circulating the *Chronicle of the Lithuanian Catholic Church*. Five brave and brilliant men had gone on trial in December 1974 for this precise crime and the case was designed to bring an abrupt end to the activities of the Lithuanian activists. So they thought. Nijole was arrested just after the five and was under interrogation when they were brought to trial, of which, miraculously, an almost complete transcript appeared in the very next issue of the *Chronicle*, which the trial had set out to suppress for all time.[16] The *Chronicle* was soon to make Nijole's an international name and her imprisonment cause for widespread anti-Soviet feeling in the West.[17] At her trial Nijole said in her defence speech:

> The truth does not need to be defended, as it's omnipotent and invincible! ... For the truth I'm prepared not only to lose my freedom, but would joyfully even sacrifice my life… The *Chronicle* is like a mirror which reflects all the crimes of atheists against those who believe in God. Nothing evil likes to look at its own image, it hates its own reflection… This is the happiest day of my life. Today I'm standing at the side of Eternal Truth, Jesus Christ … How can I not be happy, when Almighty God has shown that light triumphs over darkness and truth over lies and falsehood?[18]

Sentenced to six years, three in labour camp, three in exile, Nijole was first held for seven days in a damp underground cell, where she caught a severe chill and a fever. Then she had to endure 28 days on the train from Vilnius to Mordovia (in south-eastern European Russia, but these prisoners' rail transports ran with insufferable slowness). Locked in the iron cages with her were hardened criminals, the place swarming with lice, and the prisoners receiving salt fish, bread and water only.

In the camp her health further failed, yet she held on and enjoyed brief periods of remission. During these she would, according to the testimony of another prisoner, walk around the camp singing at the top of her voice to cheer up the men in their camp nearby. Everybody liked her, it was said. She could even charm the guards into carrying messages from the women over to the men.[19] Presumably, this, too, is how her letters reached the outside world, via their addressee, Birute, a friend in Vilnius. Among her voluminous letters she wrote:

> I am grateful to those whose efforts have led to my being here. I have learned and experienced much, and it is all to my benefit. The good Lord truly knows best what I need … How good it is that the small craft of my life is being steered

---

16   Bourdeaux, *Land of Crosses*, pp. 264–293.

17   For the full story, including a large selection of documents, see *Land of Crosses*, pp. 271–3 & 282–91. See also Philip Walters and Jane Balengarth (eds), *Light Through the Curtain* (Lion Publishing, Tring, 1985), pp. 124–7.

18   Bourdeaux, op. cit., p. 272.

19   Walters and Balengarth (eds), op. cit., p. 124.

by the hand of the good Father. When He is at the helm, nothing is to be feared. Then, no matter how difficult life may be, you will know how to resist and to love. I can say that 1975 has flown by like a flash, but it has been a year of joy for me. I thank the good Lord for it.

There is not a great deal of dust in our section, although the material from which we sew gloves is dusty with glass powder. The work is oppressive in its monotony, and frequent mechanical defects add to this. [Describing many spells in and out of hospital, she continues:] I complete my norm because I work in a single shift. I can begin sewing at 6 a.m. and finish at 10 p.m.... I am fortunate and contented. We have many old women and sick people, so I rejoice that I have been brought here in accordance with my calling – to nurse and to love. Although I long greatly to see you all, it will be hard for me to leave here. It will be distressing to leave people who have become so near and dear to me, but the good Lord does indeed care for us most of all. I receive letters not only from acquaintances, but also from some whom I have never met.[20]

She was told that over three hundred letters had arrived from the UK, but the camp authorities sent them back. She survived to go into exile in Siberia, where she worked first as a cleaner, then – denied the right to work officially as a nurse, but doubtless playing her part – as a hospital orderly. She revelled in the beauty of the local countryside, especially the Angara River. Nijole served her full sentence of six years and then returned to Vilnius to live with her brother, Jonas where she played an active role in the life of her local church.

I first met Nijole by chance on Gediminas Square in Vilnius on my first visit in 1989 and then again in 2005 and 2007. It was the spirit of these indomitable people, with whose story I began my Introduction, which convinced me irrevocably of their ability not only to hold out, but also to win through.

Irina Ratushinskaya

World publicity had already raised Irina Ratushinskaya's profile to international status. She was not a natural dissident. She graduated in physics from Odessa University and became a primary school teacher. A gifted poet, with firm Christian convictions, she tried to inculcate her own standards in her pupils. Although she singularly failed to conform, it is a mystery why she was singled out for such inhuman treatment. Perhaps it was the way her Orthodox faith shone out to all around her. One might have expected that she would receive an intimidating rebuke by the KGB and be dismissed from her job. Instead she found herself confronting the full force of the Soviet law. Poetry in Russia was always dangerous.

In April 1983 Irina faced the court, charged with 'agitation carried on for the purpose of subverting or weakening the Soviet regime', for which she received a

---

20   Bourdeaux, op. cit., p. 290.

sentence of seven years in a labour camp in Mordovia, followed by five years of internal exile. She was 29.

After her release she described conditions in the 'small zone' of the camp in a remarkable book, *Grey is the Colour of Hope*, one of the finest pieces of Russian prison literature in a crowded field.[21] This restricted area, a kind of prison within a prison, was set aside for particularly dangerous female political criminals; her companions were almost a roll call of prominent women dissidents of the time. She describes them with occasional humour and much insight, as they helped and sustained each other in conditions almost beyond imagining. Between them they could have formulated a theoretical democratic future for the Soviet Union. Irina recounts her friendship with Lagle Parek, a survivor of years of persecution, who would later become the first Minister of the Interior in free Estonia.[22]

Even in prison Irina was able to continue writing. Deprived of paper, she would scratch her poems on bars of soap, commit them to memory, erase them and reconstitute them when eventually paper came to hand. Somehow she smuggled them out to her redoubtable husband, Igor Gerashchenko, and he relayed them to the world. They made a huge impact. Sally Beamish was not the only composer to set a cycle of her poems to music ('No, I'm not afraid', 1988). After Irina's death Sally wrote to me: 'The inspiration I found in Irina's poems led to my first major work – and a significant step for me in finding the confidence to become a full-time composer.'[23]

In her prison poetry Irina was able to capture the atmosphere of the prison camp in a remarkable way, which comes over even in translation, and she could find joy in the simplest experience:

> *And I will tell of the first beauty*
> *I saw in captivity.*
> *A frost-covered window! No spy-holes, nor walls,*
> *Nor cell-bars, nor the long endured pain –*
> *Only a blue radiance on a tiny pane of glass,*
> *A cast pattern – none more beautiful could be dreamt!*
> *The more clearly you looked the more powerfully blossomed*
> *Those brigand forests, campfires and birds!*
> *And how many times there was bitter cold weather*
> *And how many windows sparkled after that one –*
> *But never was it repeated.*[24]

Emigration to the UK soon followed her sudden release. Medical checks revealed the extent of her physical suffering: she was told that she would not be able to bear

---

21   Irina Ratushinskaya, *Grey Is the Color of Hope* (Hodder & Stoughton, London, 1989).

22   Ibid., p. 195.

23   Private email.

24   Irina Ratushinskaya, *No, I'm Not Afraid,* p. 132.

children. However, miraculously and with the help of medical science, in 1993 she gave birth to twins, Sergei and Oleg.

Irina's immense popularity in the West would fade and invitations to speak would become less frequent. She and Igor decided that they would like to bring up the boys as Russians. The Yeltsin regime took some time to give them Russian citizenship, but they settled into a reasonably comfortable way of life, supplemented by the royalties she received from her writing. Irina continued to write, not least scripts for sitcoms, and give an occasional poetry reading, but her plans for a satirical novel in which dogs, crows and rats took over the world from people were cut short at an early stage by the onset of cancer. She died on 5 July 2017, aged 63.

Mustafa Dzhemilev

The Soviets – and then the Russians – did their best to change a peaceful Muslim people, the Crimean Tatars, into terrorists, but without success. Mustafa Dzhemilev was twice exiled from his homeland in the Crimea, the first time aged six months, the second seventy years later. He was born in 1943 under the brief German occupation of Crimea during the Second World War, a side-show in the conflict which was to have devastating consequences. Stalin accused these people of collaboration with the Nazis and, in retribution, the whole population of the Crimean Tatars was exiled in sub-human conditions, so that around half of them died either during the transport in cattle trucks or in Uzbekistan, where they were dumped, with no immediate means of survival.

One of the few Muslim ethnic minorities in Europe, the Crimean Tatars have a remarkable history. They are survivors of the Golden Horde, the warriors from the East who subdued most of Asia and even some parts of Europe, especially Kiev and some Russian territory. They adopted Islam in the fourteenth century, but Russia fought off the 'Tatar yoke' in 1480.

The Crimean Tatars have known two short spells as an independent country. The first was after the Crimean War, when they gained this freedom for nine years, before incorporation into the Russian Empire. The second was in December 1917, when they declared themselves as the first Islamic democracy, only to be crushed by the Revolution a month later. The succeeding period was economically harsh, with a famine in 1921, followed by a worse one after the enforced collectivisation in 1931–3. During this second time of oppression most of the political and religious leadership was executed.

Simferopol had been a centre of Islamic Tatar learning and Bakhchisarai, a city imbued with beauty and culture, was renowned for its friendly welcome for visitors. Among these was Pushkin, who celebrated its fountains and its women in one of his finest poems. The Soviets destroyed their history, so what had the Crimean Tatars done to deserve their fate of genocide? While some served in the Red Army during the war, others joined a German brigade – but was it a surprise that they were looking for something better than the fate which had befallen their people over the previous twenty years?

Mustafa Dzhemilev, growing up far from his homeland, had to learn this history from the adults around him. At the age of 18 these stories inspired him. Almost miraculously, he longed to be a free Muslim in a free society. He founded a Union of Young Crimean Tatars, which cost him the next twenty years of his life. During this time he held the longest-recorded hunger strike in Soviet political history – 303 days – during which his captors kept him alive by force-feeding him. He was never free from interrogation and intimidation, as he furthered the cause of his people, both religious and political.

During this time Keston was closely in touch with Crimean émigrés and we monitored all the information sent to us about their struggle. In May 1989 Gorbachev signed a decree permitting the return of the Crimean exiles, who now numbered about a quarter of a million. Some had been able to make their way back over the previous two decades, but their status had not been formally resolved. Dzhemilev continued to be their natural leader and he negotiated with the now-independent Kiev government. He had some success and it seemed as though his long period of struggle was at an end; many improvements were being achieved, including the founding of the Mejlis, a parliament for the Tatar people. History had made false promises, however. In 2014 a lesser-known consequence of the Russian grab of Crimea, followed by the falsified referendum, saw the loss of these political gains. The Mejlis now has to meet in exile in Kiev. Dzhemilev was in Ankara when the Russian invasion took place. On his attempted return he was shown an unsigned decree banning him from entry to the country and a return to his own property. He attempted a second return by a different route but found his access blocked.

In all the political debates and criticism of Russian action in Crimea, one of the major themes should have been the deprivation of the rights of a whole people, albeit a minority in terms of size. But here is an issue which will never disappear, as long as the illegal occupation of Crimea persists. In other contexts Russia has underlined its positive relations with its significant Muslim minority. That does not apply to Crimea, where Islam is suppressed. Mustafa Djzhemilev stands for religious, as well as political, freedom for his people.

Chapter XVII
Oxford: Mixed Hopes

Such was the excitement of 1988 that I decided to take a sabbatical year to write an account of Gorbachev's new deal and how it was affecting religion. I applied, successfully, to the Leverhulme Trust for a grant. St Edmund Hall elected me as a Visiting Fellow. The dons not only welcomed me warmly, but also wanted to hear my ideas on the changing world as it unfolded.

The family moved to Iffley, where we rented a tiny cottage. I had to find a quiet workspace in another house in the village away from the distractions of my three-year old son, Adrian, and three-month old daughter, Lara Clare. Lorna and I loved living in a beautiful environment by the Thames and close to Oxford. Eventually, through the friendships we made, Iffley became our permanent home.

My research assistant, Suzanne Oliver, newly graduated from Oxford and now working at Keston, was relaying new material almost daily, as it flooded in. Behind her was the detailed work of many other researchers, all of whom stood solidly behind the project.

I thought of *Gorbachev, Glasnost and the Gospel* as the most important piece of work which I had done to date and such was the interest in the publishing world that some seven or eight translations were under discussion. I was, after all, writing at the fulcrum of history and recording, more as a journalist than a researcher, the many events as they took place.

The fall of the Berlin Wall, the Velvet Revolution in Prague and the bloody events in Romania followed in quick succession as the communist regimes collapsed like dominos. The BBC regularly, sometimes almost daily, interrupted my writing with requests for briefings and interviews. Fortunately many of the interviews were done at the local studio in Summertown.

By the summer of 1990 *Gorbachev, Glasnost and the Gospel* was complete and had just gone to the printers.[1] Lorna and I were preparing our permanent return to Chislehurst. On almost the last day before we were due to leave, Oxford's Theology Faculty invited me to a meeting to discuss to the new possibilities for links with Russia. On the agenda was a new scheme to invite to Oxford young theologians from Eastern Europe whom political circumstances had deprived of the possibility of full study in their homeland.

'We would like you to be a member of our team setting up this project. Your archive and experienced group are essential for us.' So went the conversation and I was bursting with excitement. This was the launch of the 'Oxford Theological Exchange

---

1   Hodder & Stoughton, London, 1990.

Programme' (OTEP) and I was invited to be a founding member; I would continue in this capacity for nine years until my retirement.

'We need you here – Oxford is a natural home for Keston.' The voice was that of Oliver O'Donovan, Canon of Christ Church and one of Oxford's leading theologians, whom I had known and greatly respected since I gave the Chavasse Memorial Lectures at Wycliffe Hall in 1976. Also at the meeting was another Canon of Christ Church, Rowan Williams, who had a considerable knowledge of the Russian Orthodox Church and, unknown at the time, was about to be elevated to the bishopric of Newport. With Bishop (later Metropolitan) Kallistos Ware in the room adding his assent, the challenge to me was overwhelming.

We discussed the decline of the work in Oxford on the Russian Orthodox Church. From the 1950s to the 1970s there had been a group of scholars who had collectively propelled the university into perhaps the world's leading role in research and lecturing on the subject, but the tradition had not been maintained. There was now a good chance of reversing this, as they explained, using the momentum generated by the excitement flowing from the fall of the Berlin Wall and the dissolution of the Soviet bloc. Oxford could honour the names of Professors Nicolas Zernov (now deceased), Dimitri Obolensky and John Fennell (both retired).

Also, the 'Campaign for Oxford' was in full swing and the group even mentioned the possibility of finding funding for the OTEP project, provided it could be included in the university's ambitions to raise £270 million. Keston would find a niche somewhere in the university's loose structure (exactly where was left open). Keston's Archive would enrich and build on Professor Zernov's legacy, the House of St Gregory and St Macrina in Canterbury Road, which housed his life's work. Here, too, were the modern Russian Orthodox Church and, next door, St Theosevia's, a study centre. There was also the Fellowship of St Alban and St Sergius, devoted to relations between the Anglicans and the Orthodox, which had recently moved to Oxford from London. St Antony's College, with its tradition of Soviet Studies and its developing Russian Centre, were a mere stone's throw from Canterbury Road. Forming a link with an established university had always been one of Keston's core aims, but it had not been realised up to this point.

Nicholas Goodrick-Clarke later came to Keston to address a meeting of the full Council. He was then working for the Campaign for Oxford and he enthusiastically presented a plan for bringing Keston to Oxford. He was so persuasive that the Council decided, on a unanimous vote, to take the most important decision in its twenty-year history – to say yes to the invitation to move everything, sell Keston College and purchase property in Oxford. It would entail a change of name, because Keston could not be a 'college' in the Oxford sense of the word. We quickly decided on 'Keston Institute'. Goodrick-Clarke pointed out that the University gazette and diary listed a loose grouping of 'associated institutes, not governed by the University', a status which would suit us admirably, listed, as we would be, beside the Jewish centre and the Islamic institute.

With hindsight, our Council was beguiled by the offer without insisting on something in writing. We took Goodrick-Clarke at his word. Also, it was abundantly clear to us that the decline of financial support for our work, however unjust at the precise time when it could expand into exciting fields of direct cooperation with newly developing religious enterprises in the East, was beyond our control and would continue. Keston College, on Keston Common, would come to seem more and more isolated, with a dwindling number of scholars to staff it. The closest co-operation with a great university was on offer.

The die was cast. Before us lay a huge undertaking and, unsurprisingly, the responsibility was going to lie almost entirely with me. The attempt to establish our work in perpetuity in Oxford was to cost me the final nine years before my retirement and explains why I wrote no new books during this period (I did manage to edit some collaborative volumes, but my written contributions were minimal).

The most immediate problems concerned staff. Not all, by any means, would be able or willing to come to Oxford. At the same time I had to counteract the idea that, because of the downfall of communism, Keston had 'finished' its work. The sudden, though to me inevitable, collapse of the Soviet Union which immediately followed in 1991 merely reinforced this popular view. We would never enjoy such a coverage again, nor engage such a numerous and talented workforce as we had had for the last fifteen years in Kent. The compensation, we hoped, would be working alongside world-class scholars in theology and politics. In retrospect, I was taking on, as my sixties approached, a task which should have fallen to a younger person. Whatever the sadness of what was to come, what we were to achieve in Oxford undoubtedly preserved not only Keston's Archive, but also its ability to carry out new programmes.

We would sadly miss such wonderful colleagues as Michael Rowe, Alyona Kojevnikov, Grazyna Sikorska, Bob Hoare and Arvan Gordon. Alex Tomsky had already left to become, for a short time, Director of the UK branch of Aid to the Church in Need, before leaving to make his home in Prague during those heady days of new freedom. Perhaps the keenest loss – someone we could not even begin to replace – was the cement of Keston's sometimes shaky fabric, Mavis Perris. She had been my secretary and PA, administrator, PA to Philip Walters and much else, through thick and thin, over some fifteen years. Without Mavis, I doubt whether Keston would have survived to 1990.

Those who did make the move kept the work going for years under difficult circumstances. Malcolm Walker bore a weighty burden, first packing up the archive and library, then putting it into store, having selected a small part to go immediately to Oxford. Further packing and unpacking followed, without any assistance. Philip Walters moved with his family and put all his efforts into keeping the research and publishing going at a time when we were unable to continue the Keston News Service. He shared the administrative burden with me.

Jane Ellis made the move, but soon left the full-time employ of Keston in order to work for a doctorate at St Antony's College. Her early death prevented her from bringing this project to fruition, but her legacy lives on. When Christopher Andrew and Vasili Mitrokhin produced their masterly study of the KGB, *The Mitrokhin Archive*, Jane's work provided the main pillar of the authoritative chapter entitled, 'The Penetration and Persecution of the Churches'.[2]

We lost, too, most of our Council, who considered that with the change of location we needed new faces, more representative of our academic work and the influential people who wanted to see us in Oxford. The Revd Bill Broad, a parish priest from Hartlepool, who had long had a close association with our work, stepped in as temporary Chairman, before Professor Michael Kaser took over for most of the 1990s. One factor, which seemed so promising, was that the University followed up on Goodrick-Clarke's verbal promise by appointing two observers to the Council, a gesture of intent to integrate Keston's work into the University. These were influential people, faithful to our cause, but as the heady events of 1985–91 receded into the past, so did it become more difficult for them to help our progress. We did not become part of the Campaign for Oxford, as had at one time been mooted. However, Canon George Patterson, a modern historian, former Dean of King's College, Cambridge, and Dr Catherine Andreyev, a distinguished military historian of the Soviet Union, both at Christ Church, did their best for us. The scholars who had expressed such initial enthusiasm for our cause either moved away (Oliver O'Donovan, Rowan Williams) or lost enthusiasm and drifted away.

The real bugbear of the period immediately after the decision to move, however, was our inability to sell a property which we had lovingly restored and converted at considerable cost. Its great attraction – its location in the middle of Keston Common – was also now a millstone. Surrounded by greenbelt land, it could not be redeveloped and there was only a small space for accommodation, the former headmaster's house. It hung around our neck for a year, unoccupied, vulnerable and depreciating all the time. I could never bring myself to set eyes on it again for years after we moved: I felt that my lifeblood had circulated in it. Much later there was planning permission for redevelopment as residential accommodation, and, as I write, we have just installed a plaque, visible from the road and marking the years of Keston's occupation of the building.

Gorbachev, Glasnost and the Gospel appeared in September 1990, nearly a year after the Berlin Wall came down. It became obvious that the Soviet Union was not going to survive. In August 1991, with the failed coup, this became certain. Sadly, Gorbachev's demise led to an abrupt closure of all discussion of the eight translations which had been mooted and in the event only the Finnish one appeared. I always thought this extremely short-sighted, because the transformation of life for Soviet believers was a topic of broad interest and no other single book has told the story. Further, it was a corrective to the many who would now attribute the major changes in Soviet religious life to the collapse of communism at the end of 1991, rather than to the late 1980s, when

---

2   Penguin, London, 1999, pp. 634–61.

the most significant changes took place. A new and liberating law was passed, after all, in 1990 and it was under Boris Yeltsin that the restrictions on religious freedom, soon to be intensified, began again.

The failure to secure the translations under negotiation was a grim dose of realism telling us that our new life in Oxford would not be easy. However, I did believe that a compensation would now be my open access to Russia – and so it proved to be. There was another frustration, though. The final chapter of the Gorbachev book set out a blueprint for the kind of relations which the churches of the West could and should have developed with their Russian counterparts. Chapter 9 – and we remind ourselves that this was published while the Soviet Union was still in place – described the immense new opportunities which now prevailed. *Miloserdiye* ('charity', *caritas*, literally 'dear-heartedness') was, from 1988, a word occurring frequently in the Soviet press. The agencies of the state were by this time openly admitting the huge lacunae in the provision of care for the vulnerable. The major denominations, Orthodox, Protestants and Catholics, as well as starting to rebuild their structures, were at the same time desperate to begin to fill the needs in ways which they were now permitted to exploit.

I covered all this in the book, highlighting, for example, the way in which Mother Teresa of Calcutta had sent in her Sisters of Charity to begin to take destitute people in off the streets. She herself, an Albanian by origin, visited the Soviet Union no fewer than three times in the second half of 1989, before illness forced her to send deputies, but not before she had been able to assess the needs with her own eyes and experience. I wrote about prison visiting, the needs in hospitals, psychiatric clinics and old people's homes. A section on children talked not only of the appalling conditions in orphanages (and institutions to which children had been removed from their parents for political reasons), but also of the opportunities in general education, where religion could now be taught in any school, but there were no textbooks or teachers specially qualified to take advantage of these new openings.

The Search for Property

In Oxford we were forced to rent property and found inadequate, but conveniently located, former parish offices belonging to St Barnabas Church in Jericho, close to the city centre. The hopes that one of the Oxford colleges might find or subsidise accommodation were never fulfilled. Our almost non-existent reserves were dwindling through 1991, but thanks to the patience and loyalty of many of our supporters, who at their peak had numbered some 12,000 worldwide, we just kept in the black, as we had done after many close calls in the past. We lost too many supporters, though, who not only thought our work was done, but seemed to gain the impression that we would now be 'part of the rich set-up' of one of the world's foremost universities. Those who remained loyal to us shared our vision for the future. In 1992 we both managed to sell Keston College and also found an imposing but dilapidated house which we could convert to our use: 4 Park Town in the 'academic heartland' of North Oxford, almost opposite Canterbury Road and 400 yards from St Antony's College.

The Hon. Bobby Wills (whose Dulverton Trust had supported Keston in the past) approached me, with an offer. Since he had used the Park Town property as an educational charity, the Farmington Trust, we could secure permission to use it partly as offices, partly as housing. Its twelve rooms (not counting kitchens and bathrooms) had been poorly converted into flats some time before, but we hoped that we would eventually be able to restore the property to its full glory, as we had Keston School. Bobby Wills negotiated hard, but I was determined to see the deal through. Eventually we settled on £500,000, which was an enormous sum at the time, especially as, almost in despair, we had to let Keston College go to a commercial concern for just half that.

We had now to embark on a serious fund-raising campaign, which I approached with trepidation, although various helpers vigorously shouldered the immediate responsibility. Our subject having dropped so far down the popular agenda, it was impossible to gain much new support, but with generous help from a number of trusts with which we had had a long relationship, and a loan of £100,000 at below the going interest rate from the Bishopsdown Trust (the Templeton Prize money well invested), we managed to raise the requisite sum, signed on the dotted line and, with an enormous sigh of relief, became owners of a desirable North Oxford property. It was a decision and an effort which guaranteed the eventual survival of what was now Keston Institute.

Restoration of 4 Park Town

We had nothing in hand to begin the restoration of our new building to its Victorian splendour. It was one thing to look at the stately rooms, but another to start working in them. Yet again, as initially in Kent, we occupied a building without adequate heating. I was more shocked than I expected at the state in which the Farmington Trust had left it. We had had, of course, a survey which warned us of many problems, but it was these which had allowed me to negotiate a price with Bobby Wills. The possibility of having students living in the top (fourth level) of the building had seemed exciting, but when some of the boxes of documents and periodicals were stored there (after all, the total space was less than half of what we had had in Kent) the prospect of using it for this purpose receded and thus the hope of supplementing our income disappeared.

However, the most urgent need was to provide adequate space for the offices and archives. It was into this that we put our meagre resources and even then they were exhausted long before we had finished the work. My brother, Neil, who had his own building firm in Cornwall, brought his skills to bear, and we then had three floors which were convenient to work in. As in so many old houses in Oxford, there was a semi-basement reached by steps at the side and Neil ensured that this area was damp-proof and safe for the archive. The main floor was at the level of a short flight of steps at the front and there was another set of rooms above this. All these were in a reasonable state of repair. In front there was a gravel forecourt, but behind a neglected garden which had once been beautiful.

We knew from the survey that the roof was defective and we would need some £80,000 to repair it. I found myself both exhausted and daunted by the prospect of trying to raise such a sum. After a lifetime of fund-raising to support the academic work of a team of people I was bereft of new ideas and became increasingly convinced that new blood was needed: new ideas for the approaching twenty-first century.

In the heady post-communist days there was always the compensation of the excitement of developments in our field, a whole new world of possibilities for the churches. We soon discovered that, to our surprise, specific study of the churches in Eastern Europe was only a minority interest. St Edmund Hall welcomed me back and elected me as a permanent member of the Senior Common Room. This was a privilege, giving me access to all the facilities of my old college. I had keys to the library, the senior common room and the right to dine among the Fellows, many of whom had become friends during my earlier return as a Visiting Fellow. The Hall was still convivial, interested in my work and delighted to welcome the guests, mainly from Eastern Europe, whom I frequently introduced. If it had been a wealthy college there is just a chance that it might have provided the security that our work permanently required.

Jane Ellis and I were both invited to lecture at one of the Monday afternoon seminars held week by week during term at St Antony's College. Professor Michael Kaser, a leading economist, was one of the few who showed a practical interest in religion, but he was soon to retire. I became a 'Senior Associate Member', which gave me the right to dine there after the Monday lectures, which covered a wide variety of subjects and attempted to follow the rapidly developing political scene in the – now disintegrated – Soviet bloc. There was much to be learned there and, for a time, I was able to keep my knowledge of developments up to date. I was always surprised, however, that the Centre for Russian Studies there did not include anyone with a primary interest in religion.

One bright spot was the success of OTEP. Keston contributed substantially to the cost of bringing over the first Russian Orthodox student, who came for a year. We felt, perhaps misguidedly, that this would help establish our permanent status in the university. A succession of ambitious students from almost all countries of the former Soviet bloc arrived in Oxford, nearly all of them interested in one way or another in the work of Keston. There were several female students, lay people as well as ordinands, and some recently ordained. Among them was a female Protestant pastor from Hungary, Erzsebet Komlosi, who lived at Wycliffe Hall and became a popular figure there. From Bulgaria there was a scholar, Inna Merdzhanova, who studied the relations between Islam and Orthodoxy in her country. These students represented, over the years, every major denomination and on the committee which selected them we always tried to achieve a balance of nationality and religious tradition. We tried to ensure, but of course could not insist, that all candidates would return to work in their country of origin. One who did not, but achieved an outstanding career as a psychiatrist and theologian at Balliol College was Dr Alex Popescu, who has contributed much to Oxford and to our work.

A splendid supplement to this was Keston's introduction of a parallel and slightly more flexible scheme: to select our own special students to work for shorter periods (sometimes as little as a month) within our own specific field of interest. This brought some gifted young people to Oxford and, after returning, they began to form a nucleus in various countries who knew about and valued the work of Keston. It was a modest but promising beginning to making our work better known in the countries which it primarily concerned. It is sad that, in more recent years, we lacked the resources to build on this, but, much later, our Council selected and financed students to study in our archive when it moved to Baylor University. This continues today.

Naturally, we could no longer maintain a publication called *Religion in Communist Lands*, illustrious though its history had been. Philip Walters and I decided to change the name to *Religion, State and Society*, but cover the same ground, hoping, *inter alia*, to describe the transformation, for the first time in history, of atheist states into ones where religion was fully free. This, I think, worked for a time, but we suffered from the lack of permanent staff researching on the subject and there was little contribution from other scholars in Oxford. We also lacked the resources to publicise our journal in Eastern Europe, where we did not gain the subscribers we had hoped.

Eventually *Religion, State and Society* became divorced from what was going on at the Institute and we sold the title for £10,000 to the academic publisher, Taylor and Francis. It became more academic, more sociological, perhaps less reader-friendly, than *Religion in Communist Lands* had ever been. However, every issue continues to note that this publication was founded by Keston College. When Philip Walters retired from Keston he continued to edit it until his own retirement, maintaining a raft of worldwide contacts and advisers.

Political and Academic Progress

After a period of quietus our work began to make progress again. The European institutions, at last, started to look seriously at the subject of human rights in the former communist bloc. The Organisation for Security and Co-operation in Europe (OSCE), which had not done much in the field of human rights since the Paris 'Helsinki Review Conference' of the summer of 1989, where I had been an official Foreign Office delegate, began to reorganise itself. Warsaw was chosen as the headquarters for the office monitoring human rights and, representing the Foreign Office, I began to make regular visits there. My main contribution was to have discussions with the Vatican delegate and with him propose, successfully, that the subject of religion was so complicated that it needed its own special sub-division. This led to the establishment of a working group, but there were insufficient funds for its members to meet often. There I established a relationship with Professor Cole Durham, from Brigham Young

University, Salt Lake City, who had an acute grasp of legal codices and followed intently the development of new legislation on religion country by country.

Another initiative of the time was an invitation in 1993–4 from the European Union, via the FCO, to become a member of a so-called 'High Level Experts' Group on Foreign Policy'. Our brief was to produce a paper which would help the EU to move towards formulating a common foreign policy, especially with regard to the newly independent nations of Europe. 'High-level' it may have been, but I found a low level of knowledge among my colleagues about the realities of post-Soviet Russia. I visited Brussels for these short meetings almost every month for a year, but the task we were set was hopeless from the outset. The paper we eventually produced predictably sank without trace. I was reduced to writing a supplementary contribution, not included in the final text, on the subject of human rights and religious liberty. A large budget must have been expended on this exercise, but from the beginning it was clouded by bureaucracy, lack of leadership and no sense of urgency. I was surrounded by personnel from various foreign ministries who seemed to be procuring work as they eased themselves into retirement. What Keston could have done with a tenth of the money thus expended!

A different and much more important contact was with Emory University, Atlanta, Georgia. Professor John Witte invited me in January 1996 to a conference to discuss the study for which he had received funding from the Pew Charitable Trusts (Philadelphia). This was to be a multi-faceted project studying missions in the world as it approached the third millennium. John asked me whether Keston would take over the work on the former Soviet Union, to which, of course, I readily agreed.

I found myself for the first – and only – time in charge of a considerable budget, which was to be expended on drawing together a team of experts for two conferences, a year apart, in Oxford. At the second we would review each other's work, prior to submitting it for publication. It was a fine opportunity to call together some of my closest colleagues, and both the planning and the eventual outcome were exciting. The volume appeared in good time and lived up to my highest expectations.[3] As editor, I was deeply involved in my most serious academic project in the six years since finishing my Gorbachev book. There was a problem, though. While mission work in Russia lacked any strategy or real rationale, this work should have been essential reading for all those involved, whether in the mission field or at home. In the event, the book made little impact and I doubt whether the calibre of missionary work improved as a result of it. It would have been good if funds had been available for a follow-up conference involving some of the mission leaders. However, it was an opportunity to bring over from Russia some of the promising post-communist generation of scholars beginning serious study of religion in Russia.

---

3   John Witte and Michael Bourdeaux (eds), *Proselytism and Orthodoxy in Russia: the New War for Souls* (Orbis Books, Maryknoll, NY, 1999).

My contact with the Pew Charitable Trusts was valuable for the future also: I applied for a grant on behalf of Keston to study the internal developments in the field of religion in Russia since the collapse of communism. I wanted to build on the work which had been begun, totally under-funded, in Moscow by Sergei Borisovich Filatov. He was setting out on the study, with a small group of gifted colleagues, of religion in the regions of Russia as it was developing in the post-communist era. My application was successful and this inaugurated what was to become Keston's principal study in years to come. No one had ever undertaken such a project before and no other country, I think, has ever been subjected to such scrutiny.

Chapter XVIII
Through Trials, New Opportunities

The events of the dying Soviet Union might have rung the death-knell for Keston College. Other, more famous, institutions were to collapse or see the dispersal of their library and archive. This was the plight of the invaluable resource of the Great-Britain-USSR Association library, while leading institutions like the Russian department of Glasgow University or the School of Slavonic and East European Studies at London University suffered such drastic cuts as rendered them virtually unrecognisable, compared with their former status. Even today this trend has not been reversed.

How did Keston survive? At times we teetered on the brink, but ultimately we were able to maintain the Archive and to contribute, as in the past, to an increased understanding of Russia.

I did truly believe that my new book, particularly the last section referred to earlier, would be read and taken up as a stimulus, providing at least the beginnings of guidelines for aiding the Russian churches in their emerging freedom. Sadly, though, it soon became obvious that the churches of the West had their own agendas. A flood of foreign missionaries, mainly but not exclusively American, so often lacking the language and any fundamental knowledge of Russian culture, began to inundate not only Moscow, but the provinces and the newly independent states, too. Looking back in 2019, I am sure that these incursions increased the isolationism of the Russian Orthodox Church and exacerbated its hostility to Protestantism.

Peter and Anita Deyneka had been waiting and preparing for an opportunity to work directly in Russia, which followed the decades when the focus of their ministry had been on radio broadcasts. Training Russian missionaries, rather than becoming missionaries themselves, was now top of their agenda and their educational programmes have been influential and successful. They worked for the Slavic Gospel Association, but later set up Peter Deyneka Ministries. After Peter's death, Anita took hold of both reins and has provided a prime example of how foreign Protestants could and should work in Russia. They organised summer camps even in some of Russia's most difficult regions, such as Chechnya, and later concentrated on supporting orphans and trying to provide them with foster families.

Another avenue for direct aid opened up for Aid to the Church in Need. They invited me to participate in some eventful ecumenical work. Fr Werenfried van Straaten, its now aged but still sharp and active founder, could see that the virtual abolition of religious education blocked the progress of the Russian Orthodox Church. His Board designated financial support for helping establish new institutions and they invited me to act as an adviser. As I result I made frequent visits to their head office at Königstein, near Frankfurt.

I wrote them a report and began to look into the practicalities. I gave them the names of some individuals in Russia with whom I believed it would be possible for them to work. Later Fr Theo van der Voort, a Dutch convert to Orthodoxy, moved to Königstein, but he discovered that some of the money was being used to fund anti-Catholic propaganda, so eventually the aid programme had to cease.

At the time of our move to Oxford, my new bishop, Richard Harries, had been designated by Lambeth Palace (Archbishop Runcie) as the person primarily responsible for developing relations with the Orthodox Church in the new circumstances. Direct aid came within this brief. There were meetings and delegations, even a bilateral conference in Oxford on the needs and possibilities, to which I received an invitation to one session only. Despite some reciprocal visits, the enthusiasm among British Anglicans soon petered out, leaving one substantial achievement: a scholarship administered at Lambeth to bring over one Russian Orthodox scholar each year for study at a British university, a complement to Oxford's OTEP scheme. There were scattered initiatives at parish and diocesan level.

Conferences

As I look through my travel record of the early 1990s, a flood of memories comes back, but it would try the reader's patience to do more than list some of the new opportunities which presented themselves.

Once, in 1974, I had spoken at an evangelical conference designated the 'Lausanne Conference', memorably sharing the platform with Archbishop Janani Luwum, who gave one of his last powerful public speeches before being murdered by Idi Amin. In July 1989 there was a follow-up conference, designated 'Lausanne II', convened in Manila, Philippines, where the focus was on the Russians who were able to attend without having to be selected by the Soviet regime. This was the first-ever foreign trip which Fr Gleb Yakunin was able to make. We spent time together on outings, such as white-water rafting, and I shared his joy at his being able, finally, to speak without constraint.

In the summer of 1990 I went on a long train journey to visit the countries of the former Soviet bloc, which were now fully accessible without visas. Over three weeks in July and August I met a variety of believers in East Germany, Czechoslovakia, Hungary, Romania and Yugoslavia. Particularly interesting was my visit to Serbia, where, on behalf of Oxford University, I interviewed the son of an Orthodox priest whose application for an OTEP scholarship in the second year was successful.

To live for a few days in the house of a Serbian Orthodox priest was an intense experience. No hospitality could have been warmer, but at each meal, in succession, there was a tirade by the head of the household against the (Croatian) Catholics, the Protestants, the (Bosnian) Muslims and the ecumenical movement. As a guest in that house I learned a great deal about the exacerbated feelings of inter-communal hostility which had come to the fore after the death of Tito. One had the certain premonition that something unpleasant was about to happen, which not even our diplomats or political commentators had foreseen. The scale of the ensuing tragedy in Yugoslavia shocked me, but I had witnessed a warning of what was to come.

I had several visits to Sandhurst to lecture to successive groups of army chaplains. This led to a lecture, at the end of 1991, to a small conference of chaplains at Lübbecke, near Hanover. After the collapse of the Soviet Union, the British army in Berlin established friendly relations with their Russian counterparts. Indeed, they revelled in the association and in the freedom of the Russians to accept invitations to anything they suggested. It must have been a challenge to the Russians in February 1992 to attend a lecture by a foreigner on the role of religion in those climactic events, but the welcome could not have been warmer and they took part enthusiastically in the session. It was, indeed, a unique occasion, which could have taken place only during the briefest window in time.

In July I addressed the European Youth Parliament in Strasbourg and reflected on how useful it would be if the powers-that-be in Brussels put more money into such enterprises and less into bureaucracy. This imaginative scheme was able, for a short time, to bring together students from the newly independent countries. They had residential courses, too, at Radley College, near Oxford, and I received several invitations to participate in these. In a small way these courses contributed to the democratic development of the countries which were now free and I emphasised the positive role religion had played in recent events.

In January 1993 I went to 'St Petersburg' for the first time, all my previous visits having been to 'Leningrad', but now there had been a plebiscite on the change of name. 'Open Christianity' organised this visit and I was able to catch up with some of the fundamental changes which were taking place. Just two months later (20–24 March) I was again invited to an 'Experts' Conference', where various Russian legal representatives met in a remote (ex-KGB) conference centre at Lesnye Dali, accessible from Moscow, to discuss legislation on religion. I contributed my opinion, not to be heeded, that it was time to abandon the idea that registration was essential for the local congregation to be considered legal. At the time, I did not realise that among these 'experts' were people who regretted the degree to which Gorbachev's 1990 law had conferred virtually unlimited freedoms on the religious communities. The former atheist establishment was out of work and they wanted their jobs back, now as legal experts. I would have spoken more forcefully and issued warnings, if I had known; but even a harder-hitting contribution from me would not have changed the direction of thinking, which eventually led to the imposition of Yeltsin's retrogressive new law of 1997. This was a prelude to a flood of new restrictions, naming Orthodoxy, Islam, Judaism and Buddhism as 'traditional' Russian religions, but excluding Catholicism and Protestantism.

New and interesting parts of Russia and associated countries were opening up to organised tourist groups. We took advantage as Keston supporters were eager to travel. For a short time only, it was possible for foreign friends to join Russians in examining the Soviet Union's record on human rights and religious liberty, so I began to organise holidays in Russia, Ukraine and the Baltic States. In a sense they were pilgrimages and Keston personnel took the lead. They were a glorious opportunity to present *in situ* some of the knowledge we had acquired over the years. Lorna and the children joined me on some of these adventures and they remain, vivid, in all our memories.

I was most excited by the opening up of the Russian waterways to foreign tourists. The long route linking Moscow to St Petersburg had originally been completed in 1937 by Stalin's use of slave labour on the Moscow-Volga Canal. During the Soviet period it was barred to foreigners, as a route of strategic significance (not to mention enquiries which might have been made about its construction). Now, however, this clouded past was a subject of fascination and occasionally there were memorial plaques to those who had lost their lives in the enterprise. Much of the way, however, is via rivers and lakes rather than constructed canals and the route wends its stately way through some of Russia's most memorable and typical scenery, a succession of forests, fields and riverside villages, punctuated by majestic monasteries (St Cyril of the White Lake and the Valaam Monastery, for example) and some of the finest cities: Yaroslavl, Kostroma, Nizhny Novgorod and Uglich.

The travel agency Noble Caledonia was supportive of all we did and I highly estimated their efficiency and standards. They were, in the early 1990s, heavily promoting cruises on the 'Waterway of the Tsars'. The first such trip took place over two weeks in July–August 1994. It was a great success. I found it an emotional experience to be lecturing on board a comfortable small ship as the countryside slid by. We observed the poverty caused by collectivisation. The ruined churches were, in some places, under reconstruction. There was invariably a warm and personal welcome as we stopped briefly at some of the small villages. An especial privilege was to have Sir John Lawrence and his wife on board and this was the last of his many visits to Russia.

Later I organised a cruise specially for Keston supporters. It was moving for our pilgrims to have the opportunity of meeting face to face some of the courageous figures about whom we had written. I introduced them to Fr Georgi Edelstein at his village church some thirty miles from Kostroma, the closest his bishop would allow him to the big city. In Moscow Alexander Ogorodnikov, Fr Gleb Yakunin and the Roman Catholic bishop, Tadeusz Kondrusiewicz, came on board to meet the passengers. Their visit and our discussions welded us into a group of pilgrims. We were so much more than tourists come to gaze at the sights and this was, undoubtedly, one of the most successful Keston enterprises.

We publicised two further successful river trips – down the Volga (which I did not lead myself) and from Kiev on the River Dnieper to the Black Sea and Crimea. I also accompanied Keston pilgrims by coach through the Baltic States, when I was able to lead prayer at the Hill of Crosses, central to the faith of the Lithuanians, about which I had written nearly twenty years earlier. In my experience, this was one of the most holy sites I had ever visited. It celebrated both the faith of the people and their tradition of intricate wood sculpture. It had been a constant battle ground, with the Soviets constantly bulldozing it, followed by a succession of restorations, with crosses being secretly 'planted' by night. Now the power of its imagery was overwhelming.

Then in May 1995 I paid my first visit to the Russian European Arctic in conjunction with a remarkable conference convened in Kirkenes (Norway) on co-operation between the northern countries of Europe (Norway, Sweden, Finland and Russia). I flew via Tromsø and Kirkenes to Murmansk, then by train south to the benighted (one-time Finnish) town of Kem, whence I embarked for my first visit to an ex-labour camp, the great island monastery of Solovki, now back in the hands of the church. I almost failed to make it. After we had waited all day for transport, the little 'cutter', as the Russians called it, had only six passengers besides me. We set off in the evening, but it was going to be light all night. About halfway into the three-hour journey a dense fog descended. The captain had, apparently, been navigating visually and lost his way. With the midnight sun hugging the horizon, there was a bright, uniform glow through the fog around all 360 degrees. We struck a rock. I had noticed a cupboard marked 'lifejackets' and I led a charge below deck to open it. It was empty. Fortunately, the hull had not been holed, but the propeller and steering gear had been damaged and it looked unlikely that we would make much more progress. However, the fog lifted. The captain re-started the engines and was able to progress with a kind of crab-like crawl: he could propel his craft in a semi-circle, then cut out the engine and steer manually, using the generated momentum to correct his course (he could now see the islands).

We reached the Solovki Monastery in the early hours of the morning, still majestic in its ruined splendour. Piles of fallen masonry lay everywhere. The massive walls were in disrepair and the several churches were roofless. A night watchman found me a monastic cell, formerly occupied by political prisoners and unchanged since. The next morning Abbot Iosif received me. The experience left an indelible mark: of thanksgiving that my life had been preserved; of renewed determination to help the Orthodox Church in the immense task of rebuilding, not just here, but everywhere. The boat was now out of service and it looked as though I would not be able to get back to Norway for the conference, which was my reason for being in the Arctic. However, eventually a tiny plane arrived and flew me to Arkhangelsk, some 200 miles in the direction opposite to my destination. From there I changed airports and found a plane flying north to Murmansk, where I was just in time to meet up with a group of Russians who were going on to the conference over the border in Norway. We travelled by minibus along the Great Northern Highway, passing the stretch of coast where once Finland had had direct access to the Arctic Ocean, a sector of land which the Soviets had conquered and where the Russians still rule. I saw the ecological calamity in the town of Nikel, where mines and their processing plants belched incessant pollution into the atmosphere. I had time to meet the editor of the local newspaper, who told me that almost the whole population suffered from respiratory problems. The only difference from the communist period was that now he could write about it. We changed buses at the border, crossing by foot what had, until recently, been one of Russia's most impenetrable frontiers, the only place, apart from the long frontier with Turkey, where a NATO nation directly abutted the former Soviet Union.

The conference in Kirkenes dealt largely with ecological issues. On the way there we had also seen a mineshaft – from a safe distance – where, allegedly, nuclear waste was simply thrown in from the rim. My Russian friends, especially the priest, Fr Georgi Edelstein, were astonished to see how, just a few miles west of Nikel, the Norwegians could develop at Kirkenes, on the same band of mineral reserves, a spotless town which seemed a world away from conditions on the other side of the border.

The conference itself was remarkable. It was inspiring to witness the desire, on both sides, to co-operate in the Arctic region, establishing friendly and practical relations. Offers of help from the various Scandinavian countries followed one after the other. When one reflects on such encounters a quarter of a century later, it brings one up sharply to reflect on what the 'new Europe' might have become.

New Opportunities

In those exciting days 'twinning' was often on the agenda and Keston frequently provided advice. Modern Tring (Hertfordshire) and ancient Pskov would seem to be unlikely partners, but the enthusiasm of one person, the Revd. Janet Ridgeway, proved what could be done. The Anglican parish established a link, through the advice of Jane Ellis, with Fr Pavel Adelheim, a dynamic parish priest. He was seriously disabled as a result of a contrived accident in the prison camp, where he had 'sat', to use the Russian expression, leading to his loss of a leg, but he always made light of his disability. He was an outstanding pastor and an ecumenist. There were reciprocal visits to Tring, during which deep friendships were formed. On one occasion we enjoyed the warmth of his company for several hours at Keston in Oxford. Fr Pavel particularly wanted to minister more effectively to the young people in his parish, so his British friends bought him a minivan to enable him to transport his young converts to village centres. The local bishop did not approve and tried unsuccessfully to stymie Fr Pavel's efforts.

Eventually, in 2013, a disturbed young man presumed on his hospitality, turned on him and fatally stabbed him with a kitchen knife in his own house in the presence of his wife. The circumstances were never fully investigated and this tragic event leaves many unanswered questions. Why was this outstanding pastor murdered? In Tring I spoke in his memory in the presence of the parishioners who had supported Fr Pavel's ministry.

Twinning with Russian parishes has long since been abandoned, but I was personally involved in one ambitious diocese-to-diocese effort – Exeter to Yaroslavl (on the Volga, east of Moscow). The cathedral authorities were planning an ambitious 'millennium tour' for 2000, a three-city enterprise with concerts in each place. I became an adviser because I had a connection with the cathedral, where my daughter Lara Clare was a chorister. The tour was planned for boys and men, so she would not be going, but when I first knew about it, all the contacts were with the twinned city of Yaroslavl. I was brought on board to help with venues in Moscow and St Petersburg, which I did, and I found myself as travelling interpreter. This was one of my most satisfying visits to Russia. There had previously been one-centre visits by Anglican cathedral choirs, but this was the first full-scale tour. Not only did all go very well, but, in the absence of printed programmes, I had to introduce every concert in Russian. I was thrilled to witness – and hear – the professionalism of so many sub-teenage boys and the reception was warm everywhere. It was a privilege to establish relations with Protestants and Catholics, as well as the Orthodox.

I had arranged the three locations in Moscow: a Catholic church (St Louis, close to the Lubyanka), the Anglican church of St Andrew (for a concert and Sunday morning service), and our only appearance in an Orthodox church. The redoubtable Fr Georgi Chistyakov, priest of the church of SS Cosmas and Damian, who has since died, summoned his parishioners on a week-day afternoon. When we arrived he was carrying benches into the main body of the church, so that everyone could sit down. The church was soon packed. As I announced the items, each time Fr Georgi gave an impromptu commentary on the theology of what we were about to hear. The boys couldn't understand what he was saying, of course, but much enjoyed his presentations, because they thought he bore an uncanny resemblance to Ken Dodd. We made the pages of *Izvestia*, such a former bastion of atheism, which called the boys a 'choir of young cardinals', because of the scarlet robes they wore.

We went by road to Yaroslavl, which is twinned with Exeter, and I had much more opportunity to see its wrecked churches (with some rebuilding in central areas) than I had had when I visited it on the waterways trip. Because of the twinning, the civic authorities took over, treated us like visiting stars, and relieved me of any local responsibilities. We sang, therefore, in secular venues, but our leader, Canon Neil Collings, organised a visit for a small group to the cathedral of 'St Nicholas the Wet', in a deleterious state and which Exeter was helping to rebuild.

We travelled on by overnight train to St Petersburg, where the boys had to perform the next evening without, in most instances, having slept. Here the whole choir revelled in singing an unaccompanied Bach motet in the restored Lutheran church on the Nevsky Prospekt. On my last visit to it, in 1960, the floor had been ripped out and a swimming pool installed. It felt almost as though we were re-consecrating the building. Everywhere I met new people and left lovely friends behind.

BBC Broadcasts

Opportunities for journalism began to open out in the second half of the 1990s, once editors realised that Russia was still of interest to the general public. Thus I was able to write occasionally for the Saturday religion page of *The Times* (on Cuba, Ukraine and Georgia). But my most significant contribution to the media was the opportunity to write obituaries for *The Guardian* of Eastern Europeans and some westerners who had supported them. This was a privilege, for each time I revisited the history of the time and emphasised the bravery of the contributions so many had made. Among the westerners of whom I wrote were Jane Ellis, Sir John Lawrence, Metropolitan Anthony Bloom, Fr Sergei Hackel, Professor Dimitri Obolensky and Fr Werenfried van Straaten. Among the East Europeans were Catholicos Karekin Sarkissian of Armenia, Fr Dmitri Dudko and Cardinal Todea of Romania. There were many others.

The most special privilege of all, however, was an ongoing series of radio broadcasts for the BBC. This came about, initially, because the religion department in Manchester decided to commission a series of four broadcasts of *Sunday Worship* from around the world to mark the millennium. The Revd (now Canon) Stephen Shipley came to see me early in 1999 to ask if I would advise him on the possibility of doing one of these in Russia. This led to a kind of Indian summer in my work, the opening out of a new field of possibilities.

I responded with enthusiasm and the BBC decided to commission a programme from Russia. They preferred not to broadcast from Moscow or St Petersburg. I felt strongly that we should inform the External Relations Department of the Moscow Patriarchate of our plan at the earliest opportunity and did so on my next visit to Moscow. Archbishop Kirill, who was later to become a Metropolitan and then Patriarch, received me and warmly invited us to Smolensk, his diocese. He reiterated what I already knew: there was a vibrant Orthodox community and we would receive a warm welcome. Kirill had the reputation of being an enterprising diocesan bishop, who had established one of the most vigorous of the new theological seminaries in Russia. We discovered that the cathedral had a fine choir and Kirill was keen to invite us to come.

So it was that our broadcast was scheduled for the last Sunday of the second millennium and we made arrangements, beginning with what the BBC calls a 'recce'. Stephen Shipley became a valued colleague, with whom I went to Russia eight times between 1999 and 2008. Now retired, he was a producer of worship on radio of imposing musical knowledge, secure judgement and – so important for such enterprises – cheerfulness in adversity and technical competence. This enabled him, as a one-man team, to replicate what the complex technology of an outside broadcast van can do, manned by several staff.

We first visited Smolensk (with the clothes we stood up in, our suitcases having been temporarily mislaid) in September 1999 to hear the choir, meet possible participants and set a date for a return visit and recording. The Dean of the theological seminary invited me to give a lecture (in Russian), with a request to recount my autobiography. The response was predictably lively and this is the only time I have been invited to lecture in a Russian Orthodox seminary. There was a dearth of English speakers in Smolensk, but we found one or two who could participate in the programme. Alex Samsonov became a friend, an accomplished young singer, who was keen to help us in an exciting enterprise. He assisted Stephen with setting up the equipment and we were so impressed that we invited him informally to join our team at the next three locations for future broadcasts. The outstanding character we met was Mother Ivana, a nun, who commanded her little world with authority, while being warmly disposed to all whom she met. She was determined not to be outdone by the lively seminary for young men and had established her own institution for educating female church singers and choir trainers. Stephen's music drew us together and it was not long before he was playing the piano, with the students dancing round the room to the waltz from the *Nutcracker Suite*.

The recording itself went well. At our second visit at the end of November 1999 snow had fallen, so Stephen could not resist the opportunity of recording the crunch of my footsteps in the park as I walked up to the Glinka memorial. The turn of the millennium was an excellent time to reflect on history, so I spoke of Smolensk as a frontier town, where Napoleon was defeated, where Russian Orthodoxy had often vied with Polish Catholicism for supremacy, and whence the River Dnieper headed south to Kiev, the route by which the faith had originally reached this part of what was now the Russian heartland. I went on to recount the devastation of religion in the region first by Stalin and then by Nikita Khrushchev in the early 1960s.

Metropolitan Kirill, later to be elected Patriarch, has his critics, but he, with his dominating personality, played a unique role in the rebuilding of the structure of church life in this diocese. He invited us to dinner. The three of us were alone, relaxed and speaking English, which Kirill does well, having attended a language course in Birmingham. He agreed to record something about the life of his diocese.

The eventual programme was well received by the BBC and this led to the inauguration of what became an informal biennial series. In the summer of 2001 we twice went to the Arctic of European Russia. On my previous visit the main topic of conversation with Fr Iosif, Abbot of the Solovki Monastery, had been the return of three icons owned by the Revd. Roy Lambert and his wife Elizabeth. Roy was a retired Anglican clergyman living in Cirencester and they had been supporters of Keston for some time. On one visit to Oxford they brought the icons and told their story.

Elizabeth's grandfather had been a naval chaplain on a ship which was docked in Arkhangelsk in 1918, when a fugitive monk had fled from a monastery which was under attack. He salvaged these icons and handed them to Canon Arthur Twidle for safe keeping. They remained in the family and many years ago he gave them to Roy and Elizabeth as a wedding present. They were not sure exactly where the icons had come from, but I was easily able to identify that their origin was Solovki, because there was an inscription on the back of one of them. One also represented Ss. Savva and German, the founders of the monastery.

Roy and Elizabeth followed the post-Gorbachev renaissance of the Orthodox Church with interest and excitement. They took a visionary decision: to return the icons to Solovki, with the request to me to organise it. This, in fact, took several years, because I had always hoped to involve television in the enterprise. The whole scenario could have been visually stunning and provided the framework for a splendid modern history of the Church. But that was not to be and my efforts came to nothing. However, Stephen and BBC Radio 4 were keen to take it on as their next project.

Our next trip, in May 2001, took us from St Petersburg to Arkhangelsk. It was too early in the year for the regular transport routes to be in operation, but there was a *podvorye* ('dependent monastery') of Solovki on the mainland and we made our basic arrangements there. We also booked a three-day cruise to Solovki for July, when we would go with Roy and Elizabeth and they would return the icons. Abbot Iosif was in Moscow. We visited him on the way back and worked out the arrangements in great detail, including the precise dates and an outline of the ceremony which would take place.

As we made the wonderful approach to the islands by sea, the domes and towers of the monastery gradually appeared above the horizon, in blazing colours in the crystalline arctic light. I recorded a piece on deck, reading an extract from Solzhenitsyn which described the islands as they used to be and this would become the introduction to the programme. When we arrived in Solovki we had a shock. We had expected to be welcomed at the gates of the monastery. Instead we were rudely challenged by a guard, who was reluctant to let us in at all. We asked to be taken straight to Abbot Iosif, but received the reply that he was away.

Eventually we were allowed in and Iosif's deputy received us. He had never heard of our visit. We had arrived on the Saturday morning and the hand-over had been designated for the next day. The monk was clearly moved by what he saw emerging from the boxes professionally packed, but he claimed he had no authority to accept them without the say-so of Abbot Iosif, who was in Moscow and was unlikely to return that weekend. Much diplomacy and urgent persuasion ensued, with an eventual agreement that the icons would be handed over at the end of the *krestny khod*, the procession right round the walls at the end of the liturgy. So it happened. Roy gave a moving speech, recorded and broadcast, but no announcement was made at the preceding liturgy of what would follow, so the regular worshippers and pilgrims had no idea of the meaning of this deeply symbolic act (restoration of the Russian Church's desecrated history, ecumenical reconciliation between Anglicans and Orthodox). Nevertheless, the hand-over took place and Stephen's expertise produced a moving programme. I was able, of course, to reflect on Russian Church history in the light of the terrible deeds which had occurred in this place, one of Lenin's and Stalin's worst prison camps.

I am puzzled to this day as to what was the true reason for this errant behaviour on the part of a senior figure in the Russian Orthodox Church. Some part of the explanation may well lie in the fact that the Solovki Monastery does not come under a diocesan bishop, but is directly under the authority of the Patriarch of Moscow. Did Alexi II try to veto this act of reconciliation between the churches? Or was it a snub to me, who was still seen by the authorities as a *bête noire* who had exposed the misdeeds of the Patriarchate in communist times? Or maybe we were mistaken for Catholics

– Pope John Paul II had just visited Ukraine and his words and actions had deeply upset the Patriarchate. Or maybe it was a simple bureaucratic mix-up, with Abbot Iosif having genuinely forgotten the careful and enthusiastic agreement he had made two months earlier with Stephen and me. Even this was not quite the end of the story. The programme was scheduled for transmission on the Sunday after 9/11, leaving no alternative to postponing it. Eventually it went out in the middle of the winter, which was slightly odd for a programme which at more than one point celebrated the endless sun of the midsummer days.

Whatever the tribulations of this visit to the Arctic, it wasn't that long before once again the BBC asked me to go to Russia, to make a programme celebrating the 300th anniversary of the foundation of St Petersburg in 1703. This time, though, there were to be two programmes, with BBC Radio 3 joining in to commission one of its regular Wednesday afternoon choral evensongs (it would be designated 'Orthodox Vespers').

We went in April and May 2003 and worked with two magnificent choirs, those of the Cathedral of the Kazan Mother of God and the Transfiguration Cathedral. As was our wont, *Sunday Worship* included a great deal of documentary material. It was a thrill beyond words for me to stand on the steps of the Kazan Cathedral on Nevsky Prospekt and to record the introduction, to the sound of church bells, while looking at the Lutheran and Catholic churches on the opposite side of the street, which had been in ruins but were now restored or in the process of rebuilding, as was happening with St Catherine's Catholic Church. This, to me, symbolised the ecumenism which had, at certain times, weighed against the extreme nationalism of the Moscow-dominated church.

I was able to bring in contributions from some notable ecumenical figures of the day, such as the lay educator and former political prisoner, Vladimir Poresh, and Fr Vladimir Fyodorov, one of the city's leading ecumenists. Most moving of all, though, to me, was simply paying a return visit to this great church which I had known as a desecrated wreck over forty years earlier, housing the appalling 'model' atheist museum, paradigm for the whole Soviet Union. Fr Pavel Krasnotsvetov and the clergy were enthusiastic about our project, flexible in helping us achieve it, and assisting in every possible way. We were shown areas of the church inaccessible to the general public and watched the careful process of restoration, joining in the prayers of the layman who was building a new iconostasis. There was bustle everywhere: there were only ten days to go before the official celebration of the anniversary, with world leaders scheduled to arrive as guests of recently elected President Putin.

We had already recorded the choir of the Cathedral of the Transfiguration. This would be nearly all music, but with a quiet commentary from me simply indicating the course of the action for the BBC Radio 3 listeners. This was due for transmission on the day of the Feast of the Transfiguration, which happened to be a Wednesday in 2003. (So it was in 2017, when the BBC paid us the honour of repeating it for the Feast of the Transfiguration.) The recording session with the choir of the Kazan Cathedral took place late at night, when the vast space of the interior had fallen silent. The choir was on wonderful form and I was deeply moved by the voice of Darya Semenkova, the soprano soloist.

As we were finishing the session, we heard the boom of a thunderstorm outside. We asked the night watchman to call a taxi for us to go back to the Agora, an ecumenical centre with accommodation, which had been established by the Cornish visionary and long-time St Petersburg resident, Kenneth Rundell. The taxi arrived, we splashed through the torrential rain, opened the taxi door and all three piled inside (Alex Samsonov was with us as an essential helper). We drew up at the Agora, got out, Stephen paid and was just going round to the boot to pick up not only his irreplaceable equipment, but also the result of several days of recording, not to mention his passport and tickets in his briefcase. The driver revved his engine and drew away. I've never seen a fifty-year-old man run quicker, but Stephen failed to catch up with the taxi. We were shocked and horrified. Was it robbery? Or was it a simple mistake? We didn't know the firm and there are dozens in St Petersburg. Alex began ringing round in despair, but it was hopeless. Then I found a scrap of paper: it had the number of our original taxi on it. We took another taxi back to the Kazan Cathedral, where Fr Krasnotsvetov knew exactly which company had been contacted and my scrap of paper identified the vehicle. We rushed back to the Agora and a few minutes later the taxi arrived with – as it seemed to us – all the wealth we possessed on earth. It was a near-disaster, but the kindness and determination of the Russians involved saved the day.

Aside from the behind-the-scenes adventures, we considered these two broadcasts to be our most successful yet. This led to 2005, when I was commissioned to do another two programmes, making now six in all, for Russian Easter (1 May) and the Feast of the Exaltation of the Cross (14 September), to be broadcast also on the World Service. It was time to go to Moscow. This would be the seventh visit which Stephen and I would make together, this time an extended one of ten days instead of setting up the broadcasts with a preparatory visit. This time there were no adventures, but we carefully researched which church should be our focus, the range of choice in the capital obviously being vast.

I had seen the transformation of the Danilov Monastery from a juvenile prison in 1960 to the magnificent headquarters of the Russian Orthodox Church with its complex of cathedrals and churches, thirty years later. Therefore our decision to broadcast from it was deeply symbolic for me. In addition, there was a male (secular, not monastic) choir, which proved to be magnificent and which collaborated with us at every point. For the introduction to my BBC programme, I briefly recounted the history of the monastery.

Our concentration was on the amazing music, the renaissance of the Church and the chance to feature the voice of the Christian poet, Irina Ratushinskaya, whose life I described previously. We tried to bring the essence of Russian Easter into homes around the world. To enter into the spirit of the special vespers for the Exaltation of the Holy and Life-Giving Cross (as the Russians call it) was an experience which would leave me with a feeling of true accomplishment, a broadening of my own spiritual experience and a deeper understanding of Russian devotion to the faith.

There would be an eighth and final visit in April 2008. By this time Russia – especially its young people – was becoming more aware and inspired by the life and ministry of Fr Alexander Men', who had been murdered in 1990, perhaps the last victim of communism's assault on the Church. Fr Alexander had been a friend of Fr Gleb Yakunin since their student days together. They both became priests at about the same time, but their paths diverged. In contrast to Fr Gleb's open opposition to anti-religious policies, Fr Alexander chose a different kind of ministry. He concentrated on teaching young people, but in the quietest possible way, so as not to arouse the ire of the authorities. His gatherings took place mainly at his home in the distant Moscow suburb of Semkhoz, where he lived in the country house which was his wife's property. At the same time he travelled, in his later years, some half an hour on the train to his church, where his devoted parishioners followed him in all the observances of the traditional liturgy. Unbeknown to almost everyone, including the KGB, he acquired immense learning from a private library carefully assembled. In the quiet of his study he wrote numerous books and sent them secretly abroad, where they were printed in Belgium and secreted back into Russia.

None of this caution prevented him from frequent interrogation by the KGB, but he avoided imprisonment. He was ready to take advantage of the new opportunities which Gorbachev's Russia offered and I once called him the 'apostle of *glasnost'*. Almost overnight he became the Orthodox priest whom everyone wanted to hear, either in lectures or on TV, and he often spoke in institutions which had, until recently, been strongholds of the Communist Party. In September 1990 he was walking to catch the train to his church for the early morning liturgy when an assailant (possibly two) attacked him with an axe. He crawled back to the gate of his house, where he died. His murder, seemingly an act of revenge by the dying regime, was never solved.

Nearly a decade later I sat and recorded an introduction to my BBC programme in the quiet, inspiring atmosphere of his study. Stephen and I then visited the church built on the site of his murder, where the parish priest and his daughter recorded a talk. Finally we went to the church where Fr Alexander had spent the last part of his ministry.

This programme was a fitting end to this series. We had, I hoped, done justice to this outstanding pastor and teacher. My eight visits had provided an opening and a stimulus for a new chapter in my life. During Keston's heyday all my broadcasts had been short interviews, during which I always had more to say than the occasions offered. Now here, spread over almost a decade, were repeated opportunities to present something of the riches of Orthodox spirituality to a world public. We had contributed something positive to Anglican–Orthodox relations. I fulfilled an ideal, formulated in my early life, of speaking positively at length about the Orthodox Church.

Pope John Paul II

In April 2005 the BBC had provided me with other – and completely unexpected – opportunities. It was known that Pope John Paul II was dying. On Friday 1 April, I was in the BBC Oxford studio reflecting on his achievements as the end approached. But he clung on to life. Next morning, I received a call from London: would I come to Bush House and stay there for as long as it would take? This wasn't easy, as I was due to go to Moscow for the Easter recording on the Monday, but I could not say no. My privilege was to talk on the World Service at Bush House during the final hours of the Pope's life. Preceding this, I had continued to note that all the media attention was on his conservative theology and policies, while I wanted to talk about the explosive effect he had had on European events during the first ten years of his reign, leading up to the founding of Solidarity in Poland. Curiously, this enormous contribution to the world – certainly one of the strongest strands in the concatenation of forces which led to the eventual collapse of communism – was being, in the main, ignored, as the branches of the media vied with each other to pay tribute.

I aimed at redressing this balance. I was immensely impressed by the professionalism of the large team in the newsroom communicating with correspondents all round the world: not only their technical proficiency, but also their seriousness – not a word out of place when they were off air. I was designated as the 'presenter's friend', which meant that when the Pope died I would go into the studio and be a continuity person. If there were any hitch or hiatus, the presenter would turn to me and ask for a contribution. From time to time I was called into the studio to engage in live dialogue with various other contributors in foreign places. I had seen shifts come and go during the day, but, just as I decided I must leave, news of the death came through. I moved straight into the studio again and must have had at least fifteen minutes during that first hour to talk to the world about the life and achievement of Pope John Paul II. What an immense privilege this was, a unique opportunity which could never be repeated.

The Stasi

I would love to have had access to my KGB files in Moscow, but I had to make do with those of the German Stasi. My visit to Berlin was in June 2006 and this account was written for the Council at the time.

After several months of negotiation and waiting, permission at last came through. The Stasi held its archive in a building right in the centre of the former East Berlin, just off what used to be the Karl-Marx-Allee. With great efficiency, I was ushered to a desk already laid out with the Keston files. An employee pointed out a handbook listing under which section our files are held.

Every page has an individual stamp from the German researchers who had verified the authenticity of the documents. It would be easy, therefore, to note if any page had gone missing. There are 618 pages, if you include scraps of paper, divided between six files of unequal size. These proved to be more notable for what they did not say rather than for what they contained. The general impression is one of dull bureaucracy. With one possible exception, there were no astonishing revelations, no flights of imagination or construction of a narrative, no revealing personal profiles, no competent analysis of what we were really doing. Instead, one has the image of rows of backroom boys (or, more likely, girls) systematically perusing newspapers and Keston publications, cutting and pasting. There is page after page of repetition, much of it verbatim and in carbon – or photocopy – of earlier entries. I did not count, but I estimate that under half of the total pages contain new material. Once they had made up their mind what we were doing, they repeated this doggedly from the 1970s through to the last entry in February 1989.

The revelation was the Stasi's analysis of Keston's *raison d'être* and it is based on an unbelievable misconception. Because we began our work officially in 1969, they attribute its genesis to the Soviet suppression of the Prague Spring (they do not call it that, of course) the previous year. They repeat this endlessly, without ever once hinting at the true motivation, the impact of my study year in Moscow (1959–60), when I had witnessed the persecution of the Church at first hand. Although this year is noted in my 'biography', nothing is made of it. This proves that the Soviet KGB failed to transmit details to the Stasi of my Moscow year, which is an interesting point. Clearly, I was not as important as I had imagined!

My personal contact with East Germany had been minimal, though we covered it in our publications with the help of retired schoolteacher, Arvan Gordon. I once crossed from West to East Berlin via Checkpoint Charlie and was held – though not interrogated – for the best part of an hour. This episode had vanished from my memory, but here it came vividly back to life. The most memorable images in the Stasi trove were a series of photocopies of every single page of my passport, showing all the stamps we used to acquire in those days. Nothing remarkable there! Oh, yes there was. We had stiff black passports then and every double page was held open by a set of Stasi fingers, of which there was a record about thirty times.

I took detailed notes of what the files contained and they are reproduced in the appendix. I doubt whether I shall live to see my KGB file in Moscow.

Chapter XIX
A New Director

I had looked on my retirement, aged 65 in 1999, as a period of less frenetic activity, perhaps an opportunity to reap some rewards and certainly the time to hand on many responsibilities to others. The reality was different. After the turn of the Millennium, events became increasingly difficult. We were now in the email era and I printed out a blizzard of them, all preserved. What follows, therefore, is a foreshortened view, recording the sequence of events and omitting what could have been dozens of convoluted pages involving personalities. This story, in all its detail from my point of view, exists, secure in the archive of Baylor University. Maybe some future historian will revisit these years of crisis for Keston and retell the story from a different perspective.

Even before my retirement my relationship with Oxford University was failing to move forward. The real blow came after the Registrar came to see me, spent nearly a whole morning talking, but then wrote a letter in which he said that we would not be granted 'associated status' with the University. This was no reflection on the work of Keston, he stated, but it was simply that the list of 'Institutions Associated with University' had been closed. We do not know whether the university observers on our Council had reported back negatively, but I think not. Word came to us quietly (though this cannot be proved) that the closure of the list was due to the unprecedented expansion of the Centre for Islamic Studies. This was garnering support from the Arab world for a major building, eventually erected in Marston Road. The Oxford Centre for Hebrew and Jewish Studies enjoyed this status, too, and our work would have fitted so very well into this pattern. These were rich institutions and it did not help our cause that we were so poor.

Sadly, our relations with the missions, providing both fellowship and financial support over nearly twenty years, were also in decline. The reason is easy to see: they no longer needed a research and information service to help them decide on policies. They could now send their people freely into all the countries in which they had an interest and these would bring back all the information which was needed. Further, of course, church leaders from Eastern Europe could now visit the West. Undercover and dangerous work simply ceased to exist, but we, with more staff available, could have done more than we did to maintain our friendships with the missions and build new ones with churches in the East.

I did not feel I had completely fulfilled my mission, but I was exhausted and was only too conscious that I lacked new ideas to lead Keston into new territory. As Keston had always paid a full contribution to my Anglican clergy pension, and it would become available on my 65th birthday, I felt that 19 March 1999 should be the date on which I would make way for a younger person, someone, I hoped, who could bring fresh vision and enthusiasm to the work, not least in fund-raising.

When I told the Council of my intention, there was an initial attempt to dissuade me, but I informed them that they really were asking the impossible. I suggested a compromise: I would withdraw completely from all administrative responsibility and work as an 'ambassador at large' for Keston, devoting attention to all the opportunities and challenges which were still there in abundance in our 'new Europe'. Our home in Iffley, would become my new base.

As events turned out, the days before my retirement were some of my busiest. From 15–18 February I was in Vilnius, Lithuania, at the invitation of President Adamkus, to receive an accolade: the Order of the Grand Duke Gediminas. This was a joyous occasion, because my fellow-honorands included Fr Gleb Yakunin and Sergei Kovalyov, both of whom had done sterling work for Lithuanian freedom during the years of occupation.

Conferences in Königstein and Vienna immediately followed. Then there was a delightful 'farewell' residential conference in my honour, organised principally by Michael Kaser, held at Cumberland Lodge, Windsor.

However, I was not well and I celebrated the day of my retirement in hospital. A metal plate in my leg, put there following an old injury, had to be removed. After a short period of recovery, I went to America to give a lecture at DePaul University, Chicago, followed by a conference at the University of Helsinki. The latter had ambitious plans, which never worked out, for an ongoing study of the role of religion in the collapse of communism.

The next month, July, I went to Moscow for a consultation with a new Moscow team, which we were setting up, to work on the 'Encyclopaedia project'. Sergei Filatov had recruited several new young researchers, among whom Roman Lunkin would become a world expert on Protestants in Russia. This project would be a major focus of Keston's work up to the present.

Sir John Lawrence died at the end of the year. On more than one occasion he had said, with his prophetic voice, that there was no substance in communism and it would collapse like a house of cards. He had forecast that he would live to see the end of it (which he did), but also to see the new millennium (which he did not). He died on 30 December 1999 – but on 1 January the leading obituary in *The Times* was John's.

Larry Uzzell

It is obvious, in retrospect, that my successor would take on a difficult – perhaps impossible – job. Eschewing modesty, I reflect that Keston College was my concept and I poured into it my energy and commitment over a period of thirty years. Carrying out my vision would, it goes without saying, have been impossible without the most supportive of mentors and a devoted staff. But by the time I was 65 these halcyon days were long past. I had struggled to maintain a core of the work during a time of declining support and diminishing national interest in Russia. My retirement was due just when we needed an input of new energy and ideas.

Could I have delayed my retirement? My life in Iffley was beginning to provide new perspectives, particularly in music, where I had, in 1996, started a music society, hard work, but it offered great rewards.

I felt, though, that I still had some energy to devote to the work of Keston, both in writing articles for the press, including book reviews, and undertaking a limited amount of travel, such as I was indeed about to do with my series of BBC broadcasts. The Council accepted my proposition to work independently but it became obvious later that some of them would have preferred me to have retired completely.

I had known Larry Uzzell for several years, an American convert to the Orthodox Church, who had learned Russian and gone to Moscow to work on human rights issues for the Jamestown Foundation. He applied for a job with us, wanting to work for our Moscow office. He did this successfully for about two years. Following Jane Ellis's death, it had not always been easy to find the right personnel to run it, but when Larry came on board all seemed set fair and it was funded by, alongside the scholarship scheme, a project which we could promote with excitement. Larry fulfilled his brief to a high standard, sending back a stream of balanced and documented reports, which we incorporated into the News Service, which by now had resumed publication.

The Council decided to look for my successor nearly a year before my retirement. The post of Director had been publicly advertised and interviews took place at 4 Park Town on 29 July 1998. I did not wish to participate in the selection process, but at the insistence of Michael Kaser, our Chairman, I sat in on it. In the event, of all the candidates Larry was the one who set out a positive plan for Keston's future and promised to back up his vision with a fund-raising campaign in the USA, where he maintained strong links. The panel swiftly decided to appoint him.

He took up the appointment on 1 April 1999 and we had some good hand-over meetings, after which I left 4 Park Town to begin my role as ambassador at large. My only real contact with Larry was at meetings of the Council, which happened infrequently. I retained my formal membership of it, which was probably a mistake. I did want to ensure, though, that my activities were in accordance with their wishes and I reported on my work.

The excitement generated by Larry's move from Moscow to Oxford was palpable. Everyone felt he was the man to guide us into a new era, a strong and attractive personality, single-minded in his devotion to Russia and to the work of Keston Institute.

For a year from May 1999 Larry did not ask me for in-depth assessments of Keston's work to date. This was his style and I respected it. I was away for some time in the summer organising my parents' joint funeral and sorting out their affairs.

It came, therefore, as a shock to be told that, at a meeting of a sub-committee of the Council in December 2000, which I had not attended, Larry had criticised me to the members. His words, as reported back to me, were: 'Michael has persistently refused to carry out the assignments which I have set him.' This apparently referred to the plan of my editing an issue of *Religion, State and Society*, which I had not been able to do, due to my absence in Cornwall.

Next came a vocal criticism, severely worded, of the fact that I had given space to Metropolitan Kirill to speak in my radio programme from Smolensk. Larry expressed the view that Kirill's record as head of the Department of External Affairs was so negative that I should have exposed this in the broadcast. He did not explain how I could have done this in a programme from Kirill's own diocese and which, in any case, was presented as an act of worship. Larry himself was a member of the Orthodox Church of America, which is in communion with the Moscow Patriarchate, so his stance on Kirill was difficult to understand. It emerged later that Larry was opposed to any work I might do for the BBC, as this did not form part of his plan for the development of Keston.

I imagined that I had the freedom to use any residual energy and influence I possessed to continue speaking and writing for Keston, but Larry's objections and criticisms came one after the other, almost all by email, some trivial, some major. I found the actual work I was doing a stimulus, but in personal terms I sank into depression as I tried, in vain, to assess what Larry's motives were.

Losing 4 Park Town

Reviewing the events of 2000–1, and attempting to find the key to what went wrong, I still have no adequate answer to many questions. By the summer of 2001 there was a complete loss of trust, not only between Larry and me, but eventually between several members of the Council and myself, too.

There were questions about the chain of command: as Director, Larry was making staff appointments. He appointed and dismissed staff – and not only in Moscow – with no reference to the Council. The most notable example of this was when he dismissed Roman Lunkin, an outstanding member of our Encyclopaedia team (which I was directing) without telling me. Thus, when I went with Roman on a visit to Kaliningrad in September 1999, I had no idea that, before we set out, he had already ceased to be a part-time member of the Keston staff.

There was unquestionably also an ideological issue. Larry believed that the only way forward for Keston was to focus, virtually to the exclusion of everything else, on the deterioration in the field of religious liberty in Russia and many other countries of the former Soviet Union. None of us on the Council wanted to see that excluded from our work, but we also believed that the Archive was now a testament to recent history and unique in the world. It needed preservation, adequate housing and funding.

Larry had originally committed himself to this undertaking, outlining plans he would develop in the USA. Such support never materialised.

Instead, before, in my view, exhausting all the possibilities, he persuaded the Chairman of the Council to sell 4 Park Town, where the Archive was well housed and conveniently located The roof was indeed in a parlous state and we had not begun to raise any of the £80,000 needed to repair it. But we could have explored other possibilities. It was known that property prices had risen steeply and we would be able to sell at a substantial profit, but before doing so the Council of Management should have made a cast-iron plan for the future of the Archive. In the event, responsibility for its relocation was placed on the desk of Philip Walters, a major undertaking which he tried his best to solve.

The decisive meeting took place while I was in Solovki making my programme for the BBC, so I could not express my views. All I could do was register a vote against *in absentia* (for which there is no provision in our constitution, so it did not count). Two Council members, the Russian émigré Leonid Finkelstein and Xenia Dennen, abstained. All the rest voted in favour. In retrospect, but I was feeling too depressed to think clearly, I should have called an Extraordinary General Meeting, for which I could easily have gathered enough members' signatures, with the purpose of properly debating an issue which was central to Keston's future.

The sale, well handled by Council member, Christopher Walton, went ahead when property prices reached a new height and realised £1,460,000. Of this, £100,000 was owed to the Bishopsdown Trust in repayment of the low-interest mortgage. The interest on the remainder was supposed, when invested, to cover our rental costs, but it never did. Larry went to America for a lengthy spell, having asked Keston's administrator, to help Philip Walters solve the problem of relocation. In the event, the Council did not receive a detailed report on the suitability of the proposed new premises at 38 St Aldate's Court. This was part of a new office block in a superb location, too small, but so central that the first-floor office looked out, at the back, on to a field which was part of the extensive domain of Christ Church. The drawback, of course, was that the cost was prohibitive; to me, the move seemed to toll the death-knell of Keston.

There were other major changes at the time. Larry repeatedly pointed out that our original mission was to defend religious liberty. With this in mind – and on his own authority – he appointed a full-time expert on the now-independent countries of the former Soviet Central Asia. His brief was to roam freely among these countries and to report back to Keston on violations of religious liberty, an excellent idea, but the Council received no report on the cost of this, even after it had begun. With now substantial money in the bank, the Council did not raise the question. The new staff member never visited Oxford, so the Council did not meet him.

There were now gaps on the Council of Management and Larry was asked to suggest new members. We needed people with a new vision and expertise to make the best of our changed situation. In the event, Lord Raymond Asquith, a businessman with interests in Ukraine, was his sole new appointee.

As a modern historian, I particularly valued the record, in our Archive, of the changes we had lived through. It was now only partially available due to lack of space. In a memo I wrote, I outlined the historical context and the significance of the changes which had come about since the advent of Gorbachev and then the collapse of the Soviet Union. Larry repeatedly instructed me to abandon this approach and concentrate exclusively on current violations of religious liberty.

I saw a danger signal here. The Council discussed the issue, agreeing that we should not change our focus, but did nothing to implement their decision. I pleaded that my perspective, focussing on the more historical aspect of our work, fitted like a hand into a glove, with Larry's detailed documenting of violations of religious liberty, but the Council did not resolve this issue. Larry asked me to stop writing obituaries for *The Guardian*, claiming that this gave the general public the impression that Keston was 'interested mainly in the past'.

During 2002 Keston's affairs became more complicated and unpleasant. A propos of my planned trip to Solovki for the BBC, I quote an email received from Larry: 'Keston's core agenda [is] religious freedom. As a matter of conscience, next time I won't be able to give you the benefit of the doubt. We simply can't afford to spend Keston's scarce resources on activities that actually undermine our mission by whitewashing the authoritarian Moscow Patriarchate… It seems to me that a broadcast from Solovki that does not prominently discuss the martyrs… would be like a broadcast from Auschwitz barely mentioning the Holocaust.' Enough said: this was about a programme I had not even made and which would give me the opportunity of reflecting on the tragic history of the monastery under communist rule.

Looking back, I am convinced that the Council could and should have acted decisively to resolve these issues as they arose. As it was, they were reluctant to interfere with the way in which Larry ran Keston, allowing him to have free rein and imposing no financial control. Nor did they insist that he should pay more attention to the fund-raising which had been such an essential part of his brief when he was appointed.

By now our funds were rapidly dwindling. Larry announced his forthcoming marriage and consequent plans to spend more time in America. Would he be likely to continue as Director?

Faced with a financial crisis, the Council began to consider restructuring the work. Philip Walters came up with a plan for safeguarding the Archive. He contacted the University of Leeds, where there was an excellent tradition of Soviet Studies and one of whose senior people, Jonathan Sutton, had once worked temporarily at Keston. The idea that emerged was that the Archive should go, in its entirety, to Leeds, together with Malcolm Walker, the archivist, and Philip himself, who would continue to edit *Religion, State and Society* from there. The News Service would be taken over by some other sponsoring body. I would receive some of the residual funds to build up a team of translators of the Encyclopaedia, now an expanding project, and I would edit the result.

There was a fraught meeting of the Council, which after a debate, heard out my alternative plan: to keep the Archive in Oxford and develop a link with an Oxford college. I had had several positive meetings with heads of colleges, archivists and Soviet specialists. Eventually it was Regent's Park College which offered the hope of forging a fruitful collaboration.

The Council invited Jonathan Sutton to present his case to them, but at the outset there was obvious embarrassment in the room. He failed to appear. The Council had received nothing in writing from Leeds and it never became known what lay behind this change of plan. In the event, Regent's Park College was not able to find sufficient space to house the Archive.

Larry began to fly in from America just to attend Council meetings, but he seemed to be losing interest in Keston's affairs. He offered his resignation, which several members of the Council did not want to accept. There was much confusion, with the emergence of two factions. Some members wished to dismember Keston, others to retain Larry's services whatever the cost. There was a tangible sapping of morale.

Several unpleasant meetings passed. Michael Kaser reported that he had made Larry an offer. He suggested that a considerable sum from Keston's investment should be made available to help Larry promote and fund *Keston News Service* from his new post (whatever that should be) in the USA.

Michael Kaser and several others resigned. Heroically, Xenia Dennen, stepped into the breach as our affairs were disintegrating and saved the day, with her clear judgement and grasp of where Keston's real interests lay. Xenia avoided dismemberment of the work and ensured that it would live on in Oxford for a few more precarious years.

On the day that Larry Uzzell resigned, in December 2002, the *Keston News Service* staff, who had remained loyal to Larry throughout, also resigned en bloc. Instantaneously, *KNS* reappeared under a new name, *Forum 18*, published from Oslo and continuing in more or less the same format as previously. To this day it continues its reportage by email. Its financial sources are secret.

Chapter XX
A Secure Future

Like Leonid Brezhnev, we had our period of 'stagnation', though it lasted less long than his. After Larry Uzzell's resignation in 2002 we had five years in the restricted premises in St Aldate's, during which Xenia and I focused on seeking a satisfactory permanent home. I devoted time to writing the first draft of my memoirs.

Larry's appointed successor was Davor Peterlin, a Croatian Baptist who joined us at a difficult time. He was an academic who did not know Keston's history and encountered difficulties on many fronts. Keston was in limbo, reduced to a skeleton. Malcolm Walker paid detailed attention to the Archive and devoted time to visitors who came to work in it. Philip Walters continued his editorial work on *Religion, State and Society*.

After many false starts, exploratory discussions in the UK, Europe and then further afield led us to consider moving the Archive to universities in Cardiff, Gloucester, Prague, Helsinki and Harvard, among others, but for various reasons all these discussions came to nothing.

There were, however, compensations, with some of the work presenting challenges unlike anything we had done before. Ideological opposition had largely disappeared, the problem now being indifference rather than hostility

Vilnius

A significant development came about in our relations with Lithuania when the Mažvydas National Library in Vilnius invited Keston to display some of its Lithuanian documents to the public. Our visit took place in November 2005. President Valdas Adamkus received our group which comprised Davor Peterlin, Xenia Dennen, Malcolm Walker, and Lorna and me. We were welcomed into the Presidential Palace and Mr Adamkus made a speech of considerable warmth. Journalists asked questions, cameras flashed and I spoke impromptu.

The staff had worked hard on ensuring the safe transit of a representative collection of Lithuanian documents. In many instances, even those who had compiled and signed them did not know their eventual destiny. But we had collected and preserved them, waiting, although we could not possibly have known it at the time, for just such a day.

There were moving scenes at the library, especially in relation to the collection of 17,043 signatures on one document, a simple appeal to Leonid Brezhnev for religious liberty in Lithuania, dated 1971. The curators of the exhibition had mounted it superbly, set out in a long glass case, so that people could read their own signatures of the time, a poignant reminder of an age of oppression, now in the past. Former political prisoner, Sigitas Tamkevičius, now Archbishop of Kaunas, told us the story at the formal opening of how he had circulated the text secretly in multiple copies round the parishes. He then entrusted a layman, Petras Plumpa, to take it to Moscow to hand in to Brezhnev's office. However, along the way Plumpa had second thoughts. This thick file of paper would, he knew, disappear without trace into the maw of the KGB archives. What was the purpose of that? He decided to look for an alternative. He found a Western journalist, so the amazing compilation ended up on my desk, and thence came to the Keston Archive. Its temporary resurfacing in Vilnius caused a real stir. People came to us in tears, saying they had found their own signatures there or those of relatives who had subsequently died. Allowing people to revisit their past through these documents was unprecedented in the history of Keston.

When looking at the list of signatures, I was struck by the fact that we had preserved a document central to Lithuania's campaign for religious liberty and political freedom. Later, I was asked if we might consider returning it to its place of origin. The next year our Council debated this and – for the only time – decided to give away an original document, and one of our most important, on condition that our Lithuanian friends could make a facsimile for us. Eventually this was done, so I had the joy in July 2007 of taking the original back to Lithuania for the second time and putting it in the hands of its begetter, the Archbishop of Kaunas, with whom I stayed. During our breakfasts together we reflected on many strange facets of history, not least that we were sitting in the former headquarters of the KGB, now his residence.

The Encyclopaedia Project

As mentioned earlier, the idea originated with Moscow academic Sergei Borisovich Filatov. He was trained as a sociologist of religion, learning his craft as a researcher during the communist period, but he never became an atheist and later wanted to evaluate all aspects of how religion was embracing a new world of opportunities.

The aim, at first, was to visit all accessible regions of Russia, from the Baltic to the Pacific and write up information, based on face-to-face interviews, on all religions including paganism and new American imports, such as Mormonism and Scientology. Sergei built up a small core team and invited additional experts, for example on Islam, when they visited the relevant region. He concentrated on the Orthodox Church and its offshoots, while Roman Lunkin concentrated on the many Protestant denominations. I went on two early *komandirovki* ('trips'), with Roman to Kaliningrad and with the team to Yakutsk, in the far east of Siberia. Xenia Dennen became a member of the team and made many dozens of such visits, acquiring a breadth of knowledge, which, added to her deep love of all things Russian, has given her a unique perspective on religious life in the post-Soviet era.

The team would arrive unannounced in a region. First, Sergei approached the office of the local bishop, while Roman called on the local governor and Protestant leaders. Xenia's presence as a 'westerner' with fluent Russian would sometimes disarm the more cautious interviewees and allow discussion to open up, yielding surprising insights.

The team completed the first edition of the Encyclopaedia: the volumes covered Russia denomination by denomination and offered a compendium of information current during the first decade of the new millennium. The series also covered Russia region by region, giving a break-down of what religions were present in each (there were 89 regions at the outset of the project). Only some difficult areas, such as Chechnya, where the team might have been at risk, were left unvisited, as well as the vast area of the Siberian north, inhabited mainly by reindeer and their scattered herdsmen.

Encyclopaedias on contemporary issues are always open-ended. After ten years of field research, Sergei Filatov embarked on a further series, entirely geographical. Instead of concentrating on themes, he began producing an 'atlas', describing each region of Russia in alphabetical order. The result was a set of volumes which not only went into more detail than the first series, but also traced developments, often rapid, since their previous visits. Apart from the first three years, Keston has provided the entire funding, including travel costs and fees to the researchers. At the time of writing, this work is continuing. A whole volume on St Petersburg is in preparation, but Moscow is yet to be tackled. Completion of the work is still several years in the future, as is fulfilment of a plan to present the essential findings in English.

Here is an example of the richness of new information contained in the research. In a lecture Xenia described religion in Karelia, territory annexed from Finland in 1940:

> A tradition of tolerance was established in the early days of *perestroika* by an official, Boris Detchuyev, who was in charge of official policy towards religion in 1987 when church–state relations in Karelia dramatically improved thanks to him. As early as 1989–1990 he and officials from the mayor's office visited all the main religious groups in Petrozavodsk, and apologised for all the devastation caused by the atheist campaigns of the communist authorities. He firmly supported freedom of conscience. Today Viktor Birin is head of the Department for National Policy and State-Confessional Relations, and responsible for official policy on religion. Birin continues this tradition of tolerance. The local authorities cooperate with the Orthodox, Lutherans, Pentecostals and Adventists and invite representatives from all religious groups to round-table discussions and seminars. Even an International Day of Tolerance (16 November) is officially observed in Karelia.

The following quotation, relating impressions of the team's visit to Kamchatka, on the Pacific coast of Siberia, illustrates the variety of humanitarian work being done by the Orthodox Church in Russia. Xenia reported:

> The priest in charge of social work, Fr Viktor Muzykant, told us about a sisterhood of 25 women, the Martha and Mary Sisters, who helped care for the

disabled, the elderly and those in hospital. This community of women (they were not nuns) had existed for ten years. In the centre of the city the church ran a youth centre, founded in 1999, which had a chapel, and a youth camp for 9–18-year-olds out in the country on land belonging to a convent. Some work was being done with prisoners: a priest regularly visited inmates and ran a community for former prisoners in the countryside, where members helped locals with building work and repairs. The church allocated volunteers to three feeding stations in the city where medical help and clothing were also provided, and planned to found a centre for single pregnant women with a view to preventing abortions. The local authorities welcomed the Orthodox Church's help in the social field and were able to provide some funding with state grants for non-commercial organisations.

Such involvement in a society still suffering from the after-effects of communism is widespread, though not universal. The Encyclopaedia is particularly strong in assessing the openness – or otherwise – of local bishops to co-operating and building relations with Protestants and Catholics. It is encouraging to report that the team has been able to operate for so many years free of constraint, while not all welcomes have been equally warm. My theory is that the Moscow Patriarchate itself learns from the project and perhaps it will acknowledge this one day.

The Encyclopedia takes readers into areas of religion in Russia which are largely unknown and unexplored. For example, the rise of Protestantism in many forms is present throughout and the revival of Catholicism can be studied nowhere except in the work of the team. A fascinating byway is the revival of paganism which is occurring in many different places and unrelated forms. Here is an example from the Mari El region in northern European Russia, a report by Xenia Dennen, on the team's visit, dated November 2015:

> As a Mari [President Vladislav Zotin] shared the hopes of his people, who began campaigning for national recognition and official acceptance of Mari paganism. Pagan priests (*karty*) started to take part in official ceremonies. During Zotin's inauguration as President (1991) only an Orthodox bishop was supposed to have offered a blessing, but in the end under the pressure of a national political campaign a *kart* was allowed to bless the new President as well. Immediately after his inauguration Zotin signed a law protecting 'sacred groves' throughout Mari El and regularly began attending pagan animal sacrifices, which much displeased the Orthodox clergy.

Baylor University

Xenia's and my efforts were shortly to bring about the most significant change in the history of our work. We finally struck gold in our quest for a permanent home for the Archive. In February 1972 I had responded to an invitation to give the Dawson

Lectures on Church and State at the Dawson Center at Baylor University (both named after a benefactor). My host was James Wood, a Baptist academic who had built up a department which paid especial attention to religious liberty and church–state relations.

Thus it was that when Professor Wallace Daniel heard that Keston's Archive was seeking a home, my earlier contact with James Wood at Baylor encouraged him to contact us. James had long since retired, but Wallace introduced himself to me by email as a historian at Baylor who was now making Russia the focus of his research. He visited our archive towards the end of 2006 and talked about possible collaboration. The next February, Xenia and I flew out to inspect the possible premises at Baylor. Making the decision was not difficult for the Council, because no alternative was by then on the table, but everyone was impressed by our account of the splendour and suitability of the rooms and their location in the heart of the campus. Equally important was the guarantee that this transfer would be at Baylor's expense. There would be a legal agreement, under which we would assign ownership of the Archive to Baylor and they would undertake to make provision for it and promote it.

The decision once taken, events moved fast. The director of the work at Baylor was to be Professor Christopher Marsh, a historian who read both Russian and Chinese, and devoted an enviable supply of energy to the physical task of moving the Archive. He brought a team of four to St Aldate's, hiring a shipping container, putting it in a car park close by and setting about the task of transferring all the books and documents to it for onward transport by land, sea and then land to Baylor. The group worked unstintingly to complete the work in three days. Malcolm Walker had to relinquish, in addition, some seventy boxes which he had never had time to unpack since their transfer from Kent all those years earlier. They contained the working archives of the various researchers who had left Keston at the time of the move to Oxford. At Baylor the unpacking of these boxes has been a measured exercise, demanding many hours of reading often in a foreign language, and assigning their contents to relevant files. Sadly, my personal archive, carefully saved by Mavis Perris, but never integrated into the main body of research, disappeared, possibly discarded at Park Town, when a major reduction of our holdings took place.

Soon after the unpacking of the archive, Christopher Marsh arranged a conference to inaugurate the new era for our work, inviting Lorna and me to meet some of his associates. James Wood, long since retired, came from the East Coast; we shared memories and it was a happy occasion. Thirty-five years after my first visit, the Dawson Center, with its splendid space and outlook, was renamed the Keston Center for Religion, Politics and Society. Its reading room bears my own name.

A succession of people looked after our documents and books. There was to be a complete re-cataloguing of the archive and – most importantly – its rehousing in permanent acid-free files, together with the removal of all paper clips and staples, which endangered the future of fragile materials. Keston's books, while kept in the

Keston Center, were integrated into the university library system. Gradually important documents are being digitised and made available online.

This undertaking has continued with commendable persistence. The latest description of its progress comes from a private email from Professor Kathy Hillman, which I quote: 'Gradually important items are being digitised for preservation and availability online. To date, all 4,500 photographs have been digitised and approximately one third of the *samizdat,* with the addition of metadata in progress.'

Kathy Hillman, a native Texan, has been Director of the Center since 2012. She has put immense energy into integrating the body of Keston's work into the university. With the degree of Master of Library Science, she has applied professional standards to this development of our work. Her first degree was in communications, followed by postgraduate business studies. She also serves as Associate Professor and Director of Baptist Collections and Library Advancement for the Baylor University Libraries.

Her Baptist faith has led to her holding a number of prominent positions such as serving as President of the Baptist General Convention of Texas. She also writes extensively for a variety of publications.

We have a formal agreement that both Baylor and Keston are represented on each other's board and council of management. Between 2007 and 2017 I visited Baylor seven times. Kathy comes annually to one of our meetings in Oxford and either Xenia Dennen or another representative of Keston UK visits Baylor reciprocally. Thus we receive comprehensive reports on progress at Waco.

Keston UK sponsors occasional postgraduate researchers to visit Baylor and they are normally housed on university premises, but Kathy and her husband John have added a treasured personal element to this hospitality. These scholars write reports on their research for us to publish in the *Keston Newsletter.* Larisa Seago, the Curator of the archive, devotes time, like Malcolm formerly, to welcoming visitors and locating the materials they request.

Julie deGraffenried is an academic at Baylor who teaches courses related to the archive and she is vigorously promoting it. My hope is that eventually the Board will identify a benefactor who will endow a full-time lectureship in the subject.

Professor Wallace Daniel was promoted to a senior position at Mercer University, Atlanta, Georgia, soon after he had been the prime mover of securing our archive for Baylor. He has frequently returned to give lectures and uses the archive to continue his own writing (biographies of Fr Alexander Men' and now, in preparation, Fr Gleb Yakunin). No one has ever written more persuasively about Keston's work and its archive than Professor Daniel, so it is worth quoting a substantial extract from his essay:

> The memories stored in the Keston Archive are often not the most pleasant aspects of the past, but collectively they comprise a nearly unparalleled record of struggle, courage, and commitment to certain values in extremely difficult circumstances. They fill in important gaps in Russia's national story that otherwise would remain unknown.

Periods of war and revolution are notorious for destroying key components of a nation's memory. Equally destructive are government attacks on ways of thinking and believing that seek to obliterate the past. In the Soviet Union, for most of the twentieth century, Russian Orthodoxy and other forms of religious belief suffered one of the greatest assaults on religion in history. As a result, a great deal of Russia's national story has been lost from view, feared gone forever, or remains still to be reconstructed. Such losses particularly apply to individuals and groups whose views did not conform to the government's desired paradigm. Their voices are essential parts of the mosaic of life in the former Soviet Union and, they comprise the raw materials out of which the future of religious liberty, human rights, and the Russian Orthodox Church will be built. The Keston Archive offers a rich trove of documents that speaks directly to these themes… the collection must be preserved and made accessible. Baylor University committed itself to those goals.

Why Baylor?… First, the University has a long-standing commitment to religious liberty and to freedom of conscience. This commitment to freedom of the mind and the spirit to discover the truth, without political force and outside compulsion, speaks to the core principles of Baylor's heritage. Michael Bourdeaux's book, *Patriarch and Prophets*, illuminates the struggle of groups and individuals for religious liberty in the former Soviet Union. The legal separation of church and state has long been a key theme in Baylor's history. The university and Keston share common commitments.

Second, while Baylor historically is connected to the Baptist Church, its approach is ecumenical… The materials in the Keston Archive do not represent a peripheral source to the University, part of a marginal interest, but of central importance. The University has a very large concern with the study of religion, and it goes beyond an academic one; it is part of the University's expressed goals, what it takes most seriously, what it sees as most vital to humanity, community, democracy, and civil society.

Third, one can only appreciate the courage, the energy, and the spiritual vision that went into the preservation of the materials in the Keston Archive. The University is committed to preserving and expanding the archive, to digitizing the entire collection, to organizing all the materials in the archive, and to making the archive accessible to students and scholars internationally…

Archival work lies at the heart of original historical research. The Keston Archive needs to be better known. It is a rich, underexplored resource for scholars in Russian, European, and world history and for those who want to gain a larger, more complete picture of the history of religion, human rights, and religious liberty. Some of the findings there will surprise the scholar. The collection is huge, and the scholar who spends time exploring its holdings will be richly rewarded. Michael Bourdeaux has spoken eloquently about the heroism and self-sacrifice of courageous individuals and groups whose voices comprise central parts of a fascinating, multi-dimensional history, which, in this post-Cold War period, is in need of re-examination. The Keston Archive offers a rich source for that project to begin.

These remarkable words, a tribute from one of the foremost scholars working in Keston's field, set out a perspective, the horizons of which I could not have envisaged when I began this journey nearly seventy years ago.

Afterword

I began this memoir by claiming that the unseen hand of God was present in my life, guiding it throughout. The fact that I did not mention this, chapter by chapter, does not mean that I forgot His presence. Rather the opposite. It is obvious that divine intervention was never far away and, at times, directly controlled a series of events which led me to found Keston College and sometimes reassured me and pointed the way forward. Even at the most difficult moments, when I was close to despair, I was never alone. I came through these, feeling an inner strength, as a result of prayer, which I did not know I possessed.

When I was young, the feeling of being singled out was strongly present. How could it be that the events which qualified me for my career unfolded in sequence? Being drafted on to the National Service Russian course was miraculous. Then selection for the first year-long exchange with Soviet students followed in my twenties, at the first time in my life when I was free to benefit from this. When my calling – in its simplest form, to use my knowledge of languages in the service of the Church – seemed to be flagging, there was another life-changing event: my encounter in Moscow with the two women from Pochaev in Ukraine, who urged me to be their voice and speak for them.

Acquiring the old school at Keston for the work of the College seemed, at first, an opportunity beyond my grasp, but the good will of Rochester diocese made it possible. Despite being on a blacklist for Soviet visas for two periods of ten years, this did not prevent my presence in Moscow for the dramatic beginning of liberation for the churches – the Millennium of the Baptism of the Eastern Slavs in 1988. My first visit to Lithuania to participate in the re-consecration of Vilnius Cathedral followed quickly afterwards.

The last 25 years have been less dramatic, but still clearly under a guiding hand. The compensation for not being able sufficiently to interest Oxford University to use Keston's resources was moving to Iffley. Here we found a lovely house and became part of a vibrant community, where we brought up our two children. Making a contribution to the life of the parish has been personally fulfilling for Lorna and me, but it has opened special opportunities for her. We have the privilege of worshipping in one of England's most beautiful medieval churches where we are encouraged and enfolded by a tolerant and inclusive Anglicanism.

Finally, the move of our archive to its permanent home at Baylor University in Texas (2007) was an event beyond my remotest dreams when I first visited the university more than three decades earlier. This has cemented a precious tie with Kathy and John Hillman and a new group of friends. Their hospitality on my visits, and those of other

Council members, has been unforgettable. My greatest hope is that Baylor's resources will become better known and used by a new generation of scholars from Russia and the countries of Eastern Europe.

Reflecting on fifty years of work for freedom of religion for those denied it, I think of what Keston has done for Catholics, Protestants and, perhaps especially, for the Orthodox Church. To this day, it may be that this is not fully recognised. As recently as 2016, my erstwhile colleague from our studies in Moscow, Avril Pyman, writes of the 'scathingly anti-Orthodox stance' of Keston.[1] The truth, of course, is the exact opposite. One only has to cite our translation and publication of such works as *The Unknown Homeland* and *An Early Soviet Saint: The Life of Father Zacharia* to prove the case. These classics of Russian spirituality remain little known in Russia, but they will one day gain recognition.

Interjecting a personal aside, I note that there are aspects of my life which could have been greatly expanded in these memoirs, but I had to concentrate on the history of Keston, beginning with an explanation of how, without my knowing it at the time, I was led towards this goal. I would have liked to pay more attention to my two wives, Gillian and Lorna, without whom I would have achieved nothing. Gillian lived for only 44 years, but her span was full of rich experiences. Lorna, without question, devoted herself to a man whose life, without her, might have disintegrated. She showed me that dark times and obstacles along our path could, by faith, be turned into blessings.

I'm sorry not to have been able to write about my four children, so different from each other, and enhancing my life in their contrasting ways.

There are also many friends whom I would have liked to mention, but could not. They include Gerald Brooke, with whom I studied in Moscow, and whose efforts to help the Russians cost him several years in a Soviet prison. His undiminished idealism led him, much later, to assist the British Government's Know-How Fund in its efforts, during those open years of the 1990s, to develop a Russian democratic system.

There is also my Cornish friend, Jonathan Ball, whose brilliance as an architect gave him the initial stimulus to establish the Eden Project.

Kevin Grant, a distinguished journalist and published poet, has been a long-time friend and adviser bringing wit and good humour into our conversations. The Bishopsdown Trust owes him a particular debt for the careful way in which he evaluated applications. Roland Bryan devoted many years of his retirement to administrating Keston College and then serving as Secretary to the Bishopsdown Trust.

I have been blessed with a long life, so, like others of my generation, I have seen changes in the world beyond imagining. It is hard to think back now to the fact that my early education was played out against the background of the Second World War, in which some of the most cultured nations of Europe were tearing each other apart for the second time in a century.

---

1   *Metropolitan Anthony of Sourozh: A Life* (Lutterworth Press, 2016), p. 119.

My reading about Russia today – its politics, personalities and power struggles – makes me think that, in one sense, little has changed. But were I to visit Russia again now, I am certain I would encounter the same warmth, hospitality and openness to discuss and exchange ideas which I experienced when younger.

I took the decision early on not to attempt to evaluate President Putin's Russia or Patriarch Kirill's Orthodox Church. Even if I had the knowledge, these tasks would have been for another book. Suffice it to say that, for a brief window in the early 1990s, Russians had a chance to establish a democratic system. They were open to reforms, but sadly these hopes have come to nothing. The cycle of history will roll on, however, and an opportunity will appear again, no one knows when, but democracy will be forged by a new generation for whom 'one word of truth shall outweigh the whole world'.

Appendix to Chapter XVIII

As an appendix, I include my edited summary of the contents of the Keston Stasi file for those who wish to have more detailed information, including the classification numbers.

HA XX/4, No.73 (318 pp. retrieved from stack 21/1/06)

1. The first reference is to *Religion in Communist Lands*, No.1, 1986. It's handwritten, listing Philip Walters as chairman of the editorial board, giving the impression he's the 'head man'. Jane Ellis: editor. My name spelled (as so many times, but not always) Bordeaux.
2. International Board, patrons.
3–4. Staff, Council.
5. 'Report' dated Berlin, 25/8/83. This is typed and my name correctly spelt. Keston founded 1968 (wrong) as CSRC – result of Czech events. Keston has a 'fascist past' (no explanation of what this means).
6–7. Tribute to our competence ('Analysefähigkeit'). We had three 'directions':
    (a) UK centre with branches worldwide, concentrating on 'former British Empire'.
    (b) Building up church contacts in socialist countries – 20% of our staff trained in E Europe.
    (c) From 1979 we strengthened the 'unofficial' side of our work (this means reading *samizdat*, but doesn't use the term). KC sends in money, printing materials, photocopiers, medicine, religious articles. *[They obviously confused us with someone else, possibly Aid to Russian Christians, but ARC did not do all this.]* KC report for Madrid Helsinki Review Conference.
8. Names 60 contact groups inside and outside socialist countries.
9. KC's 'study and research' programme: press, *samizdat* translations, publications, presentations – e.g. to NATO states, international conferences, lectures.
10. The 'moving force' from the beginning was 'Pfarrer Bourdeaux', supported by 'Rev' Paul Ősterreicher *[sic – misspelt]*, especially with regard to the Christian Peace Conference *[nonsense]*. In 1982 MB 'gave up being director' in order to become 'International Director'. There was a financial crisis that year, solved by help (unnamed source) from USA; Paul O disagreed with this, so he left KC. *[This is also nonsense – but he receives no significant other mention throughout these texts. I had thought they would make a big thing of the connection.]*

11.	KC Council in 1983.

11.   KC Council in 1983.

12.   Financial support from Dutch churches, ACN, Billy Graham (true, but one-off).

13.   'International Structure' – branches in USA, NZ, Australia, Canada *[diagram makes it seem as if we're massive!]*

14–15.   Contacts: Underground Evangelism, Aid to the Church in Need, Open Doors, Bukovsky, Hruby (NY), Russia Cristiana (Bergamo).

16.   Radio Liberty.

17.   KC Information Department: Michael Rowe; DDR – Arvan Gordon, Peter Hebblethwaite *[they have a 'thing' about him – his name comes up several times, whereas in fact he had very little to do with KC, except to fall out with Alex Tomsky!]*; CZS, Poland – Tomsky. Bourdeaux, Lorna is listed as 'Assistant from early 1981'.

18.   Publications – careful list and description.

19.   MB CV – many mistakes, no date of birth. 1959 Moscow mentioned in one line.

21–7.   Staff list of August 1983, listing Peter Hebblethwaite again! One is Xenia Johnston-Howard! List includes casual writers for *RCL*.

28–82.   Our publications. *Frontier* March–April 1987 is photocopied, also *The Right to Believe* 1/87, *Keston News Service* 11/12/86, 1985 fund-raising brochure, photostat of front cover of *RCL* Winter 86. Photocopies of articles based on KC reports in German-language publications (*Idea* and *KNA*).

83.   The first sign of actual intelligence-gathering. A certain 'Tom' had been asked to make contact with KC. He reports back in Dresden on 27/5/86. He had subscribed to KC materials on 17/3/86, costing £37, for which he receives Stasi reimbursement.

84.   Glaube in der 2 Welt.

86.   Letter from Oberst Zörner to Wiegand – seems to be a covering letter for all of above.

87–9.   *Idea* (German journal – photocopies).

90–1.   More intelligence-gathering. Hand-written notes from a conference at Keston 19–21/4/85.

93–6.   Conference invitation, as sent to Professor B. Schottstadt in Berlin (with his address).

97.   KC calendar of events.

103.   Stasi perception of KC's 'anti-DDR activities'

119.   Profile of Peter Reddaway (4/7/83), concentrating solely on his work on Soviet psychiatric prisons.

126–8.   One of the more interesting sections. KC's plan to send three groups of tourists to Luther celebrations in DDR, 1983. Arvan Gordon to lead first group, MB the third. *[this never happened]*

129–32.   Breaks off to insert photocopy of *Right to Believe* 2/87.

134–68.   1/8/83 35 identical slips of paper requesting info. on MB (misspelt and giving address as Mourfield House, Prace [Praze] – my parents' address, which I left in 1960!). Resulting report is dull and brief, referring back to 1976.

177.   Back to Arvan's group – gives rooming list and includes Caroline Cox and John Pridmore, both subsequently prominent. Itinerary in DDR. Group 'unofficially' organised by KC. They had a 'search task'.

214–37.   Interesting again – but truly boring, too. MB had day-pass on 16/5/82 to visit East Berlin from West. Notes that I was in Berlin to umpire a tennis tournament. At point of entry 'Kirchenmaterial' was discovered, but the import was 'permitted' – 2 Russian Bibles and maps of USSR. Instructions found to visit Aktion Sühnezeichen (contacts named) – from Nicky [Crane]. I behaved well!! 'Der Burger verhielt sich ruhig und kam allen Aufforderungen nach' (I behaved calmly and fulfilled all requests). But then follows something amazing: a complete photostat of my passport of the time, every single page, with all the foreign stamps, with the fingertips of the Stasi official holding the passport flat for filming. The complete document is very heavy, due to the photographic paper used.

241.   MB wins Templeton Prize *[no comment]*.

244.   16/10/86 Gillian – who had died almost ten years earlier – is listed as my 'Ehefrau'. Here begins perhaps the most interesting section in the whole archive – only four pp. to 247. I'm listed as a member of NTS (the one-time West German-based anti-communist organisation, for allegedly working for which Gerald Brooke was imprisoned for five years 1965–9). [*I never was a 'member'*].This is 'information from a Russian fraternal organisation'(!). MB is active with Radio Free Europe – travels and sells books(!). Lorna is his wife. Lists my trips to the USSR and my books. I'm a PhD *[thanks for crediting me with an honour I did not have!]*. In 1965 I organised an 'Agentnetz' in Poland and prepared secret writing materials for it. [*I did indeed visit Poland 20–26 April 1965. I visited Cardinal Wyszynski, but this is not mentioned. Why not, if they knew so much?*]

251.   The file peters out with two pages from the back of my passport listing currency exchange (as happened in those days).

252–317. This is amazing, but nothing to do with Keston. A complete photocopy of *'Places of Worship in Moscow and Leningrad'*, a private publication by John Innes.

HA XX/4 No.540

252.   (Begins with this page.) Oct. 1977. 6 pp. – 'Information Bulletin' on KC – lists Council, International Board, staff. This document is repeated *ad infinitum* elsewhere.

HA XX/4 No.11474

1157–8.   Two pages only. Thumbnail sketches (undated) of Marite Sapiets, Andrew Lenox-Koningham [Conyngham], Nikolai Koshewnikow [Kojevnikov – who never had any connection at all with KC – indeed, I think I met him only once]. Listed as 'NTS', as is 'Aljona', then his wife. Allis [sc.Ellis] Jane Elisabeth. These sketches are brief and totally unrevealing. It's noted that Jane's visa was blocked in 1985.

HA XX/4 2772

This is listed as an 'Information Document' on Keston-Kollege, England (KC) and dated 22/7/83. It begins with p.6 and has 41 pages, properly bound as a file fair copy, but in the main repeating information in other parts of the file.

7.   An organisation with 'real expertise' was considered necessary to unite information flow and inform worldwide – including Taiwan and Singapore [*nonsense!*]. China and DDR included in the research plan.

8.   ARC was an 'unofficial arm'.

18–24.   Structure and staff (surprising mistakes).

25.   Peter Reddaway campaigns for 'Freedom for Sakharov'.

26.   MB CV again – I note that they completely miss my studying Russian during National Service.

HA XX/4 1896 (56 pp., 25/8/83)

1–29.   Carbon copy of 2772 on thin paper.

30–1.   Continues on thicker paper.

32.   Small-format note prefacing photocopy of a big Keston publication, *Christians East and West Unite* (?Feb 89). [*I had forgotten what an amazing document this was – 35pp. – real harbinger of the collapse of communism. In the year of the breaching of the Wall the Stasi must truly have known from this that the 'writing was on the wall'. Perhaps our work had some effect in DDR after all.*]

35.   How to send letters to prisoners.

55–6.   How to set up a KC support group.

HA X/4 2771 (195 pp. of immaculately produced and bound photocopies – but often of poor originals).

25.   This is more interesting: long document translated from Russian and marked '*streng geheim!*' (top secret – the ! is original). Undated. CSRC is, in the Anglo-Saxon area, the most significant ('*am bedeutendsten*') E–W church organisation. My name spelt correctly and misspelt on same page.

26–7.   'Ideological diversion' is main aim. Raymond Oppenheim (ex-American chaplain in Moscow) quoted as saying that KC reports on 'church representatives' in socialist countries. Programme of visits to East led by Nicky Crane and Jane Ellis.

28.   Contacts – UE, Licht im Osten, G2W, etc. KC has 2,000 subscribers [*many more, actually*]. Financial resources – correct. [*NB no accusation that we received money from CIA.*] Jan. 79 'development plan' quoted.

29.   UE – profile of Joe Bass. Its London base in is Mayfair ('most expensive area'). [*Irrelevant to KC*].

30.   Christian Solidarity International, ACN (led by *Warenfield* – sc. Werenfried – van Straaten (not listed as monk or cleric). Mentions UE-Wurmbrand conflict – KC 'refuses to be involved' [*correct*].

64–70.   Something different: photocopy of handwritten notes – in German – by someone who came to KC on 11/8/77. [*I couldn't read the writing.*] My Lubbock Road address is given (only time). This document looks systematic and seems to be the basis of other typed reports.

71–98.   Press reports, both in German and English. On p. 89 our *Post-Nairobi Documentation* is mentioned.

99.   Strange page with names blocked out – but doesn't look important.

167–8.   Interesting – this must be translation from Russian. Handwritten list of our founding Council, with many mis-transliterations. I'm down as 'Maikl' (crossed out and 'Michael' written above) Burgo [*sic*]. 'Former Fletscher [*sic*] Inst.' mentioned as being closed in 1971. [*NB. This is the only mention of this.*] Dated April 1971 – so seems to be the earliest report included.

171–6.   Typed version of some of above, where a certain 'Grubb' is described thus: 'Vor 1945 Offizier des britischen Geheimdienstes' [*not blocked out!*]. [*We had no meaningful contact with Sir Kenneth Grubb, a leading Anglican layman.*]

182–3.   Report of 11/6/74 – repeats much, but Grubb really has got them going – this is where the whole text on him is printed and not blocked out.

Index of People

Aczel, Tamas 108, 110
Adamkus, President Valdas 279, 285
Adelheim, Fr Pavel 268
Alban, St 79, 100, 254
Aldiss, Brian W 96
Alexander, Stella 144, 193
Alexi I, Patriarch 110, 237, 240
Alexi II, Patriarch 272
Alton, David 141
Alton, Reggie 46
Amin, Idi 264
Anatoli and Alyosha 56
Anderson, Paul 82, 106-7, 111, 130, 160, 165
Andrew, Brother 138-9, 145, 196, 214
Andrew, Christopher 212, 256
Andrews, Caroline 163-4
Andreyev, Dr Catherine 256
Andreyev, Nikolai 37
Andropov, Yuri 211-12, 221, 227
Antonov, Boris 230
Antony, Bishop 87-8
Armstrong, Baron Robert 162
Armstrong, Sir Thomas 48-9
Arnold, Revd John 127, 140, 183, 186, 188, 192-3
Ascherson, Neal 156
Ashworth, Norma 150
Asquith, Lord Raymond 282
Atkins, Dennis 128

Bach, J S 62
Baillie, Isobel 27
Balengarth, Jane 236, 248
Ball, Jonathan 294
Bardinet, Alain 23
Barinov, Valeri 237, 244-6
Bartha, Bishop 190
Bartolomei, Fr 70
Bass, Joe 104, 196, 217-18, 300
Bax, Martin 187
Beamish, Sally 250
Bear, Fr 93
Beecham, Sir Thomas 48-9
Beeching, Dr Richard 1
Beeson, Revd Trevor 184-5
Beethoven, Ludwig van 48

Bennett, Alan 33, 38, 39
Beran, Cardinal 172, 237
Bere, John de 43
Berenson, Bernard 46
Berlin, Isaiah 61
Berlioz, Hector 48
Berman, Lazar 62
Bermingham, John de 43
Bird, Thomas (Tom) 111, 130
Birin, Viktor 287
Birute, friend of Nijole Sadunaite 248
Blachnicki, Fr Franciszek 157
Blacklaws, Moira 132, 135 ·
Blanch, Stuart 51-2
Blane, Andrew 111, 130
Blay, Alf 43
Blit, Lucjan 132, 184.
Bloom, Metropolitan Anthony 100, 270
Bociurkiw, Prof Bohdan 121-2, 136
Bolsover, George 34
Bondarchuk, Sergei 232
Bondarenko, Iosif 204, 207
Bonhoeffer, Dietrich 183, 236
Booth, Revd Alan 127, 129
Borodin, Alexander 48, 61, 62
Bottoms, Revd Walter 118, 184
Boult, Sir Adrian 27
Bourdeaux family and friends 1-7, 31-2, 40, 79, 120-21, 133, 150, 159, 168-9, 228, 253, 258, 269, 280, 293-4
Bourdeaux, Gillian (née Davies) 60-61, 74-81, 92-5, 120-21, 129, 131, 133, 141, 149-50, 294, 298
Bourdeaux, Lorna (née Waterton) 152, 159, 163, 169, 227-8, 232, 244-6, 253, 266, 285, 289, 293-4, 297-8
Boyce, Bruce 48
Brahms, Johannes 49
Branover, Herman Gertsovich 243
Brazhnik, Ilya 118-19
Brezhnev, Leonid 101, 113, 115, 148, 211-12, 221, 285-6
Brittain, RSM 31
Britten, Benjamin 26, 61-2
Broad, Revd Bill 256
Brooke, Gerald 294, 298

Index of Places

Africa, East 159
Albania 157, 199, 214
America *see* Latin America, South America, USA
Ann Arbor 130
Arkhangelsk 267, 271-3
Armenia 51-2, 63, 74, 76, 270
Australia 100, 120, 146-7, 153, 155, 160, 218, 297

Bahamas 163-4, 168, 170
Baikal, Lake 151
Bakhchisarai 74, 251
Baltimore 150
Barashevo 223
Baylor University, Waco 64, 103, 116, 127, 129, 139, 146, 155, 236, 260, 278, 288-92
Beirut 51, 91
Belgium 123, 129, 275
Belgrade 52
Belorussia 56, 89, 113
Bergamo 92, 297
Berlin 188, 222, 253-6, 265, 276-7, 296-8
Berrian Springs 130
Birobidjan 242
Bishopsdown 131-3, 136, 142, 169
Black Sea 74, 225, 266
Bodmin 30, 33-4, 39-40
Boston 121, 159
Brazil 95
Brigham Young University 260
Bromley 131-2, 146, 154, 247
Brussels 261, 265
Bucharest 75, 145
Bulgaria 66, 108, 259

California 14, 104, 121, 133, 159, 218
Camborne 1, 4-5, 9, 12, 14-15, 26, 165
Cambridge 28-41, 45, 50, 100, 154, 194, 256
Cape Town 131
Charlton 93-4, 120, 131
Chatham House 170, 173, 179-81
Chechnya 263, 287
Chequers 161-2
Chernobyl 194, 222
Chicago 120, 279
Chiemsee 189
China 55, 127, 143, 146, 158, 199, 299
Chislehurst 120, 123, 128, 131-2, 145, 150, 205, 253
Chistopol 224

Clowance 2-11
Copenhagen 139, 176, 216
Cornwall 2-30, 34, 39-43, 77, 93, 133, 149-50, 169, 201, 258, 281
Coulsdon 30-32, 37
Crail 41
Crewe 28
Crimea 74, 225, 251-3, 266
Cuba 283
Czechoslovakia 108, 110, 117, 156, 183, 189-90, 215, 218, 220, 264

Damascus 91
de Paul University 279

East Germany 108, 143, 186, 188, 214-15, 264, 277
Echmiadzin 63, 74
Emory University 261
Enfield 76-81, 84, 91, 94, 98
Erie, Pennsylvania 121
Estonia 52, 72, 143, 212-13, 246, 250
Ethiopia 172
Exeter 141, 268-9

Finland 246, 267, 287
Forest of Dean 75, 93
Foxton 35-6
France 23, 44, 79

Gediminas Square xiv-xv, 249
Geneva 87, 91-2 , 100, 106-22, 128, 172, 175-82, 194-5, 215
Georgia 73-4, 270
Germany 23, 29-30, 147, 179, 189, 206
Gorky *see* Nizhny Novgorod
Gorny 89
Greece 75

Halki 52
Hanover 23, 265
Hayle 1-2, 5
Hednesford 29-30, 41
Helsinki 59, 139, 149, 161, 163, 174-5, 224, 242, 260, 279, 285, 296
Holland *see* Netherlands, The
Hungary 41, 108, 183, 185-6, 193, 215, 220, 259, 264
Hydepark 163